Praise for PassPorter®

"A nifty travel guide that works overtime as a planner, organizer and journal..."
– Jacky Runice
Daily Herald–Chicago

"[PassPorter] is a brilliant travel aid... the most practical, sanity-saving guide you could take along to Disney World."
– Stephanie Gold,
Amazon.com

"[PassPorter] has become the Bible for those of us who want to experience Walt Disney World to the max."
– Kim Cool,
Venice Gondolier Sun

"Vacationers who want to enjoy all that Disney World has to offer should make sure they take along this PassPorter guide."
– ForeWord Reviews

I give PassPorter an A+. It's very organized! The data and facts are presented in a deceptively simple and clear format.
— Anne DeMallie
in Massachusetts

I truly fell in love with my PassPorter. I carried this book with me everywhere I went and it gave me great information! Thank you!
— Bethan Langlois
in Louisiana

We love completing the daily memories section with our daughter at the end of each day. The PassPorter is just SO MUCH FUN to use!
— Susan Coward
in Mississippi

PassPorter is a GREAT planning guide! Why didn't I buy it before?
— Juli Dennis
in Ohio

Silver Award Wi
Guide Book Catego
1999 Lowell Thom
Travel Journalism Compet
Society of American Travel Writers Foundation

WINNER

What's New in the 2004 Edition

Major Enhancements:

- **Full color, fold-out maps** of the four major Disney theme parks, printed on heavier paper to stand up to rugged use
- **Color, self-stick tabs** to mark your chapters in whatever way you prefer for quick and easy reference
- **Three times more photos** than our previous edition—many of which include your authors in the picture, too!
- **Personalization labels** to custom-design your PassPockets to your own vacation
- **Fun stickers** to brighten up your PassPorter and mark important pages, events, and memories
- **Coverage of the recent changes** throughout the "World"—thanks to our later production schedule, this is the most up-to-date 2004 guidebook available!
- **Disney changes highlighted** with a light blue background to mark significant additions and changes to Walt Disney World since our last edition
- ✓ **Expanded coverage** of reservation procedures and policies, package vacations, children's programs, and special occasions
- **More coupons and offers** for your favorite Disney-related services, such as MouseEarVacations.com and DVC By Resale

Fun New Features and Information:

- Updated PassPockets offer more flexibility, including space for cruise vacation information
- ✓ Four-page sneak peek at Saratoga Springs Resort (spring 2004)
- Sneak peeks at upcoming attractions, including Stitch Escape!, Soarin' Over California, Stunt Show, and Expedition: Everest
- ✓ Updated "Vegebility" (vegetarian) ratings for eateries
- More new reader tips, magical memories, and stories
- More peer reviewers to ensure accuracy and thoroughness

...and much, much more! Visit us at http://www.passporter.com for a complete list of what's new and changed in PassPorter 2004!

PassPorter®
Walt Disney World® Resort
2004 Edition

The unique travel guide, planner, organizer, journal, and keepsake

Jennifer Watson,
Dave Marx,
and
Allison Cerel Marx

PassPorter Travel Press

An imprint of MediaMarx, Inc.
P.O. Box 3880, Ann Arbor, Michigan 48106
877-WAYFARER
http://www.passporter.com

PassPorter® Walt Disney World® Resort–2004 Edition
by Jennifer Watson, Dave Marx, and Allison Cerel Marx

P.O. Box 3880, Ann Arbor, Michigan 48106
877-WAYFARER or 877-929-3273 (toll-free)
Visit us on the World Wide Web at http://www.passporter.com

PassPorter® Walt Disney World® Resort is not affiliated with, authorized or endorsed by, or in any way officially connected with, The Walt Disney Company, Disney Enterprises, Inc., or any of their affiliates.

While every care has been taken to ensure the accuracy of the information in this travel guide, the passage of time will always bring changes, and consequently the publisher cannot accept responsibility for errors that may occur. All prices and operating schedules quoted herein are based on information available to us at press time. Operating hours, maps, resort policies, future attractions, admission fees, and other costs may change, however, and we advise vacationers to call ahead and verify these facts and any others which are subject to change. The authors and publishers of this book shall not be held liable for any information (valid or invalid) presented here and do not represent The Walt Disney Company.

PassPorter® Walt Disney World® Resort is authored and edited by Jennifer Watson, Dave Marx, and Allison Cerel Marx. The information presented is for your personal vacation planning. Any stated opinions are ours alone, unless otherwise noted, and do not represent The Walt Disney Company or anyone else. Materials submitted and credited by persons other than ourselves are here with their permission and any associated rights belong to them.

Any and all written messages, suggestions, ideas, or other information shared with the authors in response to this guide shall be deemed and shall remain the property of PassPorter Travel Press.

Special Sales: PassPorter Travel Press publications are available at special discounts for bulk purchases for sales premiums or promotions. Special editions, including personalized covers and excerpts of existing guides, can be created in large quantities. For information, write to Special Sales, P.O. Box 3880, Ann Arbor, Michigan, 48106.

ISBN 1-58771-012-9

10 9 8 7 6 5 4 3 2 1

Printed and bound in Hong Kong

About the Authors

Name: Jennifer Watson

Date of birth: 10/09/68

Residence: Ann Arbor, MI

Signature: Jennifer Watson

Jennifer Watson fell in love with Walt Disney World on her first visit as a teenager in 1983. She has since returned more times than she can count on her fingers and toes, visiting every park, attraction, resort, and restaurant at least once. As author of over a dozen popular books, she yearned to write one about Walt Disney World but felt no interest in churning out yet another travel guide when there were so many excellent books already available. When she hit upon the idea of the PassPorter, she knew she could offer her fellow vacationers something unique and valuable. With the help of the PassPorter, Jennifer has organized gatherings at Walt Disney World for individuals, groups, and families of all ages. Jennifer would like to live in Cinderella Castle, but happily settles for Ann Arbor, Michigan where she makes her home with Dave and their adorable Alaskan Malamute, Kippi.

Dave Marx may be considered a Renaissance Man, a jack-of-all-trades, or a dilettante, depending on how you look at things. He took a 20-year hiatus between his early journalism training and the commencement of his full-time writing career. Beyond co-authoring numerous books with Jennifer, he's been a radio writer/producer; recording engineer; motion picture music editor; broadcast engineering supervisor; tax preparer; cab driver; whitewater safety and rescue instructor; developer and instructor of online publishing courses; and newsletter editor and promotions chief for an online forum. He has also co-authored and contributed to numerous books about America Online and the Internet. He discovered the "World" (Walt Disney World, that is) in 1997 and spent more than six months there over the following five years. Dave is from New Jersey, and now makes his home in Ann Arbor, Michigan.

Name: Dave Marx

Date of birth: 04/07/55

Residence: Ann Arbor, MI

Signature: Dave Marx

Name: Allison C. Marx

Residence: New Jersey

Signature: Allison

Allison Cerel Marx ("Allie") is a veteran visitor to Walt Disney World (and Dave's 11-year-old daughter). She has a maniacal grin, especially when spinning one of Mad Hatter's teacups at top speed. She's camped at Fort Wilderness, hung out in the Treehouses at the Disney Institute, celebrated New Year's Eve 1999/2000 in the Magic Kingdom, and photographed animals at the Animal Kingdom Lodge Resort. She shares her "A-OK!" ratings and ever-popular "Allie's KidTips" notes for attractions in the Touring the 'World' chapter. Allie also offers her thoughts on the childcare clubs on property.

PassPorter Team

Our Expert Peer Reviewers and Researchers—This group of extremely knowledgable experts, each widely acknowledged as a leader, painstakingly checked our text and maps and helped us ensure PassPorter's accuracy, readability, and thoroughness.

Steve Baker enjoys assisting others in vacation planning as a PassPorter message board guide. Steve became addicted to Disney at the age of 7 and now visits the "World" annually. He is husband to Susan and father to three.

Joanne and Tim Ernest are message board guides at PassPorter, where they enjoy discussing the magic of Disney with readers. They have two boys, David and Andrew, and are veterans of over a dozen trips to Disney.

LauraBelle Hime has made sixteen trips to Disney World and Disneyland. She travels solo as well as with young children (her kids and grandkids), adults, and families. She is also a message board guide at PassPorter Online.

Deb Koma, a Virginia-based writer, discovered the magic of Walt Disney World relatively recently. Since then she has made up for lost time, and is now a veteran of over twenty Disney trips, with many more on the horizon.

Bruce Metcalf has loved and studied Disney parks since 1958. He works at a major Central Florida theme park and co-writes the delightful "Iago & Zazu's Attraction of the Week" at http://aotw.figzu.com.

Michelle Nash is an Instructional Technologist who has loved Walt Disney World since her first trip in 1975. Since then she's been over ten times. She is also a PassPorter message board guide and the mother of one son, Todd.

Sandy Schubert is a frequent visitor to Walt Disney World and a PassPorter message board guide. She is married to Andy and has two sons, Chris and Craig, who is a recent alumnus of the Walt Disney World College Program.

Cindy Seaburn and her husband Russ make several weekend visits a year to Walt Disney World. As a PassPorter message board guide, Cindy enjoys chatting with others about all the excitement found at Walt Disney World.

Ann Smith is a PassPorter.com message board guide. She is wife to Jim and Mom to Jamie, Brendan, and Shelby, who are all equally addicted to Walt Disney World and try to visit at least twice a year.

Jeff Spencer enjoys helping fellow Walt Disney World fans on Disney-related Internet discussion groups. For Disney trip reports, tips, links, and other excellent Disney information, visit http://home.hiwaay.net/~jlspence.

Deb Wills is a recognized expert on Disney and the founder of the popular Unofficial Walt Disney World Information Guide at http://www.wdwig.com. Deb publishes the "All Ears" newsletter and contributes to discussion groups.

Printer: Magnum Printing, Ltd., Hong Kong (thank you, Anita Lam!)
Visibility Specialists: Kate and Doug Bandos, KSB Promotions
Sorcerers' Apprentices: Kim and Chad Larner, Jeanne Beroza, and Carolyn Tody
Special thank yous to Tom Anderson, Mariska Elia, Dave Hunter, Miguel Piedra, Than Saffel, Susan Shumaker, Peter Stepniewicz, Rick Sylvain, and Dirk Uhlenbrock.

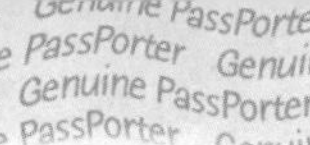
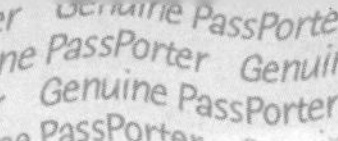
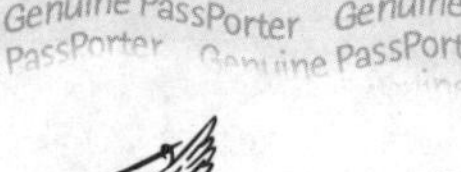

Acknowledgments

A "world" of thanks to our readers, who've contributed loads of tips and stories since PassPorter's debut. A special thanks to those who generously allowed us to include their contributions in this edition:

Anne DeMallie, Bethan Langlois, Susan Coward, and Juli Dennis (page i); Jennifer McGhinnis, Shelly Andersen, Blair Barbesin, and Susan Robertson (page 12); Judy Waldy, Maria Gallagher, Vickie Owens, and Kalliope Mulchi (page 24); Margaret Wellman, Tom Anderson, Steve Baker, and Debbie Hill (page 112); Jeri Hall, Jacquelyn Boyles, Susan Beaty, and Gregory Rose (page 198); Cynthia Olsen, Liz Myrato, and Lisa Frieman (page 240); Kris Powell, Tami Romano, and Carolyn Tody (page 260); Lori Enders, Cindy Seaburn, Kathleen Dahm, Jessica Sims, Patricia Chandler, and Melinda Brickhouse (page 279). May each of you receive a new magical memory for every reader your words touch.

PassPorter would not be where it is today without the help and support of the many members of the Internet Disney fan community. Our thanks to the friendly folks below and to all who we didn't have room to include!

- RADP (news://rec.arts.disney.parks newsgroup).
- Deb's Unofficial Walt Disney World Information Guide (http://www.wdwig.com).
- Unofficial Disney Information Station (http://www.wdwinfo.com). Thanks, Pete!
- Adults at Walt Disney World (http://www.adultsatwdw.com). Thanks, Rose!
- Badger's Disney Countdown (http://nhed.com/countdown). Thanks, Ed!
- Disney Vacation Planning (http://www.solarius.com/dvp). Thank you, Paul!
- Disney World: The Unofficial Online Guide (http://wdisneyw.co.uk). Thanks, Joanne!
- DisneyZone (http://www.disneyzone.actusa.net). Thanks, Kimmi!
- eGuides to Go (http://www.eguidestogo.com). Thanks, Andy!
- Hidden Mickeys of Disney (http://www.hiddenmickeys.org). Thanks, Tom!
- Intercot (http://www.intercot.com). Thank you, John!
- LaughingPlace.com (http://www.laughingplace.com). Thanks, Doobie and Rebekah!
- Magictrips.com (http://www.magictrips.com). Thank you, Ada!
- MousePlanet.com (http://www.mouseplanet.com).
- MouseSavers.com (http://www.mousesavers.com). Thanks, Mary!
- Our Laughing Place (http://www.ourlaughingplace.com). Thanks, Ahnalira!
- Priority Seating Calculator (http://pscalculator.net). Thanks, Scott!
- Spencer Family's Disney Page (http://home.hiwaay.net/~jlspence). Thanks, Jeff!

A special thank you to the Guides (moderators) of our own message boards: Steve Baker, Michelle Clark, Joanne and Tim Ernest, Kristin Grey, LauraBelle Hime, Debbie Hendrickson, Christina Holland-Radvon, Robin Krening-Capra, Marcie LaCava, Don Lefebvre, Michelle Nash, Allison Palmer-Gleicher, Susan Rannestad, Sandy Schubert, Cindy Seaburn, Ann Smith, Nate Stokes, Suzanne Torrey, Sara Varney, Suzi Waters, Brant Wigginton, Debbie Wright, and the 6000+ readers in our amazing community at http://www.passporterboards.com.

A heartfelt thank you to our family and friends for their patience while we were away on trips or cloistered at our computers, and for their support of our dream: Carolyn Tody; Tom Anderson; Fred and Adele Marx; Kim, Chad, Megan, and Natalie Larner; Dan, Jeannie, Kayleigh, Melanie, and Nina Marx; Gale Cerel-Marx; Jeanne and David Beroza; Gordon Watson and Marianne Couch; George Louie; Tracy DeGarmo; Ben Foxworth; and Marta Metcalf.

Last but not least, we thank Walter Elias Disney for his dream.

Contents

List of Maps, Worksheets, and Charts

Contents

(continued)

Congratulations!

First, congratulations are in order—you're going to Walt Disney World! You are about to embark on an experience that will amaze and, hopefully, delight you. This isn't an ordinary, run-of-the-mill trip—after all, you're going to spend your vacation in the heart of Mickey Mouse land!

The Walt Disney World Resort is a world unto itself, full of heralded amusements and hidden gems. Yet the very fact that it is so vast can make a visit to Walt Disney World seem more like a race in a maze than a relaxed vacation. And worse yet, pleasant memories of a great vacation may disappear beneath the stress and worries that accompanied it.

Happily, after fifty-plus trips to Walt Disney World we've learned to dispel our stress with one simple and enjoyable task: **planning ahead**. In fact, it is no task at all—planning is as much fun as the vacation itself. Planning gave birth to the PassPorter concept. Originally, Jennifer made itineraries on her computer and placed them in a binder. During the trip she kept the binder handy, using it to store passes, brochures, and receipts. After the vacation, these organizers had turned into scrapbooks, full of pixie-dusted memories and goofy smiles. When Jennifer's writing career took off she didn't have the time to create binders for every trip. She wished for a simpler version that she could use each trip without a lot of fuss. It was on a Disney bus that the idea came to her. She could make an easy-to-use, book-based version and offer it as a resource to fellow vacationers!

Now, after much work, you hold PassPorter in your hands. The first edition of PassPorter debuted in 1999, creating a sensation in the Disney fan community, winning eight national awards, and helping tens of thousands of vacationers plan great vacations. This edition, our sixth, is our best yet!

It is our greatest hope that PassPorter helps you "discover the magic" through your own eyes, as it did for us. To get you in the spirit, read "Disney Dreaming" on the next page and prepare for your adventure!

Smiles and laughter,

Jennifer, Dave, and Allison

We'd love to hear from you! Visit us on the Internet (http://www.passporter.com) or drop us a postcard from Walt Disney World!

P.S. As a favor to loyal readers who want their new editions a bit sooner, we finished this edition's updates in October 2003, a month earlier than usual. We expect some exciting news just over the horizon, so be sure to consult our updates at http://www.passporter.com/customs/bookupdates.htm.

Disney Dreaming

A good part of the fun of going to the Walt Disney World Resort is the anticipation before your trip! To really get you into "Disney Dreaming," we present some of our favorite tips to feed your excitement and prepare you for the adventure that lies ahead. This is magical stuff—don't blame us if you get the urge to hop on the next plane to Orlando.

Watch a Movie
Disney movies—animations and live action alike—capture the Disney spirit wonderfully. Rent your favorite from the local video store and settle in for a cozy evening. You can also request a free vacation planning video of the Walt Disney World Resort— call Disney at 407-934-7639 to order your free video. (To get a free Disney Cruise Line video, call 888-325-2500.)

Go shopping
Pay a visit to The Disney Store, found in major shopping malls. The stores' delightful theming, classic characters, and foot-tapping music really get you in the spirit. You can buy park admission at a discount, and special offers may be available with the Disney Visa card (see page 10).

Reminisce
If you've visited the "World" before, think back to your vacation and the things you enjoyed most about it. Dig out your souvenirs, photos, and home movies and view them with fresh eyes. If you used a PassPorter last time, go through your PassPockets carefully to refresh your memory and find the notes you made "for next time." If you haven't gone to Walt Disney World before, talk to all the friends and family members who have gone and get their impressions, tips, and stories.

Network With Others
Disney fans tend to gravitate towards online services and the Internet. If you've got an Internet connection, you'll find many Disney sites—even one for PassPorter planners! (See page 7 for more information.) No access to the Internet? Look to your communities for other vacationers who'd like to swap ideas and plans—try your workplace and school.

Plan, Plan, Plan
Few things are better than planning your own trip to the Walt Disney World Resort. Cuddle up with your PassPorter, read it through, and use it to the fullest—it makes planning fun and easy. PassPorter really is the ultimate in Disney Dreaming!

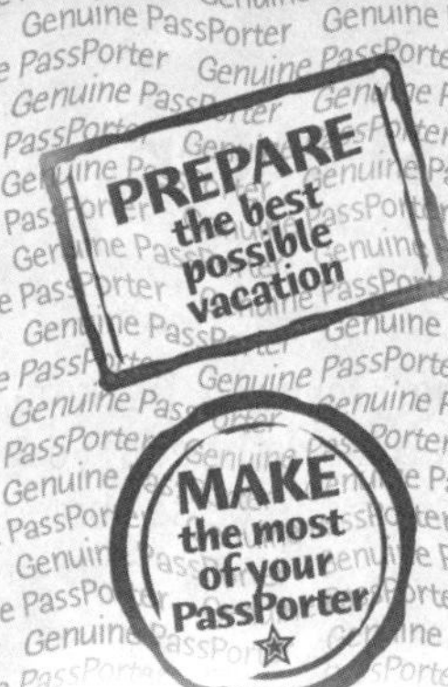

Planning Your Adventure

Planning is the secret to a successful vacation. The vast Walt Disney World Resort is not designed for procrastinators or last-minute travelers. Good planning is rewarded by a far more magical Disney experience. Planning is also wonderful fun. It increases the anticipation and starts the excitement months before the vacation begins.

Planning begins with learning about the Walt Disney World Resort. Your PassPorter has all the information you need for a great vacation, and then some! Written to be complete yet compact, the PassPorter can be your only guidebook or act as a companion to another. You can use it in a variety of ways: as a travel guide, a vacation planner, an organizer, a trip journal, and a keepsake. We designed it for heavy use—you can take it with you and revisit it after your trip is a fond memory. Personalize it with your plans, notes, souvenirs, and memories. We even crafted it with extra room in the binding to hold the things you'll squeeze and jam into the pockets along the way. The PassPorter is the ultimate Walt Disney World Resort guide—before, during, and after your vacation.

This first chapter helps you with the initial planning stage: gathering information and budgeting. Your PassPorter then continues through the planning stages in order of priority. Sprinkled throughout are ways to personalize your trip, little-known tips, and magical Disney memories.

Above all else, have fun with your plans, both now and when you reach the Walt Disney World Resort. Leave room for flexibility, and include time to relax and refresh. Despite the temptation to see and do it all, an overly ambitious plan will be more exhausting (and frustrating) than fun. Don't get so bogged down with planning and recording that you miss the spontaneous magic of a Disney vacation. As Robert Burns so appropriately said, "The best laid plans of mice and of men go oft astray." Use your PassPorter to plan ahead so you can relax and enjoy your vacation, no matter what it brings.

Planning With Your PassPorter

Each important aspect of your vacation—budgeting, traveling, packing, lodging, touring, and eating—has a **special dedicated worksheet** in your PassPorter. Don't be shy, we designed these worksheets to be scribbled upon at will. Not only do they take the place of easy-to-lose scraps of paper, they are structured specifically for your vacation.

When you start planning your trip in your PassPorter, **use a pencil** so you can erase and make changes. Use a permanent pen once your plans are definite to avoid smudging. You can **keep a pen handy, too**! Slip it inside the book's spiral binding. The pen's pocket clip holds it in place.

Additions and significant changes at Walt Disney World since our 2003 edition are highlighted in blue, just like this paragraph! This is not to be confused with general changes to PassPorter—almost every page changed!

Your PassPorter is most useful when you keep it handy before and during your vacation. It fits compactly into backpacks and shoulder bags. Or, tuck your PassPorter into a **waist pack** (at least 6.5" x 9" or 17 x 23 cm).

Your PassPorter loves to go on rides with you, but try to **keep it dry** on Splash Mountain and Kali River Rapids. The heavy cover offers good protection, but a simple resealable plastic bag (gallon size) is a big help.

Personalize your PassPorter! **Write your name** under the front cover flap, along with other information you feel comfortable listing. Your hotel name, trip dates, and phone number help if you misplace your PassPorter. Under the back cover flap are places for your important **phone numbers**, **reminders**, and **addresses**. Use the checkboxes to mark items when done. The **label page** at the end of the text is a new feature—use the labels to personalize your PassPockets and attach the tabs to mark your chapters!

Two tools you may find helpful for planning are a **highlighter** (to mark "must-sees") and those sticky **page flags** (to mark favorite pages).

It's normal for the **handy spiral binding** in your PassPorter to rotate as you flip pages. If this causes your binding to creep up, you can easily rotate it back—just twist the binding while holding the pages securely.

Your PassPorter's **sturdy cover** wraps around your book for protection, and you can fold it back and leave the book open. The binding is a bit bigger than necessary to fit your stuff. We crafted a pocket for each day of your trip (up to eleven days), plus special ones for your journey, lodging, and memories. Read more about these "PassPockets" on the next page.

Note: Most of the tips on these two pages apply to the regular edition (spiral-bound); if you have a deluxe edition (ring-bound), visit http://www.passporter.com/wdw/deluxe.htm

Using Your PassPockets

In the back of your PassPorter are fourteen unique "PassPockets" to help you plan before you go, keep items handy while you're there, and save memories for your return. Just record your trip information and itinerary on the front, store brochures, maps, receipts, and such inside, and jot down impressions, memories, expenses, and notes on the back. Use the PassPockets in any way that suits you, filling in as much or as little as you like. You can even personalize your PassPockets with the included labels!

Read the advice or tip.

Use the pockets as printed, or personalize with a label.

Write your itinerary here, including times, names, and confirmation numbers. Or just record what you did.

Jot down things you want to remember, do, or visit.

Make notes before you go or add notes during your trip.

Store items you want to have on hand during your trip, or things you collect along the way, in this roomy pocket. Guidemaps, brochures, and envelopes all fit inside.

Slip small items in this smaller slot, such as receipts, claim tags, and ticket stubs.

Write the day of the week and the date for quick reference!

Record memories of your vacation to share with others or to keep to yourself. You can jot these down as you go, or reminisce at the end of the day.

Keep track of photos taken so you can find them later!

Watch your expenses to stay within a budget or to track your resort charge account balance.

Remember all those great (or not so great) meals and snacks by noting them here. You can even include the price of the meal or snack, too!

What did you forget? What do you want to do again? What would you like to try next time? What wouldn't you touch again with a ten-foot pole? Make a note of it here!

Use the Vacation-At-A-Glance page just in front of your PassPockets to record park hours, showtimes, meals, or anything that helps you plan your trip. And if you prefer to travel light, don't be shy about removing a PassPocket and carrying it around for the day instead of your entire PassPorter. Just tuck it back in here at the end of the day! (If you have the spiral version and feel uncomfortable about tearing out a PassPocket, you may prefer our ring-bound Deluxe Edition with looseleaf pockets—see page 284.)

Finding Disney Information

The PassPorter can act as your **first source** of information for the Walt Disney World Resort. It can also be a companion to other Disney books you may already own or purchase later. Either way, we like to think it packs a lot of information into a small package. Everything you need to know to plan a wonderful Disney vacation can be found within its pages.

Do keep in mind that the Walt Disney World Resort is constantly changing. We've taken every step to ensure that your PassPorter is as up-to-date as possible, but we cannot foresee the future. So to help your PassPorter remain current, we **make free updates available** to you at our Web site (http://www.passporter.com/customs/bookupdates.htm). If you have ideas, questions, or corrections, please contact us—see page 260.

Oodles of **travel guidebooks** are available if you have a hankering for second opinions. We highly recommend these guidebooks: "The Unofficial Guide to Walt Disney World" (for irreverence and detail), "Birnbaum's Walt Disney World" (for the official line and color photos), "Walt Disney World for Couples" (for sweet romance), and "Hassle-Free Walt Disney World" (for touring plans). You'll find something different in each.

Call the **Walt Disney World Resort** at 407-WDISNEY (407-934-7639) when you need answers to specific questions. In our experience, their representatives are very friendly, but they rarely volunteer information and won't offer opinions. Prepare questions in advance. If the person you reach doesn't have an answer, call back—several times if necessary. Don't hesitate to ask for a manager if you can't get the information you need.

Travel agents whom you know and trust can be an excellent source of information, such as the service-oriented MouseEarVacations.com (see coupon on page 282). Also check with **membership organizations** that arrange travel, such as AAA (see page 11).

Magazines and newsletters about Disney are also available. The "Disney Magazine" covers all things Disney, including the parks. Subscribe for $20 for eight issues (two years) at 800-333-8734. Annual Passholders (see page 10) receive a periodic newsletter from Disney. ALL EARS™ is a free unofficial e-mail newsletter that comes out weekly with news, reviews, and reports—subscribe at http://www.allearsnet.com. We also offer our own bi-weekly e-mail newsletter with book updates, features, tips, and deals—subscribe at http://www.passporter.com/news.htm. "Mouse Tips" is a more traditional newsletter on paper—subscribe for a special rate of $11/year at Box 383, Columbus, OH 43216.

Exploring a Whole New World Wide Web

The ultimate source of information, in our opinion, is the **Internet**. Of course, this requires a personal computer with a modem, a network connection, or "WebTV," but with this you can connect to millions of vacationers happy to share their Disney knowledge.

The Web offers hundreds of Disney-related sites. In fact, **PassPorter** has its own Web site with updates, tips, ideas, articles, forums, and links. Visit us at http://www.passporter.com. More details are on page 281.

As you might expect, Disney has a Web site for all things Walt Disney World at http://www.disneyworld.com. While **Disney's official Web site** doesn't offer opinions, it is an excellent source for basic information, including operating hours, rates, maps, and resort room layouts. Late changes to operating hours are best verified at 407-824-4321, however.

We also highly recommend several **unofficial Web sites**, which we frequent ourselves when planning a trip. We introduce these Web sites as appropriate throughout the book (check pages 272–273 in the index for a full list), but one special site deserves mention now: **All Ears Net** (also known as WDWIG) is a comprehensive and up-to-date collection of information about the Walt Disney World Resort, often contributed by other Disney vacationers and enthusiasts. All Ears Net is located at http://www.wdwig.com. Tell Deb we said, "Hi!"

Another source of information (and camaraderie) is **discussion groups**. PassPorter has its own set of message boards with an active, supportive community of vacationers at http://www.passporterboards.com–come chat with us and ask your questions! Fans also congregate at Pete Werner's **Unofficial Disney Information Station** at http://www.wdwinfo.com, as well as at John Yaglenski's **Intercot** at http://www.intercot.com and Rich Koster's **DisneyEcho** at http://disneyecho.emuck.com. We also recommend **rec.arts.disney.parks (RADP)** newsgroup at news://rec.arts.disney.parks. Last but not least, those of you on **America Online** should pay a visit to the Disney message boards at Keyword: TRAVEL BOARDS.

E-mail lists are yet another valuable Internet resource, allowing you to observe and participate in discussions from the safety of your e-mailbox. We host a discussion list and a newsletter list (with regular features)–subscribe for free at our Web site. Many other mailing lists are available, including the wonderful **DisneyDollarless** list for Disney fans on a budget–subscribe at http://www.disneydollarless.com.

Budgeting For Your Vacation

There's nothing magical about depleting your nest egg to finance a vacation. Too many Disney vacationers can tell you that money worries overshadowed all the fun. Yet you can avoid both the realities and worries of overspending by planning within a budget. Budgeting ahead of time not only keeps you from spending too much, it encourages you to seek out ways to save money. With just a little bit of research, you can often get **more for less**, resulting in a much richer, more relaxed vacation.

If you purchase a **vacation package**, you have the advantage of covering most of your major expenses right up front. And while package prices haven't offered a real savings in the past, they've recently gotten better and can be excellent deals. Beyond finding a package with a great deal, planning each aspect of your vacation yourself usually saves you more money, as we show you throughout this book. You can learn about vacation packages on page 30 and inquire into prices with the Walt Disney Travel Co. at 800-828-0228 or on the Web at http://www.disneytravel.com.

Your **vacation expenses** usually fall into six categories: planning, transportation, lodging, admission, food, and extras. How you budget for each depends upon the total amount you have available to spend and your priorities. Planning, transportation, lodging, and admission are the easiest to factor ahead of time as costs are fixed. The final two—food and extras—are harder to control, but can usually be estimated based on your tastes and habits.

Begin your vacation budgeting with the **worksheet** on the following page. Enter the minimum you prefer to spend and the maximum you can afford in the topmost columns. Establish as many of these ranges as possible before you delve into the other chapters of this book. Your excitement may grow as you read more about the Walt Disney World Resort, but it is doubtful your bank account will.

As you uncover costs and ways to save money later, return to this worksheet and **update it**. Think of your budget as a work-in-progress. Flexibility within your minimum and maximum figures is important. As plans begin to crystallize, write the amount you expect to pay (and can afford) in the Estimated Costs column. Finally, when you are satisfied with your budget, **transfer the amounts** from the Estimated Costs column to the back of each PassPocket. Note that each PassPocket also provides space to record actual expenses, which helps you stay within your budget.

Budget Worksheet

Use this worksheet to identify your resources, record estimated costs, and create a budget for your vacation. When complete, transfer the figures from the Goals column to the back of each PassPocket.

	Minimum		Maximum		Est. Costs	
Total Projected Expenses	$		$		$	
Planning:						
Phone Calls/Faxes:						
Guides/Magazines:						
Transportation:	*(transfer to your Journey PassPocket)*					
Rental Car:						
Fuel/Maintenance/Tolls:						
Travel Tickets:						
Shuttle/Town Car/Taxi:						
Stroller/Wheelchair:						
ECV/Golf Cart:						
Parking:						
Lodging:	*(transfer to your Rooms PassPocket)*					
Enroute Motel/Other:						
Resort/Hotel:						
Admission:	*(transfer to appropriate PassPocket)*					
Theme Park Passes:						
Water Park Passes:						
DisneyQuest Passes:						
Pleasure Island Passes:						
Guided Tours/Other:						
Food:	Daily	Total	Daily	Total	Daily	Total
Breakfast:						
Lunch:						
Dinner:						
Snacks:						
Groceries/Other:						
	(transfer to each daily PassPocket)					
Extras:						
Souvenirs/Clothing:						
Gratuities:						
Vacation Wardrobe:						
Other:						
Other:						
Total Budgeted Expenses	$		$		$	

Money-Saving Programs

You can save real money on a Walt Disney World Resort vacation by taking advantage of these money-saving programs. Some require a membership fee, but they often pay for themselves quite quickly. *Note: The Disney Club program ended on December 31, 2003, and American Express cardholders no longer receive discounts or special perks at Disney.*

Disney's Visa Card—This new credit card from BankOne gives cardholders special discounts on Disney resorts and packages, and onboard credits on the Disney cruise. The card itself has no annual fee and earns "Disney Dream Reward Dollars" equal to 1% or more of your purchases. You can redeem your dollars quickly for Disney travel, entertainment, and merchandise. Another perk is the "pay no interest for 6 months" offer on Disney packages and cruises. We have Disney's Visa ourselves and while the "rewards" are just average, the available discounts can be great. Visit http://disney.go.com/visa or call 877-252-6576 for more information.

Annual Pass (AP)—An Annual Pass (regular or premium) saves big money on admission if you plan to visit for more than eight or thirteen days in a one-year period (depending on the pass), at which point it becomes less expensive than conventional admission. It may also deliver great discounts (up to 50%) at selected Disney resorts. The discounts alone may be worth it! See pages 116–117 for details and call Disney at 407-934-7639 for prices.

Florida Residents—Those of you with proof of Florida residency (such as a valid Florida driver's license) often enjoy great savings on Disney tickets, resorts, cruises, and more. The deals are so good we're almost tempted to move to Florida. Visit http://www.disneyworld.com for more details.

Disney Dining Experience (DDE)—Available only to Florida residents with a valid Florida driver's license or I.D. card, this program offers 20% discounts at most Disney table-service restaurants, plus free parking after 5:00 pm and half price Pleasure Island admission. Membership is $75/year (with an extra $5 off for annual passholders and cast members). Renewals are $60/year. Call 407-566-5858 to order (allow 2-3 weeks).

Disney Information Center at Ocala—If you're driving from the north, stop at Disney's Information Center off I-75 in Ocala for occasional deals on accommodations. Open 9:00 am to 6:00 pm. Call 352-854-0770.

Disney Vacation Club (DVC)—This timeshare program may save money for families who plan ahead. See pages 102–103 for details.

Tip: Sections highlighted in light blue (like the one below) indicate additions or significant changes at Walt Disney World since our previous edition!

Advance Purchase Park Admission Discounts—Buy your Disney park tickets in advance and save! At press time, you can save 7%-10% off the price of Park Hopper passes (see pages 116-117 for pass details). Get your advance purchase discounts at Disney Stores outside of Florida, Disney Specialist travel agents (such as MouseEarVacations.com—see page 282), via the Web (http://www.disneyworld.com), or by phone (407-934-7639). If the tickets need to be mailed, expect a mailing charge of $3 per order. If you do buy your tickets in advance, be sure to write down the pass reference number(s) in your PassPorter in the event you lose them.

Disney "Postcard" Specials and Advertisements—Disney frequently offers lodging discounts in direct mail and mass media advertisements. These offers may be sent to previous Disney guests, or may appear in newspaper or TV ads. These offers usually have eligibility requirements, such as residence in a particular state, or can only be used by the person who received the mailing. If you receive an offer, be sure to save it for your records. You'll need the "coupon code" and perhaps an I.D. number to make your reservation. Be sure you are eligible for the offer—if you show up at Disney and can't prove eligibility, you'll lose your "deal." Visit http://www.mousesavers.com for an excellent listing of current offers.

Orlando Magicard—This free card offers discounts on many non-Disney shows and park tickets, as well as rental cars and hotels. Call 888-416-4026 or visit http://www.orlandoinfo.com/magicard and allow 3-4 weeks.

American Automobile Association (AAA)—Members enjoy discounts ranging from 10%-20%, including tickets (when purchased in advance). Contact your local office, call 800-222-6424, or visit http://www.aaa.com.

Money-Saving Tips

- ✔ *MouseSavers.com is a Web site dedicated to cataloging available Disney discounts and deals. Webmaster Mary Waring has built a huge following, both at http://www.mousesavers.com and through her free monthly newsletter.*
- ✔ *If you are flying, check the newspapers and the Internet for fare sales—they occur more frequently than you might think and offer savings. Expedia.com (http://www.expedia.com) also has great deals on fares and hotel rooms!*
- ✔ *If you are driving or arriving late in the evening, consider staying a night at a less expensive motel your first night.*
- ✔ *You can save money on meals by eating only two meals a day, as Disney portions tend to be quite large. Bring quick breakfast foods and snacks from home to quell the munchies and keep your energy up.*
- ✔ *Always ask about discounts when you make reservations, dine, or shop. You may discover little-known specials for AAA, Disney Visa Card, Florida residents, Annual Passholders, or simply vacationers in the right place at the right time.*
- ✔ *Join the DisneyDollarless community for more money-saving tips—you can subscribe for free at http://www.disneydollarless.com.*

Plan It Up!

Use these tips to make planning your vacation fun and rewarding:

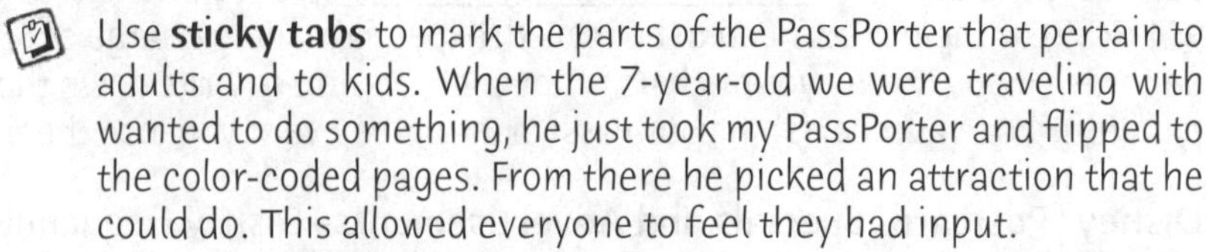

Use **sticky tabs** to mark the parts of the PassPorter that pertain to adults and to kids. When the 7-year-old we were traveling with wanted to do something, he just took my PassPorter and flipped to the color-coded pages. From there he picked an attraction that he could do. This allowed everyone to feel they had input.

– Contributed by Jennifer McGhinnis, a winner in our 2003 Reader Tip Contest

If you have access to the **Internet**, make it a point to get online once a week for the latest dish on the "World." We have many trip reports from fellow vacationers posted on our message boards at http://www.passporterboards.com. MousePlanet also offers trip reports at http://www.mouseplanet.com/dtp/trip.rpt.

Before setting out on a trip, **call your credit card company** and let them know you are traveling. Often if the credit card company sees several purchases from different places on consecutive days they will think your number has been stolen and will cancel the card to avoid further charges. You can avoid unpleasant and embarrassing surprises at the cash register by letting them know your itinerary.

– Contributed by Shelly Andersen, a winner in our 2003 Reader Tip Contest

Magical Memories

"Our last trip to Walt Disney World was also the first for our two children, so my wife decided to make the experience for them really special. About 1½ months before we were scheduled to leave my wife had the kids' favorite Disney characters 'write' them a letter (on character themed letterhead she created) and she mailed each of them a letter once a week. Each week the kids would get a letter from Cinderella, Snow White, Sebastian, Simba, Goofy, and of course she saved Mickey and Minnie for last. The look of joy and excitement on the kids' faces was worth all the work she put into this. It also drove the kids nuts! They wanted to leave for Disney each day they received their letter. It was the perfect build up for the kids and to be honest, their excitement got my wife and me just as excited to leave."

...as told by Disney vacationer Blair Barbesin

"I wanted our Walt Disney World trip to be extra special, and with four children, I also wanted it to go very smoothly. I planned for months. I planned and planned and then planned some more. We had a fabulous trip–I couldn't have been more pleased with our experience. But the crowning touch came on the last day. My son Nathan looked around and said, 'Mom, thanks for planning such a great vacation.' And without missing a beat, my oldest son Aaron observed (at the tender age of 9)... with great sincerity... 'Yeah! I think this has been the best week of my LIFE!' I knew then and there that we would be returning in another year." *...as told by Disney vacationer Susan Robertson*

Getting There (and Back!)

FIND many ways to get to Disney

PACK just what you need to bring to Disney

So, you promised your family a trip to visit the Mouse, or for the tenth time today you've gleefully thought, "I'm going to Disney!" Eventually the moment of truth arrives: just *how* are you going to get there?

Traveling in this age of tightened security requires more planning and patience, but you'll discover it is quite easy to get to the Walt Disney World Resort. The path to Orlando, Florida is well traveled by cars, planes, trains, buses, and tours. On the other hand, "easy" isn't always convenient or inexpensive. Choosing the best and most affordable way to get to Disney can take some doing. And we can help!

In this chapter we walk you through the process of making your travel arrangements. We brief you on weather, attendance levels, park hours, and seasonal rates so you can pick the best time to go, or make the most of the date you've already chosen. You'll find descriptions of each major path to the Walt Disney World Resort, and a worksheet to help you pick a route and make your reservations. Then it's time to get packing, with the help of our special packing lists. Finally, we help you smile and enjoy your journey with tips for having fun along the way.

What we won't do is take up space with the phone numbers of airline and car rental companies or travel directions from every city. You can find that information in your phone book or on the World Wide Web. Just jot down numbers and notes on the worksheet, and transfer the winners to the appropriate PassPocket in the back.

It's important to note that traveling is generally less flexible than lodging, which is in turn more costly. Thus, we find it works much better to make traveling decisions before finalizing hotel arrangements. However, you may prefer to skip to the next chapter and shop for your lodging first. Just return here to tailor your travel plans to your lodging choice.

Your journey begins...

The Best of Times

Most Disney veterans can tell you, in no uncertain terms, that some times are much better than others to visit the "World." We wholeheartedly agree, but there's more to it. While there are certainly times of the year that are less crowded or more temperate, only you can decide the best time to visit. To help you decide, we charted the **fluctuating factors** for each month below. If you ask us, the best time to visit is November–February, but avoid the holidays, when parks fill to capacity. Three-day weekends are also to be avoided whenever possible. The latter half of August and September are uncrowded, though you'll battle the heat. For links to temperature and rainfall data, visit http://www.passporter.com/wdw/bestoftimes.htm.

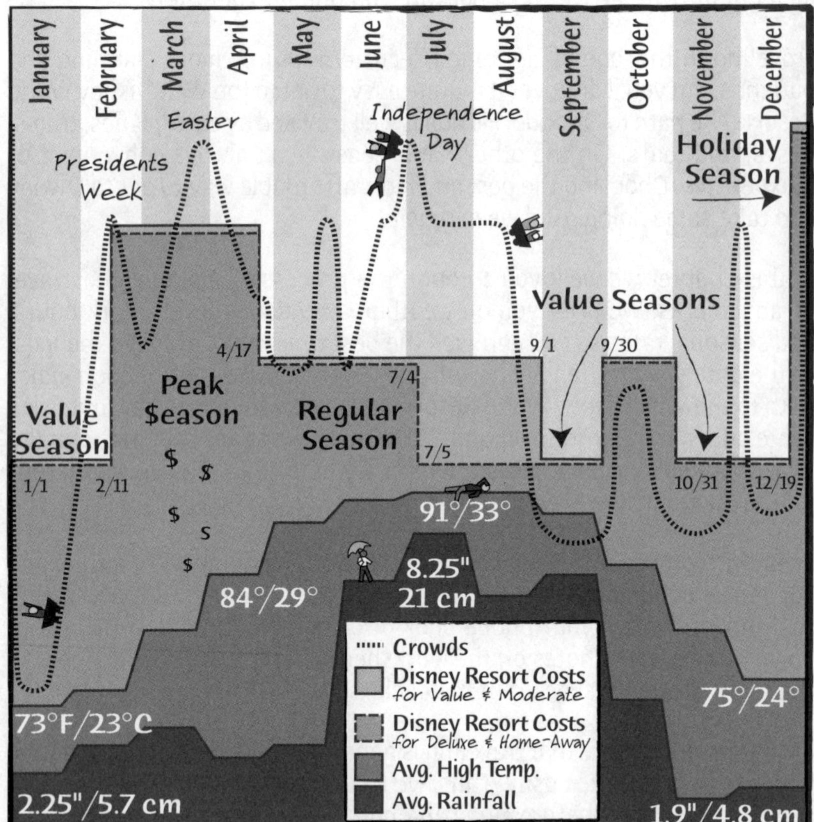

2004 Disney resort cost seasons are as follows:

Value Season *is Jan. 1– Feb. 11 (all), Jul. 5–Sep. 29 (deluxe and home-away), Sep. 1–29 (value and moderate), Oct. 31–Dec. 18 (all);* ***Regular Season*** *is Apr. 18–Jul. 4 (deluxe and home-away), Apr. 27–Aug. 28 (value and moderate), Sep. 30–Oct. 30 (all);* ***Peak Season*** *is Feb. 12–Apr. 17 (all);* ***Pre-Holiday Season*** *is Nov. 19–Dec. 19 (Ft. Wilderness only); and* ***Holiday Season*** *is Dec. 20–31 (all).*

Getting There

One of the major hurdles to a Walt Disney World Resort vacation is figuring out how to get there in the first place. Many of us think along the traditional (and expensive) lines first, and become discouraged. It doesn't have to be like that. There are **more ways** to get to Disney than you probably realize. Below we describe each, beginning with the most popular. At the end of the list, on pages 20–21, a worksheet gives you space to make notes, jot down prices, and note reservation numbers. When your travel plans are finalized, record them on the first PassPocket.

By Car, Van, Truck, or Motorcycle

Most vacationers arrive at Disney in their own vehicle. It's hard to beat the **slowly rising sense of excitement** as you draw closer, or the freedom of having your own wheels once you arrive. Driving may also eliminate the concerns you or family members may have with air travel. And driving can be less expensive than air travel, especially with large families. On the down side, you may spend long hours or even days on the road, which cuts deeply into your time with Mickey.

If you opt to drive, carefully **map your course** ahead of time. You can do this with a AAA TripTik—a strip map that guides you to and from your destination. You must be a AAA member (see page 11) to get a TripTik, but that is easily done for $40-$55/year (visit http://www.aaa.com for more information). If you're driving, we heartily recommend "Along Interstate-75" (Mile Oak Publishing, http://www.i75online.com) and/or "Drive I-95" (Travelsmart, http://www.drivei95.com). I-95 drivers should also visit http://www.usastar.com/i95/homepage.htm. Or try a trip routing service, such as AutoPilot at http://www.freetrip.com **Tip**: Have exact change ready for the many Florida toll roads. You can get toll prices at http://www.dot.state.fl.us/turnpikepio/TollCalculator/tollrates.htm.

If you live more than 500 miles away, **spread your drive out** over more than one day, allotting one day for every 500 miles. Arriving at Walt Disney World overly road-weary is no way to begin a vacation. If your journey spans more than one day, decide in advance where to stop each night and make reservations accordingly. Check that your air-conditioning is in good working order. Secure rest areas are available once you hit the Florida border, making it a bit easier to drive at night. And be sure to compare the price of driving versus flying, too.

By Airplane

Air travel is the fastest way for most to get to Orlando—and it's a great way to strengthen the air travel industry and the U.S. economy. Plus, air travel may be less expensive than you think if you know the tricks to getting an **affordable flight**. First, be flexible on the day and time of departure and return—fares can differ greatly depending on when you fly and how long you stay. Second, take advantage of the many "fare sales"—to learn about sales, visit airlines' Web sites or travel sites like Expedia (http://www.expedia.com), Orbitz (http://www.orbitz.com), or Travelocity (http://www.travelocity.com). Third, try alternate airports when researching fares. Fourth, be persistent. Ask for their lowest fare and work from there. When you find a good deal, put it on hold immediately (if possible), note your reservation number on page 21, and cancel later if necessary. Finally, don't stop shopping. If your airline offers a cheaper fare later, you may be able to rebook at the lower rate (watch out for penalties).

Try your **airline's Web site**—you can experiment with different flights, sign up for fare sale e-mails, and you may get a discount for booking online. Or try Priceline (http://www.priceline.com) where you name your own price for a round-trip ticket (but once your price is met, Priceline chooses your flight times and you can't cancel).

Once you reserve a flight, **make a note** of the reservation numbers, flight numbers, seat assignments, and layovers on your first PassPocket. To arrange **ground transportation** from the airport, see page 19.

Our Top 10 Flying Tips, Reminders, and Warnings

1. Visit http://www.tsa.gov for travel security news and updates.
2. Check the status of your flight before departing for the airport.
3. Pack (or pick-up) a meal for the flight, as most domestic flights have discontinued meal service for security reasons.
4. Pack sharp or potentially dangerous items in checked luggage (or just leave them at home). This includes pocket knives, knitting needles, sport sticks (i.e., pool cues), lighters, or flammable items such as aerosol hairspray. If you must bring needles or syringes, also bring a note from your doctor. Nail clippers and tweezers are now fine to keep in your carry-on.
5. Keep your luggage unlocked for inspections, or it may be damaged.
6. Limit your carry-ons to one bag and one personal item (purse, briefcase, etc.) and assume they will be searched.
7. Plan to arrive at the airport two hours prior to departure.
8. Curbside check-in may be available, but you may need to obtain a boarding pass from your airline's customer service desk anyway.
9. E-Ticket holders should bring a confirmation and/or boarding pass. If you don't have one, print it from your airline's Web site.
10. Keep your ID handy. We carry ours in PassHolder Pouches (see page 285).

Getting Around the Orlando Airport

Orlando International Airport is a large, sprawling hub and one of the better (and cleaner) airports we've flown into. When you arrive, your plane docks at one of the **satellite terminals** (see map below). From there, follow the signs to the automated **shuttle** that takes you to the main terminal—there you'll find **baggage claim** and ground transportation. Once you reach the main terminal (Level 3), follow signs down to baggage claim (Level 2). Shuttles, taxis, town cars, rental cars, and buses are found down on Level 1 (take the elevators opposite the baggage carousels). Each shuttle and bus company has its own ticket booth, so keep your eyes open. If you get lost, look about for signs or an information desk that can get you back on track.

As your authors used to live in entirely different parts of the country, we became quite good at **meeting up at the airport**. It's best to meet your party at their baggage claim area as you won't be allowed past security without a valid boarding pass. The trick here is knowing which airline and baggage claim area. Use the map and airline list below, or call the airport directly at 407-825-2001. Be careful when differentiating between side A and B's baggage claim. Gates 1-29 and 100-129 use side A, while gates 30-99 use side B. Check the arrival/departure boards in the main terminal for flight status, too! Other meeting spots are the Disney Stores inside the terminal (see stars on map below), or an airport restaurant (especially good for long waits).

For **more details** on the Orlando International Airport, call 407-825-2001 or visit http://www.orlandoairports.net. Page travelers at 407-825-2000.

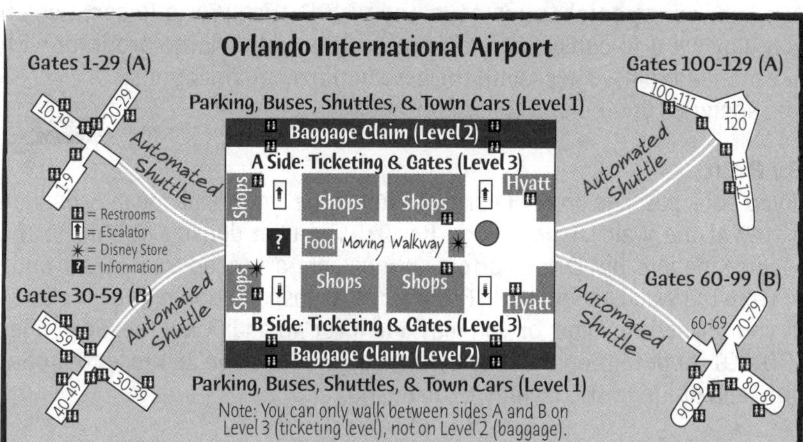

American Airlines, America West, Continental, SunWorld, Thomas Cook, and TWA use gates 1-29; Air Canada, ANA, Northwest, United, and USAir use gates 30-59; Delta, British Airways, Midwest, Song, Sun Country, and Virgin Atlantic use gates 60-99; and AirTran, jetBlue, Southwest, and Spirit use gates 100-129.

By Train, Bus, Tour, and Boat

By Train

The train is a uniquely relaxing way to travel to the Walt Disney World Resort. **Amtrak** serves the Orlando area daily with both **passenger trains** and an Auto Train, which carries your family and your car. The **Auto Train** runs between suburban Washington DC and suburban Orlando (Sanford, FL). Other trains may go through to Kissimmee, which is a closer, less-crowded station for vacationers bound for Walt Disney World. Prices vary depending upon the season, the direction, and how far in advance you make your reservation. The Auto Train is also available one-way, and in many seasons one direction is less expensive than the other direction. You may need to take a taxi or town car (see page 19) from the train station to the Disney property. Hertz rental cars are available from the Sanford and Orlando stations, but not the Kissimmee station. For Amtrak reservations, call 800-USA-RAIL or visit them at http://www.amtrak.com.

By Bus

Buses make good economic and environmental sense. **Greyhound** serves Orlando and Kissimmee. You can take the local LYNX buses from there, but it's not easy (for more information on LYNX, see the next page under "Riding a Bus"). Buses take longer to reach a destination than do cars driving the same route. Fares are lowest if you live within ten hours of Walt Disney World. For fares, schedules, and tickets, call Greyhound at 800-231-2222 or visit them at http://www.greyhound.com.

By Tour

A number of **special tours** go to the Walt Disney World Resort, which you may want to consider if you prefer to go with a large group or with like-minded folks. Check with the associations, organizations, and societies you belong to, or contact a travel agent.

By Boat

If you book passage on the **Disney Cruise Line**, your package may include a stay at the Walt Disney World Resort. The boat doesn't pull up to the Magic Kingdom, but Disney offers optional, pre-arranged transfers to and/or from the Walt Disney World Resort—this transportation may be included in your cruise package, or you may add it for an additional fee. See pages 100–101 for details on the Disney Cruise, and see page 284 to learn about our field guide to the Disney Cruise Line.

By Everything Else!

The list of ways to get to Disney is really endless. Consider traveling under your own power—bicycles! Combine business with pleasure, or make your pleasure your business, as we have.

Are We There Yet?

Once you reach Orlando, you need to continue about 20 miles before you actually reach the Disney property. Here are your options:

Taking a Shuttle or Town Car

A number of shuttle companies stay in business largely by transporting guests to and from Disney. Shuttle stands are located at the Orlando International Airport (Level 1), but all other pickup points require advance notice. The major shuttle operator is Mears (800-759-5219). We prefer and recommend a **town car**, however. The town car driver greets us at baggage claim, carries our luggage, drives us to our hotel, and charges less than it costs a family of four to use a shuttle, taxi, or rental car. We love Tiffany Towncar (888-838-2161) and highly recommend their services (we've included a great coupon for a roundtrip on page 282). If you'd like to stop at a grocery store or if you need a car/booster seat, request this at reservation. Visit http://www.tiffanytowncar.com. Two more services we recommend include YourRide (866-240-RIDE, http://www.yourride.net) and Selective Limousine (800-730-0211, http://www.selectivelimo.com)

Driving a Car

If you're driving to Walt Disney World, you'll need specific directions. You can find detailed directions through a trip routing service (see page 15) or Disney (call 407-939-4636). Fliers planning to drive a car while in Orlando should rent at the airport. We don't feel a rental car is needed if you stay only in Disney as their internal transportation system works well (see pages 118–119) and even an occasional taxi fare can be cheaper than a rental car. If you plan to go off-property often, you may find a rental car helpful. Alamo (Disney's official rental car agency), Avis, Budget, Dollar, and National are located right at the airport on Level 1 (in-airport rentals incur a 10% fee). Enterprise, Hertz, and many others are off-site and you'll need to take a shuttle on Level 1 to reach them (off-site rentals carry an 8.67% fee). The Dolphin Resort and several off-property hotels offer rental car desks, too. Inquire about all taxes and surcharges.

Riding a Bus

The regional bus system, LYNX, has limited service to the Walt Disney World property. Call 407-841-2279 or visit http://www.golynx.com. And if you need to get from your hotel to any other theme park in the Orlando area, Mears offers shuttles ($12 roundtrip)—call a day in advance.

Using a Taxi

While taxis are available, we don't recommend them for travel due to cost. Large parties may be able to ride in a taxi mini-van economically, however.

Planning
Getting There
Staying in Style
Touring
Feasting
Making Magic
Index
Notes & More

Travel Worksheet

Use this worksheet to jot down preferences, scribble information during phone calls, and keep all your discoveries together. Don't worry about being neat–just be thorough! When everything is confirmed, transfer it to your first PassPocket in the back of the book. Circle the names and numbers once you decide to go with them to avoid confusion.

Arrival date: ____________ Alternate: ____________

Return date: ____________ Alternate: ____________

We plan to travel by: ❑ Car/Van ❑ Airplane ❑ Train ❑ Bus ❑ Tour ❑ Other: ____________

For Drivers:

Miles to get to Orlando: ________ ÷ 500 = ________ # days on the road

We need to stay at a motel on: ____________

Tune-up scheduled for: ____________

Rental car info: ____________

For Riders:

Train/Bus phone numbers: ____________

Ride preferences: ____________

Ride availabilities: ____________

Reserved ride times and numbers: ____________

Routes: ____________

For Tour Takers:

Tour company phone numbers: ____________

Tour preferences: ____________

Tour availabilities: ____________

Reserved tour times and numbers: ____________

Routes: ____________

For Fliers:

Airline phone numbers: ____________________

Flight preferences: ____________________

Flight availabilities: ____________________

____

____

____

Reserved flight times and numbers: ____________________

____

For Ground Transportation:

Town car/shuttle/rental car phone numbers: ____________________

____

Town car/shuttle/rental car reservations: ____________________

____

Package ground transportation details: ____________________

____

Additional Notes:

Reminder: Don't forget to confirm holds or cancel reservations (whenever possible) within the allotted time frame.

Planning | Getting There | Staying in Style | Touring | Feasting | Making Magic | Index | Notes & More

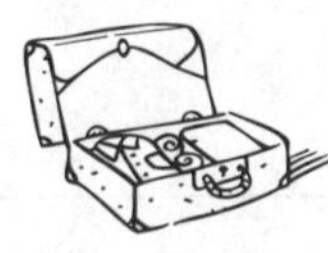

Packing List

Packing for a vacation is fun when you feel confident you're packing the right things. Over the years, we've compiled a packing list for a great Disney vacation. Just note the quantity you plan to bring and check them off as you pack. Consider carrying items in **bold** on a daily basis around the parks.

The Essentials

❑ Casual clothing you can layer—the dress code nearly everywhere at Disney is casual, even at dinner. One "nice" outfit is usually enough.
___ *Shorts/Skirts* ___ *Pants/Jeans* ___ *Shirts* ___ *Sweaters*
___ *Underwear* ___ *Socks* ___ *Pajamas* ___ ________

❑ Jacket and/or sweatshirt (light ones for the warmer months)
___ ***Jackets*** ___ *Sweatshirts* ___ *Sweaters* ___ *Vests*

❑ Comfortable, well-broken-in shoes... plus a second pair just in case!
___ *Walking shoes* ___ *Sandals* ___ *Sneakers* ___ ________

❑ Swim gear (bring one-piece suits for water slides)
___ *Suits/trunks* ___ *Cover-ups/towels* ___ *Water shoes* ___ *Goggles*

❑ Sun protection (the Florida sun can be brutal)
___ ***Sunblock*** ___ ***Lip balm*** ___ ***Sunburn relief*** ___ ________
___ ***Hats w/brims*** ___ ***Caps*** ___ ***Visors*** ___ ***Sunglasses***

❑ Rain gear (compact and light so you don't mind carrying it)
___ *Raincoat* ___ ***Poncho*** ___ ***Umbrella*** ___ ***Dry socks***

❑ Comfortable bags with padded straps to carry items during the day
___ ***Backpacks*** ___ ***Waist packs*** ___ *Shoulder bags* ___ ***Camera bag***

❑ Toiletries (in a bag or bathroom kit to keep them organized)
___ ***Brush/comb*** ___ *Toothbrush* ___ *Toothpaste* ___ *Dental floss*
___ *Favorite soap, shampoo, & conditioner* ___ *Deodorant* ___ ***Baby wipes***
___ ***Aspirin/Acetaminophen/Ibuprofen*** ___ ***Band aids*** ___ ***First aid kit***
___ ***Prescriptions*** *(in original containers)* ___ *Vitamins* ___ *Fem. Hygiene*
___ *Hair dryer/iron* ___ ***Anti-blister tape*** ___ *Makeup* ___ *Hairspray*
___ *Razors* ___ *Shaving cream* ___ *Cotton buds* ___ *Lotion*
___ *Nail clippers* ___ *Spare eyeglasses* ___ *Lens solution* ___ ***Bug repellent***
___ *Mending kit* ___ *Small scissors* ___ *Safety pins* ___ ***Insect sting kit***

❑ Camera/camcorder and more film than you think you need
___ ***Camera*** ___ ***Camcorder*** ___ ***Film/tapes*** ___ ***Storage cards***
___ ***Batteries*** ___ *Chargers* ___ ***Camera case*** ___ ________

❑ Money in various forms and various places
___ ***Charge cards*** ___ ***Travelers checks*** ___ ***Bank cards*** ___ ***Cash***

❑ Personal identification, passes, and membership cards
___ ***Driver's licenses*** ___ ***Other photo ID*** ___ ***Passports*** ___ *Birth certificate*
___ ***AAA card*** ___ ***Discount cards*** ___ *Air miles card* ___ ________
___ ***Tickets/Passes*** ___ ***Insurance cards*** ___ ***Calling cards*** ___ ________

Tip: Label everything with your name, phone, and hotel to help reunite you with your stuff if lost. Every bag should have this info on a luggage tag as well as on a slip of paper inside it. Use our Luggage Tag Maker at http://www.passporter.com/wdw/luggagelog.htm.

For Your Carry-On

- ❑ Your **PassPorter**, **tickets**, **maps**, **guides**, and a **pen** or **pencil**! Remember to pack any sharp or potentially dangerous items in your checked luggage, not your carry-on.
- ❑ **Camera** and/or **camcorder**, along with **film**, **tapes**, and **batteries**
- ❑ Any **prescriptions**, important toiletries, **sunblock**, **sunglasses**, **hats**, **bug repellent**
- ❑ Change of clothes appropriate to your destination's weather
- ❑ **Snacks**, **water bottle**, **juice boxes**, gum, favorite books, **toys**, **games**, blankets

For Families

- ❑ Snacks and juice boxes
- ❑ Books, toys, and games
- ❑ Stroller and accessories
- ❑ **Autograph books** and **fat pens**
- ❑ EarPlanes (http://www.earplanes.com)

For Couples

- ❑ Corkscrew and wine glasses
- ❑ Candles and matches
- ❑ Evening wear for nights out
- ❑ (Jacket for Victoria & Albert's)
- ❑ Portable CD player and CDs

For Connected Travelers

- ❑ Laptop and power supply
- ❑ Extension cord/suppressor
- ❑ Long phone cables, coupler, splitter
- ❑ Security cable with lock
- ❑ **Cell phones** and chargers
- ❑ **Two-way radios**
- ❑ Local access numbers
- ❑ **Handheld/Palm organizer**

For Heat-Sensitive Travelers

- ❑ **Personal fan/water misters**
- ❑ **Water bottles** (frozen, if possible)
- ❑ **Washcloth** to cool off face and neck
- ❑ Loose, breezy clothing
- ❑ **Hats** with wide brims
- ❑ **Sunshades** (for baby strollers)
- ❑ **Elastics** to keep long hair off neck
- ❑ **Sweatbands**

Everyone Should Consider

- ❑ Big beach towels (for pools and water parks)
- ❑ **Penlight** or flashlight (for reading/writing in dark places and to alleviate kids' fears)
- ❑ **Water bottles** and personal **fan/water misters**
- ❑ **Snacks** for any time of the day (plus gum, if you chew it)
- ❑ Plastic cutlery for snacks or leftovers
- ❑ **Quarters** and **pennies** (and a way to hold them) for the coin presses and/or laundry
- ❑ Plastic storage bags that seal (large and small), plus trash bags
- ❑ Address book, stamps, and envelopes
- ❑ Laundry detergent/tablets, bleach, dryer sheets, stain stick, and a laundry tote
- ❑ **Binoculars**
- ❑ Collapsible bag or suitcase inside another suitcase to hold souvenirs on your return

Your Personal Packing List

❑ ______	❑ ______
❑ ______	❑ ______
❑ ______	❑ ______
❑ ______	❑ ______
❑ ______	❑ ______
❑ ______	❑ ______
❑ ______	❑ ______
❑ ______	❑ ______
❑ ______	❑ ______

Adventuring!

Your journey is more pleasant when you consider it an adventure rather than a tiring trek. Here are our tried-and-true adventuring tips:

 Listen to **books on tape**. Rent, purchase, or even "borrow" from Cracker Barrel restaurants (return them for a partial refund). You may also want to purchase/rent a video player and movies!

 **Map your course** as you go. Create a travel journal to show to your friends and to recall your adventure.

 Bring your own **beverages and snacks** aboard the plane and live in the lap of luxury. Why not bring gum (to offset air pressure), lotion (to offset dry air), and a tape/CD player (to offset boredom)?

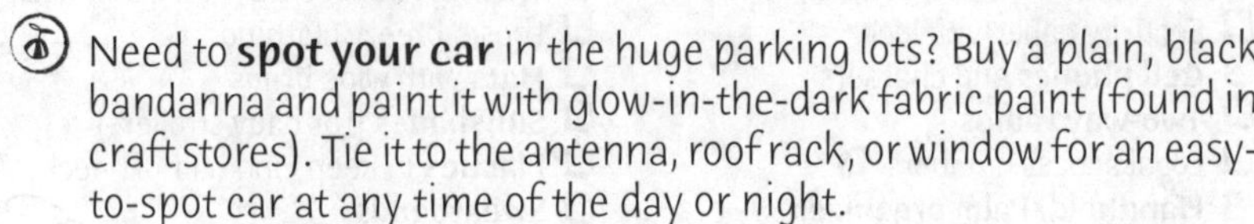

Need to **spot your car** in the huge parking lots? Buy a plain, black bandanna and paint it with glow-in-the-dark fabric paint (found in craft stores). Tie it to the antenna, roof rack, or window for an easy-to-spot car at any time of the day or night.

– Contributed by Judy Waldy, a winner in our 2003 Traveling Tip Contest

 Bring along a few padded envelopes (addressed to your home). As you **use up your film**, pop it in an envelope and mail it off to your house. This will save you from losing rolls of film (like I did in June) and from worrying about X-rays at airports.

– Contributed by Maria Gallagher, a winner in our 2003 Traveling Tip Contest

Magical Memories

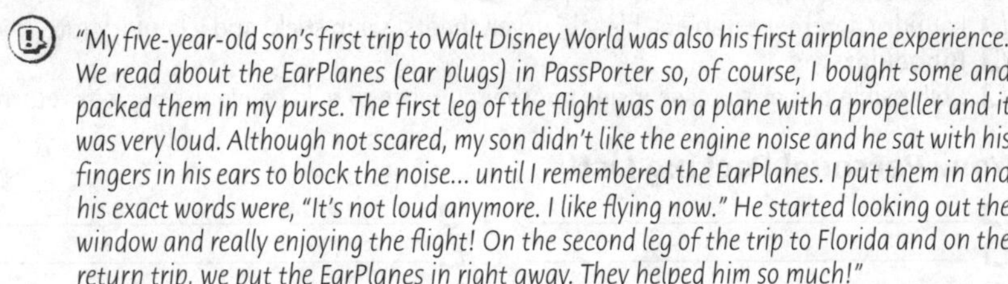

"My five-year-old son's first trip to Walt Disney World was also his first airplane experience. We read about the EarPlanes (ear plugs) in PassPorter so, of course, I bought some and packed them in my purse. The first leg of the flight was on a plane with a propeller and it was very loud. Although not scared, my son didn't like the engine noise and he sat with his fingers in his ears to block the noise... until I remembered the EarPlanes. I put them in and his exact words were, "It's not loud anymore. I like flying now." He started looking out the window and really enjoying the flight! On the second leg of the trip to Florida and on the return trip, we put the EarPlanes in right away. They helped him so much!"

...as told by Disney vacationer Vickie Owens

"It rained while we were at Disney-MGM Studios, and almost everyone in the park wore Disney-bought ponchos. My sister was the only one who had a hot pink poncho. We had no trouble finding her in the crowds. So it's no wonder that she was one of the first to be chosen from the audience for an extra in the Indiana Jones Epic Stunt Spectacular. The cast member called out, 'The lady in pink, come on down!'"

...as told by Disney vacationer Kalliope Mulchi

Staying in Style

Nowhere in the "World" is Disney magic more evident than at the resort hotels on Walt Disney World property. In fact, the resorts are so impressive that we do not often consider staying "off-property" (as hotels outside of Walt Disney World are known), and we frequently plan our visits around our favorite resorts rather than our favorite parks. Staying in a Disney resort is unlike any other hotel experience we've had, and we've visited both the exotic and the expensive. It isn't just that staying at a Disney resort provides total immersion in the Walt Disney World experience. The resorts are miniature theme parks in their own right, with hidden surprises and a remarkable attention to detail.

With over 31,000 guest rooms and campsites throughout the Walt Disney World Resort, it would take over 80 years to stay once in each room. (Sign us up!) There's something for every taste and budget. Whether you want a romantic setting, space for a family reunion, disabled access, bunk beds, or non-smoking rooms, you can find it somewhere in the "World." There are enough choices to preclude staying at a non-Disney hotel, but bargains off-property are also a factor. If you visit with friends or family, prefer to stay in another hotel, or even take a cruise, your PassPorter still serves you well–you can record your arrangements here with the same ease. We include basic information on the Disney Cruise Line, Disney Vacation Club, and off-site hotels at the end of the chapter, too.

If you've already decided to stay at a Disney resort, your PassPorter puts you a step ahead! Our Walt Disney World resort descriptions are the most comprehensive of any guidebook, and our resort maps, photos, floor plans, tips, notes, and recommendations can help the veteran vacationer as well as the novice get the most out of their resort.

To help you find your way through the staggering array of choices, we've prepared a detailed guide to choosing your resort. We heartily recommend you turn the page and take advantage of it.

Choosing a Resort

Ah, this is the fun part! Deciding which resort to stay at reminds us of choosing a dessert from a tray laden with every imaginable, mouth-watering goodie. Some are too rich for us, others aren't quite sweet enough, but there are enough choices left over to make us feel spoiled. Sometimes we stay at two or more resorts in one visit. Are you surprised?

Start with the exhaustive **Resort Checklist** on the next page. Compare it with your preferences to uncover the resorts that meet your needs. Then carefully read the resort descriptions, beginning on page 37. Each description follows the same format, allowing you to find exactly what you seek as you **compare resorts**. The first and second pages of each description list resort essentials, along with floor plans and transportation times. The third page lists the best tips, notes, and ratings for each resort—this is the "good stuff" to help you make the most out of your experience. In the Ratings section we and our readers grade each resort for value, magic, and satisfaction. An explanation of the ratings is at the bottom of this page. The fourth page features a detailed resort map and our ideas for the best rooms in the resort. Rates, addresses, and phone/fax numbers are listed at the end of each description. **Tip**: When researching resorts, use the darkest "stamp" (tab) at the top of the page to locate parks and eateries in the vicinity, which will have the same "stamp" at the top of their pages.

When you're ready, use the Lodging Worksheet on pages 110-111 to record your dates, preferences, and reservation options.

Resort Ratings Explained

We offer a variety of resort ratings in the PassPorter to help you make the best decisions. Even so, we recommend you use these ratings as a guide, not gospel.

Value Ratings range from 1 (poor) to 10 (excellent) and are based on **quality** (cleanliness, maintenance, and freshness); **accessibility** (how fast and easy it is to get to attractions); and **affordability** (rates for the standard rooms)—**overall value** represents an average of the above three values. **Magic Ratings** are based on **theme** (execution and sense of immersion); **amenities** (guest perks and luxuries); and **fun factor** (number and quality of resort activities)—**overall magic** represents an average of the above three values. We use a point accumulation method to determine value and magic ratings.

Readers' Ratings are calculated from surveys submitted by experienced vacationers at our Web site (http://www.passporter.com/wdw/rate.htm).

Guest satisfaction is based on our and our readers' experiences with how different types of guests enjoy the resort: ❤❤❤❤❤=love it ❤❤❤❤=enjoy it ❤❤❤=like it ❤❤=tolerate it ❤=don't like it

➢

Resort Comparisons

** Kitchen facilities are present only in the villas of indicated resorts*	All-Star Resorts	AnimalKing. Lodge	Beach Club/Villas	BoardWalk Inn/Villas	Caribbean Beach	Contemporary	Coronado Springs	Dolphin	Fort Wilderness	Grand Floridian	Old Key West	Polynesian	Pop Century	Port Orleans	Saratoga Springs	Shades of Green	Swan	Wild. Lodge/Villas	Yacht Club
Deluxe		✓	✓	✓		✓		✓		✓		✓				✓	✓	✓	✓
Home-Away			✓	✓					✓		✓				✓			✓	
Moderate					✓		✓							✓					
Value	✓												✓						
Rooms and Amenities																			
Total Rooms	5760	1293	785	910	2112	1041	1967	1509	1195	900	761	853	5760	3056	696	586	758	864	634
Occupancy	4	4-5	4-8	4-12	4	5	4	5	4-10	5	4-12	5	4	4-5	4-12	5	5	4-8	5
Mini bars			✓					✓		✓							✓		✓
Coffeemakers					✓		✓	✓	✓		✓				✓	✓	✓		
Hairdryers		✓	✓	✓		✓	✓	✓	✓	✓	✓	✓			✓	✓	✓	✓	✓
In-Room Safes	✓	✓	✓	✓	✓	✓	✓	✓	✓	✓	✓	✓	✓	✓	✓	✓	✓	✓	✓
Kitchen Facilities*			✓	✓					✓		✓				✓			✓	
Turndown (on req.)		✓	✓	✓		✓				✓		✓					✓	✓	✓
Eating and Drinking																			
Restaurants/Cafes	–	2	3	7	1	5	1	2	2	7	3	3	–	1	1	4	3	3	3
Character Meals			✓			✓		✓	✓	✓		✓					✓		
Lounges	3	3	3	4	1	3	2	1	1	3	1	2	2	4	2	1	2	2	2
Food Court	3	1			1		1	1					2	2					
Room Service		✓	✓	✓	✓	✓	✓	✓		✓		✓			✓	✓	✓	✓	✓
Pizza Delivery	✓										✓		✓	✓					✓
Recreational Activities																			
Beach (no swim)			✓		✓	✓	✓	✓	✓	✓		✓					✓	✓	✓
Pools	6	1	3	3	7	2	4	2	2	2	4	2	6	7	3	2	2	2	3
Kid Pool	3	1	1	1	1	1	1	1	1	1	1	1	2	2	1	1	1	1	1
Spa (Hot Tub)	–	2	5	3	1	2	1	1	–	1	2	–	–	2	4	1	1	3	5
Spa (Services)			✓	✓			✓	✓		✓	✓	✓			✓		✓		✓
Health Club		✓	✓	✓		✓	✓	✓		✓	✓				✓	✓	✓	✓	✓
Marina			✓	✓	✓	✓	✓	✓	✓	✓	✓	✓		✓			✓	✓	✓
Tennis			✓	✓		✓		✓	✓	✓	✓				✓	✓	✓		✓
Jogging Path	✓		✓	✓	✓	✓	✓	✓	✓	✓	✓	✓	✓	✓	✓		✓	✓	✓
Playground	✓	✓	✓	✓	✓	✓	✓	✓	✓	✓	✓	✓	✓	✓	✓	✓	✓	✓	✓
Arcade	✓	✓	✓	✓	✓	✓	✓	✓	✓	✓	✓	✓	✓	✓	✓	✓	✓	✓	✓
Kid's Program		✓	✓	✓		✓		✓		✓		✓					✓	✓	✓
Access and Facilities																			
Monorail						✓				✓		✓							
Disabled Rooms	288	66	10	51	22	6	99	43	13	5	67	17	126	34	16	22	8	46	10
Conf. Center			✓	✓		✓	✓	✓		✓							✓		✓
Your Favorites																			

Reserving a Room

Once you have an idea of where you want to stay at the Walt Disney World Resort, it's time to **make reservations**. A travel agent is not needed, but if you have a great travel agent, by all means consult him or her—we recommend MouseEarVacations.com, as they can often get excellent deals you may not have known about. Here's the lowdown on reservations:

Before you make your reservations, **use the worksheet** on pages 110-111 to jot down the dates you prefer to visit along with any alternates. Even a one-day change in your travel dates can open the door to a great deal. Be familiar with all resorts in your price range.

Make reservations for all Walt Disney World resorts at **407-WDISNEY**/407-934-7639 or 800-828-0228 (Walt Disney Travel Company). Disney representatives can offer assistance in English, Spanish, Japanese, French, Portuguese, and German. If you have Internet access, you can research room rates and make reservations at http://www.disneyworld.com (click on "resorts")—discounts are sometimes available on the web site, but you must follow the specific links for the specials or you'll be charged regular rates. You may also want to try Expedia or Travelocity, both of which are popular Internet reservation systems—you can visit them at http://www.travelocity.com (or keyword: TRAVEL on America Online) and http://www.expedia.com. Be sure to look for promotional rates while you're there, too! If you prefer, you can also make reservations through mail by writing to Walt Disney World at Box 10100, Lake Buena Vista, Florida 32830.

You may be able to **hold more than one reservation** for the same date, but eventually you have to put down a deposit or lose the reservation. Most reservations can be cancelled for full credit up to 45 days prior to arrival (policies vary for some discount programs). Disney will send a confirmation of your reservation.

Research **special deals or packages** by visiting MouseSavers.com (see page 11) or by calling Disney Reservations. If you have a Disney Visa card, Annual Pass, or are a Florida resident or military family, ask about those discounts, too. If your dates aren't available, ask about alternates. Sometimes you can get a discount for part of your stay. Lock-in whatever discount you can get, and book at full price for the remainder. Keep calling back, as cancelled reservations are released every morning. If a lower rate comes out later, you may be able to call back and get it applied.

Make any **special requests** at the time of reservation and again when you check-in. If you need a non-smoking or barrier-free room, a refrigerator, or a crib, request this now. If you have a particular location or room in mind (we make many suggestions later on), make sure to tell the reservations agent. It's best to make your request as general as possible. You'll have better luck requesting a "high floor with views of fireworks" than simply "room 5409." If Disney doesn't know why you want room 5409, they can't choose a suitable substitute. Disney will not guarantee a particular room or view, but if your request is "in the system" they will try their best to make your wish come true. Call or fax your resort about three days before your arrival to confirm any requests you made. We've created an easy, fill-in-the-blanks form for you to use when making phone calls (or when standing at the check-in desk) at http://www.passporter.com/wdw/resortrequest.htm.

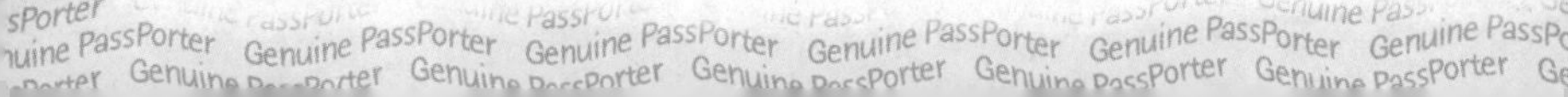

Finalize resort reservations after you make your **flight reservations**. Hotel room reservations may be changed or cancelled without penalty, whereas flight changes often incur a fee. If you wish to cancel your resort reservations without penalty, cancel no later than 45 days prior to your arrival. Cancellations within 6-45 days of your arrival incur a $100 fee. Cancellations in 5 or fewer days before your arrival are $200.

Once you've made your reservations, **record the details** on your Room(s) PassPocket, including the name of the resort, dates, type of room, price, reservation number, and any special information you want to note. This is also an ideal place to note any special requests you want to check on at check-in. Use a pencil if plans aren't final.

Typically, Disney resort reservations are held for 10-14 days without confirmation. Confirmation requires a deposit of $200, due in 14 days. Be sure to **pay your deposit** before midnight on the 14th day. Your deposit can be made over the phone with The Disney Credit Card, American Express, MasterCard, Visa, Discover, JCB, Diner's Club, or through mail or fax with the same credit cards or a personal check. The Lodging Worksheet at the end of the chapter (pages 110–111) has spaces to check off confirmations and deposits made, too! **Tip**: You may be able to request an extension on your deposit if needed.

Disney's Two Reservation Systems

Why make a toll call to Disney Central Reservations Office (CRO) at 407-WDISNEY to reserve a room when you can dial the Walt Disney Travel Company (WDTC) toll-free at 800-828-0228? Each has its strengths and weaknesses.

Central Reservations (CRO) is Disney's hotel reservation system. Its specialty is room-only reservations and selected vacation packages (they'll be happy to sell you park admission, too). CRO cannot book air travel, car rentals, travel insurance, or ground transportation. CRO has the more liberal deposit policy—the cost of one night's lodging is all that's required (due in 14 days), with a no-penalty cancellation possible up to six days prior. With less than six days notice you forfeit the full one-night deposit. Packages require full payment 21 days prior to your stay; room-only bookings can be paid-up at check-in. There's no penalty for modifying an existing reservation. The only problem with CRO (besides the cost of the phone call) is that Disney is downsizing this operation. Even though you dial 407-WDISNEY you may be connected to a Disney Travel Company agent. Make sure CRO booking policies have been applied to your reservation before you finalize it.

Walt Disney Travel Company is a full-fledged travel agency. Its specialty is package vacations with all the trimmings (see page 30). It offers a wider range of package vacations than CRO, and has access to the same "pool" of room-only reservations as CRO. Airfare, car rentals, ground transportation, and other arrangements can also be part of their service. WDTC requires full payment for your vacation 45 days in advance (even for room-only bookings), charges $100 for cancellations made between 6 and 45 days prior, and $200 for cancellations made less than six days prior. There's a $50 charge for modifying reservations within 21 days of your arrival. So, WDTC can do more for you, but it comes at a price. Disney tells us that the bulk of their reservations are through WDTC, which is why we noted their policies in the above text.

Tip: Sections highlighted in light blue (like the ones below) indicate additions or significant changes at Walt Disney World since our previous edition!

Choosing a Package

Disney's vacation packages offer the promise of peace-of-mind and luxury. Package rates may be lower than the list price for each component, but may include more components than you can possibly use. A significant number of veteran vacationers tell us they love these packages! Note that everyone in your room must be on the same package and plan. For more information and reservations, ask your travel agent, call Walt Disney Travel Co. at 800-828-0228, or visit http://www.waltdisneyworld.com.

☐ Fairytale Vacation Package

This popular package offers three or more nights accommodation, Ultimate Park Hopper tickets, and special framed character art. Rates vary by season and hotel, but at press time seven-night rates started at $499/adult, $266/junior (ages 10–17), and $212/child (3–9).

☐ Dream Maker Basic

Available year-round, you get three nights at a Disney resort hotel, an Ultimate Park Hopper ticket for each person for the length of your stay, and two trading pins and lanyards. You also get your choice of miniature golf, up to two Leave a Legacy images, a Disney character poster, or up to $25 at Planet Hollywood. From $359/adult or $188/child for three nights.

☐ Dream Maker Silver

Everything in the Basic package, plus two Magical Wishes per person per evening. Redeem Magical Wishes for dining, recreation, photos, childcare (pages 252–253), guided tours (pages 242–243), merchandise, spa treatments, and more. Add $35-68/person per night.

☐ Dream Maker Gold

Everything in the Silver package plus three meals a day, complimentary access to Disney's childcare clubs (pages 252–253), golf, free guided tours (pages 242–243), select recreation, preferred viewing locations, and Cirque du Soleil tickets. Add $94-139/person per night.

☐ Dream Maker Platinum

This all-inclusive plan is offered for guests at a deluxe or home-away-from-home resort. Includes everything in the Gold package plus concierge service, in-room childcare, itinerary planning, spa treatment, and a fireworks cruise. Add $119–199/person per night.

☐ Dream Maker Romance

Everything in the Silver package plus a 30-minute carriage ride with champagne, a special dinner at a select table-service restaurant, and your choice of Cirque du Soleil tickets, a 50-minute spa treatment, or a round of golf (and club rental). Add $149 per adult.

☐ Dream Maker Prince and Princess

Adds special kid-friendly perks to the DreamMaker Basic package, including one breakfast per person (character or traditional), bag tags, 50 Disney Dollars per child ages 3-9, and special seating at select shows (up to two). Rates are $23/adult and $64/child.

☐ Great Golf Escape

This package doesn't include park admission, but does cover your resort stay of three nights or more, one round of golf per night (with a second round at $25), transportation to courses, advance booking tee times, one 30-minute golf lesson, and club rentals starting at $40.

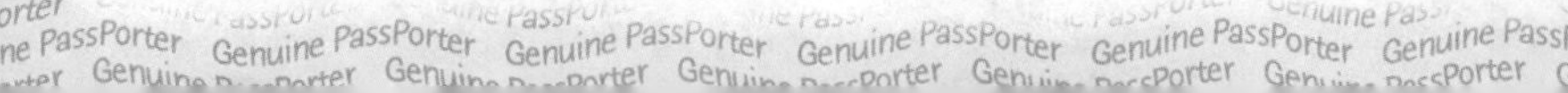

Resort Key

Resort Locations—The Disney resorts described in your PassPorter are all located within minutes of the theme parks. We organize them into four areas: Magic Kingdom, Downtown Disney, Epcot, and Disney's Animal Kingdom (use the map on the inside back cover for reference). Each resort's area is identified in its description. You can also use the blue "stamps" at the top of each page to locate all resorts in a neighborhood.

Room Locations—Room locations such as a building or room number can be requested, but are not guaranteed. However, if you note your preferences when you make your reservation, via phone or fax about three days before arrival, and again when you check in, there is a chance you will get the room you want. Resort maps and suggestions are given for each resort in this chapter. If you don't like the particular room you've been assigned, do as you would with any hotel and politely ask for another.

Room Occupancy—All resorts have rooms that hold at least four guests, plus one child under 3 in a Pack-N-Play crib. Port Orleans Riverside (Alligator Bayou) rooms accommodate up to five guests with an optional trundle bed, as do many of the deluxe resorts and the Ft. Wilderness Cabins. The two-bedroom villas in the Home-Away Resorts can accommodate up to eight. There may be an extra charge for more than two adults in a single room.

Amenities—All rooms have the basics: television with remote control, phone, drawers, clothing rod with hangers, small table, chairs, as well as simple toiletries. Additional amenities differ at each resort and are detailed later. **Tip**: If your room doesn't have a coffeemaker, alarm clock, or iron/ironing board, request it from housekeeping.

Check-In Time—Check-in time is 3:00 or 4:00 pm (varies by resort), although rooms may be available earlier if you inquire upon your arrival. If your room is not available, you can register, leave your luggage, and go play at the parks while your room is being prepared.

Check-Out Time—Check-out time is 11:00 am. If you need to check-out an hour or two later, ask the Front Desk the morning of check-out. If the resort isn't busy, they may grant your request at no extra cost. Extended check-out may also be available for an extra fee. You can also leave your bags with Bell Services and go play in the parks.

Childcare—Children's childcare "clubs" for ages 4-12 are available in each of the deluxe resorts (refer to the chart on page 27). In-room sitting is also available. See pages 252-253 for details and opinions on childcare.

Concierge—All of the deluxe resorts offer concierge services, which give you extra perks like a continental breakfast, afternoon snacks, and planning services. Concierge services are associated with certain rooms (often on the higher floors) and come at a higher rate.

Convention Centers—Several resort hotels at the Walt Disney World Resort are popular among convention-goers due to their excellent facilities, including the BoardWalk, Contemporary, Coronado Springs, Grand Floridian, Swan, Dolphin, and the Yacht Club. For more details on convention facilities, call 407-828-3200. Business Centers are available at each of the above resorts.

Data Services—All phones have data ports. Look for a local access number before you arrive. Each local call you make is 75 cents. You must include the area code (407) in all local calls. The front desk will also receive your faxes for a fee. Some resorts may be testing high-speed Internet access—inquire upon arrival.

Resort Key: Disabled Access to Information

Disabled Access—All resorts offer accommodations and access for differently-abled guests. For details and reservations, call Disney's Special Needs Department at 407-939-7807 (voice) or 407-939-7670 (TTY). Be sure to ask that "Special Needs" be noted on your reservation. Our chart on page 27 shows the number of barrier-free rooms, and the photo on page 48 shows a barrier-free guest room.

Extra Magic Hour (Early Entry)—Disney's resort guests can enter the parks up to one hour earlier than everyone else and enjoy a special character meet and greet inside the parks. Only certain attractions are open during the early entry period, however (see notes below). Here's what the early entry schedule looks like at press time:

Monday	Tuesday	Wednesday	Thursday	Friday	Saturday	Sunday
Animal Kingdom	Disney-MGM Studios	Epcot	Magic Kingdom	Animal Kingdom	Disney-MGM Studios	Magic Kingdom

Extra Magic Hour Attractions—In the Magic Kingdom, this usually includes everything in Tomorrowland (except The Timekeeper and Walt Disney's Carousel of Progress) and everything in Fantasyland. Epcot only opens Future World early (Mission:SPACE, Spaceship Earth, Test Track, and Universe of Energy). Disney-MGM Studios usually only opens Rock 'n' Roller Coaster, Tower of Terror, Star Tours, and Muppet*Vision 3-D early. Disney's Animal Kingdom opens It's Tough to be a Bug! and all of Africa.

Food—Every resort has places to eat within it, such as food courts, cafes, fine dining, and room service. All resort eateries are noted in each resort's dining section later in this chapter. Details on the table-service restaurants start on page 224. If you are looking for snack food or groceries, each resort has a general store with a small selection of foodstuffs and drinks. No gum is sold on property.

Guest Services—Each resort has a Guest Services desk where you can purchase park passes, make dining arrangements, and find answers to just about any question. You can also connect to Guest Services (and other Disney services) through a button on your in-room phone.

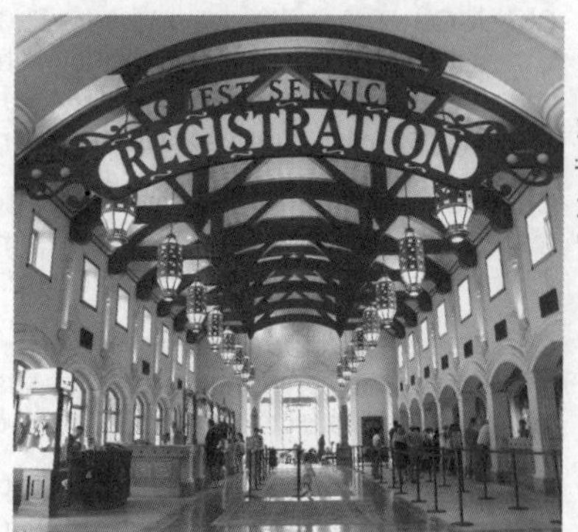

Guest Services (and Registration) at Coronado Springs Resort

Housekeeping Services—Every Disney resort has daily "mousekeeping" services, and happily provides you with extra towels, pillows, and blankets upon request, as well as a hairdryer, iron, and ironing board. If you require extra toiletries, just ask for them. For tipping suggestions, see page 34. Note that the Disney Vacation Club resorts provide reduced services to Disney Vacation Club members who are using their points.

Information—Check the Walt Disney World information channels on your in-room TV. These channels are available at every resort and offer a nice introduction for newcomers, plus a peek at what's new for veterans.

Resort Key: Ice and Soda to Pets

Ice and Soda—All resorts have ice machines within easy walking distance. Most, but not all, also have soda machines. The rule seems to be the more plush the resort, the harder it is to find a soda machine. If soda is important, pick some up before you arrive (it's cheaper anyway). Another option is to purchase a refillable souvenir mug (offered at most resorts) for free (or low-cost) refills of soda, coffee, tea, and cocoa at your resort—see page 34.

Laundry—Every resort has either coin-operated machines in a laundry room near the pool (expect to pay 8 quarters/load) or a washer and dryer in your room. Tip: Old Key West and The Villas at Wilderness Lodge offer complimentary self-service laundry facilities (no coins needed). Laundry bags and forms are available in your resort room for same-day laundering (but it's very expensive). **Tip**: Store your dirty laundry in the laundry bags.

Mail and Packages—Purchase stamps at Guest Services and in many shops; mail can be dropped off at Guest Services or placed in mailboxes. Federal Express also picks up and drops off packages. A full-service Post Office is at the Shoppes at Lake Buena Vista at 12133 Apopka-Vineland Rd., about one mile north of the Crossroads Shopping Center.

Merchandise Delivery—Resort guests can have park and Downtown Disney purchases delivered free to their resort, usually by the next day or the day after. Inquire before your purchase is rung up. Your package is delivered to your resort's gift shop for pickup, not your room. Not available for Swan/Dolphin guests.

Money—Cash, Disney Dollars, travelers checks, The Disney Credit Card, MasterCard, Visa, American Express, Discover, Diner's Club, and JCB are accepted, as well as personal checks with proper I.D. ATMs are located near the front desk. Make your room deposit over the phone or fax with the above credit cards, or by mail with a credit card or check.

Pools—Every Disney resort has at least one swimming pool. Hours of operation vary, but usually the "theme" pools close in the evenings while the "quiet" pools may stay open all night. Only guests staying at a resort can use its pool, though some resorts share pools and Disney Vacation Club members using their points have access to all but the Stormalong Bay pool complex at the Yacht & Beach Club (unless they are staying there, of course).

© Disney

The theme pool at All-Star Music Resort

Parking—Secured, free, gated parking lots are available at all resorts; the deluxe resorts also offer valet ($6/day, free to those with disabled tags). Show your resort I.D. or confirmation at the security gate—parking is reserved for resort guests and those using a resort's restaurants or recreation.

Recreation—Every resort has something to do, with many offering a wide variety of outdoor activities. You can visit another resort to use its recreational facilities (with the exception of swimming pools). Be sure to note the operating hours upon arrival or by phoning ahead.

Pets—Pets are not allowed in the parks or resorts (except for a few campsites at Fort Wilderness—see page 61) unless you travel with a companion (guide) animal. Disney kennels will board pets for $6 per day, and resort guests may board their pets overnight for $9 per night. Although the kennels are designed primarily for dogs and cats, they can also accommodate birds, ferrets, small rodents, rabbits, and non-venomous snakes. Pets in kennels must be walked three times per day by their owners. The Epcot kennel offers a dog-walking service for $2.50 per walk.

Resort Key: Refillable Mugs to Voice Mail

Two styles of refillable mugs

© MediaMarx, Inc.

Refillable Mugs—Most resorts sell thermal mugs that can be refilled free or for a small fee at your resort for the duration of your stay. If you drink a lot of soda, tea, coffee, or hot chocolate, these are a blessing—and they make fun souvenirs. Mugs are about $11 and can generally be refilled at a resort's food court or snack shop. Some resorts place mugs in your room, but if you use them you'll be charged. Mugs can't be refilled at other resorts or parks, and neither milk nor juice is a refill option. If you bring a refillable mug purchased on a previous visit back to the same resort for refills, you may or may not be allowed to refill it.

Room Service—The deluxe resorts and some of the moderate resorts offer room service. Some resorts offer a pizza delivery service in the afternoon and evenings.

Security—Security at Disney has always been good, and since 9/11 security has visibly heightened. A gatehouse guards entry into every resort, and virtually everyone who drives through the resorts' gates is questioned. Show your photo identification and resort identification, or explain that you are checking in, dining, or using the recreational facilities at the resort if you arrive by car. All resort rooms have electronic locks which open with your resort I.D. for added security. In addition, you can store small valuables in your in-room safe (most, though not all, rooms have them) or with the front desk.

Spa—Disney-speak for a hot tub. There's at least one spa at every Disney resort, with the exception of the All-Stars, Fort Wilderness, Polynesian, and Pop Century. Traditional spa facilities (massages and manicures) are available in some resorts.

Tax—Florida Sales Tax is 6.5% and is charged on all resort purchases and lodging. An additional Lodging Tax is assessed on guest rooms: 6% in Osceola County (Animal Kingdom Lodge and some parts of All-Star Resorts), 5% in Orange County (all other Disney resorts).

Telephones—All rooms have a phone and information on how to use it. Local, toll-free, and credit card calls are 75 cents each, while long distance calls are the cost of the call plus a 50% surcharge. Ouch! Use calling cards instead. Incoming calls are free.

Tipping—It's customary to tip valet parking attendants $1-2 upon arrival and departure, bell services $1–2/bag upon delivery and pick-up, and housekeeping $1/person/day. Tip: Leave your housekeeping tip on the sink in an envelope each day so it's easily spotted.

Transportation—Every resort provides its guests with complimentary transit to and from the parks via bus, boat, monorail, and/or walking path. We list each resort's options and in-transit times in this chapter.

Wheelchairs—Wheelchairs can be borrowed from every resort (inquire at Bell Services). A deposit may be required, and availability is limited. Motorized wheelchairs (ECVs) may be rented at the parks (again, availability is limited and you can only use them in the parks). Care Medical (800-741-2282—http://www.caremedicalequipment.com) or Walker Mobility (888-726-6837—http://www.walkermobility.com) both offer 24-hour rentals of wheelchairs and ECVs... and they'll deliver and pickup the chair, too!

Voice Mail—Every resort offers free voice mail that can be retrieved from your room or any other phone in or outside of the Walt Disney World Resort. You can even personalize the message callers hear when they are connected to your room. If you are on the phone when a call comes in, the voice mail system still takes your caller's message.

Disney's All-Star Resorts

Both economical and magical, the All-Star Resorts bring movies, music, and sports to life in three independent, yet connected resort hotels. The All-Star Movies, All-Star Music, and All-Star Sports Resorts are located near Disney's Animal Kingdom theme park and the Blizzard Beach water park (use the blue tab at the top of the page for parks and eateries in the vicinity).

AMBIENCE

A star-studded production awaits you at the All-Star Resorts. From the painted stars everywhere you look to the autographed photos of famous celebrities lining the lobby walls, each resort greets you as a star in its **main hall**—Cinema Hall in All-Star Movies, Melody Hall in All-Star Music, and Grandstand Hall in All-Star Sports. The halls house the registration desks, food courts, general stores, and arcades, each named and themed as only Disney can. Outside, the stars give way to larger-than-life movie, music, and sports icons, such as a towering Buzz Lightyear from Disney's Toy Story, a four-story high conga drum, and a Coke cup that could hold 240 million ounces. The themes continue with imaginatively designed pools and landscaping. Music plays in the background, providing you with an ever-changing soundtrack as you stroll through the grounds.

RESORT LAYOUT & ROOMS

The 5,760 guest rooms (1,920 in each resort) are situated in fifteen differently-themed areas encompassing a total of thirty buildings. **All-Star Movies Resort** showcases 101 Dalmatians, Fantasia and Fantasia 2000, The Love Bug, Toy Story, and Mighty Ducks; **All-Star Music Resort** features Calypso, Jazz Inn, Rock Inn, Country Fair and Broadway; and **All-Star Sports Resort** sports Surf's Up!, Hoops Hotel, Center Court, Touchdown!, and Home Run Hotel. Each of the fifteen areas features a themed courtyard created by two of the T-shaped buildings. The energetic and colorful themes of the resorts are echoed in the guest rooms, with themed bedspreads, drapes, wallpaper, and a vanity area with one sink. Rooms have either two double beds or one king bed, a TV, a small table with two chairs, and drawers. Rooms with king-size beds are also the barrier-free rooms; thus some of these rooms have only showers (no tubs). Rooms are small—260 sq. feet—but we found them adequate with the simple furnishings. Rooms have no private balconies or patios, but each offers individual climate controls. Amenities include soap, housekeeping, in-room safe, and voice mail. You can rent a small refrigerator for $10/night—request one at reservation time.

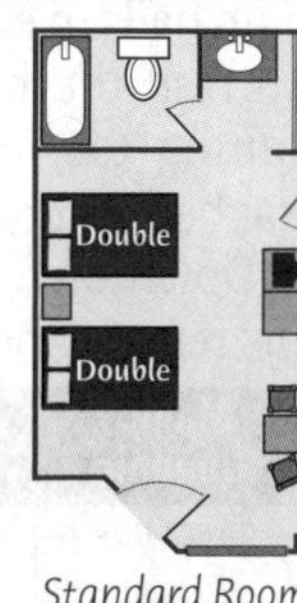

Standard Room Layout

Using the Amenities at Disney's All-Star Resorts

EATING & DRINKING

Guest room at All-Star Music

Food courts: World Premiere (Movies), Intermission (Music), and End Zone (Sports), each with four food stations plus a snack shop. Breakfast (6:30 am to 11:00 am) menu items typically include a Breakfast Platter for $5.59, a cheese omelet for $5.89, and child meals for $3.59. Lunch and dinner (11:00 am to mid.) items include a 16" supreme pizza for $17.99, a meatball sub for $5.99, a taco salad for $6.59, a cheeseburger for $5.49, and child meals for $3.99. Souvenir mugs (about $11) offer unlimited soft drink refills. A **pizza delivery service** may be available. **Walk-up bars** at each food court and main pool.

PLAYING & RELAXING

For Athletes: Well-marked paths are ideal for walks and jogs.
For Children: Quiet playgrounds are located within each resort (locations vary—see map on page 38 for playground locations).
For Gamers: Each resort's main hall has an arcade—some games reward players with tickets that can be redeemed for small prizes.
For Shoppers: Donald's Double Feature (Movies), Maestro Mickey's (Music), and Sport Goofy (Sports) offer gifts and sundries.
For Swimmers: Each resort offers a main pool and a smaller pool. Movies' main pool conjures up the fun of Fantasia, Music's main pool is in the shape of a guitar, and Sports' main pool is styled after a surfing lagoon. All main pools have children's wading pools nearby.

GETTING ABOUT

Buses (see chart below for in-transit times) are found outside the main halls in each resort. Stops are well-marked and offer benches. We find the bus service efficient, but some guests complain of waiting too long. Destinations other than those below can be reached by changing buses at Disney's Animal Kingdom (daytime) or Downtown Disney (evening). Guests may find a car useful at this resort, and ample parking is freely available around the resort.

Magic Kingdom	Epcot	Disney-MGM Studios	Disney's Animal Kingdom	Downtown Disney
direct bus ~20 min.	direct bus ~10 min.	direct bus ~10 min.	direct bus ~10 min.	direct bus ~15 min.

Approximate time you will spend in-transit from resort to destination during normal operation.

Making the Most of Disney's All-Star Resorts

Walk around the three resorts to catch all the neat props and details that make these resorts so fun. Don't forget your camera, as photo opportunities abound! Even the walkways have fun designs.

If you need an escape from the activity of the All-Stars, look for the **quiet spots** around the resorts. Relax in a hammock behind a stand of palm trees in Fantasia at All-Star Movies, or try the picnic tables in Country Fair's courtyard in All-Star Music for a leisurely lunch.

The **food courts** can get crowded at traditional meal times so stop there earlier or later in the day.

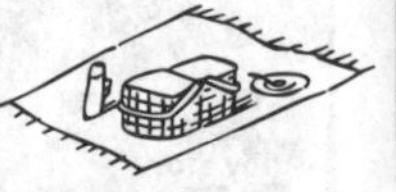

Plan to either carry your own luggage or wait a while (often 45-60 minutes) for their **luggage assistance service** to drop it off at your building. Unlike other Disney resorts, luggage is delivered at their convenience, not yours. Arrangements to pickup luggage on your departure day should be made the night before. You can borrow a luggage cart from the luggage assistance desk in the main hall, and you may need to leave your I.D. while you use the cart.

Toiletries are limited to a bar of facial soap at the sink and a wall-mounted dispenser of bodywash and shampoo in the shower/tub. You may want to bring your own from home.

Towels are not provided near the pools, so bring your own or use your room **towels**. Contact housekeeping for extra towels.

All-Star Sports **may close for maintenance** in the near future—call to check to avoid disappointment.

Check-in time is 4:00 pm. Check-out time is 11:00 am.

Ratings are explained on page 26.

Our Value Ratings:		Our Magic Ratings:		Readers' Ratings:
Quality:	6/10	Theme:	6/10	42% fell in love with it
Accessibility:	5/10	Amenities:	4/10	35% liked it well enough
Affordability:	9/10	Fun Factor:	2/10	12% had mixed feelings
Overall Value:	**7/10**	**Overall Magic:**	**4/10**	11% were disappointed

The All-Stars are enjoyed by...	(rated by both authors and readers)	
Younger Kids: ♥♥♥♥♥	Young Adults: ♥♥♥♥	Families: ♥♥♥♥
Older Kids: ♥♥♥♥♥	Mid Adults: ♥♥♥	Couples: ♥♥
Teenagers: ♥♥♥	Mature Adults: ♥♥	Singles: ♥♥♥

Finding Your Place at Disney's All-Star Resorts

ALL-STAR RESORT MAP

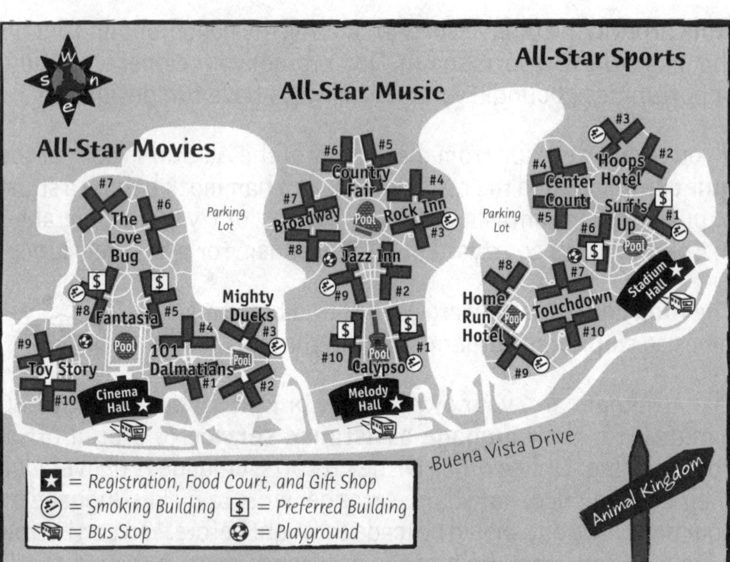

BEST LOCATIONS

Rooms at the All-Star Resorts vary only by location within the resorts and floor level. For convenience, we recommend **101 Dalmatians**, **Fantasia**, or **Toy Story** (at All-Star Movies), **Calypso** (at All-Star Music) and **Surf's Up!** (at All-Star Sports)—they are closest to the main pools, food, and transportation. Our personal preferences are **Fantasia** (at All-Star Movies), **Country Fair** (at All-Star Music), and **Hoops Hotel** (at All-Star Sports) as they are relatively quiet and have good views from most windows—the latter two are a good distance from the Main Hall, however. Quieter rooms are those that face away from the pools and are on the **second or third floors**.

RATES

2004 Sample Room Rates *Seasons are noted on page 14*

Room Type	Value	Regular	Peak	Holiday
Standard Room	$77	$99	$109	$114
Preferred Room	$87	$109	$121	$126

Tax not included in above rates. Preferred rooms are in buildings closest to the main hall (Fantasia, Calypso, or Surf's Up). Rooms may face parking lots or courtyards.

INFO

Disney's All-Star Movies/Music/Sports Resorts

1901/1801/1701 W. Buena Vista Dr., Lake Buena Vista, FL 32830
Phone: 407-939-7000/407-939-6000/407-939-5000
Fax: 407-939-7111/407-939-7222/407-939-7333
For reservations, call Central Reservations: 407-934-7639

Disney's Animal Kingdom Lodge Resort

Disney's Animal Kingdom Lodge shares the ambience of its neighboring park, Disney's Animal Kingdom (use the blue tab at the top of the page for parks and eateries in the vicinity). Guests at this deluxe resort can watch grazing mammals on 33 acres of African savanna from their balconies.

AMBIENCE

Your trek to the Lodge is rewarded as soon as you step into the atrium lobby, which offers a dramatic view to the animal reserve and "kopje" (rock outcrop) beyond. Sunlight pours in through high windows, painting the lobby's thatched ceiling and carved wooden decorations in a warm, intimate glow. African artwork, much of it museum quality, greets you at every turn. Designed by the architect behind Disney's Wilderness Lodge, the six-story hotel shares its sister resort's **rustic appeal**, but adds a welcome warmth and intimacy, even in the largest public spaces. Then, of course, there are the animals, which add a sense of delight unique to this resort.

LAYOUT & ROOMS

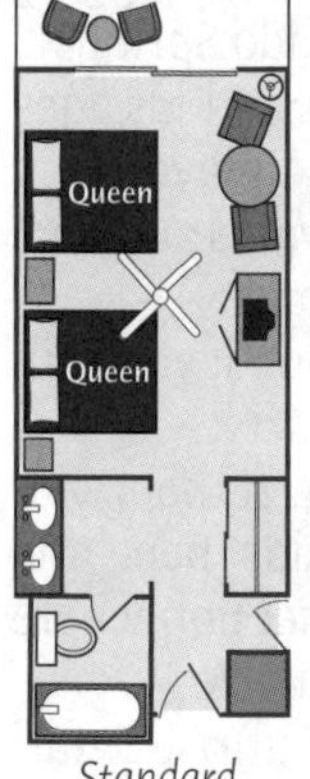

Standard Room Layout

This **horseshoe-shaped lodge**, inspired by African Kraal (corral) villages, gives all but 100 of the 1293 rooms a view of the private wildlife reserve. The rooms are vibrant with rich tapestries, hand-carved furniture, gauze hangings at the head of the beds, and Kente-inspired fabrics. Standard rooms (344 sq. ft.) have two queen beds; one king bed and a day bed; or one queen bed and bunk beds. Deluxe rooms (381 sq. ft.) add a daybed (most rooms), a make-up mirror, and a second phone. All rooms have a balcony, ceiling fan, table and chairs, armoire with 27" TV and drawers, double sinks, in-room safe, iron and ironing board, hair dryer, voice mail, and newspaper delivery.

DINING

A casual yet upscale restaurant, **Jiko**, is open for guests who want an elegantly inventive dinner. **Boma**, which means "place of refuge," offers an exciting, African-flavored dining adventure with all-you-care-to-eat buffets at breakfast and dinner. These two table-service restaurants are reviewed on page 224. **The Mara** is a quick-service cafe open all day—this is the perfect place for a fast meal. Typical breakfast menu items include breakfast pizza ($5.79), a croissant sandwich ($5.59), and a kid's breakfast ($3.99). Typical lunch/dinner items include Sugar Cane Chicken ($7.29), African House Salad ($6.59), and Fish and Chips ($9.49). Refillable mugs ($11) can be purchased (and refilled) at The Mara. Room service is also available.

Using the Amenities at Disney's Animal Kingdom Lodge Resort

LOUNGING

Victoria Falls Lounge, which overlooks Boma, serves coffees, African wines, and international beer in the evenings. The **Cape Town Lounge and Wine Bar**, inside Jiko, serves remarkable wines from South Africa. **Uzima Springs** is a poolside bar offering beer and mixed drinks. Snacks, beer, and wine are at the **Zawadi Marketplace** and **The Mara**.

© MediaMarx, Inc.

The view from a fifth floor guest room at Disney's Animal Kingdom Lodge

PLAYING & RELAXING

For Animal Watchers: Bring plenty of film for your camera—you may also want a tripod. Binoculars are an excellent idea, too.

For Athletes: Keep in shape in the Zahanati Fitness Center near the pool. Massage treatments are also offered. There are no jogging paths—drive or bus to another resort (such as Coronado Springs).

For Children: Simba's Cubhouse is a supervised club for kids ages 4–12 (see page 252). There's also the Hakuna Matata playground near the pool, storytelling at the fire pit, and daily activities at Boma.

For Gamers: Pumbaa's Fun and Games has video games.

For Shoppers: The festive Zawadi Marketplace can outfit you with sundries, foodstuffs, books, clothing, and African crafts.

For Swimmers: Soak in the Uzima Pool, an 11,000 sq. ft. pool with an African theme, waterslide (closes at 10:00 pm), kids' pool, and two spas (hot tubs). The pool features a zero-entry section where you can wade into the water. A pool wheelchair is available.

For Concierge Guests: Inquire in advance about the Sunrise Safari Breakfast Adventure, a 45-minute tour of Disney's Animal Kingdom on Tue. and Sat. for $49.95/adult or $24.95/child age 3-12.

GETTING ABOUT

Buses to theme parks and Downtown Disney (see chart below for in-transit times) are a short walk out front (see the map on page 42). Travel to other resorts via Disney's Animal Kingdom theme park (daytime) or Downtown Disney (evening). Ample parking is available, as is valet parking. This is the only deluxe resort to lack boat or monorail access to a nearby park.

Magic Kingdom	Epcot	Disney-MGM Studios	Disney's Animal Kingdom	Downtown Disney
direct bus ~20 min.	direct bus ~15 min.	direct bus ~10 min.	direct bus ~5 min.	direct bus ~15 min.

Estimated time you will spend in-transit from resort to destination during normal operation.

Making the Most of Disney's Animal Kingdom Lodge Resort

TIPS

The Lodge's own **33-acre savanna**, which is distinct from the theme park, is home to 36 species of mammals and 26 species of birds—over 330 animals in all. Guests can see zebras, antelopes, giraffes, gazelle, wildebeests, ostriches, cranes, vultures, and storks. Animals may come within 15 feet of the main observation area on the kopje, or as close as 30 feet from your balcony, day or night.

At night, the savanna is lit by **artificial moonlight**. Bring a bathrobe to visit your balcony without fear of binoculars or security cameras.

African storytelling is held nightly around the firepit. In inclement weather, storytelling moves to one of the overlooks inside. "Safari guides" are also on hand to educate guests on the animals.

Tour the resort's **African art collection**, either on your own or on a free guided tour. Ask at the front desk.

NOTES

There are **three separate savannas** (each about 11 acres) which can be viewed 24 hours a day. Each savanna has a few animal species that are unique to it. Each closes daily for cleaning and animal care, but at least two savannas are open at all times. Best viewing times are typically early to mid-morning, and dusk through sunset.

If your room doesn't have a view of the savanna, **watch the animals** from the kopje (the large observation area that extends into the savanna), the Sunset Overlook (a delightful room on the west side of the lobby), the overlook near the pool, and the alcoves along Zebra Trail and Kudu Trail (visit the second floor for outdoor viewing platforms that feature rocking chairs and high-powered binoculars).

Check-in time is 3:00 pm. Check-out is 11:00 am. No late checkouts.

RATINGS

Ratings are explained on page 26.

Our Value Ratings:		Our Magic Ratings:		Readers' Ratings:
Quality:	9/10	Theme:	10/10	65% fell in love with it
Accessibility:	5/10	Amenities:	5/10	15% liked it well enough
Affordability:	5/10	Fun Factor:	8/10	15% had mixed feelings
Overall Value:	**6/10**	**Overall Magic:**	**8/10**	5% were disappointed

Disney's Animal Kingdom Lodge is enjoyed by... (rated by both authors and readers)		
Younger Kids: ♥♥♥♥♥	Young Adults: ♥♥♥♥	Families: ♥♥♥♥♥
Older Kids: ♥♥♥♥♥	Mid Adults: ♥♥♥♥♥	Couples: ♥♥♥
Teenagers: ♥♥♥	Mature Adults: ♥♥	Singles: ♥♥♥♥

Planning | Getting There | Staying in Style | Touring | Feasting | Making Magic | Index | Notes & More

Finding Your Place at Disney's Animal Kingdom Lodge Resort

ANIMAL KINGDOM LODGE MAP

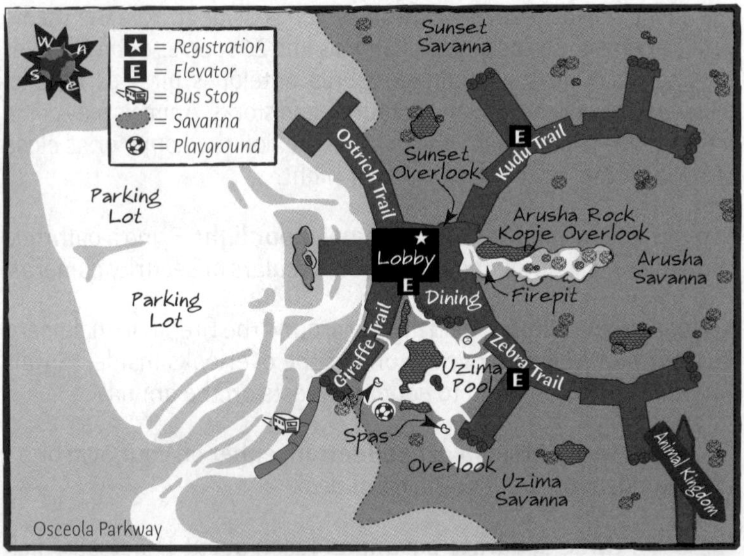

BEST LOCATIONS

Standard rooms are for up to four guests and are located on floors 1-4. Rooms come in three views: standard (Giraffe and Ostrich Trails), pool (Giraffe and Zebra Trails), and savanna (Zebra, Kudu and Ostrich Trails). **Deluxe rooms** are on floor 5 and accommodate up to five guests. If the animal watching is your main draw, reserve a savanna-view room. Rooms on the far ends of the Zebra and Kudu Trails require a long walk. **Concierge rooms** (floors 5 and 6) are also available in pool and savanna views, as are several one-bedroom, two-bedroom, and "royal" suites. Note that only the 6th floor is key-protected.

RATES

2004 Sample Room Rates

Seasons are noted on page 14

Room Type	Value	Regular	Peak	Holiday
Standard View	$199	$239	$289	$324
Standard Water/Pool View	$220	$260	$310	$345
Standard Savanna View	$275	$315	$365	$410
Deluxe Savanna View	$340	$385	$445	$500
Concierge	$425	$480	$545	$610

Tax not included in above prices. Suites start in the mid-$600's.

INFO

Disney's Animal Kingdom Lodge Resort

2901 Osceola Parkway, Bay Lake, FL 32830

Phone: 407-938-3000 Fax: 407-938-7102

For reservations, call Central Reservations: 407-934-7639

Looking for the Beach Club and Villas? See pages 93-96.

Disney's BoardWalk Inn & Villas Resort

BoardWalk Inn & Villas Resort enjoys a favored location in the middle of the action, fronting Crescent Lake between Epcot and Disney-MGM Studios (use the blue tab at the top of the page for parks and eateries in the area). The Villas are affiliated with the Disney Vacation Club (see pages 102-103).

AMBIENCE

This **"seaside" resort** takes you back to the heyday of the Atlantic City Boardwalk in the 1920s and 1930s, where carefree days floated by on the summer breeze. Reminiscent of an elegant bed-and-breakfast inn, the BoardWalk continues this impression inside with its old-fashioned furnishings and soft, muted colors. Outside, a stroll along the vibrant promenade offers great views, family fun, and more eateries, clubs, and shops than you can visit.

LAYOUT & ROOMS

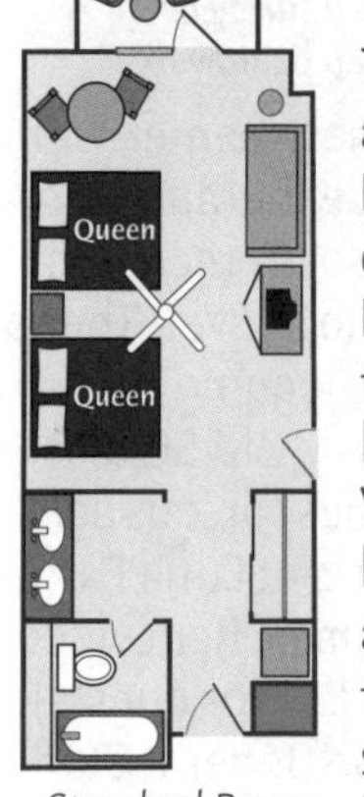

Standard Room Layout (Inn)

The two different sides of this resort offer varying accommodations, ranging from 422–1071 sq. feet. **BoardWalk Inn** has 378 rooms with one king or two queens plus a day bed or queen sofa bed, and suites. **BoardWalk Villas** feature 532 studios and one-, two-, and three-bedroom suites—studios have a kitchenette, suites have a full kitchen, big-screen TV, VCR, and washer and dryer. All rooms in the resort have a balcony or patio, double sinks, a marble vanity, a table and chairs, a sofa, an armoire, TV, ceiling fan, toiletries, hair dryer, housekeeping, turndown service (on request), voice mail, valet parking, and, in most rooms, in-room safe and newspaper delivery.

DINING

Unique to this resort is a lively entertainment complex along the waterfront promenade. This innovative mini-park offers a variety of dining options. BoardWalk table-service restaurants, detailed on pages 224–225, include **Big River Grille & Brewing Works**, a modern brewpub; **ESPN Club**, an All-American sports cafe; **Flying Fish Cafe**, fine dining with an ever-changing menu; and **Spoodles**, delicious Mediterranean food. Spoodles also has an outside counter for take-out—pick up a slice of pepperoni pizza ($3.25) or a calzone ($5.50). The **Belle Vue Room** offers a quick bite in the mornings. Two quick-service cafes round out the menu. **BoardWalk Bakery** tempts you with baked goods and coffee—try the chocolate croissant ($2.79), breakfast burrito ($3.99), or a Lunch Bag (chicken salad sandwich, whole fruit, and chips for $6.59). **Seashore Sweets** offers ice cream, cookies, fudge, saltwater taffy, and coffees.

Using the Amenities at Disney's BoardWalk Inn & Villas Resort

LOUNGING

The BoardWalk is rich with lounges and clubs. **Atlantic Dance Hall** and **Jellyrolls** (see page 193) serve up drinks and fun. In the resort itself is the **Belle Vue Room**, perfect for a quiet drink and a game of chess. **Leaping Horse Libations** is the pool bar near Luna Park. 24-hour room service is also available.

© MediaMarx, Inc.

Jennifer and Dave pedal a surrey bike down the resort's wooden boardwalk

PLAYING & RELAXING

For Athletes: Muscles and Bustles Fitness is a fitness center with exercise equipment, steam room, sauna, and massage therapies (for an extra fee). Rent bikes at Community Hall (the resort's recreation center) and surrey bikes on the BoardWalk (see photo above). There are also two lighted tennis courts and a walking/jogging circuit around Crescent Lake and along the path to Disney-MGM Studios.
For Children: Harbor Club offers supervised activities for kids ages 4-12 (see page 252). A playground and wading pool is at Luna Park.
For Gamers: Side Show Games Arcade has video games. Rent video tapes at Community Hall (free to DVC members, $3.16 for guests).
For Shoppers: Dundy's Sundries and Screen Door General Store offer the basics, while Thimbles & Threads and Disney's Character Carnival stock apparel and gifts. Wyland Galleries has collectibles.
For Swimmers: Of the three pools, the largest is Luna Park with a 200-ft. wooden "coaster" slide. All pools have spas (hot tubs).

GETTING ABOUT

Buses are boarded in the front of the resort, while **boats** depart from the marina (see the chart below for in-transit times). Travel elsewhere via a park (daytime) or Downtown Disney (evening). You can **walk** to Disney-MGM Studios, Epcot, Yacht & Beach Club, and Swan & Dolphin. If you miss the Disney-MGM Studios boat, just walk to the Swan & Dolphin boat dock before your missed boat reaches it and hop on. Parking is available, as is valet ($6/day).

Magic Kingdom	Epcot	Disney-MGM Studios	Disney's Animal Kingdom	Downtown Disney
direct bus ~20 min.	walk/boat ~10/~5min.	walk/boat ~15/~20 min.	direct bus ~10 min.	direct bus ~15 min.

Approximate time you will spend in-transit from resort to destination during normal operation.

Making the Most of Disney's BoardWalk Inn & Villas Resort

TIPS

The **Belle Vue Room** is a marvel of nostalgia. It's tucked away in a corner down the hall from the lobby on the Inn side of the resort. You'll find backgammon, chess, and checkers tables (ask a cast member for game pieces), as well as a single-malt scotch menu.

Take a stroll through the grounds of the resort, away from the busy BoardWalk Promenade itself. The **landscaping** is meticulous and often original. If you prefer the bustle of the BoardWalk, rent a **surrey bike** and tour around the promenade and lake.

The BoardWalk Inn's **Garden Suites** have got to be the most romantic in the "World." Each of the fourteen suites looks like a two-story cottage. All suites have private entrances and most have a unique garden surrounded by a white picket fence with a trellised arbor gate. Suites have a separate living room, sleeper sofa, and a wet bar on the first floor, while the open second floor has a king-size bed, a separate shower, and a large whirlpool tub.

There are several quaint **sitting areas** scattered (and sometimes virtually hidden) throughout the resort's buildings.

NOTES

Guests with rooms in the **small courtyard building** on the Inn side must use their room key to enter the building itself.

Noise and **light** levels are important considerations here due to the proximity of the BoardWalk Promenade. If these are concerns, request a room away from both the promenade and the pools.

Conference facilities are available at the BoardWalk.

Check-in time is 3:00 pm (BoardWalk Inn) or 4:00 pm (BoardWalk Villas). Check-out time is 11:00 am for both.

RATINGS

Ratings are explained on page 26.

Our Value Ratings:		Our Magic Ratings:		Readers' Ratings:
Quality:	9/10	Theme:	8/10	80% fell in love with it
Accessibility:	7/10	Amenities:	8/10	10% liked it well enough
Affordability:	3/10	Fun Factor:	6/10	4% had mixed feelings
Overall Value:	**6/10**	**Overall Magic:**	**7/10**	6% were disappointed

The BoardWalk is enjoyed by...	(rated by both authors and readers)	
Younger Kids: ♥♥♥♥	Young Adults: ♥♥♥♥	Families: ♥♥♥♥♥
Older Kids: ♥♥♥♥	Mid Adults: ♥♥♥♥♥	Couples: ♥♥♥♥♥
Teenagers: ♥♥♥	Mature Adults: ♥♥♥♥♥	Singles: ♥♥♥

Finding Your Place at Disney's BoardWalk Inn & Villas Resort

BOARDWALK RESORT MAP

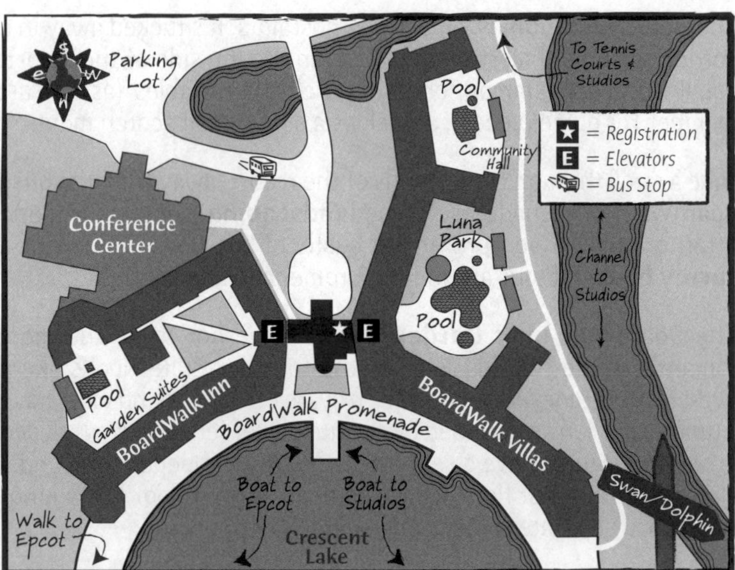

BEST LOCATIONS

It's hard to get a bad room at either the BoardWalk Inn or Villas. Request a **water view** at the Inn if you want to watch the bustling BoardWalk Promenade, but keep in mind it can be noisy. Water views in the Villas may be over the Promenade itself, but are more likely to overlook the canal leading to the Studios. **Standard views** overlook attractive courtyards or the entrance driveway (which isn't so bad as trees shield the parking areas). **Preferred views** in the Villas can overlook anything but a parking area. Rooms around the quiet pools are more peaceful than those around Luna Park.

RATES

2004 Sample Room Rates

Seasons are noted on page 14

Room Type	Value	Regular	Peak	Holiday
Standard (Inn) or Studio (Villas)	$289	$329	$394	$449
Water View (Inn)	$360	$405	$470	$530
One-Bedroom (Villas)	$390	$435	$505	$570
Two-Bedroom (Villas)	$545	$705	$890	$1010

Tax not included in above prices. Concierge-level rooms at the BoardWalk Inn begin at the low-$400's and suites begin in the mid-$500's. The Grand Villas begin in the $1300's.

INFO

Disney's BoardWalk Inn & Villas Resort

2101 Epcot Resorts Blvd., Bay Lake, FL 32830
Phone: 407-939-6200 Fax: 407-939-5150
For reservations, call Central Reservations: 407-934-7639

Disney's Caribbean Beach Resort

The free spirit of the tropics greets you at the Caribbean Beach Resort, Disney's original moderately-priced resort. Within easy distance of both Epcot and Disney-MGM Studios (use the blue tab at the top of the page for parks and eateries in the area), this large resort is popular with families.

AMBIENCE

The bright, sunny colors of the buildings and rooftops are your first sign of the **laid-back lifestyle** you'll find at the Caribbean. After you check in at the Customs House, you make your way to one of the six "islands" that encircle 45-acre Barefoot Bay. Lush tropical foliage, hidden courtyards, and white sand beaches are the setting for your lively Caribbean adventure.

RESORT LAYOUT & ROOMS

The 2112 rooms are well spread out among the six exotic "**islands**" of the Caribe—Aruba, Barbados, Martinique, Jamaica, Trinidad North, and Trinidad South. Each island has a cluster of stucco, pitched-roof buildings that make up the "village centers," all painted in their own distinctive colors. The rooms in the two-storied buildings are decorated in soft colors with oak furnishings. The beds (one king or two doubles) have posts carved into pineapples, the symbol of hospitality. Guest rooms have double sinks in the separate vanity area, a small table and chairs, an armoire with TV, a set of drawers, and a ceiling fan. There are no balconies or patios. The guest rooms here are the largest of all the moderately-priced resorts at 340 sq. ft. Amenities include a coffeemaker, toiletries, housekeeping service, limited room service, and voice mail.

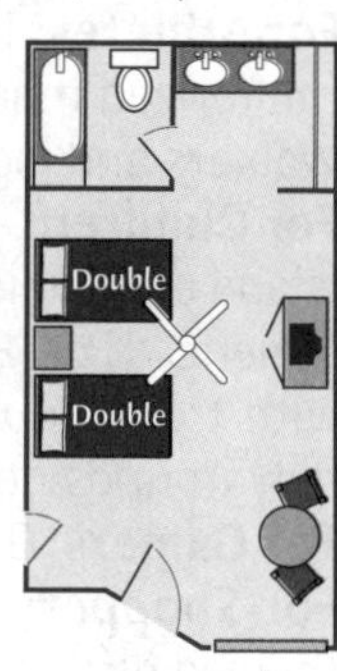

Standard Room Layout

DINING

The Caribbean Beach offers a new table-service restaurant, as well as a breezy food court and the ubiquitous pool bar. All are available in **Old Port Royale**, the resort's "towne center" housing the eateries, shops, main pool, and marina. The food court's hours are 7:00 am–11:30 pm. **Banana Cabana**, a pool bar located at Old Port Royale, offers a variety of specialty drinks ($6.50) and beer ($4.25–$5.25) during pool hours. **Bluerunner** is a limited room delivery service—typical menu items include domestic beer ($4.50), 16" pizza ($14.95), 8-piece chicken in a bucket ($13.50), tuna sub with chips ($5.49), a chef salad ($5.99), and cheesecake ($3.50). **Shutters**, the table-service restaurant, serves Caribbean-flavored fare for dinner only—see the restaurant's description on page 225.

Using the Amenities at Disney's Caribbean Beach Resort

MORE DINING

A bustling village atmosphere sets the stage for **Market Street**, the resort's newly renovated food court. Fill your trays at the various food stations, then pay at a central check-out area. Chicken, pasta, sandwiches, burgers, pizza, and baked goods are on the menu, as is French toast with bacon ($4.99), chicken Caesar salad ($5.99), double cheeseburger with fries ($6.19), veggie wrap ($5.49), kid's grilled cheese ($3.99), and carrot cake ($2.99). Get refills at the beverage island with a mug ($11).

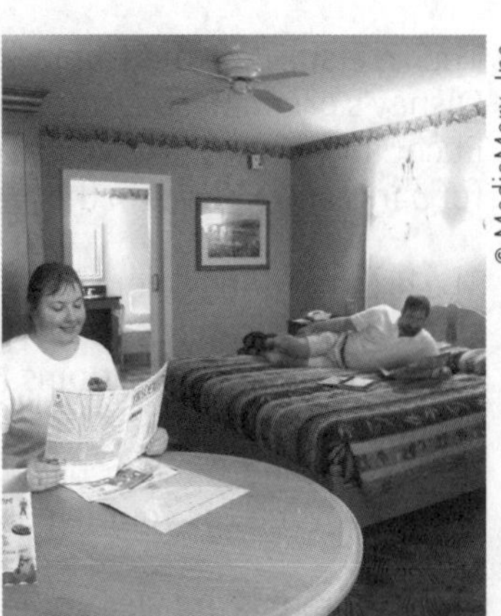

Relaxing in our king bed, barrier-free room (#2311)

PLAYING & RELAXING

For Athletes: The Barefoot Bay Boat Yard rents boats and "toobies" (motorized inner tubes). Rent a bicycle for a ride around the bay. Walkers and joggers enjoy the many beautiful paths.

For Children: A wonderful playground is located on Parrot Cay, an island in the middle of Barefoot Bay you can reach via bridges from either Old Port Royale or Aruba. Parrot Cay is a lush, exotic hideaway with tropical birds and meandering paths. There are two other playgrounds near Martinique and Trinidad South.

For Gamers: Goombay Games in Old Port Royale has video games.

For Shoppers: The Calypso Trading Post & Straw Market offers themed gifts, sundries, clothing, and Caribbean items.

For Swimmers: The theme pool near Old Port Royale features cannons and waterfalls, as well as a wading pool for kids, a spa (hot tub), and a slide. Six quiet pools are in each of the resort's "islands."

GETTING ABOUT

Transportation to the theme parks and water parks (see chart below for in-transit times) is via frequent **buses**. Other resorts are accessible by changing buses at a nearby theme park (daytime) or Downtown Disney (evening). You can also take an internal resort bus if you need to reach other areas within the resort. To go to the Customs House, get off at Barbados.

Magic Kingdom	Epcot	Disney-MGM Studios	Disney's Animal Kingdom	Downtown Disney
direct bus ~20 min.	direct bus ~15 min.	direct bus ~12 min.	direct bus ~20 min.	direct bus ~25 min.

Approximate time you will spend in-transit from resort to destination during normal operation.

Making the Most of Disney's Caribbean Beach Resort

TIPS

We stayed in this **beautiful resort** after its recent renovation and are delighted to report that it is looking wonderful! For those who visited prior to December 2002, note that the old restaurant, Captain's Tavern, has been replaced by Shutters (see page 225).

While you can't swim in the bay, the **white sand beaches** are great spots to relax. We found several hammocks set up along the beach—take some time to just kick back and watch the palm trees flutter.

You can catch a glimpse of the **Epcot globe** between Old Port Royale and Martinique—look in the evenings for a glimpse of IllumiNations.

There are "hidden" **courtyards** sporting tables with umbrellas in every "island" of the resort—finding these can be an adventure in itself, and they offer a very rewarding place to relax.

Be sure to take a trip across the bridge to **Parrot Cay** in the middle of Barefoot Bay. Beyond the lush gardens and dense bamboo stands you'll find gazebos and picnic areas.

You can rent **refrigerators** for $10/day—request when reserving.

NOTES

One of the biggest drawbacks of this resort is how spread out it is, making it difficult to get to Old Port Royale to eat or shop. You may find it easier to **stock up** on snacks and quick breakfast foods. Board the bus marked "Internal" to move around the resort a little easier.

All rooms in Martinique and Trinidad North are **Preferred Rooms** and are priced the same as a water-view or king-bed room.

Check-in time is 3:00 pm. Check-out time is 11:00 am.

RATINGS

Ratings are explained on page 26.

Our Value Ratings:		Our Magic Ratings:		Readers' Ratings:
Quality:	6/10	Theme:	6/10	48% fell in love with it
Accessibility:	5/10	Amenities:	6/10	38% liked it well enough
Affordability:	8/10	Fun Factor:	6/10	8% had mixed feelings
Overall Value:	**6/10**	**Overall Magic:**	**6/10**	6% were disappointed

Caribbean Beach is enjoyed by...	(rated by both authors and readers)	
Younger Kids: ♥♥♥♥♥	Young Adults: ♥♥♥♥	Families: ♥♥♥♥
Older Kids: ♥♥♥♥♥	Mid Adults: ♥♥♥♥	Couples: ♥♥♥♥♥
Teenagers: ♥♥♥♥	Mature Adults: ♥♥♥♥	Singles: ♥♥♥

Finding Your Place at Disney's Caribbean Beach Resort

CARIBBEAN BEACH RESORT MAP

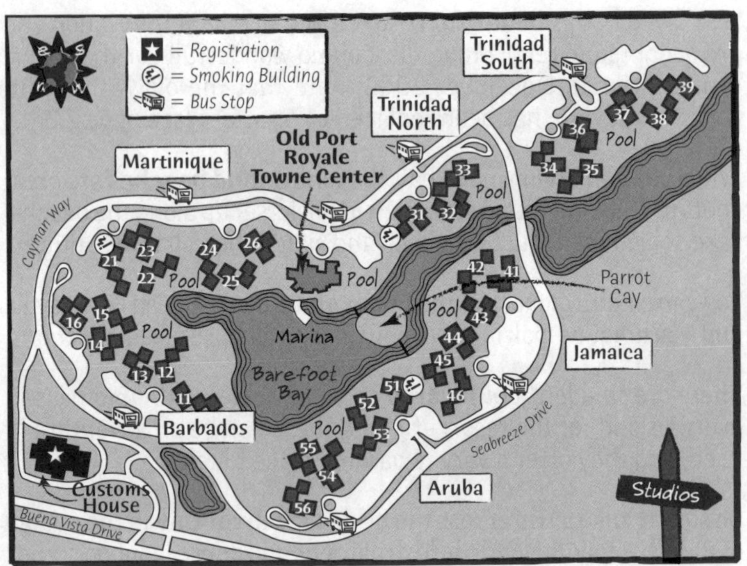

BEST LOCATIONS

Your "island" can make or break your experience. Though more expensive, we suggest you request **Martinique** or **Trinidad North**, both of which are close to Old Port Royale (dining and shopping). **Aruba** and **Jamaica**, across the Barefoot Bay bridge, are good choices if you wish to be a bit secluded. You don't need a **water view** to enjoy your room here, but if you prefer one we found the following rooms to have outstanding water views: 2524, 2525, 2556, and 2557 in Martinique; and 3117, 3149, 3225-3228, and 3257-3261 in Trinidad North. Corner rooms (with king-size beds) seem larger as they often have an extra window.

RATES

2004 Sample Room Rates

Seasons are noted on page 14

Room Type	Value	Regular	Peak	Holiday
Standard View	$133	$144	$169	$184
Preferred, Water/Pool, or King	$148	$159	$194	$209

Tax not included in above rates. King-bed rooms come in both standard or water view, and both are the same rate as a water view room. Preferred rooms (any view, any bed size) are located in Martinique and Trinidad North.

INFO

Disney's Caribbean Beach Resort

900 Cayman Way, Lake Buena Vista, FL 32830

Phone: 407-934-3400 Fax: 407-934-3288

For reservations, call Central Reservations: 407-934-7639

Disney's Contemporary Resort

The Contemporary Resort is one of the original and quintessential Walt Disney World hotels, built at the same time as nearby Magic Kingdom (use the blue tab at the top of the page for parks and eateries in the area). Bay Lake and the Seven Seas Lagoon surround the resort on three sides.

AMBIENCE

Every time we enter the Contemporary Resort, we get the sense we've entered the **center of the "World."** It isn't just the soaring architecture, the massive steel and glass tower, or the monorail running right through it, though those are all a part of it. Rather, it is akin to the feeling city dwellers boast about: everything you need, everyone you like, and every place that matters is right there. And that seems to be exactly the way Disney intended it, with the Grand Concourse housing most of the resort's services, restaurants, and shops. There's even a restaurant at the top of the tower, overlooking the "World" below. The Contemporary Resort is the future we dreamed of as children.

RESORT LAYOUT & ROOMS

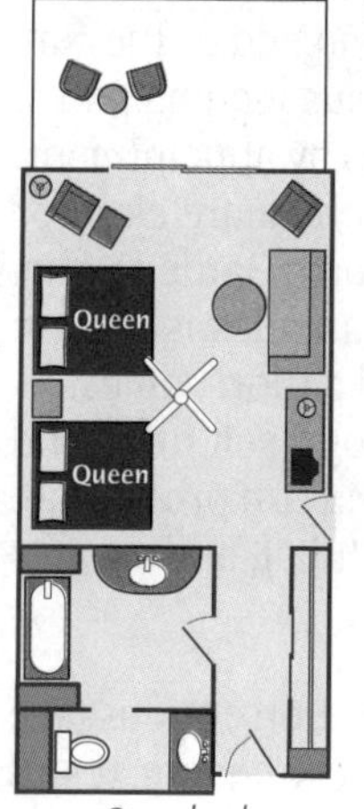

Standard Room Layout

The 1041 guest rooms at the Contemporary are housed along the outside of the 15-story, A-frame **tower** or within the two flanking, three-story **garden wings**. Spacious rooms (about 436 sq. ft.) are decorated in eclectic, vibrant colors with two queen-size beds or one king-size bed, and a daybed. All rooms have spacious bathrooms with two sinks, a massage shower head, a small table and chairs, an armoire with drawers, and a TV. Some rooms have large patios or balconies. Amenities include housekeeping, toiletries, safe, newspaper delivery, hair dryer, turndown service (on request), voice mail, and valet parking.

DINING

If your stomach feels as cavernous as the Grand Concourse, the Contemporary has great dining. Table-service restaurants (see details on pages 225–226) include **Chef Mickey's**, a character dining experience; **Concourse Steakhouse**, traditional fare; and trendy **California Grill**, the Contemporary's centerpiece. The **Food and Fun Center Snack Bar** is open early and late. Typical menu items include biscruits and gravy ($4.99), fruit plate($4.99), chicken strips ($6.59), California club wrap ($6.99), and kids macaroni and cheese with fries, chips, or fruit ($4.29). Refillable mugs are available here for $11. The **Sand Bar**, by the pool also offers drinks, sandwiches, and ice cream.

Using the Amenities at Disney's Contemporary Resort

LOUNGING

California Grill Lounge offers California wines and appetizers along with a magnificent view of the Magic Kingdom. The **Outer Rim Cocktail Lounge**, overlooking Bay Lake, offers a full bar and snacks. **Contemporary Grounds** is a coffee bar near the front desk. **Room service** is also available 24 hours a day.

Our first floor Garden Wing room was spacious and convenient

© MediaMarx, Inc.

PLAYING & RELAXING

For Athletes: The Olympiad fitness center has exercise equipment, sauna, and massage therapies. Six, lighted clay tennis courts are available. Boat rentals, waterskiing, and parasailing add to the fun. Volleyball and shuffleboard courts are available, plus jogging paths.
For Charmers: A full-service salon offers services by appointment.
For Children: The Mouseketeer Clubhouse is a childcare club for kids 4–12 (see page 253). A playground is by the North Garden Wing.
For Gamers: The biggest and best of the resort arcades is here in the Food and Fun Center, with pinball, video, and action games.
For Shoppers: The fourth floor Concourse shops sell gifts and clothing. The marina pavilion offers swimming and sun protection.
For Swimmers: Two heated pools, two spas (hot tubs), and a water slide, as well as a sand beach for sunbathers.

GETTING ABOUT

The Contemporary Resort offers myriad transportation options (see the chart below for in-transit times). For the Magic Kingdom, board the **monorail** on the 4th floor or walk the **path** on the north side (see map on page 54). For Epcot, monorail to the Transportation & Ticket Center (TTC) and transfer to the Epcot monorail. For other parks, take the **direct bus** just outside the lobby. For the Polynesian or Grand Floridian, take the monorail. For Fort Wilderness or the Wilderness Lodge, take the **boat**. For other destinations, go to the Magic Kingdom (daytime) or Downtown Disney (evening) and transfer to the appropriate resort bus.

Magic Kingdom	Epcot	Disney-MGM Studios	Disney's Animal Kingdom	Downtown Disney
monorail/walk ~20/~10 min.	monorail x 2 ~15 min.	direct bus ~20 min.	direct bus ~20 min.	direct bus ~35 min.

Approximate time you will spend in-transit from resort to destination during normal operation.

Making the Most of Disney's Contemporary Resort

TIPS

The **Electrical Water Pageant**, a whimsical parade of lighted barges and music, can be seen from the shore of Bay Lake at 10:00 pm.

The resort also offers one- and two-bedroom suites and a concierge level, all with special amenities. Among the many amenities in the **suites** (bathrobe, triple sheeting, turndown service, etc.), the two-line speakerphones are great for those who use dataports often.

We were pleasantly surprised by the tranquility of the grounds. **Stroll** around the resort and admire the view of Bay Lake.

The obvious method of transportation to Magic Kingdom is via the monorail, but consider **walking** instead on busy mornings or when the park lets out–it's much faster! The monorail goes around the lagoon clockwise, so it can take a while to reach the Magic Kingdom.

Guest rooms in the **Garden Wings** can be a hike from the Tower's restaurants and services. If this is a concern, reserve a Tower room. On the other hand, the North Garden Wing is very convenient to the buses and to the walking path to the Magic Kingdom.

NOTES

The **observation deck** on the 15th floor is open again for stunning fireworks views. There's also a viewing deck on the fourth floor.

For some, the Contemporary lacks the whimsy seen in most other Disney resorts. It feels much more like a traditional hotel. Even so, it is a very deluxe, modern, sparkling-clean hotel with a powerful presence. You'll be delighted by **subtler details** and **little luxuries**. Look for a high-speed Internet access here in the near future!

Check-in time is 3:00 pm. Check-out time is 11:00 am.

RATINGS

Ratings are explained on page 26.

Our Value Ratings:		Our Magic Ratings:		Readers' Ratings:
Quality:	8/10	Theme:	4/10	54% fell in love with it
Accessibility:	9/10	Amenities:	9/10	31% liked it well enough
Affordability:	5/10	Fun Factor:	5/10	10% had mixed feelings
Overall Value:	**7/10**	**Overall Magic:**	**6/10**	5% were disappointed

Contemporary is enjoyed by...	(rated by both authors and readers)	
Younger Kids: ♥♥♥	Young Adults: ♥♥♥♥♥	Families: ♥♥♥♥♥
Older Kids: ♥♥♥♥♥	Mid Adults: ♥♥♥♥	Couples: ♥♥♥♥
Teenagers: ♥♥♥♥♥	Mature Adults: ♥♥♥	Singles: ♥♥♥♥

Finding Your Place at Disney's Contemporary Resort

CONTEMPORARY RESORT MAP

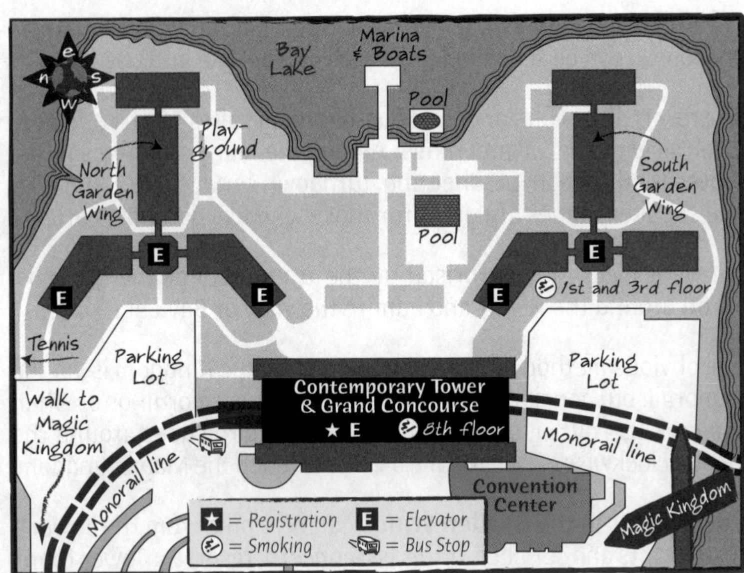

BEST LOCATIONS

If you are drawn to the Contemporary by its proximity to the Magic Kingdom and you want to **see the castle** from your room, be sure to request this specifically when reserving—only certain **Tower** rooms get this breathtaking view. The **Garden Wing** may lack the tower's excitement, but we found the rooms delightful and relaxing, especially those facing the water. North Garden Wing rooms are closer to the Magic Kingdom. Rooms fronting Bay Lake feel far removed from the bustle of the Tower. Very few of the Garden Wing rooms have **balconies**, but first-floor rooms have **patios**.

RATES

2004 Sample Room Rates

Seasons are noted on page 14

Room Type	Value	Regular	Peak	Holiday
Standard View (Wing)	$239	$264	$309	$344
Garden/Water View (Wing)	$275	$305	$355	$395
Tower Room	$335	$370	$435	$475
Tower Club (concierge)	$395	$435	$505	$545

Tax not included in above rates. Concierge-level suites (floors 12 and 14) start in the high-$300's. Suites come in garden and lake views, and start in the high-$700's.

INFO

Disney's Contemporary Resort

4600 North World Drive, Bay Lake, FL 32830
Phone: 407-824-1000 Fax: 407-824-3539
For reservations, call Central Reservations: 407-934-7639

Disney's Coronado Springs Resort

Coronado Springs is located near Disney's Animal Kingdom and Disney-MGM Studios (use the blue tab at the top of the page for parks and eateries in the area). The resort offers moderately-priced rooms and convention facilities. The resort surrounds a 15-acre lake known as Lago Dorado.

AMBIENCE

The architecture and decor traces the travels of explorer Francisco de Coronado in colonial Mexico and the **American Southwest**. Adventure awaits around every corner, from the colorful, bustling market to the Mayan pyramid overlooking the main swimming pool. Your visit begins in a sunny plaza, which leads to the large, open lobby graced by beamed ceilings, elegant columns, and intricately inlaid floors. Around the corner a festive market offers native foods, just the thing to eat on the lakeside terrace. The resort's buildings are clustered around sparkling Lago (Lake) Dorado, including the stately main building, El Centro.

RESORT LAYOUT & ROOMS

The guest rooms in this 1,967-room resort are divided into three districts. Closest to El Centro are the **Casitas**, a bustling village of three- and four-story stucco buildings painted in soft pastels. Next around the lagoon are the rustic adobe-and-wood **Ranchos**. You could imagine Zorro dashing under the porch roofs and amid the cactus, while bubbling springs cascade into rock-strewn stream beds, ultimately to disappear into the parched desert earth. Finally, you reach the tropical **Cabanas**, vibrantly colored two-story buildings with the corrugated tin roofs of a rustic beach resort. Rooms are about 314 sq. ft. and offer two extra-long double beds or one king bed, a separate vanity area with just one sink, table and chairs, armoire, and a TV. Amenities include toiletries, housekeeping, limited room service, hair dryer, iron and ironing board, coffeemaker, in-room safe, and voice mail. Newspaper delivery is available for $1.50/day. A number of junior, one-bedroom, and executive suites are also available.

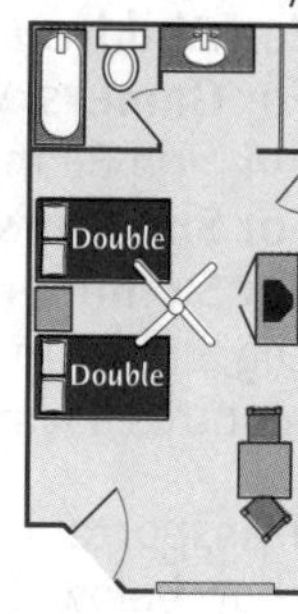

Standard Room Layout

The large 95,000 sq. ft. **Conference Center** is quite modern and generally lacks the regional character of the resort. It boasts the largest ballroom in the Southeast (60,214 sq. ft.). Several smaller-sized meeting rooms, another 20,000 sq. ft. ballroom, and patios round out the facilities. The center is currently undergoing a major expansion. A full-service business center is available.

Using the Amenities at Disney's Coronado Springs Resort

DINING

© MediaMarx, Inc.
Home on the Ranchos

Coronado Springs' dining options are the real enchilada. **Maya Grill** (see page 226) is an upscale table-service restaurant open for breakfast and dinner. **Pepper Market** is a food court dressed up like a festive, outdoor market for breakfast, lunch, and dinner. Typical menu items include breakfast burrito ($6.99), cheese omelet ($6.99), catch of the day ($11.95), chicken fajitas ($10.75), ham and cheese sandwich ($6.75), and kids chicken strips ($4.50). **Siesta's** is the poolside bar serving sandwiches, nachos, fries, and various drinks. **Francisco's** is a large lounge where you can also get light snacks and appetizers. **Limited room service** is offered in the mornings and evenings. Refillable mugs ($11) are available at the Pepper Market

PLAYING & RELAXING

For Athletes: La Vida Health Club has exercise equipment, whirlpool, and massage treatments. Boats, bikes, surreys, and fishing poles can be rented at La Marina, and there is a volleyball court. Enjoy a nature trail and the walk/jog around the lagoon.
For Charmers: Casa de Belleza offers beauty and hair treatments.
For Children: The Explorer's Playground is near the main pool.
For Gamers: Video games of all sorts are found at the two arcades: Jumping Bean (in El Centro) and Iguana (near the main pool).
For Shoppers: Panchitos has sundries, character items, and gifts.
For Swimmers: A quiet pool in each of the three districts, plus the Dig Site main pool, which is built around an ancient pyramid, and features a waterslide, spa (hot tub), and kid's pool.

GETTING ABOUT

Transportation to the theme parks is by frequent, direct **buses** (see chart below for in-transit times). There are four bus stops (see map on page 58). For other destinations, transfer at a nearby theme park (daytime) or at Downtown Disney (evening). A sidewalk connects the resort to Blizzard Beach, and it's a quick drive to both Disney-MGM Studios and Disney's Animal Kingdom.

Magic Kingdom	Epcot	Disney-MGM Studios	Disney's Animal Kingdom	Downtown Disney
direct bus ~15 min.	direct bus ~15 min.	direct bus ~15 min.	direct bus ~10 min.	direct bus ~25 min.

Approximate time you will spend in-transit from resort to destination during normal operation.

Making the Most of Disney's Coronado Springs Resort

TIPS

The **Dig Site** is really a miniature water park with delightful scenery and fun water attractions. The pool itself is huge (10,800 square feet) and there's a large sandbox that masquerades as the "dig site" of the Mayan pyramid. The 123-foot long water slide has a jaguar atop it that spits water. Oh, and they have the largest outdoor spa (hot tub) of any Disney resort—it fits 22 people!

Small **refrigerators** can be rented for $10/day. Roll-away beds are available for $15/day (but rooms are still limited to four guests). Request these with your reservations and again at check-in.

NOTES

The **Pepper Market** food court works differently than other food courts. Upon arrival, you are seated by a cast member and given a ticket. You then visit the various food stations and when you find an item you want, your ticket is stamped. You pay after your meal. A 10% gratuity is added (unless you get your food to go).

This resort goes for the sun-drenched effect and in the process seems to **lack enough shade** to protect you from the scorching Florida sun. Use caution if you are fair-skinned (as Jennifer is) or are going during the summer months.

Coronado Springs strikes us as a bit more **buttoned-down** than the other moderate resorts, no doubt due to the conference center and business facilities. While we have no major complaints, it also didn't delight us in the same way that other moderate Disney resorts have. On the other hand, some of our fellow vacationers are very impressed with the resort, especially its quality service. We definitely feel this is a great resort for business travelers.

Check-in time is 3:00 pm. Check-out time is 11:00 am.

RATINGS

Ratings are explained on page 26.

Our Value Ratings:		Our Magic Ratings:		Readers' Ratings:
Quality:	7/10	Theme:	8/10	33% fell in love with it
Accessibility:	6/10	Amenities:	5/10	41% liked it well enough
Affordability:	8/10	Fun Factor:	4/10	15% had mixed feelings
Overall Value:	**7/10**	**Overall Magic:**	**6/10**	11% were disappointed

Coronado Springs is enjoyed by...	(rated by both authors and readers)	
Younger Kids: ♥♥♥♥	Young Adults: ♥♥♥♥♥	Families: ♥♥♥♥
Older Kids: ♥♥♥♥	Mid Adults: ♥♥♥♥	Couples: ♥♥♥♥♥
Teenagers: ♥♥♥♥	Mature Adults: ♥♥♥	Singles: ♥♥♥♥

Finding Your Place at Disney's Coronado Springs Resort

CORONADO SPRINGS RESORT MAP

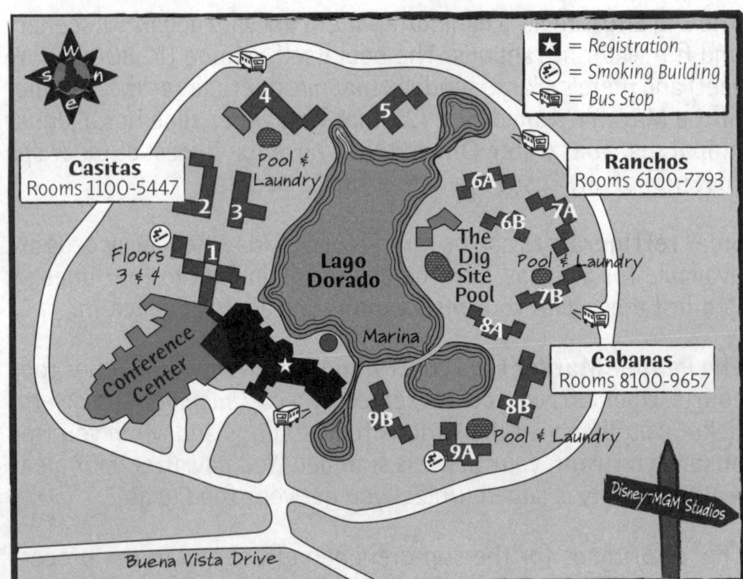

BEST LOCATIONS

The **Casitas** are the least interesting visually, but are convenient to the Convention Center—in fact, they house the only rooms that you can reach from El Centro without leaving the protection of a roof or overhang. Building 1 is the closest to the Conference Center. The charming **Ranchos** are closest to the main pool, and farthest from El Centro. We recommend buildings 6B and 8A for view and proximity to the quiet pool. The **Cabanas** are convenient to El Centro. We loved our room in building 8B (close to pools and the bus); building 8A has good views and 9B is next door to El Centro.

RATES

2004 Sample Room Rates *Seasons are noted on page 14*

Room Type	Value	Regular	Peak	Holiday
Standard View	$133	$144	$169	$184
Water View or King-Bed Room	$148	$159	$194	$209
Junior Suite (Double Beds)	$280	$325	$380	$420
One-Bedroom Suite	$560	$615	$685	$750

Tax not included in above rates.

INFO

Disney's Coronado Springs Resort

1000 W. Buena Vista Drive, Bay Lake, FL 32830

Phone: 407-939-1000 Fax: 407-939-1001

For reservations, call Central Reservations: 407-934-7639

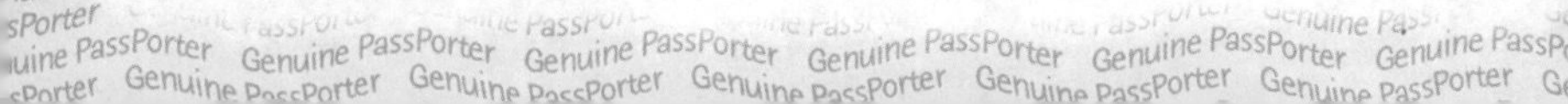

Looking for Dixie Landings? Page 79. Dolphin Resort? Page 99.

Disney's Fort Wilderness Resort & Campground

Much more than tents and hookups, Fort Wilderness is a resort in every sense of the word. It is pleasantly situated in a shady forest on Bay Lake, connected by a scenic waterway to the nearby Magic Kingdom theme park (use the blue tab at the top of the page for parks and eateries in the vicinity).

AMBIENCE

Enveloped by pine, cypress, and oak, this 700-acre campground is a **relaxing haven** after the noise and excitement of a long day at the parks. Rough-hewn log common buildings are nestled among towering pine trees and flowering meadows. Wilderness this is not, however. There are enough daily conveniences and services that the tents may be the only reminder that you are camping.

RESORT LAYOUT & ROOMS

All types of camping are available—tent, pop-up, trailer, and motor home (RV)—throughout the 788 **campsites**. Located on small loop roads connecting to larger thoroughfares, each site is relatively secluded by trees and shrubs and offers its own paved driveway, Coquina rock bed, charcoal grill, picnic table, and 110V/220V electrical service. Of the three types of campsites, partial hookups supply water, full hookups offer sewer and water, and preferred sites have cable TV, sewer, and water—preferred sites are also closest to the marina and eateries. Each site accommodates up to ten people and one car; pets are welcome at certain sites. All sites are close to very clean, air-conditioned "Comfort Stations" with restrooms, private showers, telephones, ice machines (extra fee), and laundry facilities. For guests without a tent or trailer, the 407 **Wilderness Cabins** are roomy, air-conditioned "log cabins" (504 sq. ft.) that accommodate up to six guests plus a child under 3 in a crib. Each cabin has a living room, bedroom, a full kitchen, and modern bathroom. Charmingly rustic yet comfortable, each cabin comes stocked with pots and utensils, plus a coffeemaker, stove, microwave, refrigerator, dishwasher, cable TV, VCR, phone, hair dryer, and safe. The living room has a pull-down double bed, while the bedroom has a separate vanity, a double bed, and a bunk bed. Outside is a charcoal grill, picnic table, and deck. Amenities include voice mail and housekeeping—they even do dishes! All guests staying in the Cabins must be accommodated within them; no tents are permitted outside the Cabin.

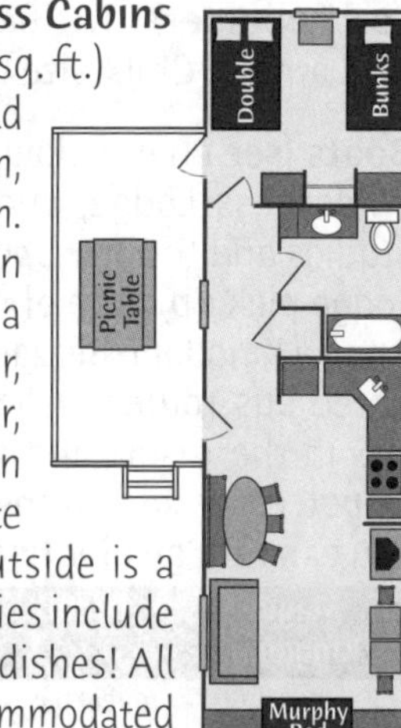

Cabin Layout

Using the Amenities at Disney's Fort Wilderness Resort

DINING

Many guests cook at their sites or cabins. If cooking isn't your thing, try **The Chuck Wagon**—it's open during the nightly campfire and serves snacks. Typical menu items: a hot dog ($2.12), popcorn ($1.89), and s'mores ($4.72). **Hoop-Dee-Doo Musical Revue** is a dinner show (see page 234). **Trail's End Restaurant** is a buffeteria (page 226). **Crockett's Tavern** serves drinks and snacks.

© MediaMarx, Inc.
Inside a Fort Wilderness Cabin

PLAYING & RELAXING

For Athletes: You'll find two lighted tennis courts, plus volleyball, tetherball, basketball, and horseshoes. Rent a boat or surrey bike at the marina, or a canoe or bike at the Bike Barn. Horseback rides ($32) at the livery (must be 9+ yrs., 48"+). Nature walks, too!
For Children: A free Petting Zoo with pony rides ($3) and a nearby playground delight kids. Free nightly campfires with Chip and Dale, and Disney movies, or go on a "hayride" ($8/adult and $4/kids).
For Fishers: Try a bass fishing excursion in Bay Lake for $165–195.
For Gamers: Two video arcades are within the resort.
For Romantics: Enjoy a relaxing, private carriage ride for $30.
For Shoppers: Gifts, sundries, and groceries at two trading posts.
For Show-Goers: Two dinner shows! See page 234 for details.
For Swimmers: Two heated pools, a wading pool, and a beach for sunbathers. Child-size life vests are at the pools (no charge).

GETTING ABOUT

Boats (see chart below for in-transit times) go to Magic Kingdom, Wilderness Lodge, and Contemporary. **Buses** to Disney-MGM Studios and the Transportation & Ticket Center (TTC)/Wilderness Lodge pick up/drop off at Settlement Depot. Buses for Epcot, and Animal Kingdom/Blizzard Beach pick up/drop off at Outpost Depot. Three bus routes—Yellow, Orange, and Purple—service locations within the resort and all stop at Settlement Depot and Outpost Depot. For resorts, transfer at Magic Kingdom or Downtown Disney. You can rent an **electric golf cart** to move about the resort easier.

Magic Kingdom	Epcot	Disney-MGM Studios	Disney's Animal Kingdom	Downtown Disney
boat ~15 min.	direct bus ~25 min.	direct bus ~30 min.	direct bus ~30 min.	direct bus ~35 min.

Approximate time you will spend in-transit from resort to destination during normal operation.

Making the Most of Disney's Fort Wilderness Resort

TIPS

Electric golf carts are very popular for moving about the resort, but are hard to get. To reserve one up to a year in advance, call the Bike Barn at 407-824-2742. Rates are $43+tax per 24-hour period.

The **Electrical Water Pageant**, a light and music barge parade on Bay Lake, can be seen from the beach at around 9:45 pm.

Seasonal, weekly, and monthly **discount rates** may be available for campsites (but not cabins).

A **car** may come in handy at this resort. Disney transportation to and from Fort Wilderness requires a transfer from an internal to external transport, making it more time consuming than most resorts. To reduce transit time, request a site in loops 100-800 as these are within walking distance of Settlement Depot and the marina.

NOTES

Motor traffic is limited to vehicles entering or leaving the resort only, though there is 15-min. parking at the Meadows Trading Post.

Bring your **groceries**, or buy them at Gooding's at Crossroads near Downtown Disney. You can pick up some items from the Trading Posts.

Pets are allowed for $3/day, but only in loops 300 and 1600–1900 (request at reservation). Pets cannot be kept in pop-ups or tents.

Creekside Meadow offers rustic **group camping** with a Comfort Station, grills, and fire pits. Tents and cots can be rented.

Campfires are not allowed at individual campsites.

Check-in time is 1:00 pm (campsites) or 3:00 pm (Cabins). Check-out time for all is 11:00 am.

Note: The two Affordability Ratings below correspond to lodging and camping.

RATINGS

Ratings are explained on page 26.

Our Value Ratings:		Our Magic Ratings:		Readers' Ratings:
Quality:	7/10	Theme:	6/10	67% fell in love with it
Accessibility:	4/10	Amenities:	5/10	28% liked it well enough
Affordability:	6 & 10/10	Fun Factor:	8/10	3% had mixed feelings
Overall Value:	**6 & 7/10**	**Overall Magic:**	**6/10**	2% were disappointed

Fort Wilderness is enjoyed by...		(rated by both authors and readers)
Younger Kids: ♥♥♥♥♥	Young Adults: ♥♥♥♥	Families: ♥♥♥♥♥
Older Kids: ♥♥♥♥	Mid Adults: ♥♥♥♥	Couples: ♥♥♥
Teenagers: ♥♥♥♥	Mature Adults: ♥♥♥♥	Singles: ♥♥

Finding Your Place at Disney's Fort Wilderness Resort

FORT WILDERNESS RESORT

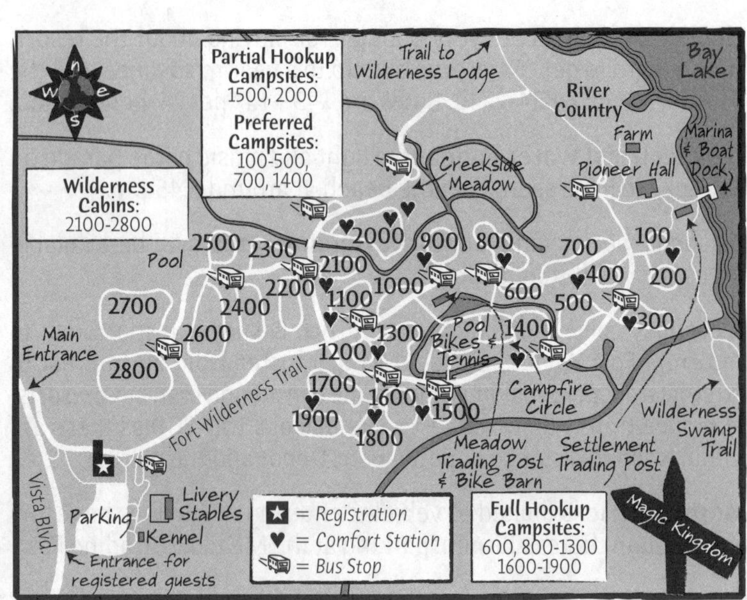

BEST SPOTS

Campsites and cabins are located on loops, which are circular drives with about 40 sites or cabins each. The most popular **Cabin** locations are on loops 2500–2700 near the west pool, though we loved our cabin on loop 2100 near a bus stop. The most popular **campsites** are on loop 400. Preferred sites are **closest to Pioneer Hall** in the 100–500, 700, and 1400 loops. **Full hookup campsites** are in loops 600, 800–1300, and 1600–1900—we highly recommend loop 800. **Partial hookups** are located in the 1500 and 2000 loops.

RATES

2004 Sample Campsite/Cabin Rates

Seasons are noted on page 14

Room Type	Value	Regular	Peak	Pre-Holiday	Holiday
Partial Hook-Up Campsite	$36	$52	$60	$40	$69
Full Hook-Up Campsite	$41	$62	$71	$45	$81
Preferred Campsite	$49	$67	$76	$53	$86
Wilderness Cabin	$229	$269	$299	n/a	$329

Tax not included in above rates. There is an additional charge of $5/night for more than two adults in a cabin, or $2/night for more than two adults at a campsite.

INFO

Disney's Fort Wilderness Resort & Campground

4510 N. Fort Wilderness Trail, Bay Lake, FL 32830
Phone: 407-824-2900 Fax: 407-824-3508
For reservations, call Central Reservations: 407-934-7639
For details: http://home.hiwaay.net/~jlspence/faq_fw.htm

Disney's Grand Floridian Resort & Spa

The most luxurious of Disney's resorts, the Grand Floridian Resort & Spa is a breathtaking Victorian hotel with turrets and gabled roofs. It extends into the Seven Seas Lagoon between the Polynesian and the Magic Kingdom (use the blue tab at the top of the page for parks and eateries in the area).

AMBIENCE

From the moment you step into the **Grand Lobby** you will feel as though you've been transported back to the 1890s and the days when the well-to-do wintered in style at grand seaside resorts. Like that unhurried time, the warm whites and soft pastels draw you in, just as the towering lobby and stained glass skylights draw your eyes upward. It is the picture of charm, romance, and luxury.

RESORT LAYOUT & ROOMS

900 guest rooms are generously spread out among five **lodge** buildings and the Grand Lobby. The luxurious rooms were recently redecorated in four different whimsical-yet-subtle themes: floral, cameo (fairies), swans (Wind in the Willows), and Alice in Wonderland. Rooms are about 400 sq. ft. and are resplendent with marble-topped double sinks and balconies or patios. Most guest rooms offer two queen-size beds and a daybed, accommodating five people. The lodge buildings also house the slightly smaller "dormer" rooms, plus suites. Amenities include signature toiletries, turndown service, mini bar, large in-room safe, hair dryer, newspaper delivery, valet parking, 24-hour room service—and best of all—big, fluffy robes to relax in after a long day at the parks.

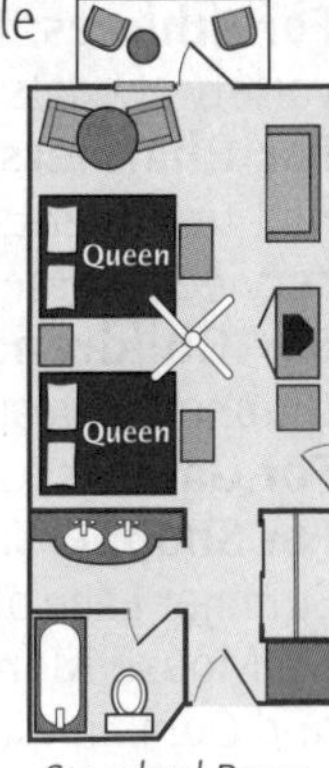

Standard Room Layout

DINING

Culinary delights await you in any of the restaurants and lounges, largely located on the first two floors of the Grand Lobby. Table service restaurants, which are described on pages 227–228, include: **1900 Park Fare**, a festive character dining experience; **Cítricos**, sophisticated Floridian and Mediterranean cuisine; **Grand Floridian Cafe**, a sun-splashed cafe with traditional fare; **Garden View Lounge**, high tea in the afternoon; **Narcoossee's**, seafood with a view of Seven Seas Lagoon; and **Victoria & Albert's**, Disney's finest restaurant. Quick service options include the **Grand Floridian Pool Bar** for snacks, and **Gasparilla's Grill and Games** for light fare 24-hours a day. Typical menu items at Gasparilla's Grill include an egg croissant ($4.79), a cheeseburger and fries ($5.99), a whole pepperoni pizza ($15.88), and chili ($3.50).

Using the Amenities at Disney's Grand Floridian Resort & Spa

LOUNGING

Lounges at the Grand Floridian include the **Garden View Lounge** which offers drinks in the evening. **Mizner's** serves cocktails and light snacks within earshot of the musicians who often perform in the Grand Lobby. The **Grand Floridian Pool Bar** also serves drinks and snacks, such as a cheeseburger with fries ($11.95) or a Cobb salad ($12.95). Visit **Gasparilla's Grill and Games** to purchase refillable mugs (about $11) and get refills.

Enjoying the themed pool at the Grand Floridian Resort & Spa

PLAYING & RELAXING

For Athletes: Two clay tennis courts are available for a fee. Rent a variety of boats at the marina. You'll also find walking/jogging paths.
For Charmers: The Ivy Trellis Salon pampers you with hair and nail treatments. The Grand Floridian Spa & Health Club is a full-service spa facility. Call 407-824-2332 for information.
For Children: A playground is adjacent to the Mouseketeer Clubhouse, a supervised program for kids 4–12 (see page 253).
For Gamers: Gasparilla's Grill and Games has a video arcade.
For Shoppers: On the first floor, Sandy Cove stocks sundries and Summer Lace offers upscale women's clothing. On the second floor, M. Mouse Mercantile has gifts; Bally offers luxury leather goods; and Commander Porter's has men's and women's apparel.
For Swimmers: A moderately-sized but relatively quiet pool and hot tub are available, as is a theme pool near the beach with a slide and play fountain. Sunbathers enjoy the beach (no swimming).

GETTING ABOUT

A **monorail** goes to Magic Kingdom as well as the Contemporary, Polynesian, and the Transportation and Ticket Center (TTC), where you can transfer to the Epcot monorail. **Boats** also take you to the Magic Kingdom and the Polynesian. For other parks (see chart below for in-transit times), use the **direct buses** in front of the resort. For other resorts, monorail to the Magic Kingdom (daytime) or bus to Downtown Disney (evening) and transfer to a resort bus.

Magic Kingdom	Epcot	Disney-MGM Studios	Disney's Animal Kingdom	Downtown Disney
monorail/boat ~3/~10 min.	monorail x 2 ~12+10 min.	direct bus ~10 min.	direct bus ~15 min.	direct bus ~20 min.

Approximate time you will spend in-transit from resort to destination during normal operation.

Making the Most of Disney's Grand Floridian Resort & Spa

TIPS

The Grand Lobby is often filled with the sound of **live music**, ranging from solo pianists to full dance bands.

Many **children's activities** are offered, including scavenger hunts, arts & crafts, story time, fishing trips, as well as the Wonderland Tea Party, the Pirate Cruise, and a cooking class (see page 244). Ask at Guest Services about the Ladybug Release Program, too!

Private dining is available for a quiet or romantic evening. You can have a meal on your balcony, on the beach, or even on a boat in the lagoon. Make arrangements in advance with room service.

For a touch of magic, end your day with a romantic, nighttime **stroll along the beach**. You may even catch the Electrical Water Pageant on the Seven Seas Lagoon around 9:15 pm.

NOTES

Four extra-special types of rooms are available. The **lodge tower** rooms have a separate sitting area, an extra TV and phone, and five windows. **Concierge** rooms offer personalized services, continental breakfast, evening refreshments, and a private elevator. Of the concierge rooms, special **turret rooms** have wet bars and windows all around, while **honeymoon suites** pamper with whirlpool tubs!

The Grand Floridian Resort & Spa is also a **conference center** with access to business services.

Even though this is a luxury resort, don't feel you need to dress up. **Casual wear** is the norm here. The only exception is Victoria & Albert's restaurant, which requires evening attire.

Check-in time is 3:00 pm. Check-out time is 11:00 am.

RATINGS

Ratings are explained on page 26.

Our Value Ratings:		Our Magic Ratings:		Readers' Ratings:
Quality:	10/10	Theme:	8/10	77% fell in love with it
Accessibility:	8/10	Amenities:	9/10	11% liked it well enough
Affordability:	2/10	Fun Factor:	6/10	10% had mixed feelings
Overall Value:	**7/10**	**Overall Magic:**	**8/10**	2% were disappointed

Grand Floridian is enjoyed by...		(rated by both authors and readers)
Younger Kids: ♥♥♥♥	Young Adults: ♥♥♥♥	Families: ♥♥♥
Older Kids: ♥♥♥♥	Mid Adults: ♥♥♥♥♥	Couples: ♥♥♥♥♥
Teenagers: ♥♥♥	Mature Adults: ♥♥♥♥♥	Singles: ♥♥♥

Finding Your Place at Disney's Grand Floridian Resort & Spa

GRAND FLORIDIAN RESORT MAP

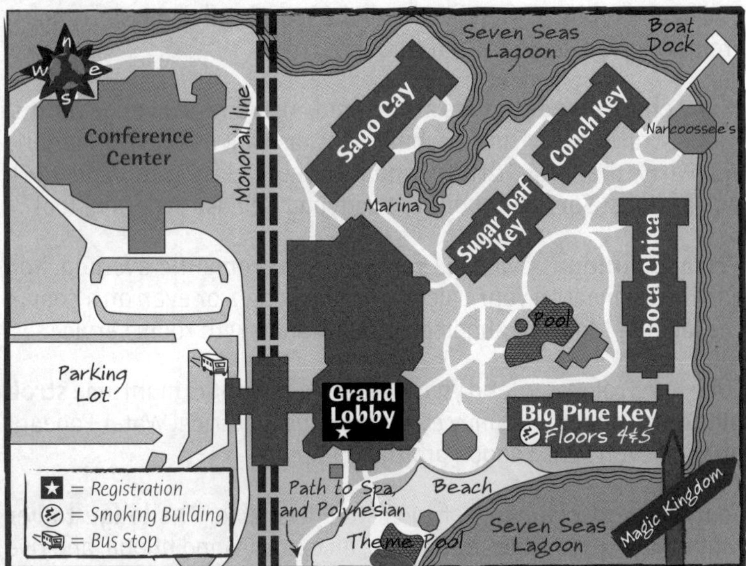

BEST SPOTS

The **dormer rooms** on the top floors of the lodge buildings may be a bit smaller (they only fit 4 rather than 5), but they feature vaulted ceilings, a secluded balcony, and a charming window above the French doors. The **best views of Cinderella Castle** come in the lagoon view rooms in Sago Cay and Conch Key lodges. Sugar Loaf Key is the closest lodge house to the Grand Lobby, but also sees the most traffic and hears the most noise. Big Pine Key is near to the beach and its lagoon view rooms offer picturesque views.

RATES

2004 Sample Room Rates *Seasons are noted on page 14*

Room Type	Value	Regular	Peak	Holiday
Garden View	$339	$384	$444	$514
Lagoon View	$400	$455	$535	$595
Lodge Tower	$415	$475	$560	$625
Lodge Concierge (Sago Cay)	$450	$520	$600	$660
Main Building Concierge	$585	$660	$740	$825

Tax is not included in above room rates. Honeymoon concierge rooms start in the high-$500's. Suites, which are available in one- and two-bedrooms, are upwards of $900.

INFO

Disney's Grand Floridian Resort & Spa
4401 Floridian Way, Bay Lake, FL 32830
Phone: 407-824-3000 Fax: 407-824-3186
For reservations, call Central Reservations: 407-934-7639

Disney's Old Key West Resort

Formerly known as the Vacation Club, the large Old Key West resort caters primarily (but not exclusively) to Disney Vacation Club members. Old Key West is located roughly between Downtown Disney and Epcot (use the blue tab at the top of the page for parks and eateries in the area).

AMBIENCE

If Disney's Grand Floridian and BoardWalk set the pace for elegant turn-of-the-century seaside resorts, this is the dressed-down, laid-back antidote. Lush vegetation and low, white **clapboard buildings** with sky blue eaves evoke authentic Key West style, and the public areas of the resort exude small-town intimacy. Quaint waterside shops and restaurants are connected by wooden walkways, and the Conch Flats Community Hall offers homey choices like table tennis and board games. The atmosphere is lively, friendly, and not at all hectic. Accommodations are spacious, comfy, and attractive.

RESORT LAYOUT & ROOMS

Intimate is not necessarily small. Old Key West is big enough to get lost in. (We speak from experience!) The resort's 761 guest "homes" range from **studios** (376 sq. ft.) with kitchenettes that sleep four adults, to spacious **one-bedrooms** (1086 sq. ft.) with full kitchens that sleep four adults, **two-bedrooms** (1392 sq. ft.) also with full kitchens that sleep eight adults, and the incredible three-bedroom/four bath **Grand Villas** (2265 sq. ft.) that sleep up to 12. All have a private patio or balcony perfect for breakfast, and all but the studios include a master suite with a large two-person whirlpool tub; a sprawling Great Room with full kitchen, dining area, and queen-sized sleep sofa; and washer and dryer. Villas sport views of the golf course, waterways, or woods. Amenities in all rooms include a TV, refrigerator, microwave, coffeemaker, and voice mail. One-bedroom and larger rooms boast a fully-equipped kitchen, big-screen TV, VCR, and in-room safe. These "homes" are an excellent choice for groups and families who wish to stay together.

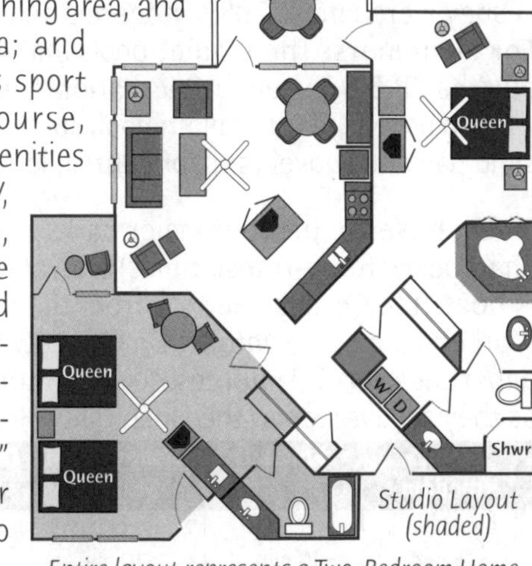

Entire layout represents a Two-Bedroom Home

Using the Amenities at Disney's Old Key West Resort

DINING

Olivia's Cafe (see page 228) is a kind of casual, small-town place loved by locals. **Good's Food to Go** over by the main pool serves up breakfasts, burgers, and snacks—typical menu items include a tuna sandwich ($6.29) and a child's sandpail meal ($5.89). Mugs are available for $5.25 (refills are $1.75). Also by the main pool, the **Gurgling Suitcase** has drinks and appetizers like shrimp fritters ($5.99), buffalo wings ($6.99), and crab cake ($7.59). **Turtle Shack** by the Turtle Pond Road pool has snacks seasonally. **Pizza delivery** is also available.

A typical villa at the Old Key West Resort

PLAYING & RELAXING

For Athletes: Tennis, basketball, shuffleboard, and volleyball courts are available. Rent boats and bikes at Hank's Rent 'N Return. Golf at the nearby course, or try the walking/jogging path. A health club has Nautilus equipment, plus a sauna and massages.

For Children: The Conch Flats Community Hall offers games and organized events for kids. Playgrounds are near some of the pools.

For Gamers: The two arcades—Electric Eel Arcade and The Flying Fisherman—have plenty of video games to keep the kids happy.

For Shoppers: The Conch Flats General Store offers general and Disney merchandise, plus groceries and sundries.

For Swimmers: Three quiet pools and a large theme pool round out the "R.E.S.T. Beach Recreation Department." A children's wading pool is near the main pool, sporting giant beach toys like a sand pail and shovel (and, of course, lots of sand).

GETTING ABOUT

Direct **buses** to the four major parks and Downtown Disney (see chart below for in-transit times) stop at the resort's five bus stops. A **boat** (the "Trumbo Ferry") from the marina also travels to the Marketplace at Downtown Disney between noon and 9:40 pm—departing every 20 minutes. To get around the resort, hop on a bus as they always stop at the Hospitality House before heading out.

Magic Kingdom	Epcot	Disney-MGM Studios	Disney's Animal Kingdom	Downtown Disney
direct bus ~25 min.	direct bus ~10 min.	direct bus ~10 min.	direct bus ~15 min.	bus/boat ~5/~15 min.

Approximate time you will spend in-transit from resort to destination during normal operation.

Making the Most of Disney's Old Key West Resort

TIPS

Some one-bedroom homes have a slight variation that can make a big difference if your party is large: there is a **second door to the bathroom** through the laundry room (see layout on page 69), which avoids the master bedroom. If this is important, request buildings 30 or higher at reservation and again at check-in.

Buildings 62-64 are the newest—they opened in early 2000. These are also the only buildings that have elevators.

The **three-bedroom Grand Villas** are luxurious (and expensive). They are two-storied with private baths for each bedroom plus an extra one for guests sleeping on the sleeper sofa. They have all the amenities of the other vacation homes, plus a 32" television and a stereo. They are phenomenally popular with families, though, so reserve as early as possible.

Hank's Rent 'N Return offers more than just bikes and boats. You can rent videos, board games, balls, and more. There are often daily activities and games—inquire when checking in.

NOTES

If you stay in a studio, you won't have a washer and dryer in your room but there are air-conditioned **laundry rooms** available near the pools at no extra charge. You can buy soap and bleach, too.

Studios guests also have **no in-room safes**, but there are safe deposit boxes at the front desk. Note that ice is available from ice machines at the bus stops.

There is **no water slide**, but kids still enjoy the pools.

Check-in time is 4:00 pm. Check-out time is 11:00 am.

RATINGS

Ratings are explained on page 26.

Our Value Ratings:		Our Magic Ratings:		Readers' Ratings:
Quality:	7/10	Theme:	7/10	93% fell in love with it
Accessibility:	5/10	Amenities:	6/10	7% liked it well enough
Affordability:	4/10	Fun Factor:	5/10	0% had mixed feelings
Overall Value:	**5/10**	**Overall Magic:**	**6/10**	0% were disappointed

Old Key West is enjoyed by...		(rated by both authors and readers)
Younger Kids: ❤❤❤	Young Adults: ❤❤❤❤	Families: ❤❤❤❤❤
Older Kids: ❤❤❤❤	Mid Adults: ❤❤❤❤❤	Couples: ❤❤❤❤❤
Teenagers: ❤❤❤❤	Mature Adults: ❤❤❤❤❤	Singles: ❤❤❤

Finding Your Place at Disney's Old Key West Resort

OLD KEY WEST RESORT MAP

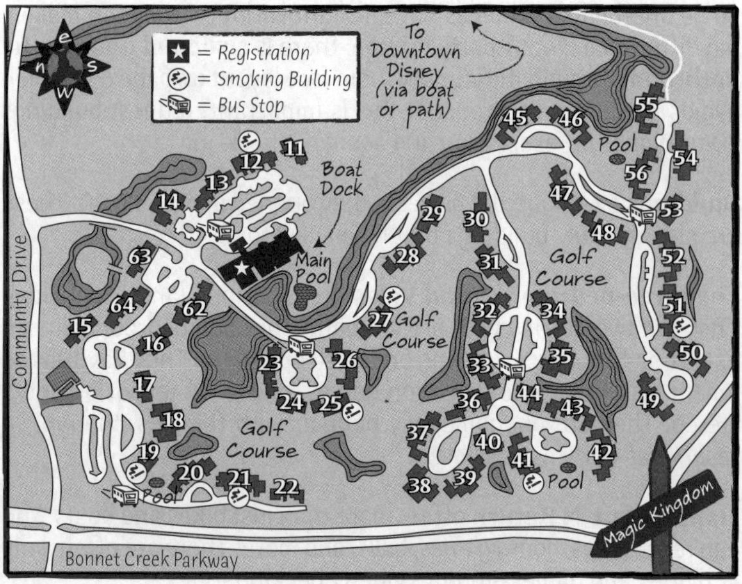

★ = Registration
= Smoking Building
= Bus Stop
To Downtown Disney (via boat or path)
Boat Dock
Main Pool
Golf Course
Pool
Community Drive
Bonnet Creek Parkway
Magic Kingdom

BEST LOCATIONS

Location is important in this sprawling resort. Though there are bus stops throughout the resort, we found staying near the **Hospitality House** to be a huge benefit. Buildings 11-14 and 62-64 are the closest (we loved our one-bedroom home in building 11), with buildings 15-16 and 23-26 also within reasonable walking distance. Most locations enjoy relative **peace and quiet**, but if you really want seclusion, 47-48 and 52-54 are nice as they are away from pools and roads, yet are near a bus stop. We suggest you avoid 30-44 as they feel remote, have traffic noise, and bus stops are often inconvenient.

RATES

2004 Sample Villa Rates

Seasons are noted on page 14

Room Type	Value	Regular	Peak	Holiday
Studio Villa	$254	$284	$329	$369
One-Bedroom Villa	$340	$385	$445	$510
Two-Bedroom Villa	$479	$560	$680	$775
Grand Villa	$1040	$1160	$1310	$1460

Tax is not included in the above rates. Three views are available–water, golf course, and woods–but with no difference in price.

INFO

Disney's Old Key West Resort

1510 North Cove Road, Lake Buena Vista, FL 32830
Phone: 407-827-7700 Fax: 407-827-7710
For reservations, call Central Reservations: 407-934-7639

Disney's Polynesian Resort

The Polynesian Resort is a lush, tropical paradise that brings the romance of the South Pacific to life. It rests tranquilly on the Seven Seas Lagoon between the Transportation & Ticket Center and the Grand Floridian Resort (use the blue tab at the top of the page for parks and eateries in the area).

AMBIENCE

The blooming gardens are your first hint of the beauty and color of the **tropics**, which are captured so splendidly here. You may not even notice that you've entered the main building, the Great Ceremonial House, with its atrium filled with falling waters, tropical plants, and the song of birds. "Aloha!" is more than a word here—it is a way of life—and you will be reminded of this again and again during your visit.

RESORT LAYOUT & ROOMS

853 guest rooms are arranged throughout **longhouses** on eleven "islands" of Polynesia. The longhouses are two- or three-stories; the first-floor rooms have patios and many of the upper-floor rooms have balconies. The lush, laid-back feeling of the resort is carried into the rooms with wicker furnishings and canopied beds. Spacious rooms (409 sq. ft.) offer two queen-size beds and a daybed, accommodating five people in a room. We particularly like the roomy bathroom with its large mirror, tub, and toilet hidden around the corner. Suites and concierge-level rooms housed in the Tonga and Hawaii longhouses offer personal service and great views. Amenities for all resort rooms include toiletries, 24-hour room service, housekeeping service, turndown service (on request), voice mail, and valet parking.

Standard Room Layout

DINING & LOUNGING

Paradise offers bounty in food, too. Two table-service restaurants (see page 228) are **Kona Cafe** offering a filling breakfast and inventive lunch and dinner, and **'Ohana** serving up food and fun with skewered meats. **Captain Cook's** Snack Company is a good place for a quick breakfast and light meals. Typical items are French toast sticks ($3.99), Polynesian-style chicken sandwich ($6.69), and kid's chicken strips ($4.29). Refillable mugs are available for $11. A family-style **character breakfast** is served at 'Ohana, too. And let's not forget the Spirit of Aloha dinner show (page 235). **Tambu**, the lounge by 'Ohana, serves snacks and drinks, **Kona Island** is a coffee bar in the mornings, and the poolside **Barefoot Bar** has drinks.

Using the Amenities at Disney's Polynesian Resort

PLAYING & RELAXING

For Athletes: Boaters rent water mice and sailboats at the marina. Joggers enjoy the Walk Around the World that partially encircles the lagoon, and a 1.5 mile path winds through the resort (ask at Guest Services for a map).

For Charmers: The Grand Floridian Spa & Health Club (see page 64) is north of the resort.

For Children: The Never Land Club is a childcare club (see page 253)—it's next to the arcade. A playground is near the main pool.

© MediaMarx, Inc.

Dave relaxes on a hammock near the Tokelau longhouse

For Gamers: Moana Mickey's Arcade offers some video games.

For Shoppers: On the first floor, News From Polynesia has newspapers and gifts; Polynesian Princess offers women's wear; Robin Crusoe's has men's apparel; Maui Mickey's has kid's apparel; and Wyland Galleries has collectibles. The second floor houses Trader Jack's (souvenirs and sundries) and Samoa Snacks.

For Show-Goers: Tucked in the back of the resort is Luau Cove, home to Polynesian-style dinner shows. More details on page 235.

For Swimmers: In addition to a quiet pool, the Nanea Volcano theme pool features a large pool "fed" by a spring, a water slide, warm water areas, underwater music, and a zero-entry section (pool wheelchair available). There's also a kids' play fountain. Alas, there is no spa (hot tub). There is a beach for sunbathing.

GETTING ABOUT

A **monorail** shuttles you to the Magic Kingdom (see chart below for in-transit times), Grand Floridian, and Contemporary, as well as the Transportation & Ticket Center (TTC). A **boat** also goes to the Magic Kingdom. To reach Epcot, take a short walk to TTC and board the monorail. To reach other parks (listed in chart below) and Downtown Disney, take **direct buses** (see map on page 74 for the relocated bus stop). To reach most resorts, take a monorail to the Magic Kingdom and transfer to a resort bus (daytime), or take a bus to Downtown Disney and transfer to a resort bus (evening).

Magic Kingdom	Epcot	Disney-MGM Studios	Disney's Animal Kingdom	Downtown Disney
monorail/boat ~10/~5 min.	walk+monorail ~10+10 min.	direct bus ~15 min.	direct bus ~15 min.	direct bus ~25 min.

Approximate time you will spend in-transit from resort to destination during normal operation.

Making the Most of Disney's Polynesian Resort

TIPS

On the beach in front of the Hawaii and Tahiti longhouses are several **bench swings** and **hammocks**. Not only are these heaven after a long day, they make ideal spots to watch the fireworks.

A **night stroll** through the resort is sublime. A very secluded spot over the rise on the beach's point is pure magic to us.

The **Electrical Water Pageant** passes right by the Polynesian around 9:00 pm. If you don't have a water-view room, take a stroll down to the beach or to the end of the dock near the marina.

The **lulling music** of the South Seas is all around you, with the notable exception of your room. If you'd like to keep these sounds, bring a portable CD player and purchase a CD in the gift shop.

Families love the Polynesian and it may get a bit **noisy** in the pool areas (near Samoa, Niue, Hawaii, Rarotonga, and Tokelau).

NOTES

The longhouses are undergoing **renovations** until May 2004, one at a time. The resort remains open during these renovations.

Walk to the Transportation & Ticket Center for the **Epcot monorail**. The monorail around the lagoon adds 20 minutes otherwise.

The Polynesian Resort shares **bus routes** with the Contemporary and Grand Floridian resorts, picking up/dropping off guests at the Contemporary first and Grand Floridian last.

Daily activities are available for kids of all ages, such as coconut races and torch lightings. Ask for a schedule upon check-in.

Check-in time is 3:00 pm. Check-out time is 11:00 am.

RATINGS

Ratings are explained on page 26.

Our Value Ratings:		Our Magic Ratings:		Readers' Ratings:
Quality:	8/10	Theme:	9/10	73% fell in love with it
Accessibility:	9/10	Amenities:	7/10	20% liked it well enough
Affordability:	3/10	Fun Factor:	8/10	4% had mixed feelings
Overall Value:	**7/10**	**Overall Magic:**	**8/10**	3% were disappointed

The Polynesian is enjoyed by...		(rated by both authors and readers)
Younger Kids: ♥♥♥♥	Young Adults: ♥♥♥♥♥	Families: ♥♥♥♥♥
Older Kids: ♥♥♥♥♥	Mid Adults: ♥♥♥♥♥	Couples: ♥♥♥♥♥
Teenagers: ♥♥♥♥	Mature Adults: ♥♥♥♥♥	Singles: ♥♥♥

Planning | Getting There | Staying in Style | Touring | Feasting | Making Magic | Index | Notes & More

Finding Your Place at Disney's Polynesian Resort

POLYNESIAN RESORT MAP

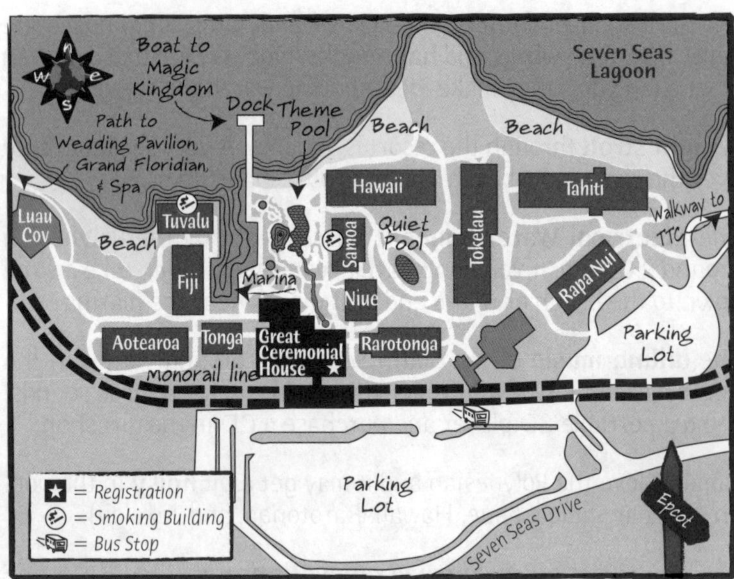

BEST LOCATIONS

All **first floor rooms** have patios and all **third floor rooms** have balconies. Most **second floor rooms** have no balconies, with the exception of Tahiti, Rapa Nui, Tokelau, and Tonga, which were built later. Particularly nice water views can be found in Tuvalu, Hawaii, Tahiti, and Fiji. The first floor rooms in Tahiti facing away from the water have pleasant, secluded patios, as do those in Rapa Nui and Rarotonga. If you opt for a standard view, we recommend Aotearoa with beautiful landscaping and an up-close view of the monorail. For added **privacy**, request a room on the top floor.

RATES

2004 Sample Room Rates *Seasons are noted on page 14*

Room Type	Value	Regular	Peak	Holiday
Garden-View	$299	$344	$404	$469
Lagoon-View	$385	$430	$505	$560
Garden-View Concierge	$390	$440	$515	$575
Lagoon-View Concierge	$470	$525	$605	$675
Suite Concierge	$495	$560	$625	$695

Tax is not included in the above rates. One-bedroom suites start in the high-$600's.

INFO

Disney's Polynesian Resort

1600 Seven Seas Drive, Bay Lake, FL 32830

Phone: 407-824-2000 Fax: 407-824-3174

For reservations, call Central Reservations: 407-934-7639

Note: Our description is based on pre-opening materials. Check our web site for updates!

Disney's Pop Century Resort

Auld acquaintance shall be remembered at Pop Century, the Walt Disney World Resort's newest value-priced resort. By the time the final phase of construction is done, each of the 20th Century's decades will be immortalized for its contribution to popular culture. Pop Century Resort is located in the Epcot area (use the blue tab at the top of the page for parks and eateries in the vicinity) on the northeast corner of Osceola Parkway and Victory Way. This resort opened in December 2003.

AMBIENCE

Whether you're eight or eighty, a **blast from your past** awaits at Pop Century. Actually twin-sister-resorts, Pop Century Classic Years and Pop Century Legendary Years surround a 33-acre lake and are connected by a scenic bridge (called the "Generation Gap"). Go from the quaint days of Main Street U.S.A. to infinity, and beyond, in eye-popping style. Each resort has its own, uniquely themed check-in lobby, food court, pool bar, and shop. Outside, giant cultural icons fill the senses, including a monumental Rubik's Cube®, a "working," billboard-sized laptop computer, and the biggest Big Wheel ever parked in a front yard. The themes continue with six imaginative theme pools. Each guest lodge building is festooned with cultural icons and "groovy" catch phrases.

RESORT LAYOUT & ROOMS

The 5,760 guestrooms (2,880 in each resort) are situated in 10 differently themed areas encompassing a total of 20 guest lodges. **Pop Century Classic Years** opened first, celebrating the decades of the 1950s, '60s, '70s, '80s and '90s. Opening later, **Pop Century Legendary Years** will take us back to the 1900s, '10s, '20s, '30s and '40s. Themed courtyards are formed between two or more of the ten T-shaped guest lodges. Each decade's theme is played out in the guest room decor, but rich, wood-grain furniture adds elegance to the fun. Rooms have either two double beds or one king bed, a large TV with remote, a small table with two chairs, and a chest of drawers. Rooms accommodate up to four guests plus one child under three in a crib (a folding crib is available on request). Rooms are small—about 260 sq. feet—but as with the All-Star resorts, the furnishings allow adequate floor space. Rooms have no private balconies or patios, but each room offers individual climate controls. Room amenities include soap, housekeeping, in-room safe, and voice mail. Inquire at check-in about renting a small refrigerator for around $10/night.

Standard Room Layout

Using the Amenities at Disney's Pop Century Resort

EATING & DRINKING

Each resort has a very large **food court**. Both food courts have a variety of food stations, plus a coffee shop. The eateries are open daily for breakfast, lunch, and dinner. For typical menu items, see page 36—we expect the menu to be similar to that at the All-Stars. Purchase a souvenir mug for about $11 and get unlimited refills from the beverage bar. A pizza delivery service should be available in the afternoons and evenings, along with seasonal snack carts.

© Disney

The 1970s at the Pop Century Resort

PLAYING & RELAXING

For Athletes: The 12' wide lakeside path is ideal for walks and jogs. The lake will not offer a marina, but we hear that surrey bikes may be available for jaunts around the lake.
For Children: Quiet playgrounds are located within each resort (locations vary-see map on page 78 for playground locations).
For Gamers: An arcade is located in each resort's main building.
For Shoppers: Both resorts offer large shops with Disney logo merchandise, clothing, sundries, and a small selection of groceries.
For Swimmers: Each resort offers one themed pool, a wading pool, and two quiet pools. Classic Years' pools are shaped like a bowling pin, a flower, and a computer, Legendary Years' pools resemble a crossword puzzle, soda bottle, and highway sign.

GETTING ABOUT

Buses (see chart below for estimated in-transit times) are outside the main buildings in each resort. Stops are well-marked and offer benches. Due to the size of the resorts we expect bus service to be prompt and efficient. Destinations other than those below can be reached by changing buses at Disney-MGM Studios or Epcot (daytime) or Downtown Disney (evening). Guests may find a car useful at this resort, and ample parking is freely available.

Magic Kingdom	Epcot	Disney-MGM Studios	Disney's Animal Kingdom	Downtown Disney
direct bus ~25 min.	direct bus ~20 min.	direct bus ~15 min.	direct bus ~15 min.	direct bus ~20 min.

Approximate time you will spend in-transit from resort to destination during normal operation.

Making the Most of Disney's Pop Century Resort

Pop Century opened in December 2003, after this edition went to press. Visit PassPorter.com for updates and **eyewitness accounts** at http://www.passporter.com/wdw/popcentury.htm.

The 33-acre lake between these resorts is an **added perk** for a value resort—the equivalent All-Star Resorts have no ponds, lakes or rivers. We also hear that the overall quality of amenities may be a bit higher than the All-Star Resorts due to "economies of scale."

Disney's Wide World of Sports is just across Osceola Parkway, so we suspect Pop Century will be a popular hotel with the many youth sports groups that compete at Wide World of Sports.

Although priced the same as the All-Star Resorts, the decorating is **a bit more upscale**. While Mom or Dad checks in, the kids can enjoy a big-screen video theater. Be sure to visit the museum-style exhibits in the main building, too.

Plan to either **carry your own luggage** or wait a while (perhaps 45-60 minutes) for the resorts' luggage service to drop it off at your building. Arrangements to pick-up luggage on your departure day should be made the night before.

Coin-operated laundries are located near each pool. Bring lots of quarters—wash loads and dry cycles are around $2.00 each.

You'll be able to **specify your choice of resorts**: "The Legendary Years" (1900s–1940s) and "The Classic Years" (1950s–1990s) when you reserve your room, with the Classic Years being the first to open.

Check-in time is 4:00 pm. Check-out time is 11:00 am.

TIPS

NOTES

RATINGS

Ratings are explained on page 26.

Our Value Ratings:		Our Magic Ratings:		Readers' Ratings:
Quality:	6/10	Theme:	6/10	Want to rate this resort?
Accessibility:	5/10	Amenities:	4/10	Visit us on the Web at:
Affordability:	9/10	Fun Factor:	2/10	http://www.passporter.com
Overall Value:	**7/10**	**Overall Magic:**	**4/10**	... /wdw/rate.htm

Pop Century will be enjoyed by...		(estimated by the authors)
Younger Kids: ♥♥♥♥♥	Young Adults: ♥♥♥♥	Families: ♥♥♥♥
Older Kids: ♥♥♥♥♥	Mid Adults: ♥♥♥	Couples: ♥♥
Teenagers: ♥♥♥	Mature Adults: ♥♥	Singles: ♥♥♥

Finding Your Place at Disney's Pop Century Resort

POP CENTURY RESORT MAP

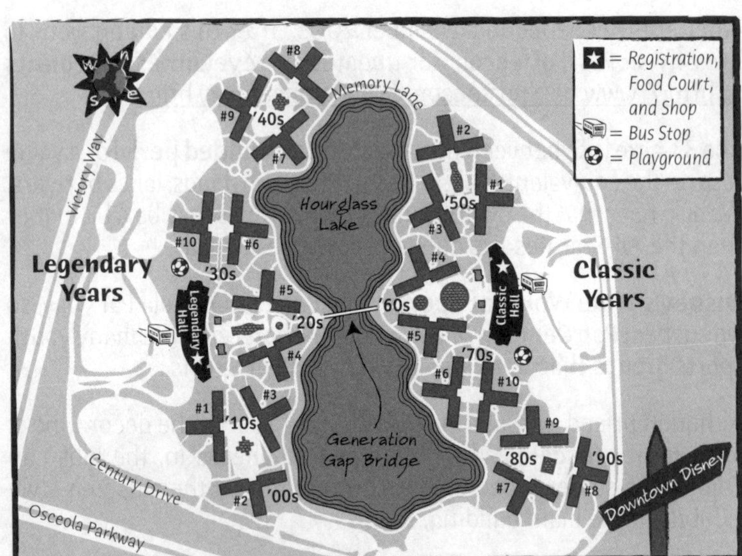

BEST LOCATIONS

Rooms at Pop Century **vary only by location** within the resorts and floor level. For convenience, we recommend the '50s, '60s, or '70s (Classic Years), and '10s, '20s, and '30s (at Legendary Years)—they are closest to pools, food, and transportation. Our personal picks are the '70s (at Classic Years) and the '30s (at Legendary Years) as they should be relatively quiet and have good views from most all windows. Note that several buildings offer excellent views of Hourglass Lake, particularly buildings #3, #4, #5, and #6. If you seek quiet, request a room on the third or fourth floors.

RATES

2004 Sample Room Rates *Seasons are noted on page 14*

Room Type	Value	Regular	Peak	Holiday
Standard Room	$77	$99	$109	$114
Preferred Room	$87	$109	$121	$126

Tax is not included in above rates. Preferred rooms are in the guest lodges closest to the main buildings (the '60s at Classic Years and the '20s at Legendary Years). There is a $10 per person charge for the third and fourth adult in a room, but no extra charge for children under 18. Rooms may face parking lots or courtyards.

INFO

Disney's Pop Century Resort

1050 Century Drive, Lake Buena Vista, FL 32830

Phone: 407-938-4000 Fax: 407-938-4039

For reservations, call Central Reservations: 407-934-7639

Disney's Port Orleans Resort
(and the former Dixie Landings)

In 2001, sister resorts Port Orleans and Dixie Landings merged into one resort known as Port Orleans. The large, moderately priced resort is located along the banks of the Sassagoula River, north of Downtown Disney (use the blue tab at the top of the page for other places in the same vicinity). Port Orleans is popular with young couples, families, and children, both for its value and for its fun atmosphere.

AMBIENCE

The romance of the Old South awaits you at Port Orleans. The resort is divided into two separate districts: the French Quarter (the smaller district and the original Port Orleans) and Riverside (the former Dixie Landings). The **French Quarter** recaptures the feeling and flavors of historic New Orleans as it prepares for Mardi Gras. The Mint is your first stop in the French Quarter, a large building with wrought ironwork details and a soaring glass atrium that safeguards the district's front desk, guest services, and shop. A step outside reveals narrow cobblestone lanes, complete with "gas" lamps, wrought-iron benches, and grand magnolia trees. A leisurely 10-minute walk along the Sassagoula takes you over to **Riverside**. Banjo music and southern hospitality greet you as you enter Riverside's Sassagoula Steamboat Company, a replica of an old riverboat depot. The depot is the crossroads of this quaint settlement, housing the district's front desk and services. Venture out along meandering paths and wooden bridges to antebellum mansions in one direction or the bayou in the other.

RESORT LAYOUT

The resort's 3056 guest rooms are scattered among the two districts, with 1008 in the French Quarter and 2048 in Riverside. Rooms in the French Quarter are housed in six large buildings (see map on page 85), each designed to resemble **rows of town houses** with differing architectural styles, varying rooflines, and facades bricked or painted in shades of blue, cream, or peach. Most buildings have their own yards and gardens in front, which are charmingly fenced with wrought iron. Down the Sassagoula in Riverside you'll find 1024 rooms gracing "Gone With the Wind," plantation-style mansions in an area called **Magnolia Bend**. These three-storied, elegant buildings are situated majestically along the Sassagoula River. An equal number of rooms are housed within crackerbox-style dwellings in the **Alligator Bayou** section. These two-storied, rough-hewn dwellings peek through the trees, with quaint paths winding through the "bayous" interspersed among them. Alligator Bayou has a more intimate feel to it than its neighbor, Magnolia Bend.

Lodging and Dining at Disney's Port Orleans Resort

RESORT ROOMS

Rooms are 314 sq. ft. in size and **decorated in three styles**. In the French Quarter you find faux French Provincial furniture, gilt-edged mirrors, and Venetian blinds. In Riverside's Magnolia Bend, antebellum rooms delight with cherry furniture and brocade settees. Riverside's Alligator Bayou rooms sport beds made of hewn "logs" and patchwork quilts. All rooms accommodate up to four and come with either two extra-long double beds or one king bed (king bed rooms are located on building corners); 963 Alligator Bayou rooms house up to five guests by offering a trundle bed for an extra $15/night (trundle beds slide out from under the double bed and fit a child or small adult). Rooms include a TV, armoire, table and chairs, ceiling fan, and a separate vanity area with double pedestal sinks. Every room has a window (corner rooms have two), but none have private balconies. Amenities include toiletries (soap and shampoo only), housekeeping, limited room service, in-room safe (most rooms), and voice mail.

Jennifer answers e-mail in her room at Port Orleans French Quarter

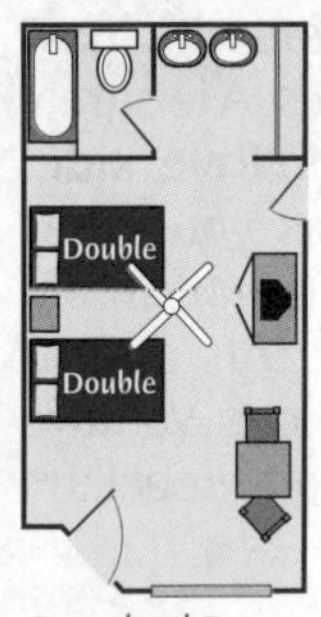

Standard Room Layout

DINING & LOUNGING

Port Orleans plays host to one of the more popular resort eateries: **Boatwright's Dining Hall**. This table-service restaurant in the Riverside district offers breakfast and dinner—see page 229. Two large food courts—**Sassagoula Floatworks and Food Factory** in the French Quarter and the **Riverside Mill** at Riverside—offer breakfast, lunch, and dinner. Typical menu items are croissants ($2.19), French toast with sausage ($4.99), beignets ($3.79 for six), roasted chicken ($8.99), chicken Caesar salad ($6.09), and kids chicken strips ($3.99). Purchase a mug for $11 and get free refills at both food courts. The French Quarter's **Scat Cat's Club** is a full-service bar with live music on the weekends, while **Mardi Grogs** pool bar has drinks and snacks. In Riverside, the **River Roost** offers specialty drinks, appetizers, and music in the evenings, and **Muddy Rivers Pool Bar** has drinks and snacks. **Limited room service** offered in the afternoons and evenings.

Using the Amenities of Disney's Port Orleans Resort

For Athletes: The Dixie Levee marina in Riverside rents pedal boats, row boats, canopy boats, and bikes (including surrey bikes). Be sure to check the rental hours early on to avoid disappointment later. Both districts offer plenty of paths for walkers and joggers, too.
For Fishers: An old-fashioned fishin' hole on Ol' Man Island in Riverside lets you hang a cane pole over a pond stocked with catfish, perch, bass, and bluegill (catch and release only). For more adventure, you can book a fishing excursion down the Sassagoula.
For Children: Two playgrounds are near the two theme pools.
For Gamers: South Quarter Games (French Quarter) has plenty of video games, as does the Medicine Show Arcade (Riverside).
For Shoppers: Jackson Square Gifts & Desires (French Quarter) and Fulton's (Riverside) stock sundries, souvenirs, and snacks.
For Swimmers: The French Quarter's Doubloon Lagoon is a moderately-sized theme pool with a huge dragon housing the water slide (you slide right down its tongue). A Mardi Gras band of crocodiles shoots water at unsuspecting swimmers. The French Quarter also has a wading pool for the young ones and a hot tub (spa) nearby. In Riverside, Ol' Man Island in the middle of the district offers a particularly nice "swimmin' hole" with a large free-form pool, complete with a waterslide and a waterfall cascading from a broken sluice. In 2003, a fun geyser was added. A hot tub and kids' wading area are also available here. Riverside also has five quieter pools spread throughout Magnolia Bend and Alligator Bayou.

PLAYING & RELAXING

Direct **buses** to the major theme parks and Downtown Disney stop regularly (see chart below for in-transit times). Buses usually pick up guests at French Quarter's single bus stop first, then go on to the four stops in Riverside. To get to other resorts and destinations, take a bus to Epcot (when open) or to Downtown Disney (evening), and transfer to the appropriate bus. A **boat** also picks up guests from Riverside and the French Quarter and goes to and from Downtown Disney Marketplace until 10:00 pm. Boats run about every 20 minutes (weather permitting) and are relaxing but leisurely. A **shuttle boat** also operates between the French Quarter and Riverside, and also goes to Downtown Disney Marketplace from 4:00–11:00 pm. Parking is available throughout the resorts.

Magic Kingdom	Epcot	Disney-MGM Studios	Disney's Animal Kingdom	Downtown Disney
direct bus ~10 min.	direct bus ~10 min.	direct bus ~15 min.	direct bus ~15 min.	direct bus/boat ~15/~20 min.

Approximate time you will spend in-transit from resort to destination during normal operation.

GETTING ABOUT

Making the Most of Disney's Port Orleans Resort

TIPS

The two **spas** (hot tubs) near the theme pools are heavenly after a long day at the parks. The spa in the French Quarter is a bit secluded (look near the laundry), but large enough for several people to soak comfortably (and sociably).

Explore the **resort's grounds** for the quaint parks and gardens scattered throughout. The French Quarter's street and park names are a treat unto themselves, with names like Mud du Lac Lane and Beaux Regards Square. An evening stroll in the French Quarter when the "gas" lamps are lit is particularly magical.

Enjoy an **evening carriage ride** through the two sister resorts. Carriages depart from in front of Boatwright's in Riverside between 6:00 and 9:00 pm. Cost is $30 for a 30 minute ride for up to four adults or two adults and two-three children.

Small **refrigerators** can be rented for $10/day, and roll-away beds for $15/day. Request these when you reserve your room.

NOTES

The **beds** are pretty high off the floor. Watch young ones so they don't fall out. If you are concerned, note that some rooms in Alligator Bayou at Riverside come with a pullout trundle bed, which you can request upon reservation and check-in. In fact, this trundle bed allows for a fifth person, making Port Orleans the only moderately-priced resort to accommodate five people.

Due to the resort merger Port Orleans has **two front desks**, one in each district. Be sure to check with Disney before arrival to find out which district's front desk you should arrive at.

Check-in time is 3:00 pm. Check-out time is 11:00 am.

RATINGS

Ratings are explained on page 26.

Our Value Ratings:		Our Magic Ratings:		Readers' Ratings:
Quality:	7/10	Theme:	8/10	69% fell in love with it
Accessibility:	7/10	Amenities:	6/10	24% liked it well enough
Affordability:	8/10	Fun Factor:	6/10	5% had mixed feelings
Overall Value:	**7/10**	**Overall Magic:**	**7/10**	2% were disappointed

Port Orleans is enjoyed by...		(rated by both authors and readers)
Younger Kids: ♥♥♥	Young Adults: ♥♥♥♥♥	Families: ♥♥♥♥
Older Kids: ♥♥♥♥♥	Mid Adults: ♥♥♥♥	Couples: ♥♥♥♥♥
Teenagers: ♥♥♥	Mature Adults: ♥♥♥	Singles: ♥♥♥

Finding Your Place at Disney's Port Orleans Resort

FRENCH QUARTER MAP

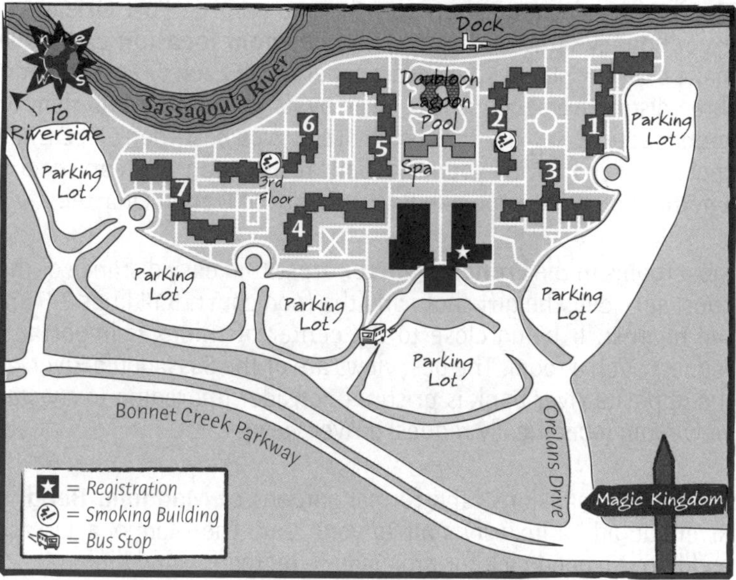

The French Quarter has a more compact, orderly layout.

RIVERSIDE MAP

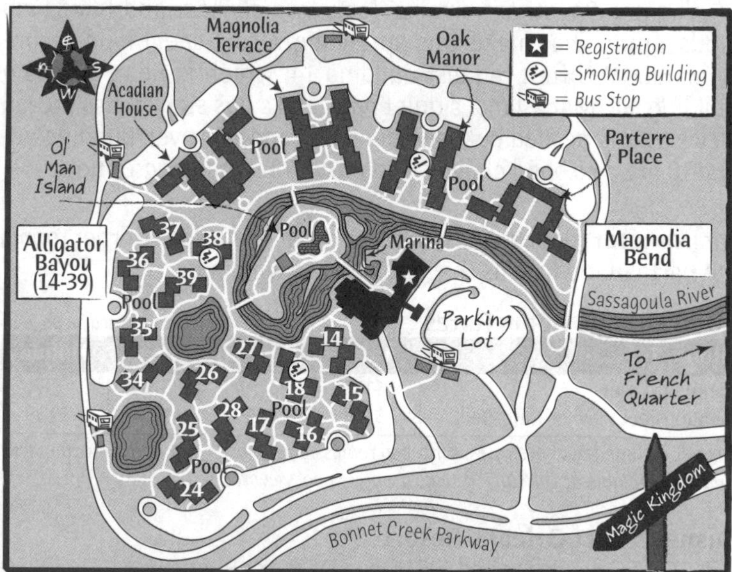

Riverside is large and meandering, with an island in the middle.

Choosing Your Room at Disney's Port Orleans Resort

BEST LOCATIONS

Thanks to the merger between the two resorts, Port Orleans is exceptionally large and sprawling and **room location** can really make a difference in your resort experience. Each of Port Orleans' three distinctive sections is beloved by its fans. There's no right or wrong section. Request the style that suits you best—don't let Disney choose for you. When you make your reservation, you can specify whether you want a room in Riverside or the French Quarter.

Most rooms in the **French Quarter** are within easy distance of the guest services, the gift shop, and the food court. Buildings 2-5 are the nearest. If being close to the center of things is important, request such a room. The best views are of the Sassagoula River, as the opposite river bank is pristine—consider upgrading to a water view room (specifically request a river view).

The grand "mansions" and formal gardens of **Magnolia Bend** in Riverside add a luxurious air to your stay. The Magnolia Terrace building is a good pick for proximity to recreation and dining.

Our personal favorite is **Alligator Bayou** in Riverside. The buildings in Alligator Bayou are smaller (only two-stories) and have lush landscaping that make this sprawling resort seem much more intimate. We often request building 14, which is near the main building, Ol' Man Island, a quiet pool, and a bus stop—it has no bad views as it is nestled between buildings and the river. Buildings 15 and 18 are also good choices—note that 18 is smoking-optional.

For a **quieter** room, request the second- or third-floor. Corner rooms are particularly nice as they provide two windows.

RATES

2004 Sample Room Rates *Seasons are noted on page 14*

Room Type	Value	Regular	Peak	Holiday
Standard View	$133	$144	$169	$184
Water/Pool View or King-Bed	$148	$159	$194	$209

Tax not included in above rates. King-bed rooms come in both standard or water view, and are available at the same rate as a water/pool view room.

INFO

Disney's Port Orleans Resort

2201 Orleans Dr. and 1251 Dixie Dr., Lake Buena Vista, FL 32830
Phone: 407-934-5000 Fax: 407-934-5353 or -5777
For reservations, call Central Reservations: 407-934-7639

Note: Our description is based on pre-opening materials. Check our web site for updates!

Disney's Saratoga Springs Resort and Spa

The Disney Vacation Club's newest and largest resort is rising across the lake from Downtown Disney, and is set to open by May 2004. Built on the grounds of the former Disney Institute, Disney's Saratoga Springs Resort & Spa offers vacation villas for vacation ownership and nightly rental.

AMBIENCE

Saratoga Springs stretches out over 65 acres of the former Disney Institute, adjacent to the Lake Buena Vista Golf Course and across Village Lake from Downtown Disney. This **Victorian-styled resort** is modeled on the historic vacation escape in Upstate New York. The fashionable elite of New York City journeyed up the Hudson on Commodore Vanderbilt's railroad to sip the health spa's waters, stroll its shady byways and cheer their race horses to victory. Disney's architects soaked up the town's Arts and Crafts atmosphere to bring its essence (minus the horses) to Walt Disney World. When finished in 2005, a dozen lodges will cluster around the resort's lakes in three districts—Congress Park (opening first), The Springs, and The Paddock, each representing the resort's theme of history, health, and horses. Other buildings survive from the former Disney Institute, including The Carriage House check-in and hospitality building, which also offers dining and shopping.

LAYOUT & ROOMS

The four, first-phase buildings of **Congress Park** are directly across the water from the Marketplace. Studio villas (355 sq. ft.) accommodate up to four guests with one queen bed, a sofa bed, sink, microwave, and a small refrigerator. The one- bedroom (714 sq. ft.) and two-bedroom (1075 sq. ft.) villas hold up to 4 or 8 guests each and offer master suites with king beds and whirlpool tubs, DVD players, sofa beds, full kitchens, and washers/dryers. The Grand Villas (2113 sq. ft.) sleep up to 12 on two levels and feature three bedrooms—the living room, dining room, and master suite (with its whirlpool tub) are on the first level, and on the second level, two more bedrooms with queen beds and private baths. All villas have a laptop-sized safe.

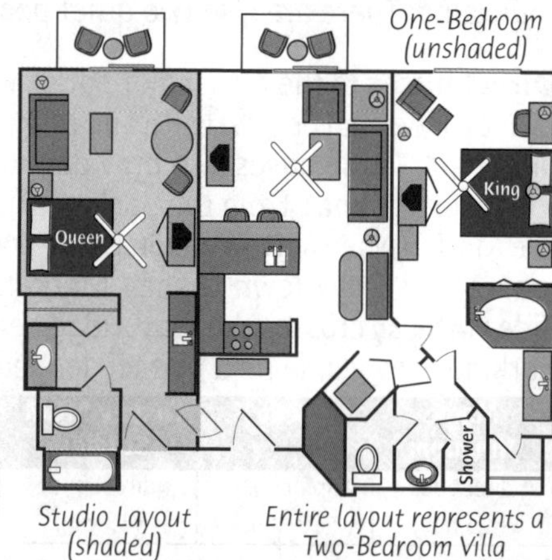

Studio Layout (shaded)

Entire layout represents a Two-Bedroom Villa

Using the Amenities at Disney's Saratoga Springs Resort

DINING & LOUNGING

Hungry? **The Artists' Palette** is a neighborhood eatery and market styled to resemble an artist's loft. Open all day, it offers pizzas, salads, sandwiches, bakery items, meals, groceries, Disney gifts, and sundries. Dine-in or take-out. More upscale than a typical food court—items ordered at the counter will be served on china plates with cutlery. **The Rocks** pool bar is open daily. The game room/lounge also has a bar.

Disney's Saratoga Springs

PLAYING & RELAXING

For Athletes: Rent surrey bikes at Horsing Around Recreation Rentals. There's also two clay tennis courts, basketball, shuffleboard, jogging path, and golf at the Lake Buena Vista Golf Course.
For Charmers: Saratoga Springs Spa (formerly The Spa at the Disney Institute) has a fitness center and a full range of spa treatments.
For Children: Organized activities are offered at Community Hall. Children's playground. Zero-entry area of theme pool doubles as kid's pool. Board games in lounge outside The Artists' Palette.
For Gamers: Win, Place or Show Arcade games in Community Hall, board games in the lounge outside The Artists' Palette.
For Shoppers: Visit The Artists' Palette for groceries and sundries.
For Swimmers: The High Rock Spring theme pool features a zero-entry/children's wading area, a 125 ft. long water slide that passes through a 20 ft. high tumble of rocks and waterfalls, two free-form hot-tub spas, and an adjoining kid's play area featuring "pop jet" fountains. There are also two quiet pools with spas (hot tubs).

GETTING ABOUT

Direct buses to the four major parks, water parks, and Downtown Disney (see chart below for transit times) stop at the resort's three bus stops. These buses also provide internal transportation within the resort. A **boat** from the dock near the Carriage House goes to the Marketplace at Downtown Disney. **Walking paths** connect the resort with Downtown Disney Marketplace and West Side (West Side pathway crosses the footbridge near the boat dock). Generous parking is available next to each lodge building.

Magic Kingdom	Epcot	Disney-MGM Studios	Disney's Animal Kingdom	Downtown Disney
direct bus ~25 min.	direct bus ~10 min.	direct bus ~15 min.	direct bus ~20 min.	walk/bus/boat ~15/10/7 min.

Approximate time you will spend in-transit from resort to destination during normal operation.

Making the Most of Disney's Saratoga Springs Resort

TIPS

This **report** is based on pre-opening information. For the latest, visit http://www.passporter.com/wdw/saratogasprings.htm.

The Downtown Disney Pleasure Island **fireworks** go off every night at midnight, and can be viewed from many guest rooms and from the Fireworks Pavilion in Congress Park. If you're concerned about the noise of the fireworks, avoid lakeside villas.

The **Main Street Railroad Station** at Magic Kingdom was modeled on the former station in Saratoga Springs, New York. The Carriage House, theater, and other nearby buildings recycled from the Disney Institute were originally modeled on the architecture of another historic Upstate New York resort, Chautauqua.

Want to **relax**? A barbecue pavilion, fireworks pavilion, formal gardens, and gazebos/fountains for "taking the waters" all add to the relaxed resort atmosphere.

NOTES

The classroom and meeting areas of the Disney Institute have been converted into the **main sales offices** and show-villas for Disney Vacation Club. The sales facility at Disney's BoardWalk will close when Saratoga Springs opens.

The **remaining villas** from the Disney Institute (Fairway Villas, Treehouse Villas and Grand Villas) will not be offered to the public for the foreseeable future. They are currently being used for internal Disney needs.

Golf carts will *not* be offered for rental to resort guests.

Check-in time is 4:00 pm. Check-out time is 11:00 am.

RATINGS

Ratings are explained on page 26.

Our Value Ratings:		Our Magic Ratings:		Readers' Ratings:
Quality:	6/10	Theme:	6/10	Want to rate this resort?
Accessibility:	6/10	Amenities:	6/10	Visit us on the Web at:
Affordability:	6/10	Fun Factor:	5/10	http://www.passporter.com
Overall Value:	6/10	**Overall Magic:**	6/10	... /wdw/rate.htm

Saratoga Springs will be enjoyed by...		(estimated by the authors)
Younger Kids: ♥♥♥♥	Young Adults: ♥♥♥♥	Families: ♥♥♥♥♥
Older Kids: ♥♥♥♥	Mid Adults: ♥♥♥♥♥	Couples: ♥♥♥
Teenagers: ♥♥♥	Mature Adults: ♥♥♥♥♥	Singles: ♥♥

Finding Your Place at Disney's Saratoga Springs Resort

SARATOGA SPRINGS RESORT MAP

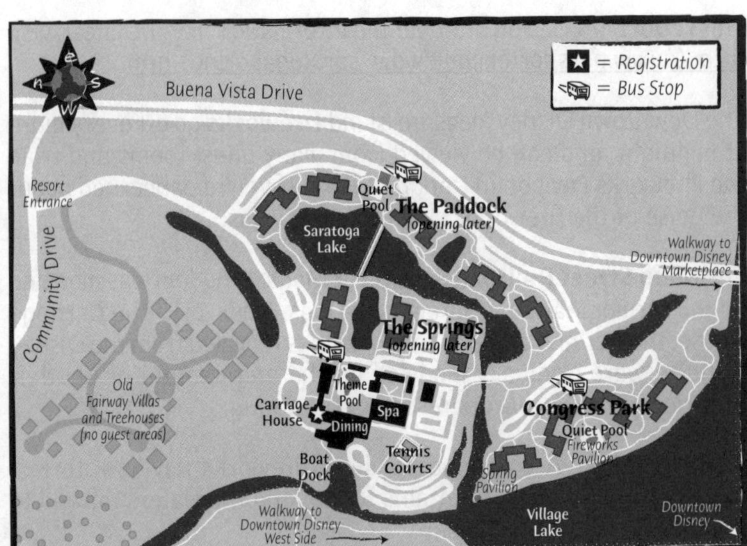

BEST LOCATIONS

There are no "preferred" or premium-priced guest rooms. Requests for particular locations will be honored when possible. Rooms in **Congress Park** (opens first) have views of Downtown Disney and/or gardens, and offer a short walk to the Marketplace, Fireworks Pavilion, and a moderate walk to The Carriage House. Some garden views include parking lots. **The Springs** (second phase) offers closest proximity to The Carriage House and theme pool areas, with views of Saratoga Lake or gardens/parking. **The Paddock** (third phase) is most spread out and distant from other facilities. Request to be close to the quiet pool and/or footbridge (to The Carriage House) if that's important.

RATES

2004 Sample Villa Rates

Seasons are noted on page 14

Room Type	Value	Regular	Peak	Holiday
Studio Villa	$254	$284	$329	$369
One-Bedroom Villa	$340	$385	$445	$510
Two-Bedroom Villa	$479	$560	$680	$775
Grand Villa	$1040	$1160	$1310	$1460

Tax is not included in the above rates.

INFO

Disney's Saratoga Springs Resort & Spa

1960 Broadway, Lake Buena Vista, FL 32830

Phone: 407-827-1100 Fax: 407-827-1151

For reservations, call Central Reservations: 407-934-7639

Looking for Shades of Green? Page 98. Swan Resort? Page 99.

Disney's Wilderness Lodge and Villas Resort

The Wilderness Lodge and Villas are nestled in a dense forest of pines on Bay Lake, accessible by waterway from the Magic Kingdom (use the blue tab at the top of the page for parks and eateries in the area). The Lodge and Villas were inspired by the U.S. National Park lodges built in the 1900s.

AMBIENCE

Ah, wilderness! Rustic log buildings, swaying pines, babbling brooks, and the faintest whiff of wood smoke from the crackling fireplace. The Wilderness Lodge pays homage to the **grand log lodges** of the Pacific Northwest, with its towering lobby, 55-foot totem poles, and deluxe rooms. The Villas at the Wilderness Lodge offer home-away-from-home accommodations for Disney Vacation Club Members (see pages 102–103) and all other guests. Architecturally, the Villas predate the existing Wilderness Lodge and draw influences from the lodges created by America's railroad workers.

LAYOUT & ROOMS

The Wilderness Lodge and the Villas offer varying accommodations, ranging from 350–1071 sq. feet. The **Lodge** houses 728 guest rooms and suites, with some encircling the cavernous lobby but most in the two wings. The cozy Lodge rooms are outfitted with pine furniture and quilted bedspreads. Most Lodge rooms have two queen beds, but some offer a bunk bed in place of the second bed. The **Villas** feature 136 studios, one- and two-bedroom suites, each with a kitchenette or full kitchen, VCR, and washer and dryer. All rooms have a balcony or patio, a small table and chairs, TV, double sinks, toiletries, in-room safe, housekeeping service, turndown service (on request), newspaper delivery, voice mail, and valet parking.

Standard Lodge Room Layout

DINING

As you would expect from a Lodge, the food here is served in hearty, healthy portions. The two table-service restaurants (see page 230) are **Artist Point** for fine dining at dinner (breakfast was discontinued in 2001), and **Whispering Canyon Cafe** for a fun, western-style adventure serving all-you-can eat meals. **Roaring Fork Snack Shop** is a self-service café serving breakfast foods, burgers, sandwiches, and snacks—purchase a refillable mug here for $11 and get free self-serve refills. Typical menu items include breakfast pizza ($5.59), smoked turkey sandwich ($5.79), chili dog with fries ($5.39), and pecan sticky buns ($2.79). **Miss Jenny's In Room Dining** is available for limited room service at breakfast and dinner.

Using the Amenities at Disney's Wilderness Lodge and Villas Resort

LOUNGING

Territory Lounge, a saloon adjacent to Artist Point, serves up beers, wines, and snacks. The **Trout Pass Pool Bar** offers cocktails and light snacks you can enjoy at tables overlooking the main pool and Bay Lake. Beer and wine are also available from the resort shop.

A waterfall flows to Silver Creek in the Wilderness Lodge courtyard

PLAYING & RELAXING

For Athletes: Rent watercraft and bicycles at Teton Boat & Bike Rentals. A bike and jogging path extends about a mile to Fort Wilderness. A health club, Sturdy Branches, is available.
For Children: The Cub's Den is a supervised program for kids ages 4–12 (see page 253). A playground is located near the beach.
For Gamers: Buttons and Bells arcade, across from Cub's Den.
For Shoppers: The large Wilderness Lodge Mercantile in the Lodge carries clothing, sundries, foodstuffs, newspapers, and gifts.
For Swimmers: Cleverly designed to seem like part of Silver Creek, a free-form swimming pool is nestled among craggy rocks and waterfalls. A water slide and wading pool, as well as two hot tubs are also available nearby. A quiet pool and another hot tub are located near the Villas. The white sand beach here on Bay Lake is ideal for relaxing upon, but swimming is not permitted.

GETTING ABOUT

You can take a direct **boat** to the Magic Kingdom (see chart below for in-transit times). Boats also ferry you to Fort Wilderness and the Contemporary. **Buses** take you directly to Epcot, Disney-MGM Studios, Disney's Animal Kingdom, Downtown Disney, and the water parks. To reach other resorts, go to the Magic Kingdom (daytime) or Downtown Disney (evening), and then transfer to a resort bus. Fort Wilderness and Wilderness Lodge share many of their bus routes, so travel to and from Fort Wilderness for the Hoop-Dee-Doo show (see page 234), horseback riding, etc. is quite convenient.

Magic Kingdom	Epcot	Disney-MGM Studios	Disney's Animal Kingdom	Downtown Disney
boat ~8 min.	direct bus ~10 min.	direct bus ~15 min.	direct bus ~15 min.	direct bus ~25 min

Approximate time you will spend in-transit from resort to destination during normal operation.

Making the Most of Disney's Wilderness Lodge and Villas Resort

TIPS

Guests staying in the **Villas at the Wilderness Lodge** register at the main Lodge registration desk.

For good rainy day activities, ask for a **kid's activity/coloring book** at the bell station or a list of **Hidden Mickeys** at Guest Services. You can also get a list of the resort's music at the Mercantile shop.

Explore the resort. Indian artifacts, historic paintings, and survey maps are displayed. Follow Silver Creek from its indoor origin as a hot spring and onward outside as a bubbling brook and waterfall, eventually making its way to Bay Lake (see photo on page 90).

Ask about becoming a **Flag Family**. Each morning a family is selected to go on the Lodge roof to help raise or lower the flag! This is popular, so inquire at check-in for a better chance.

Inquire about the **"behind the scenes" tour** at Guest Services. The walking tour explores the architecture, landscaping, totem poles, and paintings. Offered on Wednesdays–Saturdays at 9:00 am.

Watch **Fire Rock Geyser**, modeled after Old Faithful, erupt like clockwork every hour on the hour from 7:00 am–10:00 pm. The **Electrical Water Pageant** is visible from the beach at 9:35 pm.

NOTES

The lower courtyard can be **noisy** with the sounds of children and rushing water. Opt for a Lodge view if you prefer serenity.

About 37 Lodge rooms with **king beds** double as the barrier-free (handicap-accessible) rooms and have a large shower with no tub.

Check-in time is 3:00 pm. Check-out time is 11:00 am.

RATINGS

Ratings are explained on page 26.

Our Value Ratings:		Our Magic Ratings:		Readers' Ratings:
Quality:	9/10	Theme:	10/10	79% fell in love with it
Accessibility:	6/10	Amenities:	6/10	10% liked it well enough
Affordability:	6/10	Fun Factor:	8/10	7% had mixed feelings
Overall Value:	**7/10**	**Overall Magic:**	**8/10**	4% were disappointed

Wilderness Lodge is enjoyed by... (rated by both authors and readers)

Younger Kids: ♥♥♥♥	Young Adults: ♥♥♥♥♥	Families: ♥♥♥♥
Older Kids: ♥♥♥♥	Mid Adults: ♥♥♥♥♥	Couples: ♥♥♥♥♥
Teenagers: ♥♥♥♥	Mature Adults: ♥♥♥♥	Singles: ♥♥♥

Finding Your Place at Disney's Wilderness Lodge and Villas Resort

LODGE AND VILLAS RESORT MAP

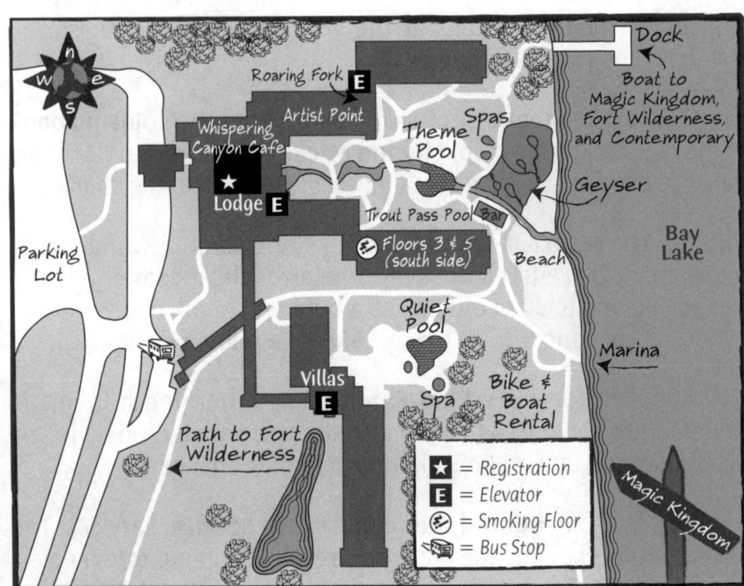

BEST LOCATIONS

Standard rooms overlook the parking areas yet are close to the Lobby. **Lodge views** overlook woods (north side) or the Villas (south side). **Top-floor rooms** facing the woods on the Magic Kingdom (north) side may catch a glimpse of fireworks. Rooms facing the **courtyard or lake** offer panoramic views and cheerful resort sounds. If you seek privacy, consider a **honeymoon suite** at the top of the Lobby, or a top-floor room with solid balcony railings. Concierge service is offered for suites and rooms on the seventh floor. **Villas** in the northeast corner offer views of the pool.

RATES

2004 Sample Room and Villa Rates *Seasons are noted on page 14*

Room Type	Value	Regular	Peak	Holiday
Standard View	$199	$239	$289	$324
Lodge View (Woods)	$219	$254	$299	$339
Courtyard View	$250	$290	$340	$385
Studio Villa	$279	$314	$379	$434
One-Bedroom Villa	$380	$425	$495	$560

Tax is not included in the above rates. Suites start in the mid-$300's.

INFO

Disney's Wilderness Lodge and Villas Resort

901 W. Timberline Drive, Bay Lake, FL 32830

Phone: 407-824-3200 Fax: 407-824-3232

For reservations, call Central Reservations: 407-934-7639

Disney's Yacht and Beach Club and Villas Resorts

Offering luxury, convenience, and added amenities, the Yacht Club and Beach Club are sister resorts. Both resorts feature a relaxing atmosphere and are located on Crescent Lake within walking distance of Epcot (use the blue tab at the top of the page for parks and eateries in the area)

AMBIENCE

These resorts evoke the charm of **bygone seaside resorts**. The Yacht Club is housed in a dove-gray clapboard building, exuding elegance and grace. The Beach Club atmosphere is casual, bringing to mind sun-filled days you might have found along the eastern seaboard generations ago. Windows in the sky blue building may gaze out upon the "beachhouses" nestled alongside the beach. A recent addition are the Beach Club Villas, which are housed in a separate building evoking the charm of Cape May, New Jersey. The Villas' clapboard walls are painted in seafoam green with white railings and columns, and gingerbread trim. Colorful pennants flap in the breeze from atop the roofs and turrets, and strings of light bulbs dangle gracefully between old-fashioned street lamps.

RESORT LAYOUT & ROOMS

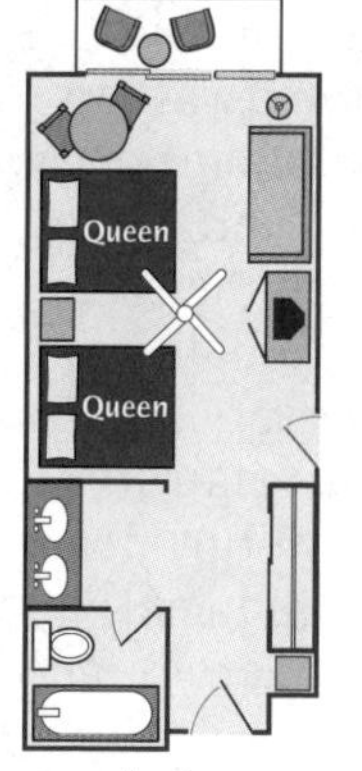

Standard Room Layout

Each of the standard rooms at the Yacht and Beach Club is housed within five floors of one deceptively large yet creatively shaped building, while the villas are located within a free-standing addition. Covered walkways connect the Villas to the Beach Club lobby. Well-appointed and understated, the standard rooms are large (380 sq. ft.) and sunny. The 634 **Yacht Club** rooms are outfitted in ocean blues, floral patterns, and antiqued wood. The 580 **Beach Club** rooms are playfully decorated in seafoam greens and cabana-striped pinks. Guest rooms have one king-size or two queen-size beds, a day bed, double sinks, a make-up mirror, a small table and chairs, and an armoire with a television and a mini-bar. Some smaller rooms have a king-size murphy bed and an extra sink and counter. Many rooms—but not all—have balconies or patios. Amenities include room service, hairdryers (most rooms), iron and ironing board, newspaper delivery, turndown service (on request), in-room safe, toiletries, voice mail, and valet parking. Beyond the standard rooms, both the Yacht Club and the Beach Club offer a luxurious concierge service with slightly larger rooms on the fifth floor. In addition, 40 special suites (20 in each resort) range in size from a junior suite to a two-bedroom suite to the ultimate Presidential Suite.

Lodging and Dining at Disney's Yacht and Beach Club Resorts

VILLAS

© MediaMarx, Inc.

The full-size kitchen in our two-bedroom villa at the Beach Club Villas

Newly added in mid-2002 are the 205 Beach Club Villas with studio, one-, and two-bedroom **villas** for Disney Vacation Club members (see 102–103) and the public at large. Studios accommodate up to four guests with one queen-size bed, a double-size sofa bed and a kitchenette (with a sink, microwave, and a small refrigerator). The one- and two-bedroom villas accommodate up to four or eight guests each and offer full kitchens, DVD players, king-size beds and whirlpool tubs in the master bedroom, double-size sleeper sofas in the living room, and washers/dryers. All villas are homey and feel like a cottage you might have on the ocean. Amenities for all villas include room service, iron and board, hairdryer, newspapers, turndown service (on request), in-room safe, toiletries, and voice mail.

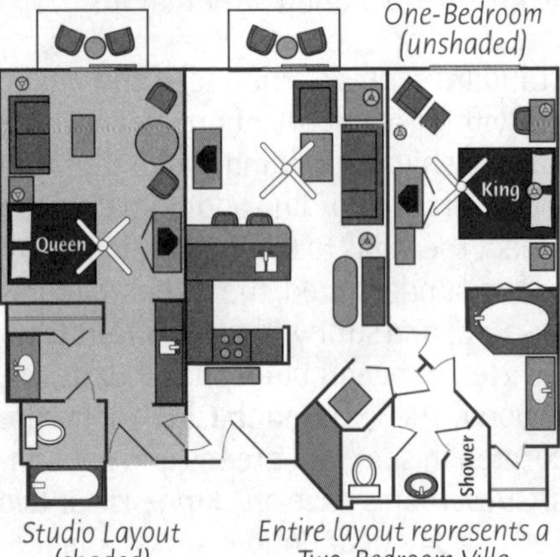

Studio Layout (shaded) *Entire layout represents a Two-Bedroom Villa*

DINING

With the Yacht and Beach Club sharing restaurants, there are more dining options here than at almost any other resort. Table-service options (see pages 230–231) include **Beaches and Cream**, a popular soda fountain; **Cape May Cafe**, a character breakfast and all-you-can-eat clambake; **Yachtsman Steakhouse** for dinner, and the **Yacht Club Galley** for breakfast and lunch. The **Crew's Cup** offers a good snack menu. For a quick meal, try **Hurricane Hanna's**, a poolside grill. Typical menu items include a grilled chicken sandwich ($6.50), garden salad ($3.50), large cookie ($2.00), and a kid's cheeseburger ($4.50). Refillable mugs are available for $11.

Using the Amenities at Disney's Yacht and Beach Club Resorts

LOUNGING

Several lounges stand ready to help you relax after a long day of playing. **Ale & Compass** and **Crew's Cup** in the Yacht Club serve drinks and munchies. **Martha's Vineyard** features an award-winning wine list and appetizers. **Rip Tide Lounge**, tucked away in a quiet corner, serves specialty drinks and a continental breakfast. **Hurricane Hanna's** is a pool bar. Room service is always available.

PLAYING & RELAXING

For Athletes: The Ship Shape Health Club is a complete fitness club offering a spa, sauna, and massage therapies. The resorts also sport two lighted tennis courts and a sand volleyball court. The Bayside Marina rents watercraft for cruises, including "The Breathless," a boat named after Breathless Mahoney in "Dick Tracy" (see page 250), and surrey bikes to ride around the lake.
For Charmers: Periwig's Beauty and Barber Shop is a full-service salon for hair, skin, and nail care.
For Children: A playground is near Stormalong Bay. Sandcastle Club offers supervised activities for children ages 4-12 (see page 253).
For Gamers: Lafferty Place Arcade has video games.
For Shoppers: Atlantic Wear & Wardrobe Emporium (Beach) and Fairings and Fittings (Yacht) offer sundries and resort wear.
For Swimmers: The three-acre Stormalong Bay water park is resort swimming at its best. Three free-form, sandy-bottomed pools create deceptively complex waterways with whirlpools, bubbling jets, "rising sands," a waterslide in a shipwreck, and two hot tubs. Stormalong Bay is for Yacht and Beach Club and Villas resort guests only (bring your resort ID). Quiet pools are located at the far ends of the resorts. The Villas has its own quiet pool, called "Dunes Cove," and a hot tub.

GETTING ABOUT

Boats (see chart below for in-transit times) depart from the marina for Epcot and Disney-MGM Studios. **Buses** outside the lobby go to the Magic Kingdom, Disney's Animal Kingdom, and Downtown Disney. Reach other destinations by transferring at a nearby theme park (day) or Downtown Disney (evening). Parking is available, as well as valet parking ($6/day). The BoardWalk, Dolphin, and Swan are all within **walking distance**, as is the International Gateway to Epcot. You could also walk to Disney-MGM Studios along the path beside the BoardWalk Villas (see map on page 46).

Magic Kingdom	Epcot	Disney-MGM Studios	Disney's Animal Kingdom	Downtown Disney
direct bus ~20 min.	walk/boat ~10/~10 min.	walk/boat ~20/~15 min.	direct bus ~20 min.	direct bus ~15 min.

Approximate time you will spend in-transit from resort to destination during normal operation.

Planning | Getting There | Staying in Style | Touring | Feasting | Making Magic | Index | Notes & More

Making the Most of Disney's Yacht and Beach Club Resort

TIPS

Enjoy a **waterfront stroll** around Crescent Lake using the boardwalks and bridges encircling it. This is a very lively place!

Request **turndown service** from housekeeping before you go out for the evening, and return to find your bedcovers turned down with a chocolate. You must specifically request this service.

A **bank of elevators** near each resort's lobby serves most rooms. If your room is at one of the far ends, look for a **single elevator or stairway** rather than trek down the hallways. If you're going to Epcot, the exit near Beach Club's quiet pool is convenient.

Yacht and Beach Club have **separate entrances** and **front desks**. Beach Club Villas guests check-in at the Beach Club's front desk.

Explore the charming **public areas**, such as The Solarium (just off the Beach Club Lobby), The Drawing Room (near the Villas' entrance), and The Breezeway (near the Dunes Cove pool).

NOTES

Be sure to bring **resort identification** with you to Stormalong Bay. Note that it can be noisy with the sounds of happy children late into the night, so avoid it and places nearby if you seek peace.

All rooms on the first floor have pleasant patios. Most rooms on the top floor have full **balconies**, as do some on the intervening floors. Be aware that some balconies are standing room-only, however. If a full-size balcony is important, request it.

A **conference center**, reminiscent of a town hall, is available.

Check-in time is 3:00 pm. Check-out time is 11:00 am.

RATINGS

Ratings are explained on page 26.

Our Value Ratings:		Our Magic Ratings:		Readers' Ratings:
Quality:	8/10	Theme:	8/10	67% fell in love with it
Accessibility:	8/10	Amenities:	9/10	24% liked it well enough
Affordability:	3/10	Fun Factor:	6/10	7% had mixed feelings
Overall Value:	**6/10**	**Overall Magic:**	**8/10**	1% were disappointed

Yacht and Beach Clubs are enjoyed by... (rated by both authors and readers)		
Younger Kids: ♥♥♥♥	Young Adults: ♥♥♥♥	Families: ♥♥♥♥
Older Kids: ♥♥♥♥♥	Mid Adults: ♥♥♥♥♥	Couples: ♥♥♥♥♥
Teenagers: ♥♥♥♥	Mature Adults: ♥♥♥♥♥	Singles: ♥♥♥

Finding Your Place at Disney's Yacht and Beach Club Resort

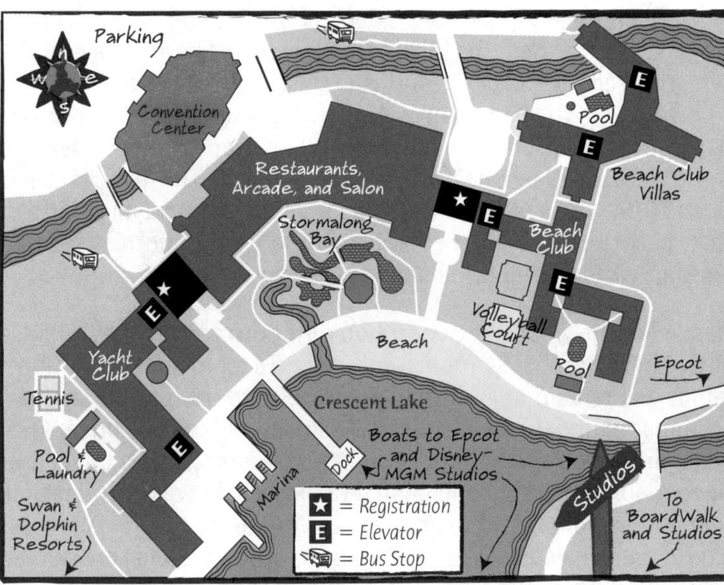

Your room location can make or break your experience. We strongly recommend you indulge in a room with a **water view** at either the Yacht or Beach Club. Specifically, try to avoid the standard-view, even-numbered Beach Club rooms between 3662-3726, 4662-4726, and 5662-5726 which overlook an ugly rooftop. You may also want to request a room **closer to the lobby** for easier access. Rooms with a king-size murphy bed are slightly smaller than other rooms. The slightly larger rooms on the Beach Club's fifth floor are concierge. Rooms at the **Beach Club Villas** have views of Epcot, gardens, or the pool, but rates are the same for all.

2004 Sample Room and Villa Rates

Seasons are noted on page 14

Room Type	Value	Regular	Peak	Holiday
Standard View or Studio Villa	$289	$329	$394	$449
Water View	$345	$395	$455	$510
One-Bedroom Villa	$390	$435	$505	$570
Two-Bedroom Villa	$545	$705	$890	$1010

Tax is not included in the above rates. Concierge rooms start in the low-$400's.

Disney's Yacht and Beach Club and Villas Resorts

1700/1800 Epcot Resorts Blvd., Bay Lake, FL 32830
Phone: 407-934-7000/8000 Fax: 407-934-3450/3850
For reservations, call Central Reservations: 407-934-7639

Shades of Green Resort
(Re-Opening in March 2004)

Shades of Green is a U.S. Armed Forces Recreational Center on Walt Disney World property, located near the Magic Kingdom theme park. Formerly The Disney Inn, this self-supporting resort is exclusively for active and retired military personnel in the Army, Navy, Air Force, Marine, and Coast Guard, as well as those in the Reserves and National Guard. Department of Defense civilians and U.S. Public Health Officers are also eligible. The resort is closed until March 2004, when it opens with bigger and better accommodations. If you visit before then you'll be lodged in the Contemporary Resort's North Garden Wing at regular Shades of Green rates.

ROOMS

Nestled in the woods **between two golf courses**, the new Shades of Green will offer 586 rooms with deluxe accommodations. Guest rooms will remain among the largest on property at 450 sq. feet, accommodating up to five guests. Features include two queen-size beds, an armoire, and a TV, plus a sitting area with a daybed or sleeper sofa and table and chairs. Rooms will have a coffeemaker, iron and ironing board, hairdryer, and an in-room safe. All rooms have either a balcony or patio. The resort (and all rooms) are smoke-free (smoking may be allowed on the balcony/patio). Eleven 1-3 bedroom suites are available, sleeping 6-8 guests each.

AMENITIES

Dining choices will include the Garden Gallery, Evergreen sports bar, a new specialty Italian restaurant (Mangino's), the new Express Cafe for quick-service meals, and room service. There's also a lounge (Eagles). Resort amenities include two lighted tennis courts, two heated pools, wading pool, playground, exercise room, arcade, and laundry facilities. You can also purchase theme park tickets. Two **buses** are available, and you can walk to the Polynesian and Transportation & Ticket Center. You must show your Shades of Green resort I.D. or military I.D. to board their buses. A car is helpful at this resort, and a new, multi-level parking structure will be built.

RATES

Rates are based on rank or paygrade and begin at **$70** for standard rooms and **$80** for pool views. You may reserve up to three rooms. Reservations are accepted up to 53 weeks in advance. **Tip**: If the resort is full for your preferred time, inquire about overflow rates.

INFO

Shades of Green Resort
P.O. Box 22789, Bay Lake, FL 32830
Phone: 407-824-3400 Fax: 407-824-3460
For more information, call 888-593-2242 or 407-824-3600
Web site: http://www.shadesofgreen.org

Swan and Dolphin Resorts

Crowned by five-story-high sculptures of swans and heraldic dolphins, the Swan and Dolphin resorts tower above nearby Epcot area resorts. Some find their design striking, others find it surreal. Westin and Sheraton, both of which are divisions of Starwood Hotels, jointly manage this pair of luxury hotels popular with business and international visitors.

ROOMS

Guest rooms feature either one bed (king-size) or two beds (queen-size at the Swan, or extra-long double-size at the Dolphin), separate vanity and bath areas, two phones, mini-bar, hair dryer, iron, and in-room safe. A mandatory "resort fee" adds a coffeemaker, free local phone calls, health club access, and newspapers. In-room movies and Nintendo are extra. Some rooms have balconies, and 195 suites offer a bit more room. Guest rooms at the Swan were renovated in 2003 and sport a modern feel and "Heavenly Beds." The Dolphin is in the process of getting a renovation, too. The sister resorts offer concierge (Royal Club Level) and conference facilities, plus many of the same amenities and benefits found at Disney resort hotels.

AMENITIES

Between the resorts, there are **15 eateries**, including Palio, Gulliver's Grill, Kimonos, and Shula's Steakhouse, plus two new restaurants, "bluezoo," opening in the spot of the current Coral Cafe, and "Fresh," opening where Juan & Only's used to be (see pages 229–230 for details).The BoardWalk entertainment district is just a stroll away, as is Fantasia Gardens miniature golf. Free **buses** serve Disney's parks and Downtown Disney, and boats run to Disney-MGM Studios and Epcot. Guests receive many of the benefits enjoyed at the Disney-owned resorts, including package delivery and the option to purchase Ultimate Park Hoppers. The things Swan and Dolphin guests can't do are charge Disney purchases to their room or get package delivery.

RATES

Rooms at the Swan and Dolphin begin in the **high-$200's**, but discounts and special rate programs are available—ask about discounts for AAA, Annual Passholders, and teachers. Great rates can be found on Hotwire.com, and won on Priceline.com (page 16).

INFO

Walt Disney World Swan and Dolphin Resorts

1500 Epcot Resorts Blvd., Bay Lake, FL 32830
Phone: 407-934-4000 Fax: 407-934-4884
For reservations, call 800-325-3535 or 407-934-4000
For more information, visit http://www.swandolphin.com

Are you looking for more details? We can't fit them all here, but more information is available. Visit http://www.passporter.com/wdw/swandolphin.htm for details.

Planning | Getting There | Staying in Style | Touring | Feasting | Making Magic | Index | Notes & More

Looking for more information? Get details on our full-length Disney Cruise guide on page 284.

Disney Cruise Line

The Disney Cruise Line set sail in 1998 with the same enthusiasm and energy you find at the Walt Disney World Resort. Each of the two ships (the Disney Magic and the Disney Wonder) have four uniquely-themed restaurants, including one for adults only. Experience Broadway-quality productions, first run and classic Disney movies, and nightclubs. Separate areas of the ship were designed exclusively for adults and children.

ITINERARY

Ships depart Disney's own terminal in Port Canaveral at 5:00 pm. Four-night **cruises** spend the next day in Nassau, followed by a full day at sea, and then a day at Castaway Cay, Disney's private island. Guests debark at Port Canaveral at 9:00 am the following morning. Three-night cruises follow the same plan, but skip the day at sea. Seven-night cruises offer different itineraries—one to the Eastern Caribbean, one to the Western Caribbean, and new "seasonal" itineraries that include San Juan, Puerto Rico, or Antigua. The Eastern Caribbean cruise includes stops at St. Maarten, St. Thomas/St. John, and Castaway Cay. The Western Caribbean cruise includes visits to Key West, Grand Cayman, Cozumel, and Castaway Cay.

STATEROOMS

Staterooms range from downright comfortable to out-and-out luxurious. Even the least expensive (there are no "cheap") rooms are decorated in glowing, warm woods, and include a television, phone, refrigerator, and in-room safe. The bright and cheery bathrooms include a hair dryer and tub. Deluxe staterooms include a split bathroom, which makes family travel especially comfortable, and 44% of all staterooms offer a verandah. Staterooms that sleep four usually have one queen bed, a single daybed, and a single berth—great for families but not so great for two couples. At the high end, the two-bedroom Walter E. and Roy O. Disney suites are a feast for the eyes, decorated with exotic wood paneling and cut crystal—they include a whirlpool tub!

RATES

Many vacationers book seven-day land/sea **packages** that include a three- or four-night cruise and three or four nights at Walt Disney World. 2004 value season packages start at $829/person (for double occupancy) for a standard inside stateroom to about $5,000/person for a Royal Suite. Third, fourth, and fifth occupants pay much less. Airfare and ground transfers are extra, but the land/sea packages include park admission. Packages with less-expensive staterooms include a room at a moderate resort, while the more expensive rate a deluxe resort. Cruise-only vacations start at $409/person.

Making the Most of the Disney Cruise Line

DINING

Your cruise includes all food onboard (including room service) and lunch at Castaway Cay. Soft drinks are extra (except when served with meals), as are alcoholic beverages. Each night you'll be assigned to a different dining room. **Triton's** (Wonder) or **Lumiere's** (Magic) is the most formal dining room, which is also open daily to all for a full breakfast. **Parrot Cay** is the informal, Caribbean-themed room, and also hosts a breakfast buffet. **Animator's Palate** is an extraordinary room, lined with black and white drawings of famous Disney characters that gradually blossom into full color. **Palo** is the ships' intimate, adults-only restaurant. The menu is elegantly continental, the service is marvelous, and the view at sunset is breathtaking. You must reserve a table at Palo ($5/person surcharge) on the afternoon that you board, and seats can go quickly. Breakfast and lunch buffets and snacks are served on Deck 9. On your first day, purchase a refillable souvenir mug and get free soda fountain refills throughout your cruise.

NOTES

You'll receive your **cruise documentation** listing your stateroom assignment a few weeks before you sail. If you have preferences, state them upon reservation and again a month before you sail.

You must show passports or certified birth certificates plus photo I.D. before boarding. Get your **papers** in order long before you depart.

All shore-side food, transportation, and entertainment in every port of call except Castaway Cay is **at your own expense**. Unless you are especially adventuresome, we suggest you either book a shore excursion (listed in your cruise documentation) or stay onboard.

Dress is mostly casual, but have a nice dress or jacket for the Captain's reception, dinner at Triton's/Lumiere's, and Palo.

TIPS

To trim your **costs** or custom-tailor your vacation, book a cruise-only passage. You can still book ground transfers through Disney.

Need to stay connected? The **Internet Cafe** has reasonable fees.

Your day at **Castaway Cay** is short. Be sure to wake up early!

Looking for more information? We have an **entire book** about the Disney Cruise! Visit http://www.passporter.com/dcl/guidebook.htm and see page 284. We also recommend the unofficial Magical Disney Cruise Guide at http://wdwig.com/cruise/cruise.shtml.

For details, visit http://www.disneycruise.com or call 888-DCL-2500.

Disney Vacation Club

Can you ever get enough of Walt Disney World? Disney Vacation Club (DVC) members are betting that they can't. DVC is Disney's kinder, gentler version of a vacation timeshare, and offers several enticing twists on the timeshare experience. As with all timeshare offerings, the DVC offers the promise of frequent, reduced-cost Disney vacations in exchange for a significant up front investment on your part.

RESORTS

Disney operates **seven Disney Vacation Club resorts**: Old Key West (see pages 67–70), Boardwalk Villas (see pages 43–46), Villas at the Wilderness Lodge (see pages 89–92), Beach Club Villas (see pages 93–97), Vero Beach (Florida coast), Hilton Head Island (South Carolina), and the new Saratoga Springs (see pages 85-88). Studios, one-, two-, and three-bedroom villas with kitchen and laundry facilities are offered (studios have kitchenettes and access to laundry rooms), as well as excellent recreational activities. Housekeeping is limited, with full services every eight days (consider these reduced housekeeping services when you compare the value of a regular hotel to a DVC ownership).

THE PROGRAM

With a typical vacation timeshare you buy an annual one-week (or multiple week) stay during a particular time period in a specific size of accommodation. DVC uses a novel **point system** that adds far greater flexibility and complexity to the process. You can use your points however you wish to create several short getaways or a single, grand vacation—at any time of the year and at any DVC or other Disney resort. Here's how it works: You buy a certain number of points at the going rate ($89 per point as of 9/2003). 150 points is the minimum and a typical purchase—so every year you'd have 150 points to apply towards accommodations. You might need 15 points/night for a one-bedroom at Old Key West weeknights during the off-season. 100 points/night may be needed for a two-bedroom at BoardWalk weekends in peak season. Just as with a regular resort room, rates are affected by size, view, location, season, and day. You also pay annual dues based on the number of points purchased. Rates vary, depending on your "home" resort—from about $3 to $5 per point—so dues on a 150 point purchase would be approximately $475–600. If you compare the combined cost of points and annual membership fees to renting comparable resort rooms at non-discounted rates, it could take about five years to recover the value of the points purchased. After that, vacations might cost half the prevailing rental rates. New contracts expire now expire in 2053.

➢

Making the Most of the Disney Vacation Club

TIPS

While you can reserve up to eleven months ahead of time at your **home resort**, you can only book seven months in advance at others.

You can **borrow points** from the next year, or save unused points until next year. You can buy more points from Disney at the going rate, or buy/sell points on the open market—we heartily recommend you try DVC By Resale (visit http://www.dvcbyresale.com or call toll-free 800-844-4099, see their details on page 283).

Don't let unused points expire! If you can't use all your points this year or prefer to use them later, you must file the appropriate form with DVC. Otherwise, those **points expire** at year's end.

You can use points to book **other Disney resorts**, Disney Cruise Line, Disneyland Paris, luxury hotels and adventure travel vacations, or barter points for conventional "swaps" at non-Disney resorts.

DVC members receive many **discounts**, including discounts at The Disney Store, resort rooms (based on availability), dining, etc.

NOTES

Point values for various resorts and seasons may fluctuate from year to year, but the **average point value** of all DVC rooms cannot increase. For maximum value, stay Sunday through Thursday nights.

Vacancies at DVC resorts are made available to **non-members**—they are booked just like regular Disney resort reservations and daily housekeeping is included. Thus, it may be very difficult to use your DVC points at a resort if your intended arrival date is 60 days away or less. Plan as far in advance as possible. Keep in mind that you can stay at a DVC property without using points, too.

The **Eagles Pines Resort**, announced in 2001, is on "hold" and is being considered alongside other, unannounced DVC projects.

To learn more about Disney Vaction Club, we recommend a helpful **unofficial Web site** at http://www.mouseplanet.com/dtp/dvc.

INFO

Disney Vacation Club

200 Celebration Place, Celebration, FL 34747-9903
Phone: 800-800-9100 Fax: 407-566-3393
DVC information kiosks are at most Disney parks and resorts.
Sales offices and models are at Disney's Saratoga Springs.
http://www.disneyvacationclub.com

Hotel Plaza Resorts

Each of the following hotels are located on Disney property across from Downtown Disney, but are independently owned and operated. A variety of discounts may be available. Some of the Disney resort hotel benefits mentioned earlier in this chapter do not apply (such as Extra Magic Hour and package delivery). Do note that all the Hotel Plaza Resorts offer scheduled bus transportation to the parks (see sidebar on next page) and are within walking distance of Downtown Disney.

Hotel Name (in alphabetical order)	*Starting Rates*	*Year Built*	*Year Renovated*
Courtyard by Marriott	**$119+**	**1978**	**1998**

With 323 standard rooms and two suites, this 14-story hotel offers clean, basic accommodations. Standard rooms come with two double beds or one king bed, balconies, satellite TV, hairdryer, iron and ironing board, coffeemaker, a large in-room safe, newspaper delivery, and toiletries. Additional amenities include Nintendo games (for an extra fee), two heated pools, wading pool, whirlpool spa, fitness center, arcade, one restaurant, one cafe, and room service. Ask about the Preferred Guest Discount card which gives discounts at many Downtown Disney eateries. Web: http://www.courtyardorlando.com. Call 800-321-2211 or 407-828-8888.

DoubleTree Guest Suites Resort	**$149+**	**1988**	**1999**

This all-suite hotel offers 229 one- and two-bedroom suites. All rooms come with dining areas, kitchenettes (refrigerator, microwave, and coffeemaker), separate living rooms with sofa beds, double-size or king-size beds, three TVs, two phones, in-room safe, hairdryer, iron and ironing board, and toiletries (no balconies). Suites accommodate up to six people (up to four adults). Amenities include a heated pool, wading pool, fitness center, arcade, one restaurant, one lounge, one pool bar, and room service. Look for the freshly-baked chocolate chip cookies upon your arrival. Web: http://www.doubletreeguestsuites.com. Call 800-222-8733 or 407-934-1000.

Grosvenor Resort	**$139+**	**1972**	**1996**

A British-themed resort offering 629 rooms in a 19-story high-rise nestled beside Lake Buena Vista. All rooms come with a VCR and wet bar in addition to the standard two double-size beds or one king-size bed, satellite TV, coffeemaker (with coffee and tea), mini-bar, in-room safe, newspaper delivery, and toiletries (no balconies). Resort amenities include two heated pools, whirlpool spa, two tennis courts (as well as basketball, volleyball, and shuffleboard courts), a European spa, fitness center, arcade, one restaurant (with character breakfasts thrice weekly), one cafe, one pool bar, and room service. The MurderWatch Mystery Theatre is held here on Saturday nights (see page 236). Kids eat free with each paying adult. You can get great rates on Priceline.com. Web: http://www.grosvenorresort.com. Call 800-624-4109 or 407-828-4444.

The Hilton	**$139+**	**1984**	**1999**

This first-class business hotel is located right across the street from the Downtown Disney Marketplace. The 814 rooms are luxurious, each offering two double beds or one king bed, overstuffed chair, cable TV, two phones, hairdryer, iron and ironing board, coffeemaker, mini-bar, newspapers, and toiletries (no balconies or in-room safes). Amenities include two heated pools, kids water play area, two whirlpool spas, fitness center, arcade, shopping area, three eateries (one with character meals every Sunday), two cafes, and one lounge, one pool bar, and room service. The Hilton is the only Hotel Plaza Hotel to offer the Extra Magic Hour perk (see page 32). Web: http://www.hotel-inside-the-park.com. Call 800-445-8667 or 407-827-4000.

Hotel Name (in alphabetical order)	Starting Rates	Year Built	Year Renovated
Hotel Royal Plaza	**$169+**	**1975**	**1998**

This hotel offers 394 standard rooms which each accommodate up to five guests and have a sitting area, balcony or patio, coffeemaker, and phone in addition to the two double beds or one king bed, daybed, cable TV, in-room safe, hairdryer, iron and ironing board, newspaper delivery, and toiletries. Note that rooms in the tower are slightly larger and offer upgraded bathrooms. Hotel amenities include a heated pool, whirlpool spa, four tennis courts, arcade, a restaurant (kids 12 and under eat free with a paying adult), a lounge, a pool bar, and room service. Of all the Hotel Plaza hotels, this is the one that gets the most rave reviews from other vacationers. Web: http://www.royalplaza.com. Call 800-248-7890 or 407-828-2828.

Hotel Name	Starting Rates	Year Built	Year Renovated
Lake Buena Vista Best Western Resort	**$99+**	**1973**	**1997**

This 18-story, Caribbean-themed hotel is on the shores of Lake Buena Vista. The resort offers 321 standard rooms (345 sq. ft.) and four suites, all of which have balconies. Rooms come with two queen beds or one king bed, satellite TV, hairdryer, iron and ironing board, coffeemaker (with coffee and tea), in-room safe, newspaper delivery, and toiletries. Other amenities include Nintendo games and premium movies for an extra fee, one heated pool, a wading pool, privileges to the DoubleTree fitness center, two eateries, two lounges, and room service. Formerly a Travelodge. Web: http://www.orlandoresorthotel.com. Call 800-348-3765 or 407-828-2424.

Hotel Name	Starting Rates	Year Built	Year Renovated
Wyndham Palace Resort & Spa	**$229+**	**1983**	**1998**

A high-rise hotel with 1014 luxury guest rooms and suites. This is the largest of the hotels on Hotel Plaza Boulevard. It's also the closest hotel to Downtown Disney Marketplace. All rooms feature balconies or patios, two double beds or one king bed, cable TV, cordless phone, coffeemaker (with complimentary coffee and tea), in-room safe, hairdryer, iron and ironing board, newspaper delivery, and toiletries. High-speed Internet access, WebTV, Sony PlayStation games, and premium movies are available for an additional fee. Resort amenities include three heated pools, whirlpool spa, tennis and sand volleyball courts, full-service European-style spa with fitness center and beauty salon, arcade, three restaurants (one with character breakfasts every Sunday), a cafe, two lounges, a pool bar, and room service. Formerly known as Buena Vista Palace. Web: http://www.wyndham.com/hotels/MCOPV/main.wnt. Call 407-827-2727.

Hotel Plaza Resort Transportation to the Parks

Guests staying at these Hotel Plaza Resorts get the added perk of free bus transportation to the four major Disney parks, Downtown Disney, and the water parks. Buses run every 30 minutes and typically start one hour before park opening and continue up to two hours after park closing. Note that buses to the Magic Kingdom drop you off at the Transportation & Ticket Center (TTC) where you can take a monorail or boat to the park entrance or transfer to a another bus to another Disney destination. Disney's Animal Kingdom buses may operate only once an hour during the slower times of the day. Within walking distance is Downtown Disney, where you can also board buses to other resorts (Disney transportation privileges are included with the Park Hopper and Annual Passes). Those bound for the water parks should check with their hotel for bus schedules. Guests who want to venture off to Universal Studios/Islands of Adventure, SeaWorld, Wet 'n' Wild, or the Belz Outlet Mall can take a shuttle for $12/person round-trip–check with your hotel on pick-up times. Many guests who stay at these hotels recommend you get a rental car–all hotels but the Best Western and Hotel Royal Plaza have a rental car desk.

Hotels Near Walt Disney World

Below are several hotels and motels near Walt Disney World (but not on property) that either we've stayed in and recommend, or at which our readers report good experiences. More hotels are listed on following pages.

Hotel Name (in alphabetical order)	*Starting Rates*	*Year Built*	*Year Renovated*
Holiday Inn Family Suites	**$114+**	**1999**	**n/a**

We had the pleasure of staying at this 800-suite resort in July 2002. Besides the resort's close proximity to Walt Disney World (just 3 miles/5 km.), the hotel offers unique and very convenient "Kidsuites" with a living room, kitchenette, master bedroom, and kids' room. The kids get a bunkbed, TV, Nintendo (fee applies), and a small table and chairs. Allie fell in love with it! If you don't have kids, you can get a room with a different configuration, such as the SweetHeart Suite (117-gallon whirlpool tub and 50" TV), the CinemaSuite (60" TV with stereo surround sound), Residential Suite (full kitchen), or the Two-Bedroom Suite (for adults or families with teens). Guests get a full, hot breakfast buffet from 6:30–11:00 am. Kids eat free when they dine with adults. The resort also has a large pool, water playground, two hot tubs, and a small miniature golf course. There is a free scheduled shuttle bus to Walt Disney World, but we found it more convenient to drive. Visit http://www.hifamilysuites.com or call 407-387-5437 or 877-387-5437. Hotel address: 14500 Continental Gateway, Orlando, FL 32821

Radisson Resort Parkway	**$69+**	**1987**	**2001**

We enjoyed our recent stay at this 718-room, 6-story deluxe hotel just 1.5 miles (2.5 km) from the gates of Walt Disney World. Guest rooms accommodate up to four guests with either one king-size bed or two double-size beds. Rooms come in either pool or courtyard views and feature modern Italian furniture and marble bathrooms. Amenities include a 25" TV, stocked mini-bar, in-room safe, coffeemaker, iron and ironing board, hair dryer, make-up mirror, voice mail, and data ports. For a fee, you can add WebTV and Nintendo. The resort has two pools, a water slide, a wading pool, and two hot tubs, as well as lighted tennis courts, fitness center, playground, and arcade. Food service includes a full-service restaurant (open for breakfast and dinner), a deli with Pizza Hut items, a sports bar, a pool bar, and room service. Note that kids under 10 eat free when accompanied by a paying adult. There is a free scheduled shuttle bus to attractions. For the best rates, visit http://www.radissonparkway.com/offers/index.asp?adsvc=02PASS or call 407-396-7000 and ask for the "Y-PASS" rate code. 2900 Parkway Boulevard, Kissimmee, FL 34747

Sheraton Safari Resort	**$85+**	**1994**	**1998**

While this isn't equivalent to Disney's Animal Kingdom Lodge, this safari-themed resort is a winner with kids and adults alike. The 489-room, 6-story hotel is located just 1/4 mile (1/2 km.) from the Disney property (you can't walk to it, but it is a short drive or ride on the scheduled shuttle). Guest rooms come in standard (one king-size or two double-sized beds), Safari Suites (with kitchenette and separate parlor), and deluxe suites (with full kitchens and large parlors). Standard rooms accommodate up to four guests, or five guests with the rental of a rollaway bed. All rooms have a balcony or patio, TV with PlayStation, two phones with voice mail, dataports, and high-speed Internet access, hair dryer, make-up mirror, coffeemaker, iron and ironing board, and in-room safe. The resort features a large pool with a 79-ft. waterslide, wading pool, hot tub, fitness center, and arcade. One full-service restaurant (Casablanca's) offers breakfast and dinner (kids under 10 eat free with paying adults), along with the Outpost Deli (for lunch and dinner), the ZanZibar Watering Hole, and room service (6:30 am–10:00 pm). Visit http://www.sheratonsafari.com or call 407-239-0444 or 800-423-3297. Hotel address: 12205 Apopka-Vineland Road, Orlando, FL 32836

Hotels Near Universal Studios

Below are the three on-site hotels at Universal Studios Florida (about 7 miles/11 kilometers from Walt Disney World property). Note that guests staying in these hotels get special privileges at Universal Studios and Islands of Adventure, such as the "Universal Express" ride access system to bypass attraction lines, priority seating at some restaurants, complimentary package delivery, on-site transportation, and more. Each of these hotels accepts pets and offers pet-related services. All of these resorts are operated by Loews Hotels (http://www.loewshotels.com).

Hotel Name (in alphabetical order)	*Starting Rates*	*Year Built*
Hard Rock Hotel	**$229+**	**2001**

If you think Hard Rock Cafe is great, this 650-room hotel really rocks. Step inside a rock star's mansion filled to the rafters with a million-dollar rock memorabilia collection. Standard guest rooms (365 sq. ft.) feature two queen beds or one king bed, cable TV, stereo and CD player, 2-line cordless phones, mini-bar, coffeemaker, in-room safe, hairdryer, bathroom scale, iron and ironing board, and toiletries. There are fourteen Kids Suites with a separate sleeping area for the kids. Hotel amenities include a heated pool with a waterslide and underwater audio system, wading pool, two whirlpool spas, sand beach, fitness center, two restaurants (including a Hard Rock Cafe with a concert venue), a cafe, a lounge, a pool bar, and room service. Web: http://www.hardrockhotelorlando.com/locations/hotels/orlando. Call 800-BE-A-STAR (800-232-7827) or 407-503-2000. Hotel address: 5800 Universal Blvd., Orlando, FL 32819

Portofino Bay Hotel	**$259+**	**1999**

Stay in this remarkably-themed resort and get a big taste of the Italian Riviera. The hotel is a deluxe recreation of the seaside village of Portofino, Italy, developed with the help of Steven Spielberg. There may be cobblestone streets outside, but luxury abounds inside. 750 rooms and suites are available, including several Kids Suites. Standard rooms come with either two queen beds or one king bed and double sofabed, cable TV, two phones, mini-bar, coffeemaker, in-room safe, hairdryer, iron and ironing board, and toiletries. Deluxe rooms offer a bit more space, an upgraded bathroom, a VCR, CD player, and fax machine. Resort amenities include three heated pools, a water slide, whirlpool spas, a full-service spa, fitness center, a Bocce ball court, four restaurants, three cafes, a lounge, and room service. Web: http://www.portofinobay.com. Call 407-503-1000 or 800-232-7827. Hotel address: 5601 Universal Blvd., Orlando, FL 32819

Royal Pacific Resort	**$209+**	**2002**

This relatively new hotel is Universal Studio's lowest-priced resort, boasting 1000 guest rooms with a South Seas theme and lush landscaping. Standard rooms (355 sq. ft.) accommodate up to five guests (four adults) and feature two queen beds or one king bed, cable TV, mini-bar, coffeemaker, in-room safe, hairdryer, iron and ironing board, and toiletries. The Club Rooms add robes, bathroom scales, turndown service, newspaper delivery, continental breakfast, and afternoon beer/wine/snacks. Resort amenities include a huge pool, kid's water play area, wading pool, two whirlpool spas, sand beach, volleyball court, putting green, fitness center, arcade, a supervised children's program, two restaurants, a cafe, a lounge, a pool bar, and room service. Web: http://www.loewshotels.com/hotels/orlando_royal_pacific. Call 888-322-5541 or 407-503-3000. Hotel address: 6300 Hollywood Way, Orlando, FL 32819

More Hotels Outside Disney

We feel we can save more at a value or moderately-priced Disney resort as there is no need for a car and we can do more in less time. Even so, you may prefer to stay "off-property" to attend a conference, visit other parks, or pay a bargain rate. Below are 33 popular hotels, motels, and inns off property. We've included starting rates for standard rooms (off-season), driving distance to Downtown Disney, available transportation to Disney, the year it was built (plus the year it was renovated, if available), if it is a Disney "Good Neighbor Hotel" (able to sell multi-day passes), a short description, web site (if available), and a phone number.

Hotel/Motel Name (in alphabetical order)	*Starting Rates*	*Distance to WDW*	*Trans. Avail.*	*Year Built*	*Good Neighbor*
AmeriSuites LBV	**$90+**	**3mi/5km**	**Bus**	**'00**	
151-suite resort with free breakfast. http://www.amerisuites.com. 407-997-1300					
Caribe Royale Resort	**$146+**	**4mi/6km**	**Bus($)**	**'97**	✔
Ten-story suite hotel with living rooms and wet bars. AAA discount. 407-238-8000					
The Celebration Hotel	**$140+**	**8mi/12km**	**Bus**	**'99**	✔
Upscale business hotel within Disney's town of Celebration. 407-566-6000					
Clarion Hotel Maingate	**$50+**	**8mi/12km**	**Bus**	**'86('99)**	✔
Five-story, 198-room hotel. http://www.clarionhotelmaingate.com. 407-396-4000					
Comfort Inn Lake Buena Vista	**$50+**	**3mi/5km**	**Bus**	**'87**	✔
Five-story, 640-room hotel. Details at http://www.comfortinnorlando.com. 407-996-7300					
DoubleTree Castle Hotel	**$90+**	**8mi/12km**	**Bus**	**'95**	✔
216-room, themed hotel. All rooms have three phones and Sony PlayStation. 407-345-1511					
DoubleTree Club Hotel	**$129+**	**1.5mi/2km**	**Bus**	**'86('99)**	✔
246 rooms and kid suites. http://www.doubletreecastle.com. AAA discount. 407-239-4646					
Embassy Grand Beach	**$269+**	**3mi/5km**	**–**	**'95**	
Secluded suite hotel, each with three bedrooms, three baths, and kitchen. 407-238-2500					
Embassy Suites LBV	**$129+**	**3mi/5km**	**Bus**	**'85**	✔
All-suite hotel with a Caribbean theme in Lake Buena Vista. 407-239-1144					
Embassy Suites I-Drive	**$139+**	**8mi/12km**	**Bus**	**'85('98)**	✔
Two-room suites with free cooked-to-order breakfasts. International Drive. 407-352-1400					
Gaylord Palms	**$320+**	**1mi/1.5km**	**Bus**	**'02**	✔
1406-room luxury resort near Disney. http://www.gaylordpalms.com. 407-586-0000					
Hawthorne Suites LBV	**$59+**	**1mi/1.5km**	**Bus**	**'00**	✔
Rooms and suites, all with free breakfast. http://www.hawthornsuiteslbv.com. 407-597-5000					
Holiday Inn Express	**$59+**	**8mi/12km**	**Bus**	**'90('99)**	✔
217-room motel with free continental breakfast bar and local calls. 407-351-4430					
Holiday Inn Maingate East	**$54+**	**6mi/10km**	**Bus($)**	**'73('99)**	✔
Standard rooms and Kidsuites. Located in Kissimmee. 407-396-4488					
Holiday Inn Nikki Bird	**$70+**	**6mi/10km**	**Bus**	**'73('99)**	✔
530-room hotel with microwaves and refrigerators, plus 75 Kidsuites. 407-396-7300					

Hotel/Motel Name (in alphabetical order)	Starting Rates	Distance to WDW	Trans. Avail.	Year Built	Good Neighbor
Holiday Inn SunSpree	**$79+**	**6mi/10km**	**Bus**	**'90('97)**	✔
Standard rooms and Kidsuites. Details at http://www.kidsuites.com. 407-239-4500					
Homewood Suites	**$99+**	**6mi/10km**	**Bus**	**'91('00)**	✔
Two-room suites with kitchen, living area, and bedroom. AAA discounts. 407-396-2229					
Howard Johnson Maingate	**$43+**	**10mi/16km**	**Bus**	**'85('00)**	✔
435-room motel with three pools. http://www.orlandohojomaingate.com. 407-396-4500					
Hyatt Regency Grand Cypress	**$285+**	**3mi/5km**	**Bus**	**'84('97)**	
750-room hotel with balconies, private lake, nature trails, and golf. 407-239-1234					
Marriott Orlando World Center	**$254+**	**4mi/6km**	**Bus($)**	**'86('99)**	
28-floor, 2000-room resort with four restaurants and a convention center. 407-239-4200					
Perri House	**$99+**	**4mi/6km**	**–**	**'89**	
Bed & breakfast with private baths. Details at http://www.perrihouse.com. 407-876-4830					
Premier Vacation Homes	**$105+**	**varies**	**–**	**'94-'99**	
Private home rentals with pools. http://www.premier-vacation-homes.com. 407-396-2401					
Quality Inn Plaza	**$49+**	**6mi/10km**	**Bus($)**	**'85('99)**	✔
1,020-room hotel with "semi suites." http://www.qualityinn-orlando.com. 407-996-8585					
Quality Suites Maingate	**$99+**	**6mi/10km**	**Bus**	**'90('99)**	✔
One- and two-bedroom suites with living rooms and kitchenettes. 407-396-8040					
Radisson Inn LBV	**$74+**	**2mi/3km**	**Bus**	**'90('00)**	✔
200-room hotel with balconies. Located in Lake Buena Vista. 407-239-8400					
Ramada Inn Maingate	**$49+**	**6mi/10km**	**Bus**	**'80('98)**	✔
391-room hotel with two pools, tennis, basketball, exercise room. 407-396-4466					
Red Roof Inn	**$40+**	**5mi/8km**	**–**	**'89('97)**	
Basic budget lodging with a good reputation. Located in Kissimmee. 407-396-0065					
Residence Inn	**$119+**	**8mi/12km**	**Bus**	**'86('98)**	✔
All-suite, business-oriented hotel with "family fun" suites and full kitchens. 407-345-0117					
Rodeway Inn International	**$39+**	**8mi/12km**	**Bus($)**	**'75**	✔
315-room, budget hotel. Details at http://www.rodewayinnorlando.com. 407-996-4444					
Sheraton's Vistana Resort	**$149+**	**3mi/5km**	**Bus**	**'80('97)**	
One- and two-bedroom villas. Details at http://www.sheraton.com. 407-239-3100					
Sierra Suites	**$65+**	**2.5mi/4km**	**Bus**	**'98**	
Studio-style suites with kitchens. Details at http://www.sierra-orlando.com. 407-239-4300					
Summerfield Suites	**$229+**	**2mi/3km**	**Bus**	**'93('98)**	✔
All-suite hotel with one- and two-bedroom suites and free breakfast. 407-238-0777					
Travelodge Maingate East	**$49+**	**3mi/5km**	**Bus**	**'84('97)**	✔
446-room hotel. Details at http://www.orlandotravelodgehotel.com. 407-396-4222					

Tip: You really need a car when staying at off-property hotels. Even when shuttles to the parks are provided, the schedules and drop-off/pick-up points aren't accommodating. If you are flying to Orlando and staying off-site, be sure to factor in the cost of renting a car.

Lodging Worksheet

Use this worksheet to jot down preferences, scribble information during phone calls, and keep all your discoveries together. Don't worry about being neat—just be thorough! Circle your final choices once you decide to go with them (to avoid any confusion) and be sure to transfer them to your Room(s) PassPocket.

Arrival date: ____________________ Alternates: ____________________

Departure date: ________________ Alternates: ____________________

Total number of nights: _________ Alternates: ____________________

We prefer to stay at: ____

Alternates: ____

____

Using your preferences above, call Disney's Reservations phone line at 407-WDISNEY (407-934-7639) and jot down resort availabilities in the table on the next page. It works best for us when we write the available days in the far left column, followed by the resort, view/type, special requests, rate and total cost in the columns to the right. Draw lines between different availabilities. Circle those you decide to use, and then record the reservation numbers, as you'll need them to confirm, cancel, or make changes later. The two columns at the far right let you note confirmations and room deposits so you don't forget and consequently lose your reservation.

Additional Notes:

Collect information on lodging in the table below. We've included some sample notes to show you how we do it, but you're welcome to use this space in any way you please.

Dates	Resort	View/Type/Requests	Rate	Total	Reservation #	Confirm by	Dep.
7/10 - 7/13	Port Orleans	Water View (Riverside)	$164	$492	2635 1419 8419	2/14/04 ✓	✓
7/11 - 7/14	All-Star Movies	Standard (Fantasia)	$99	$297		2/15/04	

The Last Resort

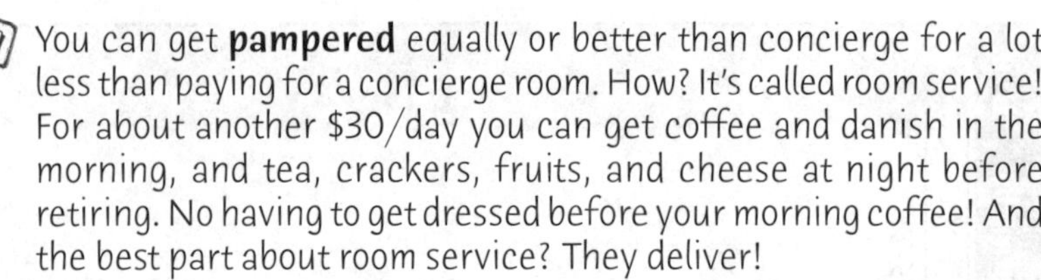

You can get **pampered** equally or better than concierge for a lot less than paying for a concierge room. How? It's called room service! For about another $30/day you can get coffee and danish in the morning, and tea, crackers, fruits, and cheese at night before retiring. No having to get dressed before your morning coffee! And the best part about room service? They deliver!

– Contributed by Margaret Wellman, a winner in our 2003 Lodging Tip Contest

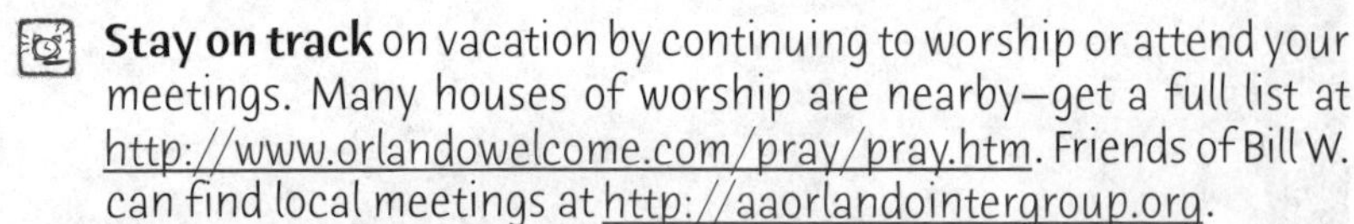

Stay on track on vacation by continuing to worship or attend your meetings. Many houses of worship are nearby—get a full list at http://www.orlandowelcome.com/pray/pray.htm. Friends of Bill W. can find local meetings at http://aaorlandointergroup.org.

To put into **perspective** just how vast Walt Disney World really is, the cities of Buffalo, New York City, Grand Rapids, Miami, Newark, and San Francisco are all smaller. In fact, Walt Disney World is larger than the countries of Nauru and San Marino combined! Things are not just around the block here. *– Contributed by Tom Anderson*

Magical Memories

"Disney's Animal Kingdom Lodge is one of our family's favorite places to stay as it truly immerses you in its rich, African theme while providing spectacular vistas from your resort room of the wildlife. A favorite pastime of our most recent stay at the Lodge was to head out to the Arusha Rock Overlook each evening to enjoy the African story telling by the fire pit. My children were completely spellbound by the tribal nature of this area, and they specifically commented that it distinctly reminded them of the setting of a very popular reality television show where individuals face eviction near a fire pit. One evening after returning to the Lodge late after a day of touring, we were disappointed to find the fire pit area eerily empty of guests—alas we'd missed that evening's storytelling. My youngest son, always trying to find light in any disappointing situation, exclaimed, 'Well, aren't you glad we weren't here to get voted off like the rest of the people did?' We all laughed so hard that we were concerned we'd start a stampede on the savanna!"

...as told by Disney vacationer Steven Baker

"We are from England and our last trip was on 1st October 2001, just two weeks after the Sept 11th tragedy. It was touch and go whether or not we would even be able to fly, but thankfully it was fine. We were staying at the Boardwalk Villas and when I looked out over the boardwalk on our first morning it was so eerie as it was deserted. It was so unnaturally quiet and I wondered whether we had done the right thing in coming! An American couple heard our accent and said 'Are you guys English?' to which they then said 'May God Bless you for coming.' I was stunned and thought that this was just one very thoughtful and friendly couple... but no! During our whole holiday, in queues for rides, on the bus, by the pool, Americans made a point of coming up to us and thanking us for coming at this time! I felt so touched and humbled by their heartfelt words that it just confirmed to me that Walt Disney World is the most magical place on earth."

...as told by Disney vacationer Debbie Hill

GET
where you
want to go
with ease

Touring the "World"

DECIDE what parks to visit and which attractions to see

The Walt Disney World Resort has been called many things—a world-class resort, an endless playground for young and old alike, and even a mecca to capitalism—but we have never heard it called boring.

The "World" (as it is known to insiders) began in 1971. Opening on October 1st of that year, it offered a small fraction of what we enjoy today: the Magic Kingdom park and the Contemporary, Polynesian, and Fort Wilderness resorts. It was the dream of an All-American leader, Walt Disney, who didn't live to see opening day. Yet his legacy flourished, becoming the 47-square-mile wonderland we know and love today.

One of the things that makes the Walt Disney World Resort so special is the attention to detail and service. It takes tens of thousands of people, known as "cast members," working together to stage the "show" we see as "guests." You'll notice that Disney often uses special words to describe their unique services and attractions. There's nothing mundane here.

To help you recognize these terms we begin with Park Passwords, defining the "Disneyese" you'll hear and read, such as the much-touted "FASTPASS" ride reservation system. We then move on to practical matters, such as transportation and admission to the parks. Next come our detailed attraction descriptions for the four major theme parks, along with the largest theme park maps you'll find in any Disney guidebook. (They fold out!) Descriptions and maps of the smaller parks follow, along with hints, tips, and a Touring Worksheet to help you decide what to do. Don't overlook our at-a-glance attraction lists and theme park touring plans.

In the 2004 edition, we bring our popular fold-out park maps to life with vibrant color. We've also printed these maps on heavier paper so they'll stand up to rugged use—feel free to remove them from the book and carry them around the parks as you tour.

So let's go around the "World" in 86 pages! 

Park Passwords

Admission Media—Park passes (tickets). See pages 116–117 for pass details and rates.

Attraction—An individual ride, show, or exhibit.

Baby Services—Special centers are found in each of the major parks. All restrooms (men's included) support diaper changing.

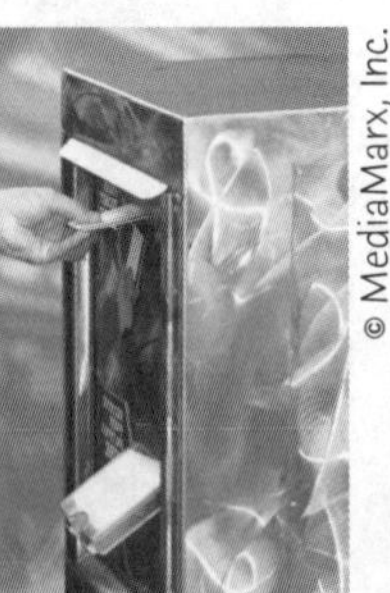

A FASTPASS machine

Cast Member—All Disney employees are "cast members"—they wear white nametags with their names and hometowns.

Disney Dollars—Disney's own currency, good throughout the Walt Disney World Resort.

Extra Magic Hour (Early Entry)—Resort guests can enter certain parks one hour early on certain days. See page 32 for details.

ECV—Electric Convenience Vehicle. You can rent these four-wheel scooters at the parks and elsewhere. See "wheelchairs" on page 35.

FASTPASS—Disney's popular ride "reservation" system (see below).

Making the Most of FASTPASS

Tired of waiting in long lines? Disney's FASTPASS system reduces the amount of time you spend in line—and it's free to all park guests! Just slip your park pass into a machine near an attraction with FASTPASS. Out pops your pass and a printed ticket (see sample below) that promises you a ride during a particular period some time later in the day. Depending on how many tickets have been issued to other guests, you may be able to return in 25 minutes, or hours later. When you receive your FASTPASS, look for the time you can get your next FASTPASS (you can get another at 5-10 minutes after the return time of your current pass, or in two hours, whichever comes first). When your FASTPASS return time arrives, walk up to the attraction's "FASTPASS Return" entrance, show your FASTPASS to the cast member, and walk on in. There's usually still a short wait, and you'll experience most or all "pre-show" activities. Every FASTPASS attraction has a "Standby" line, which is the regular wait-in-line queue—the wait time for the Standby queue is typically half as long as the FASTPASS return time. We recommend you get your first FASTPASS early in the day for one of the more popular rides, as FASTPASS tickets can run out on busy days. Our attraction descriptions later in this chapter indicate if an attraction has FASTPASS (look for the FP icon), and our touring plans give recommendations on which FASTPASSes to get throughout a day. Note that FASTPASS isn't always available, especially later in the day when all tickets have been issued. **Tip**: Enjoy the same ride twice! Get a FASTPASS, then get in the Standby queue. By the time your ride is over, your FASTPASS may be ready to use. Rumor has it that Disney may start issuing FASTPASS tickets for some character meet-and-greets. What a great idea!

Sample FASTPASS

Enter Any Time Between
9:45 pm
and
10:45 pm
Another FASTPASS ticket will be available after
9:50 am
10/09/03 9:25

Actual size: 2¼" x 2¾"

First Aid—First aid stations and Automatic Defibrillators are at every park.

Guidemaps—Free maps available at the parks. See also "Times Guide."

Guest Relations—An information desk, located both inside and outside the front gates of all four major parks. Guest Services at resorts provide a similar range of services.

Land—An area of a park organized around a common theme.

Lockers—Available for a fee ($5 + $2 deposit) in each park and at the Transportation & Ticket Center. Save your receipt for a new locker at another park on the same day.

Lost & Found—Lost items or children can be claimed at a central location in each park. Consult a guidemap or a cast member. Also see page 249.

Money—Pay with Disney Dollars, cash, travelers checks, The Disney Credit Card, American Express, MasterCard, Visa, Discover, JCB, Diner's Club, and Disney Visa Reward Vouchers. Disney Dollars are sold at parks, resorts, and the Disney Store. ATMs are located in the parks. Disney resort guests can charge to their room.

Packages—Purchases can be delivered or held for pickup near the park exit at all major parks, and Disney resort guests can have packages delivered to their resort free of charge. Inquire before purchasing.

Park—Disney's recreational complexes requiring admission, which include the four major parks (Magic Kingdom, Epcot, Disney-MGM Studios, and Disney's Animal Kingdom) and six minor parks (Blizzard Beach, Typhoon Lagoon, River Country, Pleasure Island, Wide World of Sports, and DisneyQuest). Descriptions begin on page 121.

Parking—Fee is $7; free to Disney resort guests and Annual Passholders. Tip: Save your receipt to park free at another Disney park on the same day.

Queue—A waiting area or line for an attraction or character greeting.

Re-Entry—Guests may exit and re-enter the same park on the same day. Be sure to get your hand stamped as you exit, and hold on to your pass.

Security—All bags are searched before entering parks.

Shopping—Shops sell Disney items, themed products, and sundries.We list the best shops in this chapter.

Smoking—Prohibited in most areas of parks, except in designated smoking areas (see photo and park maps).

Strollers & Wheelchairs—Strollers ($7-14/day + $1 deposit), wheelchairs ($7/day + $1 deposit), and ECVs ($30/day + $10 deposit) can be rented at the parks. Limited availability—arrive early, bring your own, or rent elsewhere (see page 35). Save your receipt for a free rental at another park on the same day.

Tax—Florida sales tax is now 6.5%.

Times Guide—Free weekly listing of hours and showtimes. Available when you enter the parks.

© MediaMarx, Inc.

A Magic Kingdom smoking area

Park Passes

Disney offers many admission options. It's safest to budget **$55.38**/day for adults and kids ages 10+ (**$44.73**/kids 3-9), the single-day price for the major parks. Most multi-day passes emphasize flexibility over savings, so you can do more at a lower price. Here's the deal on passes (prices include tax):

Note: Rates for single-day and Park Hoppers are actual 2004 rates (last increase June 2003). Rates for Annual Passes are estimated for 2004 (last increase January 2003).

Two- and Three-Day Single Park Passes — *Actual 2004 Rates*

A two-day/two-park pass ($105.43/$84.14) saves $5 over two day passes, while a three-day/three-park pass ($155.49/$123.54) saves $10. Offered only at the park ticket windows.

Four- and Five-Day Park Hopper — *Actual 2004 Rates*

Unlimited admission to the four major parks. While there are no savings over the price of four single-day tickets, you save $22 over the price of five single-day tickets and are free to visit more than one park in a day. Save unused days for a later visit. Four-Day Park Hopper is $221.52/adult and $177.86/kid. Five-Day Park Hopper is $254.54/$204.48.

Five-, Six-, and Seven-Day Park Hopper Plus — *Actual 2004 Rates*

Unlimited admission to all four major parks, plus "options" that can be used for single-day admission to a minor park (Pleasure Island, the water parks, or Wide World of Sports). You get two options with a five-day pass ($286.50/230.04), three with a six-day ($318.45/$255.62), and four with a seven-day ($350.40/$281.18). Each option represents a retail admission worth $10–33. Save unused days and/or options for later visits.

Ultimate Park Hopper Ticket — *Actual 2004 Rates*

Only for Disney resort hotel/campground guests. Unlimited use of all major and minor parks (the water parks, Pleasure Island, DisneyQuest, and Wide World of Sports) for the duration of your stay. Ultimate Park Hoppers are about the same price as equivalent Park Hopper Plus passes. While you can't save or get a refund of unused days, you can park hop without concern for "options." Ultimate Park Hoppers are based on the number of nights of your stay. Stay five nights and six days, get a "five-night" pass that's good for all six days. Use it on the days you arrive and depart. ***Tip:*** *You may be able to buy an Ultimate Park Hopper for a day or two less than the actual length of your stay. Ask at check-in. Two nights = $179.99/$144.84, three nights = $251.17/$193.83, four nights = $289.68/$232.17, five nights = $323.76/$259.86, six nights = $356.78/$285.42, seven nights = $392.99/$315.24.*

Annual Pass — *Estimated 2004 Rates*

Unlimited admission to the four major parks for a full year, plus special privileges. An Annual Pass ($413/$350) is $29 cheaper than two four-day Park Hopper Passes. Annual Passes also kick-in remarkable discounts on resorts (based on availability) and other privileges, such as a newsletter and events. See page 10 for details. There are also annual passes for the water parks ($112/90), Pleasure Island ($62), DisneyQuest ($88/$71), and water parks plus DisneyQuest ($144/$111). You cannot share an annual pass (or any other multi-day pass).

Premium Annual Pass — *Estimated 2004 Rates*

A Premium Annual Pass ($547/$465) offers the same privileges as the regular Annual Pass plus unlimited admission to the minor parks (including DisneyQuest) for $134 more. Five minor park visits cover the added cost. A Premium Annual Pass is almost the same price as a 12-night (13-day) Ultimate Park Hopper (just $26 more), but it is good for a full year.

Tip: Sections highlighted in light blue (like the ones below) indicate additions or significant changes at Disney since our previous edition! Rest assured that all prices are updated, too!

Upgrades: Apply the unused value of a park pass to a better pass at any time. For example, apply the unused portion of a Park Hopper Pass to the cost of an Annual Pass. Visit Guest Relations in the parks or Guest Services at a resort for details.

Magic Kingdom E-Ride Nights: What if you could ride the biggest and best rides at the Magic Kingdom for three hours after most of the crowds have gone home? Would it be worth an extra $13 ($11/kids)? We think so! Guests staying at a Disney resort hotel, Swan, Dolphin, Shades of Green, or Hotel Plaza with a multi-day or Annual Pass can take advantage of E-Ride Nights. Disney announces dates about 15-30 days in advance (call 407-939-4636 for dates). Ask at your hotel or Magic Kingdom Guest Relations for availability and passes. Attractions which may be open include: Astro Orbiter, Big Thunder Mountain Railroad, Buzz Lightyear, Country Bear Jamboree, Haunted Mansion, Space Mountain, Splash Mountain, Tomorrowland Transit Authority, and possibly Stitch Escape! (opening in late 2004). Note: You must use a park pass along with an E-Ride Night Ticket.

Advance Purchase Discounts: Available if you buy certain Park Hopper passes from Disney's Web site, The Disney Store, or with resort reservations. A $3 shipping charge per order may be charged. Discounts vary, but are generally 7%–10%. See details on page 11.

AAA: Members (see page 11) can expect a 5% discount on some passes. You must purchase Park Hoppers directly from AAA to get the discount.

Florida Resident Discounts: It pays to live nearby. Florida Resident Seasonal Passes work like Annual Passes, but with blackout dates in busy seasons. There are some other special deals for Florida residents only.

Military/Civil Service Discounts: Discounts of roughly 7%–8% may be available on admission–check with your Exchange shop or MWR (Morale, Welfare, and Recreation) office. Some offices may need to pre-order your tickets, so we advise you check with them well in advance. Keep an ear out for special programs for active military personnel–in the latter half of 2003, Disney offered all active military personnel a free five-day park hopper, with discounted admission for up to five family members or friends. To check on any current specials, visit http://www.disneyworld.com/military.

Online Ticket Brokers–These folks sell legitimate, unused park hoppers at great rates. Try http://www.ticketmania.com (877-822-7299) or http://www.floridaorlandotickets.net (888-723-2728). Be wary of others hawking tickets, including eBay and timeshares.

Kids Ride Free (Well, Some Do): Kids under 3 are admitted into the parks for free (and get a free ride if the ride allows someone that small). Anyone 10 and over is considered an adult in the eyes of the ticket booth. Passes for kids ages 3-9 cost about 20% less than adult passes. Also, the option-filled pass you buy for yourself is usually more than your child needs, especially if you use childcare programs (detailed on pages 252–253).

Pass Comparison Chart: Options and prices for your number of days in the parks.
(Prices are the 2004 costs of adult, non-discounted passes, including tax)

Pass Type Days:	1	2	3	4	5	6	7	8	9	10	11	12	13	14
Single Day/Single Park	$55	$105	$155											
Park Hopper				$222	$255									
Park Hopper Plus					$287	$318	$350							
Ultimate Park Hopper		$132	$180	$251	$290	$324	$357	$393	$425	$457	$485	$506	$521	
Annual Pass								$413 →	→	→	→	→	→	→
Premium Annual Pass													$547 →	→

For more details and updates, visit http://www.passporter.com/wdw/passes.htm

Getting Around the Resort and Parks

The internal **transportation system** at the Walt Disney World Resort is quite extensive, with buses, boats, and the famed monorail all doing their part to shuttle guests around the property. Transportation hubs exist at each major theme park and Downtown Disney, where you can reach nearly any other place in the "World" by bus, monorail, or boat. The Transportation & Ticket Center (TTC) near the Magic Kingdom forms another hub, where you can get the monorail, ferryboat, and various buses. For current route information, see our property transportation chart on the right, check the Transportation Guide (available upon arrival), or call 407-WDW-RIDE.

Bus service is the cornerstone of the Walt Disney World transportation system. It is efficient, if occasionally confusing. With a few exceptions, bus routes run every 15 to 20 minutes, from about one hour prior to park opening until about one hour after closing. Bus stops are clearly marked. Travel times vary by route. Be sure to build in extra time for travel. Tip: Special early morning "character breakfast" buses visit all Disney resorts to pick up guests—ask about it at your resort. Most buses are lift-equipped to accommodate wheelchairs and ECVs.

Dave boards one of the new buses, which can lower its front step for guests who have difficulty negotiating it

Monorail trains run along two circular routes for the Magic Kingdom. The express route visits the park and the Transportation and Ticket Center (TTC), while the resort route also stops at the Contemporary, Polynesian, and Grand Floridian resorts. A separate line connects the TTC to Epcot. Monorails run from 7:00 am until one and a half hours after park closing.

If you **drive**, you'll find ample parking at the parks. Use the map on the back flap of your PassPorter to get around the "World." **Tip**: Jot the row number and name of your parking lot in your PassPorter so you don't forget where you parked your car. Also, if you intend to take advantage of Extra Magic Hour (see page 114), we recommend you avoid driving to the Magic Kingdom—it may be difficult to get into the park early enough.

From several locales, **boats** (also known as launches or ferries) usher guests to the Magic Kingdom, Epcot, Disney-MGM Studios, Downtown Disney, and between some resorts. Boats generally depart every 15–30 minutes. At the Magic Kingdom, large ferries transport guests from the TTC to the gates, and a **railroad** encircles the park. Boats run between the Magic Kingdom and the nearby resorts. At Epcot, a "**Friendship**" shuttles between points in the World Showcase.

By far the most reliable and common method of transportation within the "World" is **walking**. You can't walk between most parks and resorts—it's too far and there are few sidewalks, making it unsafe. You will, however, walk a lot around the parks, the resorts, and even between some parks and resorts. Bring comfortable, broken-in, walking shoes!

Disney Property Transportation Chart

To get to the Magic Kingdom from...	Take the...
Polynesian, Contemporary, or Grand Floridian	Monorail (or walk from Contemporary)
Wilderness Lodge or Fort Wilderness	Boat
All other resorts	Bus
Disney-MGM Studios or Animal Kingdom	Bus to TTC, then monorail or boat
Epcot	Monorail to TTC, then monorail or boat
To get to the Disney-MGM Studios from...	**Take the...**
BoardWalk, Yacht & Beach Club, Swan & Dolphin	Boat or walk
All other resorts	Bus
Epcot or Disney's Animal Kingdom	Bus (or boat from Epcot)
Magic Kingdom	Monorail or boat to TTC, then bus
To get to Epcot from...	**Take the...**
Polynesian	Monorail (or walk) to TTC, then monorail
Contemporary or Grand Floridian	Monorail to TTC, then monorail
BoardWalk, Yacht/Beach Club, Swan/Dolphin, Studios	Boat or walk
All other resorts	Bus
Disney-MGM Studios or Animal Kingdom	Bus (or boat from Disney-MGM Studios)
Magic Kingdom	Monorail or boat to TTC, then monorail
To get to Disney's Animal Kingdom from...	**Take the...**
All resorts	Bus
Disney-MGM Studios or Epcot	Bus
Magic Kingdom	Monorail or boat to TTC, then bus
To get to Downtown Disney/Typhoon Lagoon from...	**Take the...**
Port Orleans, Old Key West, or Saratoga Springs	Boat *(DD Marketplace only)*, bus, or walk
All other resorts	Bus
All parks	Bus, boat, monorail, or walk (to a resort), then bus
To get to Blizzard Beach/Winter Summerland from...	**Take the...**
All resorts	Bus
To get to Fantasia Gardens from...	**Take the...**
All resorts *(guests at Swan, Dolphin, BoardWalk, and Yacht & Beach Club can walk)*	Travel to any park but Epcot, take a bus (or boat) to Swan, then walk
To get to Wide World of Sports from...	**Take the...**
All resorts	Go to Disney-MGM Studios, then bus
To get to Hoop-Dee-Doo Revue from...	**Take the...**
Magic Kingdom, Wilderness Lodge, or Contemporary	Boat to Fort Wilderness
Any other park	Bus to Fort Wilderness
Any other resort	Go to Magic Kingdom, then boat
To get to Disney Resort Hotel from...	**Take the...**
Any resort *(Swan, Dolphin, BoardWalk, Yacht & Beach Club are in walking distance of each other)*	Go to nearby theme park or Downtown Disney, then bus or monorail.

Note: TTC = Transportation & Ticket Center (see previous page)

Park Tips and Ratings

Check **park hours** by calling 407-WDW-INFO (407-939-4636) or by visiting http://www.disneyworld.com. Resort guests may also consult the World Update, park maps, and Times Guides on arrival.

Study the descriptions and maps to **familiarize yourself** with the names and themes of the lands before you arrive.

Check the **Tip Board** at the end of the main thoroughfare in each major park. Tip Boards are also located in Tomorrowland at the Magic Kingdom and in New York Street at Disney-MGM Studios. These tip boards are continuously updated with wait times and closings—even openings or sneak peeks of new attractions.

Plan your visit around the things that are **most important** to you or require advance planning (like restaurant seatings or show times). If you're just not sure, you can use our favorite touring plans included in each major park description as a starting point. In general, though, we feel it is more enjoyable to "go with the flow" from attraction to attraction within each land. Relax and have fun!

Park Ratings

We rate each park to help you make the best decisions. Even so, our ratings may differ from your opinions—use the ratings as a guide only.

Value Ratings range from 1 (poor) to 10 (excellent) and are based on **quality** (cleanliness, maintenance, and freshness); **variety** (different types of thing to do); and **scope** (quantity and size of things to do)—**overall value** represents an average of the above three values. **Magic Ratings** are based on **theme** (execution and sense of immersion); **excitement** (thrills, laughs, and sense of wonder); and **fun factor** (number and quality of entertaining activities)—**overall magic** represents an average of the above three values. We use a point accumulation method to determine value and magic ratings.

Readers' Ratings are calculated from surveys submitted by vacationers at our Web site (http://www.passporter.com/wdw/rate.htm).

Guest satisfaction is based on our and our readers' experiences with how different types of guests enjoy the park: ❤❤❤❤❤=love it ❤❤❤❤=enjoy it ❤❤❤=like it ❤❤=tolerate it ❤=don't like it

Magic Kingdom

The Magic Kingdom is a true fantasy land, playfully painted in bold strokes upon the canvas of the imagination. This is quintessential Disney and often the first park guests visit. It is located the furthest north of all parks, on the shore of the Seven Seas Lagoon.

AMBIENCE

The Magic Kingdom conjures up fantasy, nostalgia, youth, and most of all, **magic**. One thing it does especially well is blend the ordinary with the unusual, enhancing both to make it all seem better than reality. This giant, 107-acre playground attracts people of all ages to its bygone boulevards, tropical gardens, western saloons, and living cartoons. All roads lead to Cinderella Castle (see photo on next page), the crown of the Kingdom.

PARK LAYOUT AND HIGHLIGHTS

Five "lands" radiate like spokes from the hub of Cinderella Castle, located in the center of the park, with two more lands added on for good measure (see the fold-out map on page 124). Below are the lands in clockwise order, along with descriptions and headline attractions. See page 123a&b for our favorite itineraries and an at-a-glance list of attractions, and pages 128–136 for attraction details.

Main Street, U.S.A. *Headline Attraction:*	An early 1900s main street bustles with shops, eateries, a barbershop quartet, and City Hall. *Walt Disney World Railroad*
Adventureland *Headline Attractions:*	Walk to the beat of jungle drums in a paradise filled with pirates, parrots, crocs, and camels. *Pirates of the Caribbean, Tiki Room, Jungle Cruise, Aladdin*
Frontierland *Headline Attractions:*	Journey back to the American Frontier, complete with a fort and "mountain range." *Splash Mountain, Big Thunder Mountain Railroad*
Liberty Square *Headline Attractions:*	Step back in time to Colonial America with her presidents, riverboats, and a haunted house. *The Haunted Mansion, The Hall of Presidents*
Fantasyland *Headline Attractions:*	An enchanted, brightly-colored "small world" where elephants fly and teacups spin. *Winnie the Pooh, Dumbo, Mickey's PhilharMagic*
Mickey's Toontown Fair *Headline Attractions:*	Walk through a cartoon world to Goofy's farm, Mickey and Minnie's homes, and Donald's Boat. *Mickey's Country House, The Barnstormer at Goofy's Farm*
Tomorrowland *Headline Attractions:*	The future as imagined in the 1930s, complete with space flights, aliens, and time travel. *Space Mountain, Buzz Lightyear, Stitch Escape! (late 2004)*

Fold out the next page for touring plans and a handy attraction chart

Entertainment and Shopping at the Magic Kingdom

ENTERTAINMENT

Fun and excitement surround you in the Magic Kingdom. Live entertainment fills the streets with parades, performers, bands, and fireworks. Every afternoon the 20-minute long **Share a Dream Come True Parade** highlights favorite moments captured inside giant snow globes (see the parade route on page 124). We like to watch the parade from Frontierland or Liberty Square. The dazzling, new **Wishes fireworks show** is generally held nightly in peak seasons and on weekends at other times. Stand in front of Cinderella Castle to see Tinker Bell fly towards Tomorrowland before the 12-minute fireworks show. Mickey's Toontown Fair, Tomorrowland (near Indy Speedway), and Liberty Square are good viewing locations, too. Cinderella Castle is the backdrop for live musical stage shows, including **Cinderella's Surprise Celebration**—a fun show that spills out onto the forecourt stage, castle balconies, and even a turret! The **SpectroMagic** evening parade (if showing) adds lights and music to the fun and follows the same route as the day parade. Disney characters make appearances throughout the park, especially at park opening and after some shows. See the Times Guide for showtimes or visit Steve Soares' unofficial site at http://pages.prodigy.net/stevesoares.

Dave tries the Sword in the Stone behind Cinderella Castle

SHOPPING

Sure stops for general Disney merchandise include much of Main Street, U.S.A.—shops here are open for half an hour after park closing. Here are some of our favorite **themed shops**:

Shop	Land	What makes it special
The Chapeau	Main Street, U.S.A.	Hats with embroidered names
Disney Clothiers	Main Street, U.S.A.	Upscale yet casual Disney clothes
Agrabah Bazaar	Adventureland	Themed, open-air marketplace
Briar Patch	Frontierland	Great theme, Pooh & friends
The Yankee Trader	Liberty Square	Cooking and serving accessories
Tinker Bell's Treasures	Fantasyland	Disney costumes and dolls
Mickey's Star Traders	Tomorrowland	Sci-fi toys and gadgets

Making the Most of Epcot

If you arrive at Epcot via the **monorail**, you get a wonderful aerial view of Future World and a glimpse of World Showcase as the monorail glides on a track several stories above the park.

Your little ones will adore the **Kidcot Fun Stops** at each World Showcase pavilion. Cast members offer kids masks to color and decorate with beads and cut-outs–there's something different to add to the mask at each country. Allie loved it! Kids also love the play fountains on the promenade between Future World and the World Showcase, and behind Innoventions East. Come prepared with bathing suits under clothing and/or dry clothes and shoes.

Looking for **characters** at Epcot? Watch for a double-decker bus loaded with many Disney characters making the rounds, as well as various character meet and greets. Check your Times Guide, too!

Seniors should try to make more time for Epcot–you'll love it here!

Consider an Epcot **guided tour**. Several are offered, including Gardens of the World and Backstage Magic. See pages 242–243.

On your way out of the park in the evening, glance down at the path as you pass Innoventions–you'll discover **fiber optic lights** embedded in the pavement that make beautiful patterns.

Epcot is the dining capital of the "World." Nearly all the good stuff encircles the World Showcase Lagoon in an **international dining extravaganza**, offering everything from the upscale Bistro de Paris to tacos and beer at Cantina de San Angel. Future World offers less table-service dining, but it has a wide range of counter-service opportunities. See detailed descriptions on pages 208–214.

"**Friendships**" (boats) convey you to different points within World Showcase. You can usually get there faster if you walk, however.

Good viewing locations for **IllumiNations** go quickly. See page 150 for hints on getting the best possible view of the action.

After IllumiNations ends, step aside and wait for the crowds to thin. Take a **leisurely stroll** around the lagoon. Enjoy the music and the lights–you'll have a nice, quiet walk with very few people around. As a bonus, you'll miss the traffic in the parking lot and bus queues.

TIPS
NOTES
Planning | Getting There | Staying in Style | Touring | Feasting | Making Magic | Index | Notes & More

Getting to Epcot

BEST TIMES TO GO

The **best time to visit World Showcase** is when it first opens at 11:00 am, as most guests are still in Future World. It follows then that the **best time to tour Future World** is in the late afternoon and during dinner time (note that most attractions in Future World close at about 7:00 pm). World Showcase becomes congested in the evenings due to the many restaurants and IllumiNations show. Because of the focus on dining at Epcot, traditional lunch and dinner times are better spent at the attractions while others are eating. Along the same vein, you will find restaurants less busy and noisy if you dine before or after the normal lunch and dinner hour. **IllumiNations** is held nightly at park closing (usually 9:00 pm)—for a good view, start looking about one hour prior to showtime (see tips on page 150). If you've already seen IllumiNations, consider **dining during IllumiNations** for a quieter experience.

GETTING THERE

By Monorail—From the Magic Kingdom, Contemporary, Polynesian, or Grand Floridian, take the monorail to the Transportation & Ticket Center (TTC) and transfer to the Epcot monorail.
By Boat—From Disney-MGM Studios, Swan & Dolphin, BoardWalk, Yacht & Beach Club, boats go to Epcot's International Gateway.
By Bus—From other resorts, Disney-MGM Studios, or Disney's Animal Kingdom, buses take you directly to Epcot. From Downtown Disney, take a bus to a nearby resort and transfer to an Epcot bus, boat, or walk (tip: bus to BoardWalk and walk/boat to Epcot).
By Car—Take I-4 to exit 67 (westbound) or exit 62 (eastbound) and continue on to the Epcot toll plaza. All-day parking is available for $7 (free to resort guests and annual passholders).
By Foot—From the BoardWalk Inn & Villas, Yacht & Beach Club and Villas, Swan & Dolphin, and Disney-MGM Studios, Epcot is within walking distance. Follow the pathways towards the International Gateway entrance—it emerges between United Kingdom and France.

RATINGS

Ratings are explained on page 120.

Our Value Ratings:		Our Magic Ratings:		Readers' Ratings:
Quality:	8/10	Theme:	8/10	58% fell in love with it
Variety:	8/10	Excitement:	8/10	34% liked it well enough
Scope:	10/10	Fun Factor:	6/10	7% had mixed feelings
Overall Value:	**9/10**	**Overall Magic:**	**7/10**	1% were disappointed

Epcot is enjoyed by...	(rated by both authors and readers)	
Younger Kids: ♥♥♥	Young Adults: ♥♥♥♥	Families: ♥♥♥♥
Older Kids: ♥♥♥	Mid Adults: ♥♥♥♥♥	Couples: ♥♥♥♥♥
Teenagers: ♥♥♥♥	Mature Adults: ♥♥♥♥♥	Singles: ♥♥♥♥♥

Charting the Attractions at Future World (East)

Jennifer's Rating / Dave's Rating / Readers' Rating

Spaceship Earth [D-7] A-OK! 9 7 8

Go inside the huge geodesic sphere that towers above Epcot for a look at the development of communications technologies from cave paintings through the space age. Four-seat "time machine" vehicles take you up into the huge sphere past 65 Audio-Animatronics reenacting milestones in communication, before bringing you gently back to Earth to explore the Global Neighborhood exhibit. Adults should accompany and sit beside children. Visit at park opening or evening for shorter waits. Outdoor queue is mostly covered. Must transfer from wheelchair. **Allie's KidTip:** *"You'll love all the lights. And it's good for learning."*

Track Ride | E-Ticket | Ages 5 & up | Dark, steep incline, but gentle | Short waits | 15 min. ride

Global Neighborhood [D-7] A-OK! 3 3 5

Explore the world of modern telecommunications in this hands-on exhibit at the exit of Spaceship Earth. Sample Internet-based TV programs, place interactive phone calls (for a fee), and play communication games. Updated in 1999. You can also enter through the "backdoors" opposite Guest Relations. Some short queues. Wheelchair accessible. **Allie's KidTip:** *"I like the storytelling booth."*

Playground | B-Ticket | Ages 3 & up | Short waits | Unlimited

Innoventions East [C-6] A-OK! 6 5 6

If the latest gee whiz technology pushes your buttons, visit Innoventions—Epcot's two-part, high tech, hands-on trade exhibit. Innoventions East hosts exhibits on Internet activities (send electronic and video mail back home), forestry (play the "Total Treevia" game show), UL product testing (test the limits of products like a real UL engineer), and the House of Innoventions showcasing inventive products of the future (see the "next new thing" in home appliances). Short queues. Wheelchair accessible. **Allie's KidTip:** *"Games and shows and Aibo, a dog robot!" (For information on Aibo, visit: http://www.us.aibo.com.)*

Playground | B-Ticket | All ages | Noisy | Short waits | Allow about one hour to explore

Universe of Energy (Ellen's Energy Adventure) [B-7] A-OK! 5 6 7

Join Ellen Degeneres for a humorous crash course in energy, the stuff that powers our world. Widescreen films, thunderous sound effects, and gigantic Audio-Animatronics dinosaurs help tell the tale, sponsored by Exxon/Mobil. Ellen's cast includes Bill Nye, Jamie Lee Curtis, and Alex Trebek. Shows start every 17 minutes. Indoor queue with uncovered, outdoor, overflow queue. Small children should be accompanied by an adult. Effects may be too intense for small children and some adults. ECV must transfer to wheelchair. Wheelchair accessible. Assistive listening. No flash photo or video lights. **Allie's KidTip:** *"Dinosaurs!!! Oh, and it has a movie about energy, too. May be loud."*

Film/Ride | E-Ticket | Ages 4 & up | Dark, loud, dinosaurs | Med. waits | 8 min. intro 27 min. ride

Wonders of Life [B-7] A-OK! 7 5 7

Health and fitness take center stage at this pavilion with a thrill ride, shows, hands-on exhibits, and a healthy foods counter-service restaurant.

Pavilion | D-Ticket

Fitness Fairgrounds [B-7] A-OK! 5 3 5

Hands-on health and fitness-oriented exhibits, including sports games, fitness tests, quizzes, and demonstrations. Good refuge from the crowds. May not always be open. Inside Wonders of Life pavilion. Wheelchair accessible.

Playground | B-Ticket | All ages

Attraction descriptions and ratings are explained on page 127.

Tip: Sections highlighted in light blue (like the one below) indicate additions or significant changes at Walt Disney World since our 2003 edition!

Charting the Attractions at Future World (East)

(continued)

Jennifer's Rating | Dave's Rating | Readers' Rating

Body Wars [B-7] — A-OK! — 7 | 6 | 6

Get "shrunk" for an incredible medical rescue mission through the human body, utilizing the same technology as airline flight simulators. You'll be strapped into your seat and experience a rough ride—without really going anywhere. Indoor queue inside The Wonders of Life. Monitors show 1-min. introduction. 40"/102 cm height restriction. Young children require supervision. Health warning. Transfer from ECV to wheelchair. Closed captioning. Motion sickness warning. Non-moving rides available for ECV-bound and motion-sensitive—ask a cast member. **Allie's KidTip:** *"It's fun, but don't go on it after a big meal."*

Thrill Ride | D-Ticket | Ages 6 & up | Turbulent, bumpy, jerky | Med. waits | 5 min. ride

Cranium Command [A-7] — A-OK! — 6 | 5 | 8

Follow the progress of an inexperienced "Cranium Commando," Captain Buzzy, as he gets inside the mind of Bobby, an adolescent boy. This is a funny, fanciful film with star appearances and Audio-Animatronics characters. This show is especially appreciated by teens and their parents. Pre-show is standing only, while theater has seats. The indoor queue is located inside The Wonders of Life. Wheelchair accessible. Assistive listening devices. Reflective captioning. **Allie's KidTip:** *"It's funny. I liked the cartoon part best. It's loud in some parts."*

Show | D-Ticket | Ages 3 & up | Loud noises | Short waits | 5 min. intro, 12 min. show

The Making Of Me [B-7] — 6 | 7 | 5

Join comedian Martin Short for a humorously touching and sensitively-told film about childbirth and family life. Sex takes a backseat to romance, marriage, and family love. The "difficult" issues are deftly glossed-over. Indoor queue inside The Wonders of Life pavilion. Parental discretion advised. Wheelchair accessible. Reflective captioning. Assistive listening. **Allie's KidTip:** *"Don't go. They talk too much." (As you can see, the finer points may be lost on the young.)*

Film | C-Ticket | Ages 8 & up | Touchy topic | 15 min. film

Mission:SPACE [B-6] (Opened August 2003) — FP — 4 | 9 | 8

Prepare for your space flight at the International Space Training Center in Epcot's latest attraction. As a civilian "astronaut," you board a four-person training centrifuge to experience the sensations of liftoff and zero gravity. Your mission takes you from the earth to a Mars landing, including a 15 sec. slingshot around the moon. Sensations are intense—you could become queasy. Afterwards, Jennifer felt very dizzy, but Dave was fine. You can skip the simulator and go straight to the interactive, hands-on exhibits. Kids too young to ride enjoy the Space Base playground. Indoor, themed queue. 44"/112 cm height restriction. Young kids must be with an adult. Health and motion sickness warnings.

Thrill Ride | E-Ticket | Ages 8 & up | Disorienting | FASTPASS or long waits | 7 1/2 min. pre-show, 5 min. ride

Test Track [B-5] — FP — A-OK! — 8 | 8 | 9

Do you feel the need for speed? How does 65 miles per hour in a rapidly accelerating six-seat, open-air test vehicle on a tightly banked track sound? Learn how GM tests (and tortures) new vehicles and experience some of those tests. Wait in an incredibly noisy, slow queue and watch test gear whack auto parts. Use "singles queue" on the left for the shortest wait. Front seat offers more leg room. Indoor/outdoor queue. 40"/102 cm height restriction. Young children must be accompanied by adult. Health warning. Must transfer from wheelchair to ride. Assistive listening. Closed captioning. **Allie's KidTip:** *"It has dangerous curves. You should sit in the middle so you don't get sprayed!"*

Thrill Ride | E-Ticket | Ages 7 & up | Fast, jerky | FASTPASS or very long waits or singles line | 3 min. intro, 5 min. ride

Charting the Attractions at Future World (West)

Jennifer's Rating / Dave's Rating / Readers' Rating

Innoventions West [D-6] — 5 5 6

This is the other half of Innoventions, Epcot's two-part, high tech, hands-on trade exhibit. Tiny robot Tom Morrow 2.0 greets you at the entrance to introduce the exhibits on computing and high speed Internet technologies, e-mail postcards, Disney's interactive games, biotechnology, and a home theater demo that includes an impressive home-sized theater. Some short queues. Wheelchair accessible. **Allie's KidTip:** "Boring. The games are for little kids."

Playground | B-Ticket | Ages 6 & up | Noisy | Short waits | Unlimited

Ice Station Cool [D-6] — A-OK! — 6 5 7

Hot and thirsty? Walk through a delightfully chilly ice cave and emerge into an area where you can sample free soft drinks from around the world. The entrance is a hot weather delight, and some of these Coca Cola-owned beverages are eye openers in their own right. Self-serve machines let you sample away. You'll love some, hate others. "Beverly" will surprise you (no telling!). Wheelchair accessible. **Allie's KidTip:** "Try the watermelon soda. It's the best!"

Walkthru | A-Ticket | Ages 2 & up | Noisy, cold, sticky floor | Unlimited

The Living Seas [E-7] — A-OK! — 6 7 6

This immersion in sea life starts with a 7 min. film. Afterwards, explore hands-on exhibits and spend time marveling at the world's largest saltwater aquarium tank and artificial coral reef. View dolphins, sharks, manatees, and thousands of sea creatures. Check with a cast member for a demonstration schedule. For programs that explore the aquarium in more depth, see page 245. Rumor has it that Nemo (of "Finding Nemo" fame) may be included in the future. Indoor queue. Wheelchair accessible. Assistive listening. Reflective captioning. Closed captioning.

Pavilion | D-Ticket | All ages | Sharks! | Short waits | Allow about one hour

The Land [E-6] — A-OK! — 7 6 7

Agriculture and the environment take center stage, hosted by Nestlé. Ride, shows, food court, restaurant. "Behind the Seeds" guided greenhouse tour.

Pavilion | D-Ticket

The Circle of Life [F-6] — A-OK! — 6 5 6

Timon and Pumbaa from The Lion King set out to build the Hakuna Matata Village Resort—without regard to their ecosystem. Simba reminds them (and us) how important it is to protect the environment. Great photography. Sit in the front row for an unforgettable view. Indoor queue with benches. Inside The Land pavilion. Wheelchair accessible. Assistive listening. Reflective captioning. **Allie's KidTip:** "Simba tells us about the earth and how to take care of it."

Film | C-Ticket | Ages 3 & up | Short waits | 12 min. film

Food Rocks [F-6] — A-OK! — 6 5 5

As we go to press, we've heard a rumor that Food Rocks may close in the near future (as early as January 2004) to make way for Soarin' Over California (see page 150 for details). Food Rocks features favorite rock tunes as giant Audio-Animatronics foods impersonate famous music groups and teach about the basic food groups. Best seats are in the middle of the theater. Indoor queue features fun nutritional exhibits. Located inside The Land pavilion. Wheelchair accessible. Assistive listening. Reflective captioning. **Allie's KidTip:** "It's boring, but it teaches you not to have a lot of junk food."

Show | C-Ticket | All ages | Very loud | Short waits | 13 min. show

Attraction descriptions and ratings are explained on page 127.

Charting the Attractions at Future World (West)

(continued)

Jennifer's Rating | Dave's Rating | Readers' Rating

Living With the Land [F-6] FP A-OK!	7 6 7
Learn how modern agriculture is trying to serve the needs of a hungry world and protect the environment. Your boat cruises through a multimedia exhibit before entering Disney's amazing experimental hydroponic greenhouses. See veggies that may be served for dinner upstairs (more than 30 tons are produced annually). Flash photos are only allowed in the greenhouses. Indoor queues. Inside The Land pavilion. Must transfer from ECV to wheelchair to ride. Wheelchair accessible. Allie's KidTip: *"They have American Alligators!"*	**Boat Ride** D-Ticket Ages 4 & up Dark FASTPASS or med. waits 13 min. ride
Honey, I Shrunk the Audience [E-5] FP	8 8 8
Get shrunk by Dr. Wayne Szalinski (Rick Moranis) when a demonstration of his world-famous shrinking/enlarging machine goes awry. A funny story and spectacular visual and special effects make this a must-see show for those who aren't terrified by snakes, mice, and dogs. There's no need to sit up front. An indoor/outdoor queue leads to a touching and funny new pre-show film sponsored by Kodak. This may be too intense for children and some adults. Wheelchair accessible. Assistive listening. Reflective captioning. Allie's KidTip: *"It's scary. Take off your glasses when you get scared and just watch the TV."*	**3-D Film** E-Ticket Ages 8 & up Loud, intense FASTPASS or long waits 5 min. intro 13 min. film
Journey Into Imagination with Figment [E-5]	5 5 3
Figment, the cute purple dragon, comes roaring back to Epcot in a re-energized version of Journey Into Your Imagination. Figment and Dr. Nigel Channing (Eric Idle) team up to stimulate our imaginations with sight, sound, smell, a bit of whimsy, and music from Disney Legends Richard and Robert Sherman. Highlights include Figment's House and the final rendition of the theme song, One Little Spark. The ride still doesn't rate an "A," but you'll be charmed and tickled. Riders exit into the ImageWorks interactive playground. Indoor queue with outdoor overflow queue. Effects too intense for some children. Wheelchair accessible. Allie's KidTip: *"It seems like you get sprayed by a skunk."*	**Track Ride** C-Ticket Ages 5 & up Portions are very dark, loud, with bright flashes Med. waits 6 min. ride
ImageWorks: Kodak "What If" Labs [E-5] A-OK!	6 6 7
Hands-on sound and image exhibits and a gift shop, at the exit to Journey Into Your Imagination. Digital portraits (which can be sent via e-mail), inventive photo gifts, and a unique Kodak photo lab. "Backdoor" entrance through shop. Allie's KidTip: *"It's cool! Check out the floor piano!"*	**Playground** B-Ticket All ages Allow 30 min.

Fountain of Nations

You can't help but notice Epcot's spectacular Fountain of Nations at the heart of Future World. You may even have been cooled (or chilled) by its drifting mists. But have you really taken the time to savor this carefully choreographed water ballet? Every fifteen minutes the fountain dances to another musical number, with special seasonal music during the Christmas holidays. Thousands of water jets and lights are computer-synchronized to the rhythms and melodies. 30,000 gallons of water course through the fountain, and 2,000 gallons can be airborne at one time, shooting up to 150 feet high. While the mists are more chilling at night, the fountain's lights make the display that much more magical. Enjoy a pastry at Fountainview Café, or a meal at Electric Umbrella, and catch the show!

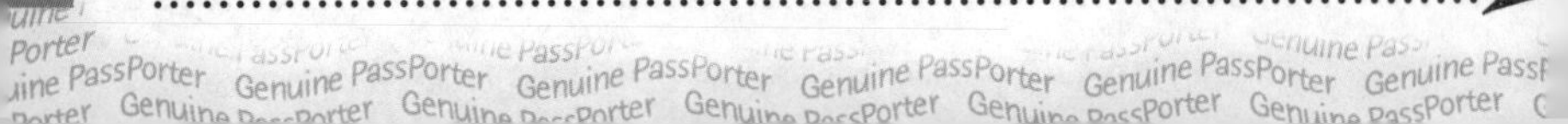

Charting the Attractions at World Showcase

(clockwise order)

Jennifer's Rating / Dave's Rating / Readers' Rating

Mexico [B-4] A-OK!	7 6 8
Enter Mexico's Mayan pyramid to find yourself in a magical, twilit village plaza with a volcano smoking ominously in the distance. Enjoy a fine exhibit of art and artifacts, eateries, a ride (see below), shops, and musicians. **Allie's KidTip:** *"Don't worry, that's not a real volcano. Looks like it, though!"*	**Pavilion** D-Ticket All ages Low light

El Rio del Tiempo [B-4] A-OK!	4 4 5
Tour Mexico's past and present as your boat drifts down the "River of Time." A combination of Audio-Animatronics, music, and short film clips tell the tale of this thousands-of-years-old culture. Highlights include a skeleton-costumed band and a fiber optics fireworks display. Your boat floats past diners at the San Angel Inn restaurant. You could call this ride the Mexican version of "it's a small world," complete with dancing dolls. Not worth a long wait. Indoor queue inside the Mexico pavilion. Transfer from ECV to wheelchair to ride. Wheelchair accessible. **Allie's KidTip:** *"Be sure to look up and see the fireworks!"*	**Boat Ride** C-Ticket All ages Dark, but very tame Short waits 7 minute cruise

Norway [B-3] A-OK!	6 6 7
This taste of Norway features a Viking ship play area, shops, the Maelstrom ride (see below), eateries, and an ancient wooden church. Tours available. Peek inside the church–it's open to the public. **Allie's KidTip:** *"The ship is fun to play in. You'll feel like a Viking. If you see a troll, rub its nose for luck."*	**Pavilion** C-Ticket All ages Allow 30 min.

Maelstrom [B-3] FP A-OK!	6 5 7
Board a boat for a refreshing ride through the Norway of fact and fancy. Trolls, Vikings, and a North Sea storm are all part of a fanciful ride that is much tamer than the name implies. The few "drops" are little more than a bounce. The Viking boats deposit you in an attractive indoor fishing village, prior to viewing a filmed travelogue that some enjoy and some don't–walk right through the theater if you decide to skip the film. Indoor queue. Must transfer from wheelchair to ride. Assistive listening. Reflective captioning. Refurbished in late 2002. **Allie's KidTip:** *"Don't be scared of the life-size polar bears."*	**Boat Ride** D-Ticket Ages 5 & up Small drops and dark FASTPASS or med. waits 15 min. ride

China [B-3] A-OK!	4 5 6
Explore China through a film (see below), art and photography exhibits, gardens, eateries, and the Yong Feng Shangdian department store. Visit a half-scale model of Beijing's Temple of Heaven. Acrobats and gymnasts perform. **Allie's KidTip:** *"When you walk into the temple to see the movie, look up."*	**Pavilion** C-Ticket All ages Allow 20 min.

Reflections of China [A-3]	7 6 7
Experience marvels of China in a sweeping, 360° motion picture. Grand scenes of the Great Wall, the Yangtze Gorge, and Beijing's Forbidden City alternate with views of bustling cities. The film–previously called "Wonders of China"–was improved in 2003 with vibrant new footage of modern China including Macao and Hong Kong. You must stand to view. Indoor waiting area with wooden benches. Wheelchair accessible. Assistive listening devices. Reflective captioning. **Allie's KidTip:** *"Don't sit down or you'll miss part of the movie."*	**Film** C-Ticket Ages 6 & up Could cause dizziness Short waits 13 min. show

Attraction descriptions and ratings are explained on page 127.

Charting the Attractions at World Showcase

(continued in clockwise order)

Attraction	Jennifer's Rating	Dave's Rating	Readers' Rating
Germany [B-1]	3	4	7
Italy [C-1]	5	4	6
The American Adventure [D-1]	6	5	7
The American Adventure Show [D-1]	7	7	7
America Gardens Theatre [D-1]	6	7	6
Japan [E-1] A-OK!	8	7	7
Morocco [E-1] A-OK!	7	6	7

Germany [B-1]

Steep-roofed stone buildings, oompah bands, eateries, and shops evoke a quaint German square. Look for the model railroad, and listen for the glockenspiel that chimes on the hour. **Allie's KidTip:** *"Find the train set in the toy shop."*

Pavilion | C-Ticket | All ages

Italy [C-1]

Disney captures the spirit and architecture of Venice in this Italian piazza. Eateries, shops, jugglers, music, and entertainers in a Mediterranean garden set the scene. **Allie's KidTip:** *"Make a good wish at King Neptune's fountain."*

Pavilion | C-Ticket | All ages

The American Adventure [D-1]

This all-American pavilion is halfway around the lagoon from Future World. Home to the American Adventure show, theater, a hamburger joint (what else?), wonderful singers, and shops. **Allie's KidTip:** *"See the fife and drum corps."*

Pavilion | D-Ticket | All ages

The American Adventure Show [D-1]

Ben Franklin and Mark Twain take you on a patriotic tour of U.S. history. A large cast of Audio-Animatronics characters including Thomas Jefferson, while Susan B. Anthony and Martin Luther King Jr. take center stage in filmed segments. Famous events are recreated and famous Americans share their ideas. Don't expect a critical view of history, however. The wide stage is easier to see if you don't sit in the front. See Times Guide for shows. Indoor queue. "Voices of Liberty" or "American Vybe" may sing. Wheelchair accessible. Assistive listening. Reflective captioning. **Allie's KidTip:** *"Look on the walls for the statues."*

Show | D-Ticket | Ages 5 & up | Dark at times | Med. Waits | 15 min. intro with singers | 30 min. show

America Gardens Theatre [D-1]

Live, musical entertainment is the hallmark of this outdoor theater on the edge of the lagoon. Check the Times Guide for show times—usually three half-hour shows daily. Seating is free, but the front rows may be reserved for "package" guests (see page 236). Shows are visible from the promenade. Seating is on benches with sycamore trees providing some shade. Wheelchair accessible. **Allie's KidTip:** *"Sit in the front because it's covered and the back is just trees."*

Show | C-Ticket | Ages 2 & up | Short waits | Most shows 30 min.

Japan [E-1] A-OK!

The sound of Taiko drummers may draw you to this pavilion, featuring traditional Japanese architecture and gardens, entertaining exhibits, eateries, a lounge, and a Japanese department store. A beautiful and peaceful retreat. **Allie's KidTip:** *"Go through the Japanese garden. The goldfish are neat."*

Pavilion | C-Ticket | All ages | Allow 20 min.

Morocco [E-1] A-OK!

Morocco's Moorish architecture, art exhibits, exotic cuisine, live entertainers, and crafts beckon to the adventuresome traveler. Much is hidden from the casual visitor—take the "Treasures of Morocco" tour for a better look. You'll find a character meet-and-greet area virtually hidden across from Restaurant Marrakesh, plus artisans and cultural representatives scattered throughout. Excellent shopping opportunities. **Allie's KidTip:** *"You'll feel like you want to go to Africa. I like the entertainers here, too."*

Pavilion | C-Ticket | All ages | No scares | Allow about 20–30 min. to explore

Charting the Attractions at World Showcase

(continued in clockwise order)

Jennifer's Rating / Dave's Rating / Readers' Rating

France [F-2] — A-OK!	7 7 7
The Eiffel Tower, cobblestone streets, eateries, shops, street performers, and a wide screen film (see below) combine to evoke the essence of France. Allie's KidTip: *"The moving statue is cool, but it moved to Italy!"*	**Pavilion** All ages D-Ticket

Impressions de France [F-2] — A-OK!	9 9 7
The beauty and romance of France's villages, cities, and countryside come to life in a breathtaking film. Fabulous scenery, wonderful 200° widescreen photography, and the best musical soundtrack at Walt Disney World (great French classical tunes), make this one of our favorites. Cool, dark theater offers seating and welcome relief. Shows on the hour and half-hour. Wrought iron benches and small exhibits make even the indoor, air-conditioned queue enjoyable. Wheelchair accessible. Assistive listening. Reflective captioning. Allie's KidTip: *"You get to see Notre Dame, like in 'Hunchback of Notre Dame.'"*	**Film** D-Ticket Ages 5 & up Dark theater, loud music Short waits 18 min. film

United Kingdom [E-3] — A-OK!	7 6 7
This is Florida's British Colony, full of quaint shops, gardens, a restful park with live entertainment (check the Times Guide for The British Invasion band—they're excellent!), a busy pub, and deliciously British eateries. Well-themed. Allie's KidTip: *"You gotta play in the hedge maze! And there's really cool music."*	**Pavilion** C-Ticket All ages will enjoy

Canada [E-4]	5 5 7
The architecture and natural beauty of Canada are captured in a 360° movie (see below), nifty waterfall, gardens, shops, eateries, and live music.	**Pavilion** C-Ticket

O Canada! [E-4] — A-OK!	7 5 6
Experience the natural and man-made wonders of Canada by way of a Circle-Vision 360° film. Swooping aerials and dramatic scenery highlight this tour encompassing the Rockies and old-world Montreal. Shows start every 20 minutes. Stand to view. Indoor queue. Wheelchair accessible. Assistive listening. Reflective captioning. Allie's KidTip: *"The animals are cute! But you can get tired of standing up for 18 minutes."*	**Film** C-Ticket Ages 5 & up Dark, a little dizzying 18 min. film

Attraction descriptions and ratings are explained on page 127.

Coming to the World Showcase: Spain?

One of the oldest topics in the Disney rumor mill is, "What will be the next World Showcase pavilion?" Norway became Epcot's 11th nation in 1988. Will Spain make that an even dozen? Spain was wooed for Epcot's 1982 opening, and hopes for a Spain pavilion resurfaced in 2002 after public statements by the Spanish government. Maybe this time it will actually happen. What might we expect? Medieval castles, Moorish palaces, fabulous art, legendary metalcraft, flamenco dancers, hearty food and drink, and the seafaring heritage of one of the world's great empires? Of course, nobody should expect the Spanish Inquisition. Whatever comes of these talks, a finished pavilion would still be several years off, so stay tuned. Watch our Web site for updates!

Making the Most of IllumiNations

IllumiNations: Reflections of Earth brings every night to a spectacular close. Brilliant fireworks and a rousing, original musical score fill Epcot's World Showcase Lagoon every evening at park closing, heralding the creation of Earth. A shower of sparkling comets paves the way, a huge globe glides across the lagoon to take center stage, and a pageant of breathtaking scenery, wildlife, and the peoples of the earth plays across a giant video display covering the continents of the globe. Lasers, blazing torches, and more fireworks tumble forth as the music builds to a rousing climax. Although the show is visible anywhere around the lagoon, there are definitely **better viewing sites**. You can judge a viewing site well in advance of the show as you stroll around the lagoon, or check our map on page 140. A clear view of the water (watch those tree limbs) at the center of the lagoon is critical, as is a clear view of the sky. It also helps if the wind is to your back or side (to avoid fireworks smoke). The bridge between France and the United Kingdom is a prime (and popular) location. Norway is another good viewing spot. Or try for a 7:30 pm priority seating at the Rose & Crown. Check-in at the podium early and request a patio table. You may get lucky with a great view. If not, enjoy your meal anyway—diners are invited outside to stand and enjoy the show. Another place to stay seated is at Cantina de San Angel in Mexico. Arrive at least 90 min. early for a lagoon-side table. We also highly recommend the excellent views from the lagoon-side patios in the UK and France, if they aren't already occupied by private parties.

The World Showcase Lagoon at dusk

New Attraction: Soarin' Over... Epcot?
Rumors have been flying for a while now, and chances are, Disney will announce this new attraction just after we go to press. Reports have this new attraction being added to The Land pavilion (Food Rocks would close to make room for the queue area), and opening in 2005. What is it? Just the most popular attraction at Disney's California Adventure park at the Disneyland Resort (California). Guests are belted into seats resembling large hang gliders and lifted skyward for a glorious flight over California's most breathtaking scenery. Your seats move to help simulate your glider's swooping flight, and with the help of an eye-filling Omnimax-style movie and other sensory input you'll be amazed and exhilarated by this fabulous attraction.

Disney-MGM Studios

Disney-MGM Studios is the Hollywood that never was. Yet it always will be, on 154 acres that spotlight the golden era of the glamorous silver screen. Disney-MGM Studios is located southwest of Epcot, and is connected to Epcot by Friendship boats.

AMBIENCE

Tinseltown never looked so good. All the glamour, glitz, and pageantry of Hollywood comes out to greet you at the Disney-MGM Studios. Disney's rendition of Hollywood Boulevard is done up in 1930s art deco architecture, and an old-fashioned water tower (complete with Mickey ears) sets the stage. And you can't miss the 122-foot tall version of **Mickey's Sorcerer's Hat**, representing the magic of show business and Disney animation. Disney-MGM Studios gives you a behind-the-scenes glimpse at movie-making as well as an opportunity to get involved in shows and tours. Celebrities may put in live appearances at Disney-MGM Studios as well, complete with a procession down Hollywood Boulevard and a handprint ceremony. There may also be chances to see upcoming movies being filmed on the actual soundstages that make their home here. The whole effect is of being a special guest at a major movie studio in the heart of Hollywood.

PARK LAYOUT AND HIGHLIGHTS

Unlike other parks, Disney-MGM Studios' layout is free-form, much like Hollywood's artistic personalities (see park map on page 154). See pages 153a&b for daily touring itineraries and an attractions-at-a-glance list, and pages 156–160 for attraction details.

Hollywood Boulevard Area *Headline Attraction:*	Stroll among the stars—this is the "main street" of Tinseltown in its heyday. *The Great Movie Ride*
Sunset Boulevard Area *Headline Attractions:*	Step back in time to the Hollywood that never was on this famous, palm-lined boulevard. *Rock 'n' Roller Coaster, Tower of Terror, Beauty and the Beast*
Echo Lake Area *Headline Attractions:*	Learn the magic behind spectacular stunts and effects, and go for a journey into outer space. *Star Tours and Indiana Jones Epic Stunt Spectacular*
New York Street Area *Headline Attractions:*	Visit a movie set evoking old-time New York City. It even has "towering" skyscrapers! *Muppet*Vision 3-D, Honey, I Shrunk the Kids Movie Set Adv.*
Mickey Avenue Area *Headline Attractions:*	Peek behind-the-scenes in soundstages, the "backlot," and animators' studios. *Millionaire, Voyage of the Little Mermaid, One Man's Dream*

Fold out the next page for touring plans and a handy attraction chart

Entertainment and Shopping at Disney-MGM Studios

ENTERTAINMENT

Entertainment is simply a matter of course at the Disney-MGM Studios. The funny, unique "**streetmosphere**" performers make their home along famous boulevards of Hollywood and Sunset, as well as Echo Lake. Dressed in 1940s-style garb, they're responsible for all sorts of on-the-street shenanigans. Keep your eyes open—you don't know when they may appear. The "**Disney Stars and Motor Cars**" parade is held each afternoon, showcasing several Disney characters. The parade route is marked on the map on page 154. Be sure to stake out your viewing spot along the parade route about 30 min. in advance. Come evening, it's Mickey versus villains in **Fantasmic!** at the Hollywood Hills Amphitheater. Fantasmic! is a spectacular mix of live action, music, and fireworks. The huge outdoor amphitheater seats 6,900 at this nightly show. Fantasmic! may be held more often during busy seasons (later shows may have shorter waits and better seating). Fantasmic! is popular with many guests, though we can take it or leave it. A Fantasmic! Meal Package may be available with special seating—see page 217.

Jennifer refuses to ride the Twilight Zone Tower of Terror again

SHOPPING

General merchandise shopping is centered near the park entrance on Hollywood and Sunset Boulevards. Nearly every major ride and attraction has its own **themed shop**, too. All of the ride-related shops can be entered without going on the ride. Here are our favorite shops:

Shop	Location	What makes it special
Crossroads of the World	Hollywood Blvd.	Guidemaps, Times Guides, ponchos
Sid Cahuenga's	Hollywood Blvd.	One-of-a-kind movie memorabilia
Celebrity 5 & 10	Hollywood Blvd.	Custom embroidery and engraving
Keystone Clothiers	Hollywood Blvd.	Quality Disney clothes
The Beverly Sunset	Sunset Blvd.	Disney Villain clothing and gifts
Animation Gallery	Mickey Avenue	Collectibles and animation cels
Stage 1 Company Store	New York Street	Quirky shop with Muppets!
The Writer's Stop	New York Street	Books! (We can't resist 'em!)
Tatooine Traders	Echo Lake	Star Wars items, fun theme

Making the Most of Disney's Animal Kingdom

Disney's Animal Kingdom is a paradise, where delightful and often subtle details can work their magic if you **take the time** to notice. This is not a do-it-all-in-a-day-or-die park. Slow down, revel in the beauty, wonder at the animals, and enjoy yourselves!

Trails lead off in all directions—don't be afraid to explore them. Keep your map handy, however, as it is easy to get turned around in this park. Watch your footing, too, as paths are winding and appear "weathered" in some places. Wear comfortable shoes.

This park is one big photo op! Bring plenty of **film** and **batteries**, and even **binoculars** for viewing animals.

Dining options here are a bit more limited than at the other parks, but quality almost makes up for quantity. The counter-service eateries are particularly good here. See the listings on pages 218–219.

If it's open, the outdoor, sheltered **seating** by Flame Tree Barbecue is a wonderful spot, whether you want to dine or simply rest. Tables and dining pavilions are set amidst lush tropical gardens.

Not all **animals** can be seen all the time. On the plus side, you'll see new ones each time, making subsequent visits unique.

Beverages sold in Disney's Animal Kingdom do not generally come with lids and straws, for the animals' safety. Consider bringing your own covered mug or bottle if you want to keep drinks.

It always seems **hotter** at Disney's Animal Kingdom than at any other park, possibly because there are so few attractions with air conditioning. Be prepared with hats, sunglasses, sunscreen, and ways to keep yourself cool, like plenty of cold water and/or a personal misting fan ($16). Take advantage of the mist-spraying fans throughout the park when you need relief. Take frequent breaks in air-conditioned spots—try the eateries, shops, or attractions like It's Tough to be a Bug! or Rafiki's Planet Watch.

Seniors should go carefully when touring this park due to the heat. Nearly every attraction is outdoors, which means there's limited air conditioning. There's plenty of shade while you stand around or watch the shows, though. An ECV is particularly helpful at this park if you have any difficulty with walking or stamina.

TIPS

NOTES

Getting to Disney's Animal Kingdom

BEST TIMES TO GO

Most guests arrive in the mid-morning and leave in the afternoon, making the **early morning and late afternoon** the best times to visit. Not only are the crowds thinner, but the park's animals prefer the cooler temperatures found in the earlier and later parts of the day, so you're more likely to see them. You may have more luck spotting animals during and after a rainstorm, too. When you **first arrive**, head for Dinosaur or Kilimanjaro Safaris to pick up a FASTPASS (or just go ahead and ride if the wait is short enough). Another strategy is to ride one of the popular attractions early and then immediately get a FASTPASS for another attraction. Check the **Times Guide** for show times and durations, and plan your day accordingly—these shows can chew up more time than you'd expect. You can use our touring plans on page 163a to give you an idea of what you can expect to do in one day. Finally, if your park pass allows it, consider spreading out your visit over a **couple of days** rather than packing it all into one. Midday is best avoided due to the big crowds, the intense heat/sun, and sleeping animals.

GETTING THERE

By Bus—All resorts, Epcot, and Disney-MGM Studios have buses that take you directly to Disney's Animal Kingdom. From the Magic Kingdom take the boat or monorail to the Transportation & Ticket Center (TTC) and catch a bus. From Downtown Disney take a bus to an Epcot-area resort and catch a Disney's Animal Kingdom bus. **By Car**—From I-4 take exit 65 (eastbound or westbound) and follow signs to Disney's Animal Kingdom parking. All-day parking is available for $7 (free to resort guests with resort I.D. and annual passholders). The parking lot is some distance from the entrance. You'll appreciate the free trams to the front gate.

Note: There is no boat or foot access to this theme park.

RATINGS

Ratings are explained on page 120.

Our Value Ratings:		Our Magic Ratings:		Readers' Ratings:
Quality:	8/10	Theme:	9/10	44% fell in love with it
Variety:	7/10	Excitement:	7/10	33% liked it well enough
Scope:	6/10	Fun Factor:	6/10	15% had mixed feelings
Overall Value:	**7/10**	**Overall Magic:**	**7/10**	8% were disappointed

Animal Kingdom is enjoyed by... (rated by both authors and readers)		
Younger Kids: ♥♥♥	Young Adults: ♥♥♥♥	Families: ♥♥♥♥♥
Older Kids: ♥♥♥♥	Mid Adults: ♥♥♥♥	Couples: ♥♥♥♥
Teenagers: ♥♥♥♥	Mature Adults: ♥♥♥♥	Singles: ♥♥♥♥

Charting the Attractions at The Oasis, Discovery Island, and Camp Minnie-Mickey

Jennifer's Rating | Dave's Rating | Readers' Rating

The Oasis [C-6] A-OK! 7 | 6 | 7

All guests pass through this lush jungle habitat of gurgling waters and exotic plants on their way in and out of the park. Many of the paths lead to small animal exhibits. Look for shady seats in a rocky grotto. Wheelchair accessible. **Allie's KidTip:** *"Can you spot camouflaging lizards anywhere here?"*

Walkthru | A-Ticket | All ages | Allow 20 min.

Camp Minnie-Mickey Character Greeting Trails [A-5] A-OK! 4 | 4 | 6

Meet Mickey, Minnie, and other Disney characters in the shade of four rustic, open-air pavilions—each character has his/her own queue. Low-key atmosphere. Bring your autograph book or use PassPorter's autograph section, and have lots of film handy. Wheelchair accessible. **Allie's KidTip:** *"Don't be shy."*

Pavilion | A-Ticket | All ages | Med. waits

Festival of the Lion King [A-6] A-OK! 8 | 8 | 9

This colorful, dynamic pageant set to music from "The Lion King" features singers, dancers, acrobats, and floats, and really sets your hands to clapping! The 1,000-seat theater-in-the-round affords many great vantage points, though we suggest you arrive early to get the best seats. Try the first or last shows for shortest waits. Lots of audience participation and lots of fun! This theatre is now completely enclosed and has air conditioning. Outdoor queue is uncovered. No external video lights. Wheelchair accessible. Assistive listening. **Allie's KidTip:** *"If you sit in the front you might get asked to play music!"*

Live Show | E-Ticket | Ages 2 & up | Long waits (check showtimes in Times Guide) | 30 min. show

Pocahontas and Her Forest Friends [B-6] A-OK! 4 | 2 | 4

Pocahontas and Grandmother Willow are featured in a conservation-themed live animal show. Seating is outdoors with light shade. First three center rows of seats reserved for kids under 11 (no parents), and volunteers are chosen. Brief glimpses of animals. Doors open 15 minutes before show. Check times guide for shows. Outdoor queue is uncovered. Wheelchair accessible. Assistive listening. **Allie's KidTip:** *"If you're not too shy, sit with the kids in the front."*

Live Show | C-Ticket | Ages 3 & up | Live animals and birds | 13 min. show

It's Tough to be a Bug! [D-4] FP A-OK! 8 | 8 | 9

Long lines snake around the Tree of Life on Discovery Island for a humorous show hosted by Flik from "A Bug's Life" and featuring a pint-sized cast of animated and Audio-Animatronics characters. 3-D effects, creepy sensations, and yucky smells can terrify the bug-wary. The queue offers close-up views of the tree's animal sculptures. Look for hilarious movie posters in the "lobby." Air conditioned, 430-seat theater. Outdoor queue is uncovered. Special effects may be too intense for some. Wheelchair accessible. Assistive listening. Reflective captioning. Note that the entrance is marked on the map on page 163. **Allie's KidTip:** *"Sit between two grown-ups just in case you get scared."*

3-D Show | E-Ticket | Ages 6 & up | Dark, smells, bug noises, "stings" | FASTPASS or med. waits | 8 min. show

The Tree of Life and Discovery Island Trails [C-3] 6 | 5 | 8

Tropical gardens and exotic animals surround the Tree of Life at the center of the park. Walk the winding paths, and get a close-up view of the tree, too. How many animals can you see in the trunk and roots? (Hint: 325, including a "hidden Mickey.") Wheelchair accessible. **Allie's KidTip:** *"The animals are cool."*

Walkthru | A-Ticket | All ages | Allow 30 min.

Attraction descriptions and ratings are explained on page 127.

Charting the Attractions at Africa and Rafiki's Planet Watch

Jennifer's Rating | Dave's Rating | Readers' Rating

Kilimanjaro Safaris [B-1] FP A-OK! **8 8 9**	
Board a safari truck to explore 100 acres of African habitat teeming with lions, giraffes, crocodiles, ostriches, gazelle, and many other live animals. Wildlife may be plentiful or scarce, since it's free to roam. Disney also includes a story line in case the animals are feeling shy, but the story loses its charm after the first ride. You should expect the ride to get very bumpy (so hang on tight). We recommend you ride first thing in the morning or late afternoon, when the animals are more active. Sit in outside seats for best views and photos. The safari closes at dusk. Outdoor queue is covered, and has overhead monitors. Height restriction for children riding in front two seats. Young children should be accompanied by an adult. Health warning. Transfer from ECV to wheelchair to ride. Wheelchair accessible. Assistive listening. Closed captioning. Allie's KidTip: *"Be on the lookout for the baby elephant (Little Red)."*	**Ride** E-Ticket Ages 4 & up Bumpy, live birds and animals, "close escapes" FASTPASS or long waits 19 min. vehicle ride
Pangani Forest Exploration Trail [B-1] A-OK! **6 8 7**	
Animal lovers will stroll enthralled through this exhibit of African wildlife in an artfully-built natural habitat. African birds, hippos, meerkats, and a troop of gorillas make their home here. Hands-on exhibits in the naturalist's hut add interest. A habitat–the Endangered Animal Rehabilitation Centre–calls attention to the African bushmeat crisis. The meerkat viewing area is especially popular, and plan to spend extra time in the aviary. Walk slowly or sit, and the wonders will unfold. Allow several hours if you love to watch animals. Early morning or late afternoon is the best time to visit. Wheelchair accessible. Closed captioning. Allie's KidTip: *"You'll love all the animals and birds!"*	**Walkthru** D-Ticket All ages Live animals, birds flying overhead Short waits Allow at least 30 minutes
Wildlife Express Train to Rafiki's Planet Watch [C-1] A-OK! **5 4 5**	
All aboard! This train at Harambe station is the only route into or out of Rafiki's Planet Watch (formerly called Conservation Station). Enjoy a ringside glimpse of the park's backstage animal care areas. A guide describes the sights as the train chugs slowly along the track. Note: Everyone must disembark at Rafiki's Planet Watch. As always, Disney's eye for detail shines forth around Harambe Station and onboard the train. The best seats are in the front row. Themed, outdoor queue is mostly covered. Wheelchair accessible. Assistive listening. Allie's KidTip: *"Sit in the front row of the train to see better."*	**Train Ride** B-Ticket All ages Glimpses of backstage Short waits 15 min. ride (each way)
Rafiki's Planet Watch [off map] A-OK! **5 6 5**	
This is the park's most remote and most underappreciated attraction, a must-visit for animal lovers of all ages. Formerly called Conservation Station, it was renamed and jazzed-up with live Animal Encounter shows, more hands-on activities, and visits from Tarzan and Rafiki. The 5-min. walk from the train station to Rafiki's Planet Watch is interspersed with fun, conservation-themed exhibits and activities. See short films, use interactive video displays, and relax in darkened rain forest "soundscape" booths. View the park's nursery and veterinary hospital. Enjoy the cleanest, most animal-friendly petting zoo anywhere (it even has a hand-washing fountain at the exit). The Wildlife Express Train from Harambe is the only way into or out of Rafiki's Planet Watch. Wheelchair accessible. Assistive listening. Allie's KidTip: *"Look for the fishes, lizards, and frogs. And go to the petting farm!"*	**Exhibit** C-Ticket All ages Backstage, educational fun Live animals Short waits Allow at least 90 minutes for a good exploration

Charting the Attractions at Asia

Jennifer's Rating | Dave's Rating | Readers' Rating

Flights of Wonder [D-2] A-OK! 7 7 7

Duck! Owls or hawks may fly right above your head during a show starring over 20 species of free-flying exotic birds and their talented animal handlers. Guano Joe, a tour guide from Anandapur Tours, adds some comic relief to this conservation-themed show. Guests are selected from the audience to join in the action. Afterwards everyone has a chance to come down to ask questions, view the "stars" up close, and take photos. Sit near the aisles for the closest animal encounters. Outdoor, shaded theater. Outdoor queue is uncovered. Theater opens 15 minutes beforehand. No food or drink allowed. Leave strollers at the door. Wheelchair accessible. Assistive listening. Allie's KidTip: *"Volunteer to go on the stage! I'm too shy to do it, but it looks like fun."*

Live Show | D-Ticket | Ages 3 & up | Live birds overhead | Med. waits (showtimes listed in Times Guide) | 25 min. show

Kali River Rapids [F-2] FP A-OK! 8 8 8

Drift through jungle mists, unexpected geysers, and smoking devastation on a somewhat daring ride in a 12-person raft. The roaring rapids boast one thrilling (albeit tame) drop. Just when you think it's all over Disney tosses in one last little surprise. You will get wet—possibly damp, more likely soaked—and there's no way to predict (or control) how much. A small storage area is available on board, but it won't keep things very dry. Some guests wisely bring a poncho and a dry change of clothing—plastic ponchos are available for sale nearby. Shoes/sandals must be worn at all times. Long lines are common, but they snake through fascinating Asian architecture rich with fine detail. 42"/107 cm height restriction. Special effects may be too intense for some children and adults. Health warning. Must transfer from wheelchair to ride. Allie's KidTip: *"Don't worry, the fire is real, but the wood is not. If you go backwards on the drop, be prepared to get soaked."*

Raft Ride | E-Ticket | Ages 7 & up | Med. drop, flames, geysers, and you will get wet! | FASTPASS or long waits | 5 min. cruise

Maharajah Jungle Trek [E-1] A-OK! 6 8 7

Walk a winding path through ancient ruins in a lush Asian setting. Tigers, tapir, fruit bats, deer, antelope, a Komodo dragon, and a walk-through aviary filled with tropical birds highlight this beautifully designed zoo. Artfully hidden barriers make you feel like you can reach out and touch the animals, but fortunately for them (and us) you can't. Cast members are on hand to enrich your animal viewing adventure. We think the tigers, aviary, and bats are the highlights, but you'll find your own favorites. Be sure to pick up a guidemap on your way in. Animal lovers may be tempted to spend hours here—bring your camera! Wheelchair accessible. Allie's KidTip: *"Tigers! How many can you find?"*

Walkthru | D-Ticket | All ages | Live animals, birds overhead | Short waits | Allow at least 30 minutes

Expedition: Everest

Disney's newest "mountain" is rising in Asia, between Kali River Rapids and the Tarzan Rocks theater. Called "Expedition: Everest," the new family attraction is slated to open in 2006, and is another "take" on a runaway mine train. This time, you'll ride up and into the 200-foot-tall Mount Everest on a rickety tea plantation train for a startling encounter with the fearsome Yeti (abominable snowman). Your train will hurtle through darkness and even backwards before you return safely to your mountain base camp. While Disney has borrowed concepts from Disneyland's classic Matterhorn, Big Thunder Mountain Railroad, and Dinosaur (among others), this has all the markings of a great, new ride.

Charting the Attractions at DinoLand, U.S.A.

Jennifer's Rating | Dave's Rating | Readers' Rating

The Boneyard [F-5] — A-OK!	7 5 6
Kids can climb, slide, crawl, scamper, excavate, and explore to their hearts' content in a funky dinosaur dig. Parents are welcome, too. One of the places at Disney's Animal Kingdom with a water spray for hot days. Keep an eye on your young ones! Bring a towel and dry clothes. Wheelchair accessible. **Allie's KidTip:** *"You can get wet here if you are hot. I love this place!"*	**Playground** B-Ticket Ages 1 & up Allow 30 min.

Dinosaur [E-7] — FP — A-OK!	7 7 8
Intrepid riders are sent back through time to fetch a dinosaur before the dinos (and the riders) become extinct. Be prepared to be bounced, jostled, and scared as your Time Rover vehicle hurtles into the past and races through a dark forest. The "pre-show" and science exhibits in the indoor queue areas make the wait interesting. Front row "outside" seats for maximum thrills, inside seats for the less bold. No flash photography. 40"/102 cm height restriction. Young children should be accompanied by an adult. Effects may be too intense for some. Health warning. Must transfer from wheelchair to ride. Closed captioning. **Allie's KidTip:** *"Cover your eyes in the dark parts if you're scared. Ask your grown-ups to tell you when a dinosaur shows up so you can look."*	**Thrill Ride** E-Ticket Ages 7 & up Dark, loud, very scary, rough and bumpy ride FASTPASS or long waits 3.5 min. ride

Tarzan Rocks! [G-4] — A-OK!	7 8 7
This rockin' live concert extravaganza features hit tunes from the animated film, Tarzan, performed by a pumped-up cast of singers, dancers, acrobats, rollerbladers, and musicians. Tarzan, Jane, and Terk swing by for part of the show. Don't look for a plot—there isn't one, just loud, solid rock and roll. Shows every 75 minutes. The outdoor, covered theater opens 20 minutes before show time. No external video lights. Uncovered outdoor queue. Wheelchair accessible. Assistive listening. **Allie's KidTip:** *"This is good, but very loud!"*	**Live Show** E-Ticket Ages 4 & up Very loud Med. waits (check times) 28 min. show

Primeval Whirl [G-6] — FP — A-OK!	7 7 8
Chester and Hester cooked up a dizzy bit of fun for Primeval Whirl, a "wild mouse"-styled coaster. Your round "time machine" car spins as it goes around tight curves, over mild drops, and even through the jaws of a dinosaur (what else?). Two identical coasters each boast 13 spinning, four-person ride vehicles. 48"/122 cm height restriction. Health warning. Must transfer from wheelchair to ride. **Allie's KidTip:** *"The dips aren't as scary as they look."*	**Coaster** D-Ticket Ages 7 & up Fast, drops FASTPASS 2.5 min. ride

TriceraTop Spin [F-6] — A-OK!	5 5 7
Dumbo morphs into a Dino! Sixteen dinosaur-shaped, four-rider cars swoop around a huge, spinning toy top. Part of Chester & Hester's Dino-Rama! (see description below). Must transfer from ECV to wheelchair to ride. **Allie's KidTip:** *"Sit in the front and make the dinosaur tilt forward or backward."*	**Ride** C-Ticket Ages 2 & up 1.5 min. ride

Chester & Hester's Dino-Rama!

Chester & Hester, the operators of DinoLand's crazy roadside-style gift shop, have created a roadside "carnival" with two attractions and about a half-dozen games of skill or chance. Play midway games for $2 a pop and maybe win a prize. Games include Raptor Race, Meteor Strike, and Fossil Fueler.

Typhoon Lagoon Water Park

Typhoon Lagoon is a 56-acre water park with lush foliage, lazy rivers, roaring waterfalls, and a huge surfing "lagoon." The water park is located near Downtown Disney West Side.

AMBIENCE

Legend has it that this was once the Placid Palms Resort in Safen Sound, Florida, a tropical hideaway nestled on a sparkling lagoon. Disaster struck when a typhoon raged through the sleepy resort, flooding the lagoon and tossing ships about. In its wake they discovered sharks in the harbor, a surfboard through a tree, and ships scattered everywhere. Most amazing was the Miss Tilly shrimp boat, impaled on a craggy mountain (Mt. Mayday) that kept trying to dislodge the boat with a huge plume of water. Water was everywhere, forming waterfalls, rapids, pools, and surf. In true Disney form, misfortune was turned into luck and the Typhoon Lagoon water park was born. Or so the story goes.

PARK LAYOUT

The park's attractions are arrayed around the its focal point, the gigantic, 2½-acre **wave pool** at the foot of Mt. Mayday. The "mountain" offers the advantage of height to several tube and body slides that slither down it. Around the perimeter of the park is a "lazy river" called Castaway Creek, offering a relaxing retreat to swimmers drifting lazily along in inner tubes. Finding your way around the park can be confusing at first—the dense foliage and meandering paths recreate the tropical look quite convincingly. Just keep in mind that one path encircles the park, and you can see Miss Tilly perched atop Mt. Mayday from almost everywhere. This park is worth exploring, too—the lush Mountain Trail on Mt. Mayday presents photo opportunities, and many hidden groves and glens offer quiet getaways.

EATING

Leaning Palms is the largest of the cafés, offering combos with burgers ($7.30), hot dogs ($7.50), sandwiches ($8.35), pizza ($9.15), wraps ($8.20), salads ($4.25), and ice cream ($2.37). A kid's peanut butter and jelly sandwich meal is $3.99 and includes chips, drink, and a sand pail. **Happy Landings** has ice cream and a fun water play area where you can take aim at the guests drifting by on Castaway Creek. **Typhoon Tilly's Galley & Grog** (open seasonally) has fish & chips, snacks, ice cream, and beverages. **Let's Go Slurpin'** offers soft drinks, alcoholic drinks, and snacks. **Low Tide Lou's** has hot dogs, sandwiches, and drinks. **Surf Doggies** offers hot dogs and turkey legs. Three **picnic areas** have shade and tables.

Charting the Attractions at Typhoon Lagoon

Attraction	Description	Jennifer's Rating	Dave's Rating	Readers' Rating	Details
Typhoon Lagoon Surf Pool [C-4] A-OK!	*Waves in the world's largest inland wave pool at the base of Mt. Mayday change every half-hour, alternating between gently bobbing swells and six-foot body-surfing waves that arrive 90 seconds apart. Youngsters enjoy the two Bay Slides to the far left, and the small tidal pools (Blustery Bay and Whitecap Cove) near the front. Observe the waves before entering.* Allie's KidTip: *"Jump up when the waves come to get carried away, but don't scrape yourself on the bottom."*	8	8	9	**Pool**; E-Ticket; All ages; Surfing waves may scare kids
Castaway Creek [Entry points: A-4, A-2, D-2, D-3, D-5] A-OK!	*Relax on a half-mile, 20-minute circuit around the park on inner tubes. Catch a free tube at one of five entrances. Note where you entered, too!* Allie's KidTip: *"This is nice and relaxing. Little kids will like the yellow inner tubes the best."*	9	8	8	**Pool**; D-Ticket; Ages 3 & up
Ketchakiddee Creek [A-2]	*Several fountains, two body slides, and a 30-sec. tube ride—just for little squirts (48"/122 cm or under). Shady, thatched-roof shelters for waiting parents.*	6	6	7	**Playground**; B-Ticket
Keelhaul Falls [A-1] A-OK!	*A slow, solo tube ride with a surprise! (Warning—ride spoilers ahead.) Rafters plunge unexpectedly into a pitch-black tunnel about half the way down.* Allie's KidTip: *"The waterfall is fun! You don't get as wet as you think you will."*	6	7	7	**Tube slide**; Ages 7 & up; C-Ticket
Mayday Falls [B-1] A-OK!	*Like Keelhaul falls, this tube ride is solo. Unlike it, Mayday Falls is fast and bumpy, twisting and turning through caves and waterfalls.* Allie's KidTip: *"This is bumpy. Think of something that is also bumpy and then you won't be scared."*	5	6	7	**Tube slide**; Ages 7 & up; C-Ticket
Gang Plank Falls [B-1] A-OK!	*Bring the family on this three-to-five person raft ride down the mountain. Watch out for waterfalls and those twisty-turny rafts!* Allie's KidTip: *"This is fun! Hold on tight because you go a little fast, but that's no problem."*	8	6	6	**Raft slide**; Ages 4 & up; C-Ticket
Humunga Kowabunga [C-1]	*This is the ultimate thrill slide at Typhoon Lagoon, shooting sliders down one of two slides in less than 10 seconds. Viewing bleachers at the bottom for observers. 48"/122 cm height requirement. Health requirement. Ages 9 & up.* Allie's KidTip: *"It's scary—don't go on it. P.S. It gave me a wedgie."*	1	5	7	**Body slide**; E-Ticket; Very fast, steep drop
Storm Slides [D-1]	*Three body slides (Stern Burner, Jib Jammer, and Rudder Buster) corkscrew through waterfalls and caves. Viewing bleachers at the bottom. Ages 8 & up.*	5	6	7	**Body slides**; E-Ticket
Shark Reef [E-1] A-OK!	*Swim with the sharks! Line up at Hammerhead Fred's Dive Shop to get your snorkel equipment (free use with park admission), shower, listen to a five-minute lesson, then snorkel across the small, chilly, saltwater lagoon. You may see a variety of fish, perhaps even three kinds of passive sharks. Bring an underwater camera. Scuba dive for an extra fee.* Allie's KidTip: *"I love the sharks!"*	9	8	8	**Pool**; E-Ticket; Ages 6 & up; Cold, salty water

Making the Most of Typhoon Lagoon

TIPS

A **refillable mug** ($10) uses barcode scanners so you can refill without cast supervision. You can purchase a new refill barcode ($5) on future visits. A Typhoon Lagoon mug can be used at Blizzard Beach and vice versa as long as you buy the appropriate refill.

You can **keep time** by Miss Tilly on top of Mt. Mayday–she blows and sprays a 50-foot plume of water every half hour!

Avoid **two-piece suits** on slides–they may come down the slide at a different speed than you. Also, swimsuits with rivets, buckles, or exposed metal are not permitted at the park. Wear water shoes–the sand and pavement can get quite hot.

Use a single-use, **underwater camera** for great photos.

Get your first taste of **scuba** in a special section of the Shark Reef. Cost is $20 for the first 30 min. and $15 for the rest of your party or for repeat dives. Pay at the booth near the dive shop. Brief lessons are provided, and parents can attend their kids without renting.

NOTES

Children under the age of 10 must be accompanied by an adult.

You can rent lockers ($5–7) and towels ($1 each). You may wish to bring your own towels from your hotel room rather than rent them at the park–the towels are practically the same size. If you do rent, get towels when you're done swimming. Changing rooms are also available. Life vests are provided free of charge (with a refundable deposit). Some personal flotation devices may be permitted.

Park hours: generally open by 10:00 am, closed at 5:00 pm or later. A one-day pass (with tax) is $33.02/adults and $26.63/kids 3–9.

RATINGS

Ratings are explained on page 120.

Our Value Ratings:		Our Magic Ratings:		Readers' Ratings:
Quality:	7/10	Theme:	8/10	76% fell in love with it
Variety:	8/10	Excitement:	7/10	21% liked it well enough
Scope:	3/10	Fun Factor:	7/10	3% had mixed feelings
Overall Value:	**6/10**	**Overall Magic:**	**7/10**	0% were disappointed

Typhoon Lagoon is enjoyed by... (rated by both authors and readers)		
Younger Kids: ♥♥♥♥	Young Adults: ♥♥♥♥♥	Families: ♥♥♥♥
Older Kids: ♥♥♥♥♥	Mid Adults: ♥♥♥	Couples: ♥♥♥
Teenagers: ♥♥♥♥♥	Mature Adults: ♥♥♥	Singles: ♥♥♥

Finding Your Way at Typhoon Lagoon

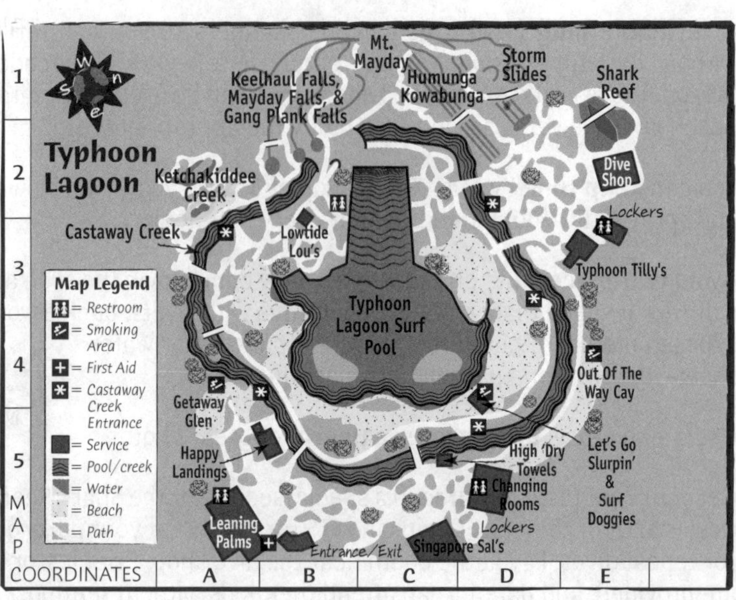

BEST TIMES

Typhoon Lagoon is very popular during the **hot months** and gets crowded fast—arrive early, as gates close when the park reaches capacity. It's also wise to stake out your beach chairs early as the good ones are grabbed quickly. We prefer to visit when it's a bit **cooler** as crowds are lighter and the water is heated. The park closes for a month in the winter (usually November or December)—call 407-560-4141 and confirm that it is open if you intend to visit the park. Beyond that, **weekdays** are better than weekends (locals love to visit the park). Visit in the **late afternoon** when the park empties a bit and the sun is less intense. The park may **close during storms**—when it re-opens it may be nearly empty. If you arrive when there are long lines, bypass them by getting your tickets at the Automated Ticket Vending Machines now available here.

GETTING THERE

By Bus—All Disney resorts have direct buses to Typhoon Lagoon. From Magic Kingdom, Epcot, Disney-MGM Studios, and Disney's Animal Kingdom, take a bus or monorail to a nearby resort and transfer to a Typhoon Lagoon bus (which may also be the Downtown Disney bus). Allow about 30-60 minutes if you travel by bus.

By Car—Take exit 67 off I-4, take the first exit and turn right on Buena Vista Dr.—the park is on the right. From Downtown Disney, turn right to Buena Vista Dr. and the park is on the left. Free parking.

Blizzard Beach Water Park

Is it a water park, or a ski resort? The Blizzard Beach water park brings the chills and thrills of a Colorado winter to the warm Florida sun. Ski jumps, toboggan rides, and slalom runs zip you past snow that never melts in Disney's most action-oriented water park.

AMBIENCE

Disney's Imagineers scattered magic white stuff over the rocks and pines of towering Mount Gushmore to create a water park that'll make you shiver on the hottest August day. Oh, don't worry, the water is always a warm 80 degrees, but just a look at some of those water slides can freeze your insides. Luckily, Disney never abandons the idea of family fun—even the meekest snow bunny will have a ball!

ATTRACTIONS

Before you "hit the slopes" you'll discover the park's **"base lodge"** facilities—the major food, merchandise, and locker room areas. Then, as you face the mountain the Tike's Peak children's area will be to your right. Straight ahead are two bridges over Cross Country Creek, the drift-along tube ride that encircles the mountain and most of the fun. Additional lockers can be found close to the action, near Downhill Double Dipper on the left, and Ski Patrol on the right. Of course, Mount Gushmore dominates the park in every way. Its slopes are home to nearly two dozen lanes of slides and flumes. Most slides can be seen from the Lodge area, but Runoff Rapids is tucked away on the back slope of the mountain. You can also watch your daredevils in comfort, from shaded grandstands at the bottom of many slides. Three footpaths and a chairlift scale the 90-foot (9-story) mountain. After your first ascent on foot in the hot, Florida sunshine you'll know why folks wait patiently for the chairlift, which takes you to the top in the comfort of a three-person, umbrella-shaded chair (32"/81 cm height restriction, under 48"/122 cm must be accompanied by an adult).

EATING

Water park meals are never fancy, which is fine when you're only wearing a swimsuit. **Lottawatta Lodge** serves up cheeseburgers ($3.65), hot dogs ($3.55), pizza ($4.95), chicken sandwiches ($4.70), Caesar salads ($6.25), and ice cream ($2.50). A kid's meal is $3.99 with a choice of mac & cheese, hot dog, or chicken strips, plus chips, drink, and a toy. **Avalunch** and **The Warming Hut** offer hot dogs, sandwiches, ice cream, and usually close before dinnertime. The thirsty line up at **Frostbite Freddie's Frozen Freshments**, **Polar Pub**, and **The Cooling Hut**. There are also **picnic areas**.

Charting the Attractions at Blizzard Beach

Jennifer's Rating / Dave's Rating / Readers' Rating

Summit Plummet [D-2] — 2 5 9

Only the boldest ride the world's highest body slide, which drops 120 feet. Go feet first, cross your arms, and it's over in eight seconds. Be prepared for a steep drop and a wedgie! 48"/122 cm height requirement. Health requirement.

Body Slide | E-Ticket | Ages 9 & up

Slush Gusher [D-2] — 3 6 8

Ninety-foot high double-bump slide is the second-tallest body slide in the park. One-piece suits recommended! 48"/122 cm height requirement. Ages 8 & up.

Body Slide | D-Ticket

Downhill Double Dipper [C-2] — 5 7 8

Race head-to-head on a half-enclosed inner tube slide. Your race results are flashed on a scoreboard. 48"/122 cm height requirement. Ages 8 & up.

Tube Slide | D-Ticket

Snow Stormers [C-2] A-OK! — 7 5 8

Zig and zag your way down this three-flume, family-friendly slalom mat slide. 12-second ride. Allie's KidTip: "Fun, but it's a little bumpy." Ages 6 & up.

Mat slide | C-Ticket

Toboggan Racers [D-2] A-OK! — 6 5 7

On your mark, get set, go! Race headfirst down an eight-lane mat slide. 10-second ride. Allie's KidTip: "Push yourself off to go down." Ages 6 & up.

Mat slide | D-Ticket

Teamboat Springs [D-2] A-OK! — 9 8 9

Whitewater-loving families can pack up to six in a large, round, river raft for a long, twisting ride—at 1,400 feet it is the longest ride of its kind anywhere. Allie's KidTip: "Hold on to the bottom of the raft when you go down."

Raft slide | D-Ticket | Ages 4 up

Runoff Rapids [D-2] — 8 7 7

Ride a tube down this twisty, turny, family-friendly course. Three different open and enclosed slides. Up to two can share a tube on the open slides. Allie's KidTip: "Pick up your behind over the bumps, or it won't feel good."

Tube slide | C-Ticket | Ages 6 & up

Cross Country Creek [Entry points: B-4, A-4, B-2, C-1, E-3, D-4] A-OK! — 8 7 7

Float around the park on a moderately-flowing creek. Enter and exit at any of seven spots around the park. Return to your starting point in 20 minutes. Allie's KidTip: "Don't get wet under the freezing waterfalls."

Pool | D-Ticket | Ages 2 & up

Melt Away Bay [B-3] A-OK! — 7 6 7

Bob in the sedate waves of a one-acre wave pool. Kids under 10 must be with an adult. Allie's KidTip: "The tide pools are cool to play in!" All ages.

Pool | C-Ticket

Ski Patrol Training Camp [D-3] A-OK! — 8 7 7

Scaled-down area for kids 12 and under. Try Snow Falls slide, Cool Runners tube slalom, and Thin Ice Training Course—a walk across a field of "ice floes." Allie's KidTip: "If an iceberg is far away, lean back to move toward it."

Playground | D-Ticket | Ages 6-12

Tike's Peak [D-5] — 6 5 7

Even the littlest ones have a miniature version of the park, with slides, wading pools, and play fountains. Must be 48"/122 cm or shorter. Ages 0-6.

Playground | C-Ticket

Making the Most of Blizzard Beach

This park has almost **no shade**. Bring (and use) plenty of waterproof sunscreen and cover-ups!

Play **miniature golf** at Winter Summerland, adjacent to the water park. See page 193 for more on this imaginative mini golf course.

Pick up a **map** on your way in to locate the lockers ($5–7) and towels ($1). Life jackets are free if you leave an ID card and/or deposit.

You'll find **chaise lounges** wherever you go, but on busy days follow the path around the back end of the mountain, where you'll find secluded lounging areas and the main entrance to Runoff Rapids.

This is the **"big thrill"** water park, so it draws a young crowd. Typhoon Lagoon is a better choice for families.

Wear **water shoes** to ward off the heat of the sand and sidewalks.

If you ride the big slides, bikinis are a very risky fashion statement. You'll have better luck with a **one-piece suit**.

The **Beach Haus** near the entrance sells just about anything you may have forgotten or lost, from sunscreen to swimsuits.

When the **summer weather** is at its hottest, the parking lots fill-up early. Use Disney buses instead, which are always admitted.

Children under the age of 10 must be accompanied by an adult.

Park hours: generally open by 10:00 am, closed at 5:00 pm or later. A one-day pass (with tax) is $33.02/adults and $26.63/kids 3–9.

Ratings are explained on page 120.

Our Value Ratings:		Our Magic Ratings:		Readers' Ratings:
Quality:	7/10	Theme:	8/10	94% fell in love with it
Variety:	8/10	Excitement:	8/10	2% liked it well enough
Scope:	4/10	Fun Factor:	7/10	2% had mixed feelings
Overall Value:	**6/10**	**Overall Magic:**	**8/10**	2% were disappointed

Blizzard Beach is enjoyed by... (rated by both authors and readers)

Younger Kids: ♥♥♥♥	Young Adults: ♥♥♥♥♥	Families: ♥♥♥♥♥
Older Kids: ♥♥♥♥♥	Mid Adults: ♥♥♥	Couples: ♥♥♥
Teenagers: ♥♥♥♥♥	Mature Adults: ♥	Singles: ♥♥♥♥

TIPS

NOTES

RATINGS

Planning · Getting There · Staying in Style · Touring · Feasting · Making Magic · Index · Notes & More

Finding Your Way at Blizzard Beach

BLIZZARD BEACH PARK MAP

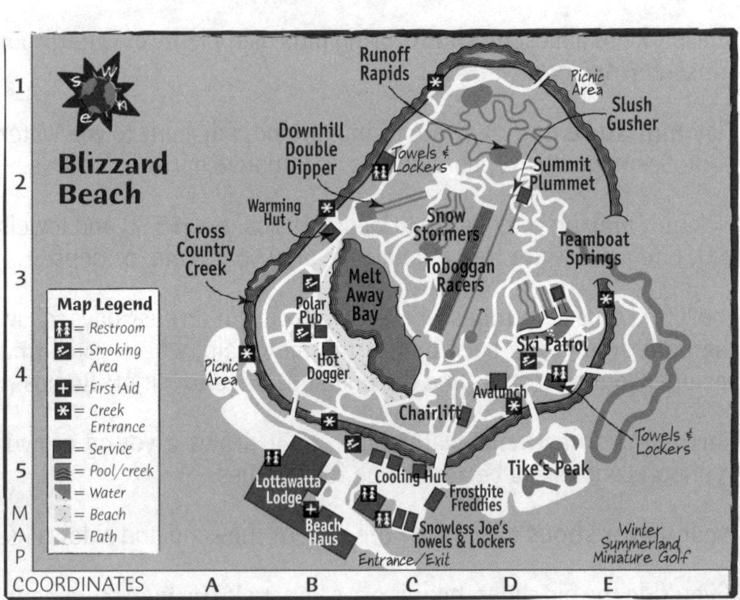

BEST TIMES

Thanks to the heated waters you'll be comfortable throughout the **cooler months**, and the sun is kinder. The crowds are thinner, but the days are shorter, and an overcast, rainy winter day can make life miserable. Note that the park may be closed on Fridays and Saturdays in the cooler months. Summer at Blizzard Beach brings **huge crowds** that arrive early in the day. If the park reaches capacity, the gates close to all. By **mid-afternoon** the crowds have thinned, as those who are worst-wilted have packed it in. That's a good time to arrive, refreshing yourself after a long morning at nearby Disney's Animal Kingdom. Operating hours vary with the season, so check before you trek. Unlike ski areas up north, the park is generally closed in January and part of February.

GETTING THERE

By Bus—All resorts and Disney's Animal Kingdom have direct buses to Blizzard Beach. From Disney-MGM Studios, take the Coronado Springs bus. From Epcot, take the Disney's Animal Kingdom Lodge bus. From the Magic Kingdom and Downtown Disney, take a bus or monorail to a Disney resort and board a bus to Blizzard Beach. We recommend you take Disney transportation when you can, because the parking lot can fill up on busy days.
By Car—From westbound or eastbound I-4, take exit 65 (west on Osceola Parkway), exiting at Buena Vista Drive. Free parking.

River Country Water Park

River Country was closed for the 2002 and 2003 seasons, and we expect it to remain closed in 2004. Check with Disney for its current status. We've left this description intact, however, as Disney continues to reserve the right to re-open it. River Country was Disney's original water park offering relaxing soaks, sandy beaches, and good, clean fun. It is located within Fort Wilderness Resort, near Pioneer Hall on the shore of Bay Lake.

AMBIENCE

River Country offered weary vacationers the chance to experience an old-fashioned swimmin' hole that even Tom Sawyer would appreciate. A private cove on Bay Lake set the stage for the fun, complete with the sort of flora and rock formations you might expect to see. The pace here was laid-back. The white sand, shady hollows, and rustic charm made for a lazy day at the lake.

ATTRACTIONS

All good things come in three's, including River Country. The first of the three sections that made up the water park was **Bay Cove**, fashioned from an inlet off Bay Lake. Its clean waters and sandy bottoms were perfect for plunging into from the rope and tire swings, ship's boom, and platforms. **Whoop 'n' Holler Hollow** made its home here with two twisting-and-turning water flumes. The inner tubes on **White Water Rapids** drifted down a gentle 330-foot long chute, with swirling whirlpools along the way to add excitement. Three smaller slides pleased the 48"/122 cm and under crowd. The second section of the park was **Upstream Plunge**, a 330,000-gallon heated pool that offered more than a simple alternative to the lake. Here the daring could venture **Slippery Slide Falls**, two short and sharply-inclined slides that ended about seven feet above the water (splash!). The third and last section of the park was **Kiddie Cove**, a miniature version of Bay Cove for the little squirts, complete with tame slides and fountains. A scenic **nature trail** also began here, offering a tour of the wetlands along the edge of Bay Lake.

EATING

River Country offered just one regular eatery: **Pop's Place** was open at lunch and dinner for an All-American selection of hot dogs, sandwiches, cole slaw, pretzels, and beverages. Typical menu items included a Chicken Strip Basket with a beverage and choice of cole slaw, chips, or fries; a kid's hot dog meal with a beverage and chips; and a brownie. During the busier months, the **Waterin' Hole** opened with a limited menu of snacks and the usual soft drinks. **Pioneer Hall** next door remains open, and has a buffet restaurant plus a trading post with snacks.

Finding Your Way at River Country

RIVER COUNTRY PARK MAP

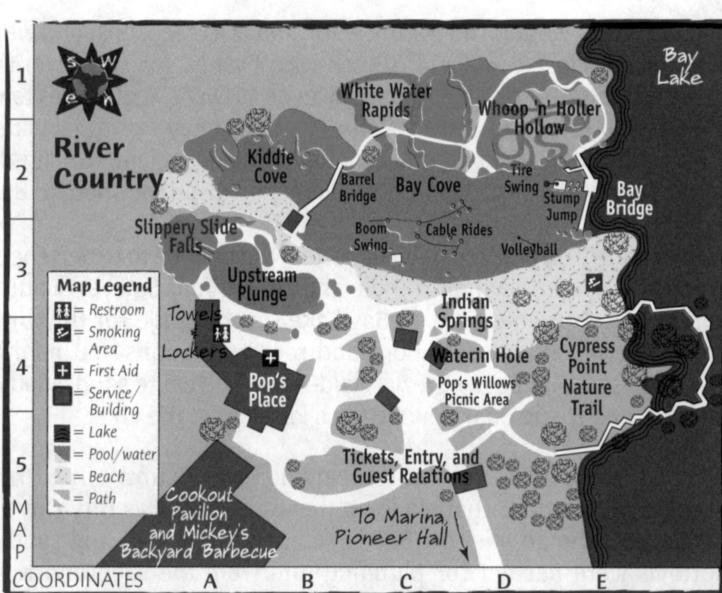

BEST TIMES

River Country was smaller and more laid-back than Typhoon Lagoon or Blizzard Beach. Crowds weren't common. **Spring and summer** were great times to visit, when the other water parks were overflowing with swimmers escaping the Florida heat. We suggested you **avoid visiting in the cooler months** as the large lake section (Bay Cove) wasn't heated. Brrr! River Country was typically open by 10:00 am and closed at 5:00 pm. It only opened on certain days of the week, and generally closed in the fall and winter. Call 407-824-4321 to check the park's status and hours (if open).

GETTING THERE

By Bus—From Disney-MGM Studios and TTC, take a Fort Wilderness bus to Pioneer Hall and follow signs. From Epcot, Disney's Animal Kingdom, or Downtown Disney, take a Fort Wilderness bus to the Outpost Depot, transfer to an internal bus, get off at Pioneer Hall, and follow signs. Resort guests should bus to a park first.

By Boat—Take a boat from the Magic Kingdom, Contemporary, or Wilderness Lodge directly to Fort Wilderness. After arriving at Fort Wilderness, River Country is located to the right. Look for the signs. We strongly recommend this route whenever possible.

By Car—Take I-4 to exit 67 (westbound) or exit 62 (eastbound) and drive four miles to the toll plaza, then follow the signs to Fort Wilderness/River Country. Parking is available, plus a free shuttle.

Downtown Disney

If "heading downtown" is your idea of rest and recreation, the Walt Disney World Resort's Downtown Disney district is a major treat. From the world's largest Disney Store to mind-boggling Lego sculptures, super dining, and thrilling entertainment, you'll have a ball Downtown.

AMBIENCE

Downtown Disney has three unique **districts**. The **Marketplace** is a charming village of shops, **Pleasure Island** thrives on its vibrant night life, and **West Side** is the urban-style shopping, dining, and fun capital of the "World." Downtown Disney's pedestrian-only streets and sprawling layout avoid the "mall" feeling completely. This is one of the brightest, cleanest, safest, and most satisfying downtowns, anywhere.

SHOPPING

Downtown Disney satisfies the urge to "shop 'til you drop." Ok, so you can shop at every theme park, but there's no admission charge here, and you'll find much more than Disney merchandise. The **Marketplace** shops are Wonderful World of Memories (Scrapbook Center), The Art of Disney, Disney's Days of Christmas, Eurospain (crystal shop), Disney at Home, Once Upon a Toy, Summer Sands (resortwear), Disney's Pin Traders, Lego Imagination Center, Pooh Corner, Studio M (portrait studio), Team Mickey's Athletic Club, and the World of Disney (the world's largest Disney Store). 2003 brought two new additions—Basin (bath and facial products) and The Earl of Sandwich (eatery). The Gourmet Pantry is gone, but a candy shop remains. **West Side** shopping features Celebrity Eyeworks Studio, Disney's Candy Cauldron, DisneyQuest Emporium, Guitar Gallery, Hoypoloi (sculpture gallery), Magnetron (magnets), Mickey's Groove (funky Disney gifts), Sosa Family Cigars, Starabilias (collectibles), Virgin Megastore, and the new Wetzel's Pretzels. Magic Masters offers top-flight magic gear, demos, and even a hidden room where guests can learn to use their magic tricks. **Pleasure Island** shops are discussed on page 190. Eateries and entertainment venues often have shops. Packages can be delivered to your Disney resort!

PLAYING

Downtown Disney builds fun into nearly every shop and restaurant, but four spots put entertainment first. Movie fans flock to the **AMC 24 Theatres Complex**, the Southeast's largest—their theaters sport stadium seating, most with retractable armrests. The innovative **Cirque du Soleil** also makes its home Downtown—see page 184. **DisneyQuest**, Disney's indoor "theme park," gets its own write-up on pages 185–188 as does **Pleasure Island** is on pages 189–192.

Feeding Your Family at Downtown Disney

DOWNTOWN DISNEY MAP

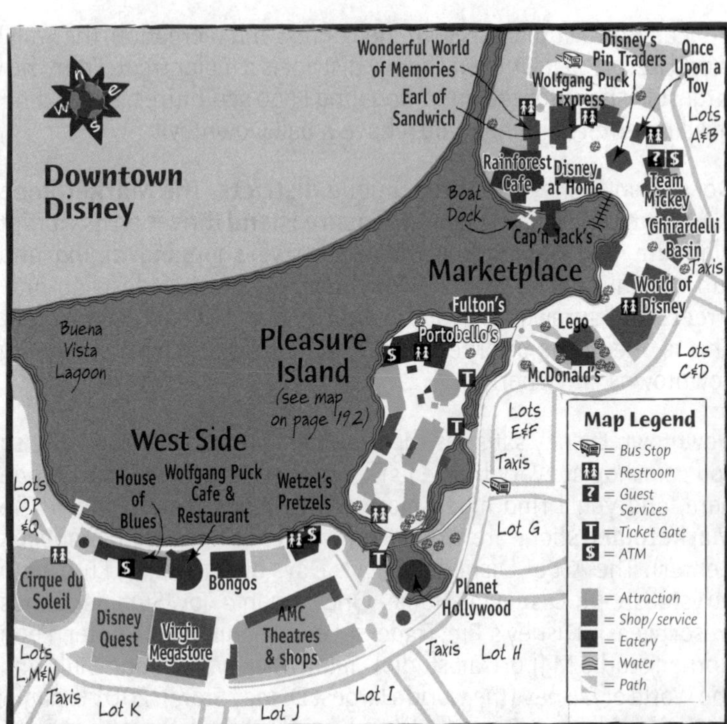

DINING

With the exception of Epcot, you won't find a more **diverse array** of dining experiences in the "World" than at Downtown Disney. For a heaping serving of showbiz, head to Downtown Disney West Side. The House of Blues serves up fabulous live music, Wolfgang Puck Grand Cafe offers famously innovative California fare, and Bongos Cuban Cafe has sizzling Latin rhythm and foods. Downtown Disney's showplace is the famous Planet Hollywood, which drips with movie memorabilia. Eateries are quieter at the Marketplace, a fine start for your night at Pleasure Island. Fulton's Crab House serves upscale seafood in a riverboat, the Rainforest Cafe cooks up imaginative fare, Portobello Yacht Club offers Northern Italian food in a casual atmosphere, and Cap'n Jack's Restaurant does seafood and steaks. Busy shoppers like the lighter fare at The Earl of Sandwich, Wetzel's Pretzels, Wolfgang Puck Express, Ghirardelli Soda Fountain & Chocolate Shop, and, of course, "Ronald's Fun House" (McDonald's). Complete descriptions of these Downtown Disney eateries begin on page 220.

Making the Most of Downtown Disney

TIPS

Once Upon A Toy has amazing decor and unique toys, including make-your-own Tinkertoys and Mr. Potatohead sets, plus a Lincoln Log version of Wilderness Lodge and a Haunted Mansion Clue game.

Kids can **play for free** at the Lego Imagination Center and in the water play fountain near the Marketplace bus stop entrance.

Little-known **discounts and specials** may be available. Be sure to ask! For example, movies at the AMC Pleasure Island 24 are $6.50 before 6:00 pm, which makes them a cool hangout on a hot day.

Every November the **Festival of the Masters** at Downtown Disney offers art exhibits, food specialties, performances, and kids activities.

Christmas brings fun activities, including an honest-to-goodness ice skating rink. There's also a toy train ride that operates year-round. And don't forget the Disney's Days of Christmas shop, open year-round.

NOTES

Of the eateries here, only Cap'n Jack's is run by the Walt Disney World Resort, so **reservations policies** differ. Most eateries and shops let you charge purchases to your Disney resort tab, however.

The Downtown Disney Marketplace and Pleasure Island **parking lots** are often packed. Try the huge West Side parking lot and use the shuttle boat (when operating) to reach the Marketplace. Alas, valet parking is no longer being offered here.

Most **shops** in the Marketplace open at 9:30 am, while West Side shops open at 10:30 am. Closing is at 11:00 pm, with seasonal variations.

For **more information** and answers to questions, call Downtown Disney Guest Services at 407-828-3058.

GETTING THERE

By Bus—Buses are available from every Disney resort. From the Magic Kingdom, Epcot, Disney-MGM Studios, or Disney's Animal Kingdom, bus or monorail to a nearby resort and transfer.
By Car—From I-4, take exit 67, then take the first exit and turn right on Buena Vista Dr. Parking is free.
By Boat—Boats may shuttle between the Marketplace and West Side seasonally. Resort guests at Port Orleans, Old Key West, and Saratoga Springs can take a boat to the Marketplace, too.
By Foot—Guests at Hotel Plaza Resorts may find it quicker to walk.

Making the Most of Cirque du Soleil

A circus has come to Walt Disney World, the likes of which you've probably never seen—magical, musical, a little mystical, and poetically graceful. Cirque du Soleil ("Circus of the Sun") from Montreal, Canada, has redefined the concept of "circus" for millions around the world and now has a company-in-residence at Downtown Disney West Side.

SHOWS

Cirque du Soleil weaves its magic with acrobats, clowns, jugglers, dancers, aerialists, lights, original music, and fabulous costumes (and not one animal). The current show, **La Nouba** (from the French "to live it up"), weaves a continuous, dream-like thread. There's a story here, but many guests hardly notice or care. This isn't Big Top-style circus, either. It has as much in common with modern dance as it does with circus. It's not for everyone (Dave likes it, Jennifer doesn't), but it adds yet another dimension to the magic.

INFO

Housed in its own **1,671-seat theater** at the west end of the West Side, Cirque du Soleil presents its 90-min. shows at 6:00 and 9:00 pm, Tues.–Sat. (Note: The show goes on brief hiatus seven times during 2004.) Tickets are $77–$87/adults and $47–$52/kids ages 3-11. Call 407-939-7600 or visit the box office. Seats are assigned based on availability, but you might get your pick at the box office. Premium-priced tickets are in the center (see blue seats below).

SEATING PLAN

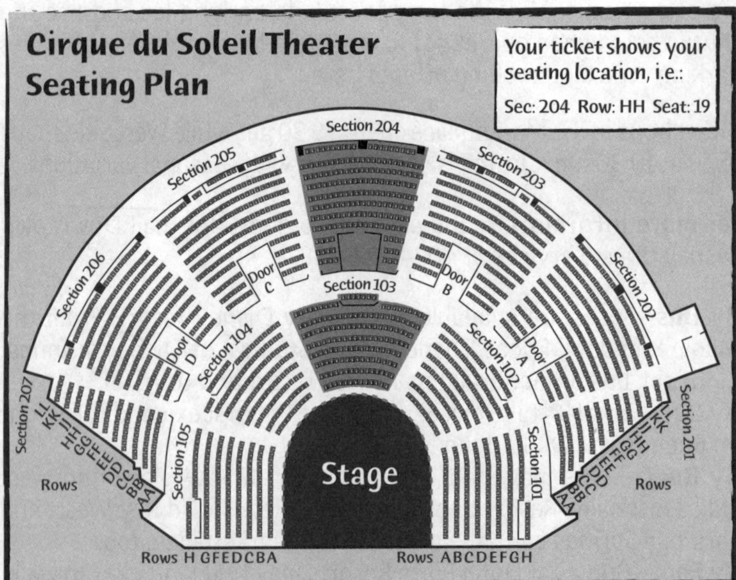

DisneyQuest

DisneyQuest is an indoor "theme park" housed in a big, blue, five-story building at Downtown Disney West Side. It features ride simulators, high-tech games, and hands-on activities for young and old alike.

Attractions run the gamut from simple video arcade games to a you-design-it, you-ride-it roller coaster simulator. Take the "Cyberlator" elevator to the Ventureport, where you can enter four zones: **Explore Zone**, **Score Zone**, **Create Zone**, and **Replay Zone**. Each zone organizes the attractions (described below) by theme. Each zone spans at least two floors, with various stairs and walkways linking them. This makes for a bewildering maze—study our map on page 188 to orient yourself before you go.

LAYOUT

Aladdin's Magic Carpet Ride [Floor 2] A-OK!	6 4 6
Don virtual reality goggles for a wild, 4-min. ride on Aladdin's magic carpet. Swoop through Agrabah and the Cave of Wonder to search for jewels and free the Genie. Motion sickness warning. Explore Zone. **Allie's KidTip:** *"Make sure your helmet is on tight so it doesn't fall off when you play."*	**Virtual** D-Ticket Ages 6 & up Dizziness

Animation Academy [Floor 2] A-OK!	7 7 6
Take your seat at a computer workstation as an instructor draws out your artistry. Hands-on lessons in drawing and/or animating characters. Several 20-minute lessons are offered. After the class, you can buy your creation. Create Zone. **Allie's KidTip:** *"Check the schedule for a class that draws a character you like."*	**Hands-On** D-Ticket Ages 6 & up Skill helps

Buzz Lightyear's Astroblasters [Floor 3]	7 5 7
Ride fully-enclosed two-person bumper cars mounted with "cannons" that shoot large rubber balls. The driver pilots to scoop up ammo, and the gunner fires on other cars to make them spin out of control. 3-min. game. 51"/130 cm height restriction. Replay Zone. **Allie's KidTip:** *"Try to hit a lot of cars so they spin around."*	**Vehicles** D-Ticket Bumpy Ages 9 & up

CyberSpace Mountain [Floor 2]	9 8 9
Design and ride your own coaster! Start by choosing a theme and designing the coaster tracks on a computer screen. Then get strapped into a two-person flight simulator to experience your coaster, or choose from a ready-made coaster. Be prepared to be shaken, rattled, and rolled on a ride more dizzying than the real thing. Simulator seats are small. 51"/130 cm height restriction. Create Zone. **Allie's KidTip:** *"If you feel sick just hit the red stop button."*	**Simulator** E-Ticket Upside down during inversions Ages 9 & up

Invasion! An ExtraTERRORestrial Alien Encounter [Floor 5] A-OK!	6 7 5
Dash across the galaxy to rescue Earth colonists from an invading horde in this simulator ride that borrows characters and fun from the popular Magic Kingdom attraction. One teammate pilots the rescue vehicle, while three other teammates keep the bad guys at bay. Great pre-show film. Score Zone. **Allie's KidTip:** *"I think kids will have more fun being a gunner than a pilot."*	**Simulator** E-Ticket Violent theme Ages 7 & up

Attraction descriptions and ratings are explained on page 127.

Charting the Attractions at DisneyQuest

Attraction	Jennifer's Rating	Dave's Rating	Readers' Rating
Living Easels [Floor 2] A-OK! — *Draw animated landscapes on a touch-sensitive screen. You can buy print-outs if you like. Create Zone. Allie's KidTip: "Use your imagination!" Ages 3 & up.* — Hands-On; B-Ticket	5	4	4
Magic Mirror [Floor 2] A-OK! — *Indulge your digital artistry as you turn a photo of yourself into a wacky portrait. Create Zone. Allie's KidTip: "Use your parent's face! It's funny!" Ages 4 & up.* — Hands-On; B-Ticket	3	3	5
Midway on the Moon [Floors 4 & 5] A-OK! — *Disney-themed versions of arcade games like Ursula's Whirlpool and traditional games like Skeeball. Purchase "points" to play ($5 for 20 credits) then redeem for prizes. Replay Zone. Allie's KidTip: "Look at all the games before you play."* — Arcade; A-Ticket; Ages 5 & up	6	8	5
Mighty Ducks Pinball Slam [Floor 3] (height restriction) — *Use body motion/weight to move a "puck" around a huge screen and "body check" opponents on this simulator. 3-min. game. 48"/122 cm height restriction. Score Zone. Allie's KidTip: "If you're tall enough but skinny it might not work."* — Simulator; D-Ticket; Ages 9 & up	5	4	7
Pirates of the Caribbean: Battle for Buccaneer Gold [Floor 1] (height restriction) A-OK! — *Yo ho, yo ho! DisneyQuest's newest attraction pits you and up to four shipmates in a 3-D simulated sea battle in quest of pirate gold. Fire virtual cannonballs against your foes, and feel the deck shudder when you take a hit. 35"/89 cm height restriction. Explore Zone. Allie's KidTip: "Shoot the ships that you pass!"* — Simulator; E-Ticket; Violent theme; Ages 7 & up	8	8	9
Radio Disney SongMaker [Floor 2] A-OK! — *Create your own hit song in a soundbooth. Combine styles and lyrics for laughs. You can buy a CD of it. Create Zone. Allie's KidTip: "Don't be shy." Ages 4 & up.* — Hands-On; D-Ticket	6	6	4
Ride the Comix [Floors 4 and 5] — *Swing your laser sword to battle comic strip villains in this 4-min., 3-D virtual reality game. Heavy goggles, sword-play, and motion sickness make this hard to play. Score Zone. Allie's KidTip: "The monsters might scare you." Ages 8 & up.* — Virtual; D-Ticket; May feel dizzy	2	3	5
Sid's Create-A-Toy [Floor 2] — *Create a demented toy from spare toy parts—on a computer screen. You can buy a real version of your creation. Create Zone. Allie's KidTip: "Boring." Ages 4 & up.* — Hands-On; B-Ticket	3	4	5
Treasure of the Incas [Floor 1] A-OK! — *Drive a remote-control truck through an underground maze—a small camera mounted on the truck gives you a visual. Allie's KidTip: "Have a grownup watch your truck through the glass floor and call out directions." Create Zone.* — Maze; B-Ticket; Ages 5 & up	5	4	4
Virtual Jungle Cruise [Floor 1] A-OK! — *Board a raft, grab a paddle, and take a 4-min. whitewater river cruise back in time on this motion simulator ride. Dr. Wayne Szalinski guides you and your teammates on this riotous journey over waterfalls and into the age of the dinosaurs. You may get a little damp. Explore Zone. Allie's KidTip: "Paddle hard."* — Simulator; E-Ticket; Paddling; Ages 6 & up	9	6	6

➤

Making the Most of DisneyQuest

DINING

You won't go hungry at DisneyQuest. The Cheesecake Factory operates two satisfying **counter-service eateries**: FoodQuest and Wonderland Café. Up on the top floor, FoodQuest (see page 222) offers an appetizing variety of pizzas, salads, burgers, sandwiches, and wraps, plus a few tempting desserts. On the floor below, Wonderland Café (see page 223) pleases the sweet tooth with a huge selection of cheesecakes and desserts, and all sorts of luxurious coffee concoctions. And while you sip your latté you can browse the Internet on limited-use computer terminals.

TIPS

First-time visitors should spend time exploring the entire place before splitting up. While you're at it, choose a **meeting place** and time. The Wonderland Café is a good choice with places to sit, and the Ventureport on the third floor is highly visible.

Allow at least **four to five hours** to tour, more if you love arcades.

Be sure to wear a **wristwatch**—it's easy to lose track of time! Also, it's faster to use the stairs to go up or down one level. On the other hand, the elevators are less disorienting than the curving staircases.

The Wonderland Café sports tables with **free Internet access**, but the custom browser makes it tough to surf at will.

NOTES

Rumor has it DisneyQuest *may* become an **ESPN Zone**.

Best times to visit are during the mornings and afternoons, and on the weekends. It gets pretty busy in the evenings, after other parks are closed. Crowds are huge on foul-weather days.

Discount admissions may be available after 10:00 pm.

RATINGS

Ratings are explained on page 120.

Our Value Ratings:		Our Magic Ratings:		Readers' Ratings:
Quality:	6/10	Theme:	5/10	78% fell in love with it
Variety:	4/10	Excitement:	5/10	22% liked it well enough
Scope:	3/10	Fun Factor:	6/10	0% had mixed feelings
Overall Value:	**5/10**	**Overall Magic:**	**5/10**	0% were disappointed

DisneyQuest is enjoyed by...	(rated by both authors and readers)	
Younger Kids: ♥♥♥♥	Young Adults: ♥♥♥♥♥	Families: ♥♥♥♥
Older Kids: ♥♥♥♥♥	Mid Adults: ♥♥♥	Couples: ♥♥♥
Teenagers: ♥♥♥♥♥	Mature Adults: ♥	Singles: ♥♥♥♥♥

Finding Your Way at DisneyQuest

DISNEYQUEST PARK MAP

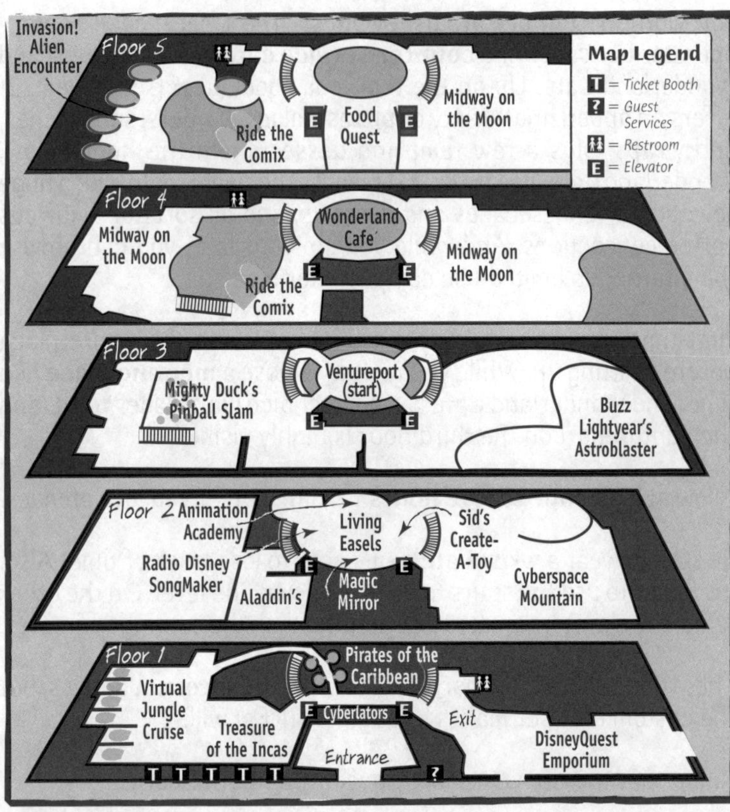

ADMISSION

In keeping with Disney's approach to park admission, you pay a **single all-day price** and enjoy unlimited use of all rides, games, and activities (excluding games that award prizes—a 20-credit card costs $5). Adults pay $33.02 for a full day admission, and kids ages 3-9 pay $26.63. Children under 10 must be accompanied by an adult, but feel free to leave the older kids here while you shop elsewhere. Annual passes are available—see page 169. DisneyQuest **admission is included** in Ultimate Park Hoppers and Premium Annual Passes, and is an option on the Park Hopper Plus passes. DisneyQuest hours are 10:30 am–11:00 pm Sundays–Thursdays, and 10:30 am–midnight on Fridays and Saturdays.

INFO

For more DisneyQuest information, call 407-828-4600 or visit http://www.disneyquest.com. There is also a DisneyQuest kiosk in Downtown Disney Marketplace that offers information.

Pleasure Island

AMBIENCE

Where can you celebrate a Times Square-style New Year's Eve every night at midnight, disco down until 2:00 am, lay back and listen to some cool, live jazz, laugh it up at a comedy club, or enjoy the camaraderie of a band of intrepid explorers? Pleasure Island! The party starts at 7:00 pm and continues until 2:00 am nightly, and admission is required (see page 191). The clubs are described below.

Club	Ratings
8Trax	8 5 6
Disco in all its Saturday Night Fever glory! The sound is classic 70s (Thursday is 80s night) the floor is packed and illuminated, and dancers are enthusiastic!	**Dance** C-Ticket
Adventurers Club A-OK!	10 10 8
In all ways, this is the most "Disney" of the clubs on Pleasure Island (and our absolute favorite). Be prepared for the unexpected, the quirky, and the hilarious. The walls are encrusted with trophies, mementos, curios, and photos amassed by the club members—intrepid explorers and wannabes all. Look closely—this is Disney, after all! You may be greeted by the club's stoic butler, the matronly Club President, or even a French maid. Different shows are held throughout the night in the Mask Room, Treasure Room, and Library. Allie's KidTip: *"The Yakoose moose drools! And they make you sing silly songs!"*	**Comedy** E-Ticket Shows run continuously from 8pm to 1am Audience participation
BET SoundStage Club	6 7 4
Contemporary music and dancing for guests 21 and over. The club is one of the smaller ones, but the intimate atmosphere can be enjoyable.	**Dance** C-Ticket
Comedy Warehouse A-OK!	9 7 9
Houses the Who, What and Wherehouse Players, a comedy troupe that delivers hilarious skits, standup acts, improv sketches, and adult humor "Disney-style." Allie's KidTip: *"This is funny, but don't sit next to the telephone!"*	**Comedy** D-Ticket Rib-tickling
Mannequins Dance Palace	7 6 6
Voted the #1 dance club in the Southeast, this is the place for the hottest dance mix and the biggest sound and lighting system. Bouncers in tuxes proof you and let in a few people at a time. Very, very loud.	**Dance** E-Ticket Must be 21+
Motion	2 5 7
A big dance floor and clean, open layout are all that distinguish this large club. Top 40 and alternative dance. Motion replaced the Wildhorse Saloon.	**Dance** C-Ticket
Pleasure Island Jazz Company	8 7 5
Offers a New Orleans setting for enjoying live jazz. There's a nice, elevated seating area outside. Wide choice of fine cigars (but you must smoke outside).	**Music** C-Ticket
Rock 'n' Roll Beach Club	8 7 6
Offers fans of classic and modern rock a crowded dance floor, live "cover" bands, and a DJ. You can also play pinball and munch-out on nachos.	**Dance** D-Ticket

Eating and Playing at Pleasure Island

SHOPPING & EATING

Pleasure Island has its share of **small boutiques**, such as Changing Attitudes (clothing), DTV (trendy fashions), Reel Finds (movie collectibles and memorabilia), Mouse House (Disney logo items and golf clothing), SuperStar Studios (star in a video/song), Zen Zone (massage beds), and Suspended Animation (Disney art). Even so, it's not the best place to do serious shopping, and a good meal is even harder to come by. Eatery details are on page 221.

Adventurers Club Member Professor Otis T. Wren puts an ichthyological curse on Dave (or maybe Dave just had one too many Jungle Juices)

PLAYING

The West End Stage is the focus of the **nightly New Year's Eve** show at midnight. A live band rocks the stage for much of the evening, and at midnight the streets are showered with confetti and fireworks. Every so often the West End Stage plays host to **big-name acts**, too. Farther down the main street the Hub Video Stage occasionally hosts performances by **smaller bands** and **energetic dancers**. The small Waterfront Stage is used on special occasions. Live and inside, you'll enjoy the **live jazz** every night at the Pleasure Island Jazz Company and straight-ahead **rock bands** at the Rock 'n Roll Beach Club. The Adventurers Club offers some **different kinds of fun**: sing-alongs, cabarets, "Fingers" the organ player, and "Balderdash" storytelling! Kungaloosh!

GETTING THERE

By Bus—Frequent buses are available from Disney resorts. From a park, bus or monorail to a nearby resort and transfer to a Downtown Disney bus. Get off at the second Downtown Disney stop.

By Car—Follow signs to Downtown Disney. Parking is free. If you intend to drink, please designate a driver. Designated drivers: As you pass through the turnstiles, let the cast member know that you're not imbibing and you may get two free soft drink coupons.

By Boat—From Port Orleans, Old Key West, and Saratoga Springs take a boat to the Marketplace and walk. All guests may use the boat between Marketplace and West Side, when it is running.

Making the Most of Pleasure Island

TIPS

As of summer 2003, all Pleasure Island clubs are **non-smoking**.

Adventurers Club can seem a little confusing at first, but just wait a while—something's sure to happen wherever you are, when you least expect it. Come with a sense of adventure and be ready to join in. You can be inducted into the club, learn the secret greeting, and sing the club song! We absolutely adore the Adventurers Club and consider it one of our favorite places at Walt Disney World. We recommend the Kungaloosh and Jungle Juice drinks!

If you find the excitement too much, or just want to go somewhere romantic with that special someone, head for our **"hidden patio."** Go down the stairs beside the Adventurers Club, or go down the stairs beside the West End Stage and turn right before the bridge.

Alcoholic beverages are even served on the streets of Pleasure Island. Adults 21 and older get wristbands to show they can drink.

A good spot to watch the **New Year's Eve show** is from the access ramp in front of Adventurers Club. Just don't block it!

NOTES

Pleasure Island is open to guests **18 years and older** (younger kids can come with a parent or legal guardian). Be sure to bring your valid driver's license or state I.D. (with photo). They really do "proof" you at the gate, and if you're over 21 you'll get a special wristband that allows you to imbibe liquor. You must be over 21 to enter BET SoundStage Club and Mannequins Dance Palace! If you bring kids, be prepared for some good-natured ribbing from performers.

Pleasure Island admission is **$21.15/person**, and is included in some passes. Ask about discounts. Clubs open from 7:00 pm to 2:00 am nightly, though some clubs may open later.

RATINGS

Ratings are explained on page 120.

Our Value Ratings:		Our Magic Ratings:		Readers' Ratings:
Quality:	6/10	Theme:	6/10	48% fell in love with it
Variety:	3/10	Excitement:	7/10	39% liked it well enough
Scope:	4/10	Fun Factor:	7/10	9% had mixed feelings
Overall Value:	**4/10**	**Overall Magic:**	**7/10**	4% were disappointed

Pleasure Island is enjoyed by...	(rated by both authors and readers)	
Younger Kids: ❤	Young Adults: ❤❤❤❤❤	Families: ❤
Older Kids: ❤❤	Mid Adults: ❤❤❤❤	Couples: ❤❤❤❤
Teenagers: ❤❤❤❤❤	Mature Adults: ❤❤	Singles: ❤❤❤❤❤

Charting Your Route at Pleasure Island

PLEASURE ISLAND PARK MAP

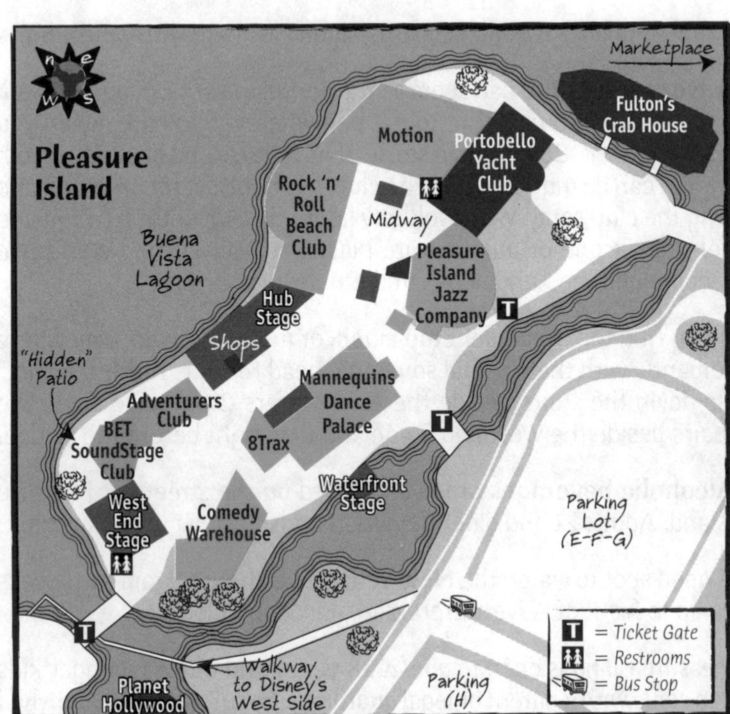

BEST TIMES TO GO

Time flies at Pleasure Island, so arrive **early in the evening** to really make the most of your visit. The clubs start hopping as soon as they open at 7:00–9:00 pm. **Comedy Warehouse** isn't the place to come for an entire evening's entertainment, but if you don't mind standing in line to enter, this is a fine place to go before you head out to other clubs. Note that Thursdays are Cast Member Nights and tend to be crowded. To escape the crowds and noise, consider the Comedy Warehouse or Jazz Company during the **busiest times** of the evening—usually between 10:00 pm and midnight. Don't miss the nightly **New Year's Eve show** at the West End Stage, beginning at 11:45 pm. Note that the West End entrance (and the "hidden patio" mentioned on the previous page) is closed before and during the New Year's Eve fireworks show. Pleasure Island is now closed **during the day**, but admission is free from 7:00–9:00 pm. Stroll through—some clubs may be open for a free "sample" and the live stage is rocking for all. You won't be able to enter most clubs without a hand stamp/wristband, however.

More Places to Play

BoardWalk—Pleasure Island doesn't have a monopoly on nightclubs in Walt Disney World—the BoardWalk resort has its own entertainment complex with clubs, restaurants, and entertainment. Jellyrolls is a dueling piano bar that serves drinks and free popcorn ($7 cover, 21 and up, smoking allowed). Atlantic Dance Hall serves specialty drinks while open-request DJ music lures you onto the floor (no cover, 21 and up, open Tuesday–Saturday). ESPN Club is a popular sports bar. Midway games and street performers add to the fun. For details and directions to the BoardWalk resort, see pages 43–46.

Celebration, Florida—Imagine what would happen if Disney created a real town and you've got the community of Celebration, located on a corner of the Walt Disney World property just a few miles from the parks. Visitors to this quaint, small town may stroll or shop, have a bite in a restaurant, take in a movie at the theater, or stay in the luxury hotel. For more information, call 407-566-2200.

Golf—The Walt Disney World Resort boasts **99 holes of golf** on five championship courses and one nine-hole course. All courses are open to the public and feature full-service facilities, including driving ranges, pro shops, cafes, and lessons. For details and to reserve tee times, call 407-WDW-GOLF. We also recommend Marc Schwartz's Unofficial Walt Disney World Golf Site at http://www.wdwgolf.com.

Miniature Golf Courses—Disney has miniature golf, too! **Fantasia Gardens**, near the Swan Resort, has two 18-hole courses. One course is based on the scenes, characters, and music of Disney's classic animated film, "Fantasia." The other is a grass course with par-three and par-four holes from 40-75 feet long. **Winter Summerland** is a miniature golf park at Blizzard Beach. It sports two 18-hole courses—one is blanketed in "snow" and the other celebrates the holidays in the tropics. Cost is about $9 for adults and $8 for children, with discounts for Annual Passholders. Hours: 10:00 am to midnight.

Fort Wilderness Resort—Here's another resort with a lot to offer! Fort Wilderness is a respite from the bustle of the parks, offering canoeing, boating, fishing excursions, biking, tennis, horseback trail rides, horse-drawn carriage rides, and hayrides. And you don't have to spend a penny to visit the petting farm (pony rides cost $3), blacksmith shop, and a nightly campfire program (with character visits and free movies). For more information on Fort Wilderness, see pages 59–62.

More Places to Play
(continued)

Health Clubs & Spas—Many of the deluxe resorts have health clubs with exercise equipment—some even offer massage treatments, steam rooms, and saunas. If you've got relaxation in mind, we recommend the **Saratoga Springs Spa** (opens May 2004) and **Grand Floridian Spa & Health Club**. These world-class, full-service centers offer many beauty and wellness treatments, nutrition and fitness counseling, and lots of pampering. Call 407-827-4455 (Saratoga Springs) or 407-824-2332 (Grand Floridian Spa).

Tennis—Anyone for a game? Tennis enthusiasts won't be disappointed—seven sets of courts are available around Walt Disney World. Our pick is the Racquet Club at the Contemporary Resort, with six, state-of-the-art hydrogrid courts. Call 407-939-7529.

Walt Disney World Speedway—Disney has its own speedway—a one-mile, tri-oval track for **auto racing**. The race track is home to the Richard Petty Driving Experience in which participants get to drive or ride at speeds up to 145 mph! In July 2002, Dave strapped on his helmet and climbed in the passenger seat of a race car for a "ride around" experience. In a flash the crew had his seat harness buckled, the photographer snapped his macho image for posterity, and he was headed out of the pit faster than you can say "zero to sixty." Dave's not a racing fan, but you don't really have to be to get a thrill out of this experience. For Richard Petty Experience details, call 407-939-0130.

Waterways (Boating, Fishing, etc.)—Water, water everywhere—and lots of things to do! You can rent boats at nearly every deluxe and moderate resort and Downtown Disney. Fishing excursions and cane pole rentals are also available in most of those same locations. See page 244.

Disney's Wide World of Sports Complex—Disney's state-of-the-art **athletic center** features a 7,500-seat baseball stadium, a 30,000-square-foot fieldhouse, a track & field complex, volleyball, tennis, baseball, softball, football, and more. With admission ($9.69/adults or $7.46/kids 3–9), visitors enjoy the Multi-Sport Experience covering sports such as football, baseball, and basketball. The 200-acre center is also home to amateur and professional sports, including Atlanta Braves Spring Training and theTampa Bay Buccaneers training camp. For more information call 407-828-FANS, or visit http://www.disneyworldsports.com.

Disney Nature Reserve—The Nature Conservancy runs this 12,000 acre hiking haven at the headwaters of the Everglades. For information, visit http://www.nature.org and search on "disney."

Deciding What To Do

Whew! We bet you're now wondering how in the world (no pun intended) you'll find the time to **fit everything** at Walt Disney World into your vacation. It's simple: you can't do it. Even a month-long stay wouldn't be enough to do and see everything. Rather than try to fit everything into your vacation, make a practical plan.

Naturally, you can't plan everything in advance, nor should you try—spontaneity and discovery are two elements of a great vacation. Yet, it is a good idea to get a feeling for the parks, attractions, and activities before you go, and to make a note of the ones you simply "must" do. This helps you **create an itinerary** and keeps you from missing the things you've got your heart set on.

First, read the preceding pages carefully to gain a solid idea of what the Walt Disney World Resort is all about. Next, **make a list** of all the things you'd like to see and do. This can be a great family activity. Make it a free-for-all, no-holds-barred event—what we call a "blue-sky session." List everything, no matter how impractical, silly, or expensive. Once you've got a good list, pare it down to the things that are most important and copy them to the worksheet on the next two pages. List the activity, where in the "World" it is located (i.e., which park or resort), its approximate cost, and any notes (including why it's on the list).

When you're done with the list, take a good look at the locations. Are several located in the same park? If so, can you do them all on the same day? Go through the list and note other patterns. With luck, you'll have a better sense of where you're headed. Next, **assign the activities** to specific days of your vacation, using the Day column on the far right. For example, on a recent trip we wanted to visit Spaceship Earth, race around Test Track, and watch IllumiNations. All those activities are at Epcot, so we grouped them together on our third day. We wrote a "3" next to each of those items, but you could write "Wed" or the date instead. If you've planned too much for one day or place, your Cost and Notes columns may help you decide which activities to keep and which to throw out or schedule for another day.

Not all activities can be decided this way, nor should they. Some choices should be **spur of the moment**. Be sure to "schedule" some free time in your trip—preferably a whole day or two. Use these techniques as a general game plan to a great vacation!

Touring Worksheet

Use this worksheet to figure out the things you want to do most on your trip. Match up attractions to determine the parks you want to visit, noting the day/date (you may wish to refer to the Extra Magic Hour schedule on page 32). Fill in the park schedule grid at the bottom of the next page once you've picked days—the park schedule can help you complete your itinerary and choose eateries (in the next chapter).

Activity	Park	Land	Cost	Notes	Day/Date

Useful Abbreviations:
MK (Magic Kingdom)
EP (Epcot)
MGM (Disney-MGM Studios)
DAK (Disney's Animal Kingdom)
BB (Blizzard Beach)
TL (Typhoon Lagoon)
RC (River Country)
BW (BoardWalk)
DD (Downtown Disney)
DQ (DisneyQuest)
PI (Pleasure Island)
WWOS (Disney's Wide World of Sports)
DS (Disney Speedway)
FG (Fantasia Gardens)
WS (Winter Summerland)
DCL (Disney Cruise Line)
VB (Disney's Vero Beach)
OFF (Off-site)
USF (Universal Studios)
IOA (Islands of Adventure)
SW (SeaWorld)
COVE (Discovery Cove)
BG (Busch Gardens)
KSC (Kennedy Space Center)
FH (Friend/Family's House)

Activity	Park	Land	Cost	Notes	Day/Date

Write your park schedule in this calendar grid—note the date in the corners.

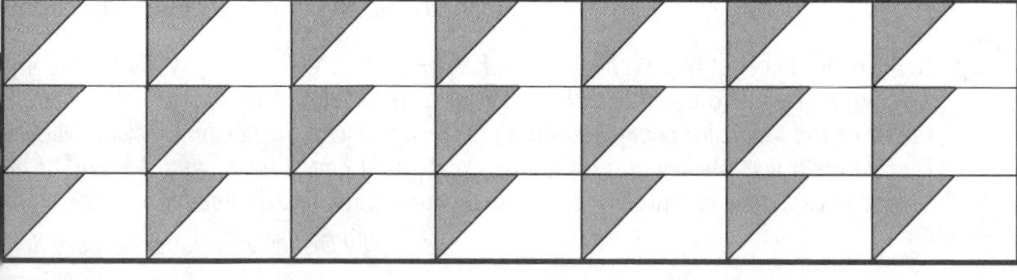

It's Not Such a Small World After All

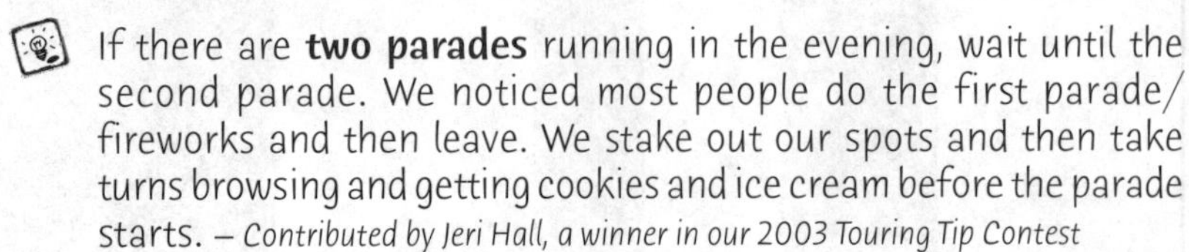

If you've read this chapter, you know that touring Walt Disney World is no simple walk in the park. Here are some tips and tricks to help you:

If there are **two parades** running in the evening, wait until the second parade. We noticed most people do the first parade/fireworks and then leave. We stake out our spots and then take turns browsing and getting cookies and ice cream before the parade starts. – *Contributed by Jeri Hall, a winner in our 2003 Touring Tip Contest*

If you need to keep in touch with others, consider two-way radios, cell phones, or pagers. You may even be able to rent them for the duration of your stay from local companies. If you use radios or cell phones, remember to turn them off during attractions.

Disney attracts vacationers from around the world. Remember that other cultures have their own **customs**.

Magical Memories

"I finally got my boyfriend to go with me to Walt Disney World. He hadn't been since his children were very small when all that was open was the Magic Kingdom. He knows that I love Walt Disney World but he didn't understand why I found it so magical. We went two weeks before Christmas and stayed at the BoardWalk. The day we arrived it was obvious he was just indulging me, but by noon the second day he was grabbing me by the hand and pulling me along so he could see the next thing! On our last morning we rode in the monorail cab on the Epcot loop and he had tears in his eyes as he told me he didn't want to leave. Now he's helping me plan his second (my fourteenth) trip and I think he's even more excited than I am."

...as told by Disney vacationer Jacquelyn Boyles

"On the second night of our much anticipated second trip to the World in June 2003, we were awaiting the start of Fantasmic! We had arrived at the theater 1 ½ hours before show time to guarantee a good seat. Unfortunately, I had picked up some kind of bug, and was fighting off the queasy feeling in my stomach as we waited for showtime. As the show began, a light breeze blew across the lake. This was followed by a soft misting of water from the 'movie screens' showing Mickey's dream. Sitting beside me, my five-year-old daughter Kaileigh gave me a nudge with her elbow and said, 'Hey, Mom, did you feel some magic get on you?' It was at that moment that I realized I most definitely did."

...as told by Disney vacationer Susan Beaty

"Our son was not yet three years of age when he went to Walt Disney World for the first time. When he saw the statue of Mickey Mouse and Walt Disney in front of Cinderella Castle at the Magic Kingdom, I asked him if he knew who the person was with Mickey. He told me it was Mickey and his daddy. 'Yes,' I told him, 'That's true!' Instead of me having to explain who Walt Disney was to a young child, he explained it to me."

...as told by Disney vacationer Gregory Rose

Feasting and Snacking

You can't have a good vacation without a good meal (or two) and your Disney vacation is no exception. Disney knows how to make your mealtimes as entertaining, adventuresome, and satisfying as the rest of your vacation experience. Disney eateries go out of their way to give everyone a unique and delicious dining experience, so you'll find that even the most exotic restaurant can please any taste, including the finicky eaters in your family. From the atmosphere to the service to the food itself, it has all been created to fill your imagination as well as your belly.

The choices can be awesome, ranging from basic hot dogs and burgers to once-in-a-lifetime elegance, from ultra-romantic dinners for two to foot-stompin' family hoedowns, and from exotic samplings of far-off places to the magic of a breakfast hug from Winnie the Pooh himself. One thing's for sure—you can't say, "There's nothing to eat around here!"

For us, meal planning is more important than choosing which attractions to visit. It's easier to jump in an unexpectedly short line at Space Mountain than it is to get a table at the better eateries.

The six basic types of Walt Disney World Resort meals are table-service restaurants, counter-service cafes, quick-service snack shops, "special experiences" (such as dinner shows and character meals), room service, and meals you fix yourself. We devote most of the space here to table-service and special dining experiences, which are more costly and require the most planning. We also include details on the counter service and snacks in the parks. Resort counter service and room service is discussed in the "Staying in Style" chapter. We can't say much about your home cooking until we're invited to your villa or campsite, though.

The chapter begins with a meal planning guide, moves to mealtime tips, park-by-park and resort-by-resort eatery reviews, the low-down on the big shindigs, and ends with worksheets to plan your meals. Bon appetit!

Deciding on Dining

If you thought selecting a restaurant in your hometown was tough, you haven't seen anything. The Walt Disney World Resort has over **300 places to eat**. But before you go running for the exit, take heart. We've been to virtually every restaurant on property at least twice (usually several times) and we offer easily-digestible descriptions and yummy ratings for you in this chapter. Better yet, we have a tried-and-true system for deciding where and when to eat.

First, decide **how often** you want to eat out. Many folks (including ourselves) bring or buy some food for snacks or meals in-room, with light breakfasts being the most practical choice. Most resorts can supply a refrigerator (for an additional fee), some include a coffeemaker, and home-away-from-home resorts have kitchen facilities, too. You can, of course, eat out every meal. We like to eat a light breakfast in our room with food we've packed or purchased, such as peanut butter and jelly on English muffins. We then do one or two special breakfasts "out" (such as a character breakfast—see pages 232–233). We often eat lunch and dinner at the parks, resorts, or Downtown Disney. Some vacationers prefer to eat a big meal mid-morning and another mid-afternoon to save time and money. More money-saving ideas are on page 203.

Once you have an idea of how often you want (and can afford) to eat out, your next task is to decide **when and where**. Revisit your Touring Worksheet (pages 196–197) and check the parks you want to visit—it is much easier to choose a restaurant in or near your day's destination. Every park offers table-service restaurants, counter-service eateries, and snack shops and carts. To help you choose from the overwhelming number of dining choices at Walt Disney World, this chapter offers descriptions of nearly all eateries. Descriptions are organized alphabetically within each park and resort to help you focus on your choices. Pick the eateries that fall within your budget, tastes, and needs—you may find it helpful to highlight or circle those eatery descriptions that interest you.

As you make decisions about your meals and the eateries you want to visit, jot them down on your **Meal Worksheet** at the end of the chapter on page 238. Make note of those table-service eateries for which advance seating arrangements (priority seating) may be made. Continue on to the next page to learn the what, when, and how of priority seating arrangements at the Walt Disney World Resort.

Tip: Sections highlighted in light blue (like the one below) indicate additions or significant changes at Disney since our previous edition! Rest assured that we updated all prices, too.

Priority Seating

Virtually every table-service restaurant within Walt Disney World allows **advance seating arrangements**, known as "priority seating," or "P.S." These are not reservations. Rather, priority seating gives you the first available table upon arrival at your specified time. This system works better than traditional reservations, which required that guests wait while there is a table free because of latecomers and no-shows. The only Disney table-service restaurants that don't accept priority seating are some Downtown Disney restaurants, Big River Grille, and ESPN Club (see detailed listings in this chapter). Additionally, some restaurants take traditional reservations, such as Victoria & Albert's, the Swan & Dolphin restaurants (see pages 229–230), and the character breakfasts at Cinderella's Royal Table and Restaurant Akershus (see pages 232–233 for reservation details/policies).

Priority seating can be made in **advance of your arrival** by calling 407-WDW-DINE (407-939-3463). Call up to 90 days in advance for priority seating at most restaurants. (Disney switched most 60-day and 120-day restaurants to 90 days in mid-2003.) We list the number of days you may call in advance for priority seating with each restaurant's description in this chapter. We also suggest you visit Scott Thomas' handy Priority Seating Calculator at http://pscalculator.net for more priority seating details. Arrangements can also be made the same day at the parks, and by touching "*88" on any Disney payphone or "55" on your Disney resort in-room phone.

When you call, you will be asked to supply the name of the Disney resort at which you are staying and your date of arrival—you can record this information at the top of your **Priority Seating Worksheet** on page 239. If you aren't staying at a Disney resort, no problem—you'll simply need to provide a daytime phone number. Also note that character breakfasts at Cinderella's Royal Table and some special meals require a credit card deposit. You will receive a **confirmation number** for each successfully arranged priority seating. Record this in your worksheet, and later transfer it to your daily PassPockets. If you are unable to get a priority seating, call back about one week before the desired date.

Due to the nature of priority seating arrangements, you should plan to **check-in at the restaurant's podium 15 minutes before** your seating time. You may also need to wait anywhere from 5-30 minutes for a table to become available, depending upon how busy it is. Some restaurants issue a pager, and most have a comfortable waiting area or bar.

If you later decide not to eat at a particular restaurant, just call Disney again and **cancel your priority seating**.

....➢

Restaurant Menu

Alcoholic Beverages—Most eateries serve alcoholic drinks, with the notable exception of those in the Magic Kingdom. Bars and lounges are located around the "World." Legal drinking age is 21 and they do check your identification. (Just ask Jennifer!)

Character Dining—Dine with Disney characters! See pages 232–233.

Children's Meals—Nearly every eatery has a children's menu at parent-friendly prices. Kid-staples like macaroni & cheese and chicken tenders can usually be had at the most exotic of restaurants—ask your server.

Counter Service—Most food at Disney is sold fast-food style. The quality does vary—it's generally worse at the Magic Kingdom and best at Disney's Animal Kingdom, the two parks where counter service is most common. At Magic Kingdom, we like Pecos Bill Cafe in Frontierland and Columbia Harbour House in Liberty Square. Disney's Animal Kingdom only has one table-service restaurant, but the counter-service food is several cuts above the ordinary. We especially like Tusker House's great rotisserie chicken, and the Flame Tree Barbecue at Disney's Animal Kingdom.

Coupons/Discounts—Don't plan on finding coupons for restaurants. Discounts for early dinners and occasionally Annual Pass and Disney Vacation Club do exist—be sure to ask your server. See the money-saving tips on the following page for more information on available discounts.

Dietary Requirements—Low-cholesterol, low-salt, low-fat, and/or vegetarian meals are a regular part of the menu in most restaurants. With 24 hours of advance notice, kosher and other special dietary needs can be met. Cosmic Ray's at Magic Kingdom has a no-advance-notice kosher menu at the check-out (ask for this at other counter service restaurants, too). We also recommend the travel guidebook, "Vegetarian Walt Disney World and Greater Orlando—Second Edition" by Susan Shumaker and Than Saffel, published by The Globe Pequot Press. The book is available through bookstores and at http://www.globepequot.com. We include Susan and Than's "vegebility" ratings—see page 204 for details on these ratings.

Dinner Shows—Disney offers several dinner shows, combining all-you-care-to-eat meals with live entertainment. See pages 234-237.

Dress—Casual clothing is appropriate for all eateries in the "World" except Victoria & Albert's in the Grand Floridian (see page 228). Several spots have "no tank top" rules. We note this in the eatery's description.

Entertainment—Some restaurants supply entertainment, while others like the Whispering Canyon Cafe and 'Ohana provide activities for kids.

Menus—Many menus can be previewed at Guest Services. Deb Wills' Web site (http://www.wdwig.com) also has a wonderful collection of menus brought back by fellow vacationers (including yours truly).

Money—Cash, Disney Dollars, travelers checks, The Disney Credit Card, Disney Visa Reward Vouchers, MasterCard, Visa, American Express, JCB, Discover, Diner's Club, and Disney Resort room charge cards are welcomed. Sales tax is 6.5% (but could increase to 7% pending a fall election). Gratuities may be applied automatically to large parties.

Smoking—Florida law now prohibits smoking in all enclosed restaurants and other indoor public spaces. Only outdoor establishments and free-standing bars (no restaurants or hotel lobbies allowed) can allow smoking, but Disney has chosen to ban smoking at most of these, too.

Time- and Money-Saving Dining Tips

- ✔ *At counter-service eateries, there are usually several lines. The line furthest from the entry is often shorter. Look before you leap.*
- ✔ *Consider eating earlier or later than traditional mealtime hours. You'll be more likely to get a seat (if you haven't arranged priority seating), or simply find the restaurant less crowded and noisy.*
- ✔ *Disney's Animal Kingdom sometimes offers a discounted meal program. The "Meal Plus" program gives you a voucher for one counter-service meal, a small soft drink, a box of popcorn (or ice cream bar), and a bottle of water for just $11.95/adults and $5.95/kids. Look for this program at the park.*
- ✔ *Every item at counter service restaurants can be ordered a la carte. If you don't want fries with that burger "meal" just ask, and you'll pay a reduced price.*
- ✔ *The Rainforest Cafe offers discounts through its Safari Club and an e-mail list—get details at http://www.rainforestcafe.com.*
- ✔ *The Disney Dining Experience is for Florida residents. It offers 20% discounts on select restaurants in the parks and resorts, reduced prices on wine tastings, and more. See page 10 for details.*
- ✔ *Resort eateries are frequently less crowded than those in the parks. Consider a visit to a nearby resort restaurant before, during, or after a park visit. The Contemporary, Polynesian, and Grand Floridian resorts are close to the Magic Kingdom, the Yacht & Beach Club, BoardWalk, and Swan & Dolphin restaurants are close to Epcot and Disney-MGM Studios, and Disney's Animal Kingdom Lodge is a short drive/bus ride from Disney's Animal Kingdom.*

Understanding and Using the Eatery Descriptions and Ratings

PassPorter's popular capsule reviews of eateries cover all table-service restaurants, as well as counter-service eateries at the parks. Our reviews include all important details, plus ratings by us and fellow vacationers. We even include snack carts. Below is a key to our eatery charts. Dig in!

Description Key

Ratings[7]

1 **Eatery Name** [D-2[2]] B/L/D/S[3] $[4] [5] [6]	#	#	#
Description offering an overview of the eatery, including comments on the theming, quality, and menu range. We try to give you an idea of what sort of foods you'll find at a particular eatery, along with typical prices and our recommendations. We also include information on the availability of lighter fare, children's meals, and alcoholic beverages. Whenever possible we describe the type of seating (tables, booths, etc.) and whether it is indoor or outdoor.	**Type**[8] Cuisine[8] Noise Factor[8] Seating[8] Avg. Wait[8] Hours[8]		

[1] Each chart has an empty checkbox in the upper left corner—use it to check off the eateries that interest you (before you go) or those at which you ate (after your return).

[2] Map coordinates—match them up to park maps in "Touring the 'World'" for locations.

[3] Meals are indicated by letters: B (breakfast), L (lunch), D (dinner), and S (snack).

[4] Dollar figures represent the average cost of a full adult dinner. Table-service meal costs include appetizer, entree, dessert, soft drink, tax, and tip. Whenever possible we also provide in parentheses the average cost of a lighter dinner, such as a sandwich, pizza, or entree salad plus dessert, soft drink, tax, and tip. Average counter-service meal costs include entree (with fries when appropriate), dessert, soft drink, and tax. Average counter-service snack prices include a snack, soft drink, and tax. Use these only as a guide.

[5] The orange symbol indicates an eatery is vegetarian-friendly, and has a good "vegebility" rating from the "Vegetarian Walt Disney World and Greater Orlando—Second Edition" guidebook published by The Globe Pequot Press (see page 202). Please note that these veggie-friendly eateries are the best bets for vegetarians in each location, especially for folks who eat eggs and dairy—but these eateries are not necessarily the best veggie restaurants in the country. For information on vegan meals and to be certain that a menu has not changed since the time of publication, please call Disney to speak directly with a chef at the restaurant in advance of your visit. Remember, too, that all the table-service restaurants can accommodate special dietary requests with at least 24 hours notice.

[6] Eateries with a reasonable selection of healthy items (low-fat/low-sodium/low-calorie) are indicated with a tape measure symbol. These are also friendly to weight watchers!

[7] The three white boxes on the right show ratings on a scale of 1 (poor) to 10 (loved it!). The first rating is *Jennifer's*, the second is Dave's, and the third is our Readers' rating. We offer our personal ratings to show how opinions vary, even between two like-minded people. You can also use our ratings as a point of reference—Jennifer likes eateries with extensive theming and well-prepared foods that aren't too exotic or spicy. Dave has more cultured tastes, enjoys unusual, spicy, and barbecue dishes, and loves seafood!

[8] The boxes on the right beneath the numeric ratings give basic information: eatery type (Table, Counter, or Buffet), cuisine, noise factor (from quiet to very noisy), seating (if priority seating is accepted, needed, suggested, recommended, or required, and how many days in advance you can call for priority seating), average wait time, and the eatery's hours.

Magic Kingdom Eateries

(park map on page 123)

Jennifer's Rating | Dave's Rating | Readers' Rating

Casey's Corner [D-4] L/D/S $10 — 5 | 4 | 7

Casey's at the bat, and there's a hot dog at the plate. Old-time stadium foods–1/4 lb. hot dogs ($3.59), fries ($1.79), brownies ($1.79), and soft drinks ($1.99 & 2.29). Most seating is outdoors; some indoor tables near a big-screen TV.

Counter | American | Open all day

Cinderella's Royal Table [D-3] B/L/D $51 — 7 | 6 | 8

For Disney magic, you can't beat dining right inside Cinderella Castle! The character breakfast at "Cindy's" is easily the hottest ticket in the Kingdom ($19.99 or $9.99/kids 3–11)–see pages 232–233. While lunch and dinner aren't character meals (and not as popular), the princess herself may visit. Menu items are named after characters from Cinderella, but the recipes aren't frivolous. The prime rib ($23-26), steaks ($25–26), seafood ($22–23), and chicken ($21) can please all, and every plate has inventive flourishes. Meals aren't quite as good as the better resort eateries, but the light through the stained glass windows makes it all worthwhile. Average price of full child's menu meal: $6.20

© MediaMarx, Inc.

Princesses Jennifer and Allie enjoy breakfast at Cinderella's Royal Table

Table | American | Med. Noise | Reservations/priority seats essential | Vegetarians should make requests before ordering | Call 90 days | ~8-10:30 am, 11:30-2:45 pm 4 pm-closing

Columbia Harbour House [C-2] L/D/S $11 — 5 | 6 | 6

This cozy inn provides cool relief and attractive decor despite the inexpensive menu. Fried chicken strips and fish with fries ($6.99), clam chowder in a bread bowl ($4.99), garden salad ($6.39), and sandwiches ($6.19–6.59) dominate the menu, but several veggie dishes–such as the vegetarian chili ($4.99)–create a rare port in the storm at Magic Kingdom. Quiet, upstairs dining room.

Counter | American | Med. noise | 11 am–1 hour before closing

Cosmic Ray's Starlight Cafe [E-3] L/D $12 — 6 | 5 | 6

Ray runs the biggest cafeteria at the Magic Kingdom. There's a wide choice of chicken ($6.49–6.99), sandwiches ($6.79), soups ($1.99), burgers ($5.49–$7.38), and salad ($6.39), but not all items are available from all stations. Families enjoy the whole rotisserie chicken meal ($15.99). Kids can get corn dog nuggets ($3.49). Toppings bar. Kosher menu, too. Singer Sunny Eclipse entertains.

Counter | American | Very noisy | Med. waits | 11 am-closing

The Crystal Palace [C-4] B/L/D $28 — 6 | 6 | 8

Little more than a stone's throw away from Cinderella Castle (but please, don't throw stones), this recently-renovated replica of a Victorian glass conservatory serves character meals all day long. Breakfast is $16.99 ($8.99/kids 3–11), lunch is $17.99 ($9.99/kids), and dinner is $21.99 ($9.99/kids). Winnie the Pooh is your host at this popular buffet. The dinner menu changes weekly, but usually offers carved meats, regional specialties such as arroz con pollo or paella, roasted vegetables, peel-and-eat shrimp, and a wide variety of salads. There's even a separate kid's buffet and an ice cream sundae "bar." Potted and hanging plants and wrought-iron tables and chairs add to the authenticity of the lovely garden setting. See pages 232–233 for details on the character meal aspect.

Buffet | American | Very noisy | Priority seats suggested | Call 90 days | Long waits | ~8-10:30 am, 11:30-2:45 pm, 4 pm-closing

Magic Kingdom Eateries
(continued)

Jennifer's Rating / Dave's Rating / Readers' Rating

Eatery	Meals	Price	Ratings (J/D/R)
El Pirata Y el Perico [A-4]	L/D/S	$10	6 6 7

Look to the sign of the Pirate and the Parrot for an informal meal near Pirates of the Caribbean. The brief menu includes nachos ($5.29), tacos ($4.79), taco salad ($5.79), and chili ($3.49). A kid's meal with a taco, cookies, and a drink ($3.49) is available. The indoor and outdoor themed seating area is shared with Pecos Bill's, so your group has more food choices. May close seasonally.

Counter | Mexican | Med. noise | 11 am-1 hour before closing

Eatery	Meals	Price	Ratings (J/D/R)
Liberty Tree Tavern [C-3]	L/D	$28	6 6 7

One if by land, two if by monorail! Disney's elegant, Colonial-styled inn serves a la carte lunches and all-you-can-eat character dinners. At lunch choose from an assortment of enticing soups and appetizers ($3.49-7.49), sandwiches ($10.29-10.99), salads ($3.99-11.79), seafood ($14.99), turkey ($13.79), and New England Pot Roast ($13.79). Kid's meals are $4.99 including drink and dessert. The character dinner resembles a Thanksgiving feast, and comes to the table on platters filled with turkey, flank steak, ham, and all the trimmings for $21.99 ($9.99/kids). See pages 232-233 for more details on the character meal. The pricey lunch menu is a good choice for an early, moderately-priced supper. Seating is at tables and chairs, and the dining rooms are well-themed.

Table | American | Noisy | Priority seats suggested | Call 90 days | Short waits | 12 pm-3 pm 4 pm-closing

Eatery	Meals	Price	Ratings (J/D/R)
Main Street Bakery [D-5]	B/L/S	$6	5 6 6

This favorite Magic Kingdom quick-breakfast and snack shop offers ever-popular fresh-baked cookies, pastries, cakes, and desserts ($1.49-5.99), hot breakfast items and sandwiches, as well as specialty coffees and other beverages. Enjoy your treats in the attractive dining area with granite-topped tables and counters, or take it outside to the tables near The Plaza Restaurant.

Counter | American | Med. noise | Med. waits | Open all day

Eatery	Meals	Price	Ratings (J/D/R)
Pecos Bill Cafe [A-4]	L/D/S	$12	7 7 6

Just the place to rustle-up a bowl of chili ($2.99), hot dog ($5.49), or cheeseburger ($5.59-7.38)—they even have a fixins' bar. Chicken wraps and salads ($4.69-7.29) please the health-conscious. Sit on the covered porch to watch the parade. Themed rooms provide delightful indoor seating, including an atmospheric "courtyard at dusk" room. El Pirata Y el Perico is next door.

Counter | American | Med. noise | 11 am-1 hour before closing

Eatery	Meals	Price	Ratings (J/D/R)
The Pinocchio Village Haus [D-1]	L/D/S	$11	6 5 5

Burgers ($5.59-7.38), salads ($4.69-$6.39), and a turkey sandwich ($7.09) don't have much to do with Pinocchio, but the Swiss-styled stone building fits perfectly with its surroundings. A burger fixings bar helps dress-up your meal, and you can substitute raw carrots for the fries. Sit outside at a patio table for Fantasyland sights; some inside tables have a view of "it's a small world."

Counter | American | Noisy | 11 am-1 hour before closing

Eatery	Meals	Price	Ratings (J/D/R)
The Plaza Pavilion [E-4]	L/D/S	$11	4 3 7

Pizza ($6.19-6.29), Italian "stacked" sandwiches ($5.69), chicken garden salad ($6.39), fried chicken strips with fries ($6.49), and kid's PB&J with chips and a drink ($3.49) are served on a shaded, open-air (not air conditioned) terrace that doubles as a shortcut between Main Street and Tomorrowland. The best tables have a panoramic view of the Castle, but the rest are unappealing.

Counter | American | Med. noise | 11 am-1 hour before closing

Eatery descriptions and ratings are explained on page 204.

Magic Kingdom Eateries
(continued)

Jennifer's Rating / Dave's Rating / Readers' Rating

■ The Plaza Restaurant [D-4] L/D/S $25	7	8	7
This small Main Street standby has all the old-fashioned ice cream parlor atmosphere you need, offering overstuffed hot and cold sandwiches including a classic Reuben ($8.99-10.49), 6-ounce burgers ($9.49 plus .49 per topping), proper malts and milkshakes ($4.29-4.49), pie a la mode ($3.99), and fountain sundaes ($3.79-5.49). Non-fat, sugar-free ice cream is available. A fresh veggie sandwich ($8.99) and the chicken and strawberry salad ($9.99) are offered as "lighter" fare. Kids meals are $4.99 with drink. Snackers and light eaters can easily split one of their huge sandwiches. Walk-up guests can expect a bit of a wait before being seated. Tables and half-booths.	Table American Med. noise Priority seats suggested Call 90 days Short waits 12 pm–1 hour before closing		

■ Tony's Town Square Restaurant [D-6] L/D $45	8	8	8
Tony's serves Italian cuisine in the heart of Main Street, U.S.A. Familiar dinner entrees include Tony's "special" spaghetti and meatballs from Lady and the Tramp ($18.49) and veal marsala ($23.49). Less familiar but perhaps more interesting are Zuppa alla Farantina (shellfish and baby vegetables in a saffron broth–$22.49), and a strip steak with gorgonzola "mac 'n cheese" ($23.99). Tony's no longer serves breakfast. The lunch menu offers pizzas, sandwiches, and salads ($11.29-$12.29), plus more elaborate entrees ($12.99-$14.99). Tony's lunch menu is a good choice for an economical, early supper. Kids meals are around $5.00. This could be the best table-service meal at Magic Kingdom.	Table Italian Med. noise Priority seating suggested Call 90 days 12–3 pm 4 pm-closing		

Selected Magic Kingdom Snack Shops and Carts

Name	Land	Specialties
Plaza Ice Cream Parlor	Main Street, U.S.A.	Hand-dipped ice cream
Aloha Isle*	Adventureland	Pineapple Dole Whips (frozen dessert)
Sunshine Tree Terrace*	Adventureland	Citrus Swirl, frozen yogurt, pretzels
Aunt Polly's Dockside Inn*	Frontierland	Ice cream, sundaes, pie (seasonal)
Frontierland Fries	Frontierland	McDonald's french fries
Liberty Square Market*	Liberty Square	Fresh fruit
Sleepy Hollow	Liberty Square	Ice cream, root beer floats, coffee drinks
Enchanted Grove*	Fantasyland	Fruit slushes, juices, Strawberry Swirls
Mrs. Pott's Cupboard	Fantasyland	Soft-serve ice cream, shakes
Scuttle's Landing	Fantasyland	Shaved ice, soft drinks
Toontown Market	Mickey's Toontown Fair	Fresh fruit
Auntie Gravity's	Tomorrowland	Ice cream, smoothies
The Lunching Pad	Tomorrowland	Turkey legs, frozen drinks

Note: Some shops and carts may be seasonal. Eateries marked with an asterisk (*) close between 3–5 pm.

Tip: Remember, opinions vary widely, especially on what constitutes a good meal. If you'd like to read reviews of eateries by other vacationers to gain their unique perspective, we recommend you visit MousePlanet's Walt Disney World Restaurant Resource located at http://www.mouseplanet.com/dtp/wdwrr. Another excellent resource are the PassPorter Message Boards at http://www.passporterboards.com. Click the "Feasting & Snacking" forum and look for messages or post your own!

Epcot Eateries

(park map on page 139)

Jennifer's Rating | Dave's Rating | Readers' Rating

☐ **Restaurant Akershus** [B-3] **B/L/D** **$32**	7 8 8
Browse an authentic Nordic buffet ($18.99 adults/$7.99 kids) in a replica of a rustic Norwegian palace. Many diners have been happily surprised by food that's both remarkably familiar and somewhat unusual. Expect cold and hot specialties such as smoked salmon, herring in many forms, Swedish meatballs, sausages, venison stew, fish in cream sauce, macaroni and cheese, red cabbage, soup, and a variety of salads. Ask for the Mickey's Child Deal ($4.99) if the kids want simpler food. Akershus' lunch is a good choice for an early supper ($13.99/$5.99). Drinks and dessert are extra. Try the Ringnes beer! The Princess Storybook character breakfast ($19.99/$9.99) offers fruit, pastries, french toast, eggs, bacon, sausage, and hash browns—see pages 232–233 for details.	**Buffet** Norwegian Med. noise Priority seats recommended Med. waits Call 90 days 8:30-10:30 am, noon–4:00, 4:15-closing

☐ **L'Originale Alfredo di Roma Ristorante** [C-1] **L/D** **$51**	6 8 7
The trompe l'oeil murals will catch your eye and so will the menu, which offers upscale Italian fare in an elegant setting—veal, seafood, and unusual pastas ($16.95–$33.95). Our most recent meal in August 2003 was the best yet, with great food and service. The hottest item is their original Fettuccine Alfredo ($17.50/$9.50 appetizer). Other first-rate choices include a salad of tomatoes, mozzarella, and mushrooms ($9.75), sinful gnocchi with gorgonzola, arugula and walnuts ($17.50, another good half-portion starter), satisfying osso bucco ($22.95), and a superior tiramisu for dessert ($5.50). The rich, expensive lunch (entrees $10.25–21.95) makes an even better early dinner. Try for lunchtime seating in the bright and cheery gallery. Child's meals $4.99-6.99.	**Table** Italian Very noisy Priority seats strongly recommended Call 90 days Med. waits 12-4:15 pm 4:30-closing

☐ **Biergarten** [B-1] **L/D** **$27**	5 8 8
Willkommen! A Bavarian town square in the midst of Oktoberfest is the setting for a hearty and satisfying German buffet ($19.99/kids $7.99). Wurst (sausages) with wein kraut, pork, chicken schnitzel, and rosemary roast chicken reign supreme at lunch. A first-rate sauerbraten and a fish entree are added at dinner. Every dish and side dish is several cuts above the typical German eatery, and each is distinctively seasoned. Musicians in lederhosen are on stage to entertain. Can you say "Gemütlichkeit"? (It roughly translates to "good feeling.") The menu has been lightened-up a little, but it isn't the place for a low-fat meal. Desserts are included, beverages are extra. There's Beck's beer on tap and a good German wine list. Lunch buffet is $14.99 (or $5.99 for kids).	**Buffet** German Very noisy Priority seats recommended Call 90 days Short waits ~11:30 am-3:45 pm, 4:00-8:30 pm

☐ **Bistro de Paris** [F-2] **D** **$66**	7 8 7
Around the corner, upstairs, and upscale from Chefs de France, this "bistro" serves a limited menu that's anything but informal. Expect a leisurely, quintessentially French meal in quiet and elegant surroundings—a far cry from the bustling restaurant downstairs. The short, classically French menu features escargot with mushroom flan ($10) and foie gras ($19) appetizers; a grilled medallion of lamb ($31), seared scallops ($29), a tender roasted veal chop ($33), rack of venison ($34), and fish of the day (market price). Desserts are outstanding ($6.75–7.50). The wine list is excellent, but the cheapest bottle is $42. Service is generally attentive, but was poor on our most recent visit. Ask for a window seat and linger until IllumiNations. No tank tops permitted.	**Table** French Very quiet Priority seats strongly recommended Call 30 days Short waits 6:00 pm-8:45 pm

Eatery descriptions and ratings are explained on page 204.

Epcot Eateries
(continued)

Jennifer's Rating | Dave's Rating | Readers' Rating

Boulangerie Patisserie [F-2] L/S $10 — 7 | 7 | 9

A quaint French bakery. Ham and cheese croissants ($2.95), a cheese plate ($5.75) and Quiche Lorraine ($4.85) make a nice, light lunch, while croissants ($1.95–2.80), eclairs ($3.50), chocolate mousse ($3.00), and fruit tarts ($3.65–$3.85) satisfy sweet tooths. Seating outside and inside Galerie les Halles shop.

Counter | French | Long waits | ~11 am-closing

Cantina de San Angel [B-4] L/D/S $12 — 6 | 5 | 7

The partly-shaded, open-air patio by the lagoon is the best feature of this taco and burrito stand. Try various platters ($6.75–7.25), nachos ($6.50), and Mexican chicken salad ($7.50). Churros ($1.89) for dessert. Vegetarians can make special requests. Enjoy a cold beer or margarita at the bar or watch IllumiNations from a lagoon-side table. Children's platter with drink is $3.50.

Counter | Mexican | Med. noise | Med. waits | ~11 am-closing

Les Chefs de France [F-2] L/D $50 — 6 | 7 | 8

Traditional French favorites such as Coquilles Saint-Jacques ($8.25), escargot ($7.95), onion soup ($4.75), duck a l'orange ($23.95), braised lamb shank ($22.95), and grilled beef tenderloin with black pepper sauce ($25.95) carry the imprint of some of France's most famous chefs. The bright, bustling brasserie atmosphere, crowded seating, and overtaxed serving staff can be at odds with the desire for a slow, enjoyable meal. Lighter lunchtime choices such as Salade Niçoise ($14.75), croque monsieur with side salad ($10.25), and Quiche Lorraine ($9.95) will keep things affordable–save the heavier entrees ($15.50–17.95) until dinnertime, even if they're more expensive then. Children's meals cost $4.45-$5.85. Chairs and half-booths. Tip: Request a table near the window for a great view.

Table | French | Very noisy | Priority seats strongly recommended | Call 90 days | Med. waits | Noon-3 pm 5 pm-closing

Coral Reef [D-7] L/D $54 — 6 | 7 | 7

Few restaurants are as breathtakingly beautiful as the Coral Reef–brightly glazed blue mosaic tiles and brushed metal shimmer in the light cast by the Living Seas aquarium, as fish of all sizes and colors swim by. The inventive seafood menu ($20–27) covers a variety of international tastes and styles, and is generally well-prepared. Meat and veggie lovers will also find foods to enjoy here ($16–$26). If only there was more elbow room, the noise more restrained, and the service more consistent. Tip: Request a tank-side table for the best views. Sweets here are special, especially for kids (they have edible Peanut Butter Playdoh). Kid's meals are $4.99–8.99. Enjoy the same view at lunch (entrees $14–22).

Table | Seafood | Noisy | Priority seats recommended | Call 90 days | Med. waits | 11:30 am-3 pm, 4:30-closing

© MediaMarx, Inc.

Dave studies the menu at Alfredo's

Electric Umbrella [C-6] B/L/D/S $11 — 4 | 4 | 6

If you're looking for basic burgers and pizza ($5.49-5.79) at Epcot, this is the place. It's also decent for healthier fare, like chicken sandwiches ($6.59) and veggie burgers ($6.09)–you can also swap your fries for an apple. The main seating area is noisy–look for quieter seating upstairs, or dine outside on the terrace and watch the fountain. Breakfast ($4.29–4.99) served seasonally.

Counter | American | Medium noise | Short waits | ~9:00 am-7:00 pm

Epcot Eateries
(continued)

Jennifer's Rating | Dave's Rating | Readers' Rating

Fountainview Espresso and Bakery [D-6] B/S $6	5 6 8
How cosmopolitan! Sip a caffe mocha ($2.79) or latte ($1.99–2.79) and nibble a croissant ($2.29–4.49), Black Forest cake ($3.99) or fruit tulip ($3.99) while watching crowds criss-cross Fountain Plaza. Mmmm! Dine inside or out. Noisy.	**Counter** French Open all day

The Garden Grill Restaurant [F-6] L/D/S $27	8 6 8
Epcot's only lunch and dinner character dining experience is tucked away in The Land pavilion. Farmer Mickey, Pluto, Chip, and Dale make the rounds of this rotating restaurant. Watch an ever-changing American landscape while you enjoy an all-you-can-eat meal. At lunch ($19.99/$9.99) and dinner ($21.99/ $9.99), the grown-ups get "homegrown" salad, sliced flank steak, roast turkey and all the trimmings, plus dessert (apple cobbler with vanilla bean ice cream) and soft drink. Some veggies come right from Disney's hydroponic gardens. Vegetarians can make special requests. Kids get chicken strips, mac & cheese, and "Dirt and Worms" (chocolate pudding with gummy worms in a cookie crumb topping). Try for a booth on the lower tier, which is closer to the scenery. Couples can get "rehitched"—ask for it when you book priority seating and again when you check in. In the afternoons you can join Mickey for an ice cream social (about $7 for adults or kids). See pages 232–233 for character meal details.	**Table** American Med. noise Priority seating not always needed Call 90 days Short waits noon-3:00 pm, 5:00 pm-8:00 pm

Kringla Bakeri og Kafé [B-3] L/D/S $10	5 6 8
This is a must stop for veteran World Showcase visitors. Have a light meal with tasty turkey, smoked ham, or smoked salmon sandwiches ($4.59–5.59). Or treat yourself to a "kringle" (sweet pretzel–$2.99), waffle with strawberry preserves ($2.49), rice cream ($2.29), or other desserts ($1.49–3.99). Beer and wine by the glass. Nice outdoor tables. Popular before IllumiNations.	**Counter** Norwegian Med. noise Long waits ~11 am–9 pm

Le Cellier [E-4] L/D $46	8 7 7
Oh, Canada! This steakhouse-in-a-stone cellar is one of World Showcase's gems. Warm lighting, brocade upholstery, and stained glass make this the coziest cellar around. The menu is very hearty, but it's not plain steaks, roast beef, and potatoes—everything is richly sauced ($17.99–$26.99). Seafood—a scallop appetizer ($8.99) and maple-glazed salmon ($18.99)—get royal treatment, and the vegetarian entree ($15.99) is very tempting. Moderately-priced lunches include excellent salads ($6.99–14.99), huge sandwiches ($9.99–14.99), and steaks, of course ($15.99–20.99). The luscious cheddar cheese soup ($3.99) is a big favorite at any time. You may also find duck, venison, and a very popular buffalo ribeye (seasonal). Leave room for dessert—chocolate "moose" anyone?	**Table** Canadian Med. noise Priority seats suggested Call 90 days Med. waits Noon-3 pm 4:30-closing

Liberty Inn [C-1] L/D/S $12	4 4 5
Hot dogs, hamburgers and chicken strips ($5.49–6.99) weren't as American as apple pie ($2.39) back in the Colonial days, but they are now. A Toppings Bar adds some relish to the basic fare, while a turkey club sandwich ($6.39), veggie burger ($6.09) and chicken Caesar salad ($6.29) provide alternatives. You can get that apple pie "a la mode" ($3.98), too! Seating indoors and out.	**Counter** American Med. noise Short waits ~11 am-closing

Eatery descriptions and ratings are explained on page 204.

Epcot Eateries
(continued)

Ratings: Jennifer's Rating | Dave's Rating | Readers' Rating

Lotus Blossom Café [B-3] — L/D/S — $10 — 3 | 4 | 5

Chinese food at Epcot leaves a lot to be desired, but the menu here has become more enticing. Try twice-cooked beef, orange chicken or Shanghai grilled chicken combo plates (all $6.59), beef and corn soup ($2.49), egg rolls ($3.19), fried rice ($3.99), and crystal noodle salad or Sichuan chicken salad ($4.99). Desserts run $1.30–2.99. Kid's meal $3.59. Covered outdoor seating.

Counter | Chinese | Med. noise | Med. waits | ~11 am–closing

Restaurant Marrakesh [F-1] — L/D — $45 — 9 | 7 | 8

Enjoy exotic food in an authentic Moroccan setting as modest belly dancers and live musicians lend even more atmosphere. Lamb and chicken are the backbone of the cuisine, either grilled, roasted, or stewed ($18.95–23.95). The flaky pastry-based appetizers ($5.95–6.95) are a must, especially the chicken bastilla ($5.95). If you've always wanted to try couscous, the Moroccan national dish of stewed meat and vegetables over steamed semolina, you'll find it is quite good here ($16.95–$23.95). Order a la carte, or choose from a variety of family-style feasts ($27.95–$29.95) at dinnertime. Plan to sample a variety of appetizers and desserts ($4.95–5.95). Check for bargain-priced specials at lunch. The kids menu is a bit exotic, offering grilled chicken with fries, beef kebabs with fries, kefta (bun-less burgers) with fries, and veggie couscous ($4.25-5.95).

© MediaMarx, Inc.

A belly dancer entertains guests during meals

Table | Middle Eastern | Noisy | Priority seats not always needed (walk-ins are often possible) | Call 90 days | Short waits | Sit at tables and chairs | ~11:30 am-3:45 pm, 4:00 pm-park closing

Matsu No Ma Lounge [E-1] — L/D/S — $37 — 7 | 7 | 8

It may be a cocktail lounge, but you can make a full meal from a variety of traditional hot and cold Japanese appetizers ($3.50–10.75) and a good selection of sushi and maki (rolls), either by the piece ($3.75–7.25) or on platters ($16.75–$21.95). The lounge is often blissfully quiet, and large picture windows overlook the World Showcase. Kick back with a sake or Kirin, and enjoy!

Lounge | Japanese | Very quiet | Med. waits | ~11 am–closing

Nine Dragons [B-3] — L/D/S — $37 — 2 | 4 | 6

Nine Dragons, decorated in traditional Chinese style with red lacquered woods and accents of gold and black, tries to cover all the Chinese favorites, but the prices are nothing like Chinatown. Many regions of China are represented by familiar menu items, including pot stickers (fried dumplings–$6.50), hot and sour soup ($3.00), mu shu pork ($15.45), scallops with black bean sauce ($18.25), lemon chicken ($18.95), kung bao chicken ($16.50), and remarkably, a traditional three-course Peking Duck dinner for two ($39) that you don't have to pre-order! Lunch now offers traditional Dim Sum service—pick plates of dumplings and other items from a cart, at $3.50-14.95 per plate. A sampler meal for two is $29.95 at lunch and $42.50 at dinner. Kid's meals are $4.75.

Table | Chinese | Med. noise | Priority seats suggested | Call 90 days | Med. waits | 12-4:30 pm, 4:45 pm-park closing

Pasta Piazza Ristorante [D-6] closed in October 2001 and is not expected to re-open soon.

Epcot Eateries
(continued)

Jennifer's Rating | Dave's Rating | Readers' Rating

Pure and Simple [B-6] B/L/D/S $10		6 5 7
The menu here in the Wonders of Life pavilion isn't as healthful (or large) as it used to be. Waffles, muffins, danish, cereal and milk, and a fruit cup ($1.79–$3.29) satisfy breakfast urges. Hot dogs and chili in various forms ($3.69–5.19) and a seasonal soup ($2.89) scratch the lunch itch. Yogurt sundaes and shakes, fresh fruit, and smoothies are low-guilt desserts ($0.99–4.29).		Counter American Noisy Med. waits ~9 am–7 pm
Rose & Crown Pub and Dining Room [E-3] L/D $37		7 6 8
They say "heck" is a place where the cooks are English, but the food in this boisterous, crowded pub is first-rate. It's so cozy inside you'd swear you just walked in out of a London fog. Traditional specialties include a meat pie sampler ($15.99), a deluxe portion of Harry Ramsden's fish and chips ($14.79), very nice salmon ($17.79), bangers and mash ($15.99), and American prime rib with Yorkshire pudding ($19.99). Start your meal (or simply snack) on a fruit and cheese plate ($5.99). Pub-style entertainers put in a regular appearance. A quieter meal with a view of IllumiNations can be had out on the terrace—request a 7:30 pm (or earlier) priority seating, check in early, request an outside table, and have a leisurely dinner. Don't forget a pint of ale, porter, or stout, an' 'ow about the lemon posset ($3.99) or toffee pudding for dessert ($4.29)?		Table English Very noisy Priority seats strongly recommended Call 90 days Long waits ~11:30 am-4:30 pm, 4:30-closing
San Angel Inn [B-4] L/D $41		7 7 7
Where but Disney can you dine at noon in a romantic, twilit Mexican plaza, while a cool evening breeze caresses your skin, a volcano steams ominously on the horizon and boats float by on El Rio del Tiempo (see page 147)? Despite the fine, authentic Mexican food, it's the atmosphere that makes San Angel Inn (pronounced "San Anhel") a favorite. For appetizers, we suggest the Queso Fundido ($9.25/two) or ceviche (marinated seafood, $7.95). For your entree try their wonderful Mole Poblano (chicken in unsweetened cocoa sauce, $18.00), mahi-mahi Veracruzana ($19.75) or the basic Plato Mexicano ($19.50). Check the Chef's Selections for tempting items that go beyond simple "Mex." Vegetarians should make special requests before ordering. The kids can choose from quesadillas, chicken strips, and cheeseburgers ($4.99).		Table Mexican Noisy Priority seats strongly recommended Call 90 days Med. waits ~11:30 am-4:00 pm 4:30-closing
Sommerfest [B-1] L/D/S $12		5 5 7
Hearty, German fare for light eaters? Sommerfest serves a daily soup ($2.89), bratwurst ($5.99), frankfurters (with sauerkraut, of course - $5.49), chicken schnitzel ($6.29), soft pretzels ($2.90), Black Forest cake ($3.79) and apple strudel ($3.09). Wash it down with Beck's beer or German wines. Seating is outdoors, within earshot of the oompah bands. Seasonal.		Counter German Noisy Med. waits ~11 am-closing
Sunshine Season Food Fair [F-6] L/D $12		6 6 8
The food court in The Land pavilion has something for every taste, including large salads ($6.39), soups ($2.89), cold sandwiches ($5.49–6.79), smoked barbecue ($6.79–7.59), stuffed potatoes ($4.69–6.29), pastas ($6.29), fresh fruit, baked goods ($1.49–3.49), ice cream sundaes, and low-fat frozen yogurt ($2.36–4.29). Wide choice of beverages. Festive, indoor seating at patio tables.		Counter American Noisy Long waits ~9 am–7 pm

Looking for Restaurant Akershus or Restaurant Marrakesh? See page 208 for Restaurant Akershus and page 211 for Restaurant Marrakesh.

Epcot Eateries
(continued)

Jennifer's Rating | Dave's Rating | Readers' Rating

Tangierine Café [E-1]	L/D/S	$14	7 7 7

Tangierine Café offers traditional Middle Eastern sandwiches and combo platters served in a delightfully-decorated, open-air café. Choose from shawarma (a grilled chicken or lamb meat loaf), roast chicken or vegetarian platters, and sandwiches & wraps ($6.95–10.95). Desserts are a deal—for $2.50 you can add baklava to your meal. A coffee and pastry counter is tucked in the back, making this cafe an excellent choice for mid-afternoon espresso and flaky, nut-filled, honey-drenched desserts. Indoor and outdoor seating.

Counter | Middle Eastern | Med. noise | Med. waits | Noon-closing

Tempura Kiku [E-1]	L/D/S	$40	5 6 8

This attractive and bustling tempura "bar" snuggles up alongside Japan's very popular teppanyaki restaurant (see below). Alas, every entree is deep-fried, or we'd visit more often. Start-out your meal with a nice variety of traditional Japanese appetizers, including sushi, sashimi, and hiyayako ($3.50–8.75), then on to the tempura—Japanese-style battered and deep-fried seafood, meats, and vegetables in various combinations, served with soup, salad and steamed rice ($12.95–24.75). Wash it all down with beer or sake. The children's meal costs $8.95. Sushi bar-style seating only.

Table | Japanese | Med. noisy | No priority seating | Medium waits | ~11 am-closing

Teppanyaki Dining [E-1]	L/D	$44	6 6 8

Meat and veggies cooked on a hot, steel-topped table by a flamboyant chef is "American food" in Japan, but don't say that too loudly at Epcot's Japan pavilion. Choose from steak, chicken, shrimp, scallops, or lobster in a variety of combinations ($16.50–31.95), and watch as everything is cooked the same way and served with the same vegetables and rice. Regardless, it's tasty, fun, and a good "adventure" for timid eaters. Vegetarians will be steered to the fresh vegetable platter ($13.95). Appetizers include chilled tofu and sushi ($2.95–8.95). Desserts are $2.95–4.50. If you're aching for "real" Japanese food, duck into the Matsu No Ma cocktail lounge for some sushi. Teppan tables are often shared by two or more parties. Children's meal is $8.95.

Table | Japanese | Noisy | Priority seats strongly recommended | Call 90 days | Long waits | 12-3:45 pm, 4:30-closing

Yakitori House [D-1]	L/D/S	$11	7 7 8

Of the Japan Pavilion's four eateries this is the place we visit most often for its tasty, filling and economical fare. This classic Japanese quick meal spot serves skewers of grilled yakitori chicken and beef as a snack, platter, or in a combo with shrimp tempura ($1.69–7.49), satisfying beef curry over rice or noodles ($5.99-6.59), and big, filling bowls of Udon noodle soup ($4.89–6.99). Wash it down with hot sake or cold Kirin beer. Dine at tables indoors or out, and take a few minutes to stroll through the nearby bonsai display. Kids meal $3.49.

Counter | Japanese | Medium noise | Medium waits | ~11 am-closing

Yorkshire County Fish Shop [E-3]	L/D/S	$10	7 8 7

Crowds have been queuing up and strolling away with Harry Ramsden's legendary Fish & Chips ($6.29), and for good reason—it's the real thing! (Dave can't resist it!) An extra side of chips is $2.59. Wash it down with a Bass ale, Guinness, or try a refreshing, hard cider (sweet or dry). Seating at patio tables is often available to the right, or visit the United Kingdom gardens to eat.

Counter | English | Med. noise | Long waits | ~11 am-closing

Eatery descriptions and ratings are explained on page 204.

Epcot Eateries
(continued)

Snacking at Epcot is every bit as diverse and rewarding as feasting in its fine restaurants. The snack carts and shops seem to appear and change regularly, however, so a definitive snack list isn't practical. Instead, we've listed our favorite treats at Epcot and where you can find them—this will give you an idea of the variety of snacks available. If you can't locate one of our favorite munchies, chances are very good you'll find a new tidbit that we haven't yet discovered!

Our Favorite Snacks at Epcot

Treat	Found At
Churros (fried dough rolled in cinnamon sugar)	Mexico (Cantina de San Angel)
Rice Cream and Vaffler (waffle with preserves)	Norway (Kringla Bakeri og Kafé)
Italian pastries and cappuccino	Italy (along promenade)
Funnel cakes (deep fried batter with powdered sugar)	The American Adventure
Kaki Gori (shaved ice with sweet flavoring)	Japan (along promenade)
Baklava (flaky pastry with honey, rosewater, and nuts)	Morocco (along promenade)
Wine by the glass	France (along promenade)
Trapper Bob's Beaver Tails (tail-shaped fried pastries)	Canada (along promenade)

Note: Some shops and carts may be seasonal.

International Food and Wine Festival

Eager to sample more international cuisine and exotic tastes? Visit the "World" in autumn, when Epcot hosts the International Food and Wine Festival. Just stroll around the World Showcase Promenade and sample food and drink at the various booths set up in front of each pavilion. The generously-sized appetizer treats range in price from $1-$6, while small plastic glasses of wine, beer, champagne, cognac, and port begin at $2 and go up from there. You can easily make a meal out of the offerings, stopping at booths whenever you discover another appetizing snack. Eating while strolling around isn't always the most relaxing, but there are plenty of benches and quiet nooks at which to munch away. In addition to the treats, you can watch cooking demonstrations by top chefs, participate in beer and wine seminars and tastings, and attend the Eat to the Beat concert series at the America Gardens Theater (no extra charge). For an additional fee (and advance reservations), you can join special wine tasting events, a Party for the Senses (a wine sipping and food sampling extravaganza), wine schools (day-long education programs), and one-hour Food and Wine Pairings. The ultimate VIP experience may be the $175 Reserve Dinners, held in a VIP dining room and featuring a VIP viewing of IllumiNations. The 9th annual festival runs from October 16 to November 14, 2004. For more information, call 407-WDW-INFO.

Disney-MGM Studios Eateries

(park map on page 153)

Jennifer's Rating / Dave's Rating / Readers' Rating

ABC Commissary [C-3] — B/L/D/S — $12 — 5 | 5 | 5

Carpeted floors, potted palms, and sleek decorating make you feel like a special employee. The International menu features fish & chips, vegetable noodle stir fry, Brazilian stew, tabbouleh wrap, Cuban sandwiches, and burgers ($5.29-6.79). Kids can get chicken or fish nuggets, and the ever-popular mac and cheese ($3.49). One of the only places to offer breakfast. Shady outdoor seating, too.

Counter · American · Med. noise · Med. waits · Open all day

Backlot Express [C-5] — L/D/S — $13 — 5 | 5 | 7

Rarely crowded and often overlooked, this backstage-themed cafeteria serves up burgers, hot dogs, chicken strips, grilled turkey & cheese, and sesame chicken salad ($5.49-6.79), plus an assortment of cakes ($3.49). The children's meal is $4.99. Pleasant indoor and outdoor seating. Perfect spot for watching the parade—stake out a table about a half-hour beforehand. Not always open.

Counter · American · Noisy · Short waits · 11 am–closing

Catalina Eddie's [G-3] — L/D/S — $12 — 4 | 5 | 6

Part of the outdoor Sunset Ranch Market mini-food court on Sunset Blvd. Cheese, pepperoni, and BBQ chicken pizzas ($6.29-6.79), a side salad ($2.19), apple pie ($2.49), and chocolate cake ($3.49) make up the menu. Outdoor, shaded (and not so shaded) seating. Nearby food stands serve McDonald's fries, fresh fruit, smoked turkey legs, burgers and ice cream.

Counter · American · Med. noise · Short waits · 11 am–closing

50s Prime Time Cafe [E-5] — L/D — $32 — 8 | 6 | 8

Clean your plate in an old kitchenette, while "Mom" serves gussied-up versions of home-cooked meals like meatloaf, pot roast, grilled and fried chicken, salmon, grilled pork chops, pasta ($12.49–18.99), and scrumptious malts, milkshakes, and sundaes ($3.29–4.79). The lunch menu adds pot pie, sandwiches and salads ($10.00–15.99) Vintage TV clips of "I Love Lucy" and "The Honeymooners" play while you eat, and your "brother" and "sister" (your servers) boss you around when your "Mom" isn't watching. This is a unique dining experience if you're willing to play along—not recommended for the overly-shy. Veggie burgers on request. The dining areas and adjoining bar/waiting area are a wonderland of '50s-vintage Formica, television sets, and knickknacks. Table and booth seating.

Table · American · Noisy · Priority seats strongly recommended · Call 90 days · Long waits · 11 am-4 pm, 4 pm-closing

Hollywood & Vine [E-5] — D — $25 — 7 | 7 | 7

This 1940s-inspired "Cafeteria of the Stars" no longer has the "star power" provided by Disney characters (character meals were discontinued in 2003), but it's a tasty and economical choice for a pre-Fantasmic! dinner. Stainless steel serving areas, comfy half-booths, metal-edged Formica tables, checkerboard floor tiles, and a mural of Hollywood in its heyday set the scene. The menu changes regularly—buffet choices may include flank steak, roast prime rib, pork loin, seafood pasta, honey-citrus baked chicken, and a fish specialty. The kids have their own buffet, and everyone can make sundaes. Dinner is $19.99/$9.99. Breakfast and lunch stopped in 2003, but may reappear. Available with the Fantasmic! dinner package at the same price (see page 217).

Buffet · American · Noisy · Priority seats strongly recommended · Call 90 days · 4:00 pm-closing

Tip: The Disney-MGM Studios' table-service restaurants may open 30 minutes earlier on Wednesdays and Sundays—check at 407-WDW-DINE.

Disney-MGM Studios Eateries
(continued)

Jennifer's Rating | Dave's Rating | Readers' Rating

The Hollywood Brown Derby [E-3] L/D $47	8	8	8

The famous Brown Derby, complete with "stars," serves enticing starters like lump crab cake ($7.99), lobster bisque ($5.99), and the yummy and original Cobb Salad ($12.99/two). Entrees include excellent pan-seared grouper with a citrus sauce, and first-rate roasts and chops ($16.99–26.99). Desserts like the famous grapefruit cake ($5.99–7.29) are quite good, and this is the place for a celebratory bottle of bubbly. The Brown Derby is the Studios' most elegant establishment. Off-white walls covered with caricatures of the stars, dark wood trim, crisp, white table linens, and attentive, formal service set the tone. Hollywood "personalities" may jazz-up the show. Fantasmic! Meal Package (see page 217). Meal with an Artist/Imagineer (see page 237).

© MediaMarx, Inc.

Dave at the Brown Derby

Table | American | Medium noise | Priority seats are strongly recommended | Call 90 days | Long waits | 11:30 am–3:45 pm | 4:00 pm–closing

Mama Melrose's Ristorante Italiano [A-4] L/D $37 ($29)	6	5	7

Mama's is a bare brick wall and checkered tablecloths sort of place. A wide variety of individual wood-fired pizzas ($11.49–12.49), light pasta specialties, and simple meats grace the menu at Mama's, which changes regularly. Veal osso bucco with risotto ($19.99); chicken parmesan ($15.99); or a grilled beef filet ($20.99) may catch your eye. The seafood pasta Fra Diavolo ($17.99) wasn't devilishly spicy or briny, but there was plenty of shellfish. Sangria, a Bellini cocktail, and desserts like spuma di cioccolata ($4.99) may catch your attention. Ask about the Fantasmic! Dinner Package, which offers a three-course dinner plus seating at Fantasmic! (see pages 153 & 217). Your little "bambini" can get spaghetti, chicken nuggets, burgers, or pizza for $4.99.

Table | Italian | Med. noise | Priority seats suggested | Call 90 days | Short waits | 11:30 am–3:50 pm, 4 pm–closing

Rosie's All-American Cafe [G-3] L/D/S $12	4	4	6

Part of the outdoor Sunset Ranch Market mini-food court on Sunset Blvd., Rosie's is really a hamburger stand offering burgers ($3.79–5.29), veggie burgers ($3.79), chicken strips ($6.49), soup ($2.59), salad ($2.19), and desserts ($2.29–$3.49). Seating is outdoors at covered picnic benches. Other stands nearby offer pizza, smoked turkey legs, ice cream, McDonald's fries, and fresh fruit.

Counter | American | Med. noise | Med. waits | 11 am–closing

Sci-Fi Dine-In Theater Restaurant [C-4] L/D $36	7	7	6

Build a drive-in theater in a movie soundstage, seat folks in replica vintage cars, serve souped-up drive-in fare, and show old sci-fi movie trailers. Would anyone buy that script? You and the kids will at this fanciful eatery. The menu is fun and portions are huge. Definitely get a shake ($3.29)—you can get "adult" (alcoholic) shakes, too. The kid's menu is classic "drive-in," but the adult menu has upscale choices like pan-seared salmon on wild rice ($16.99) and shrimp penne pasta ($16.49). At lunch try the smoked prime rib sandwich ($12.95) or apple walnut chicken salad ($10.95). The desserts are out of this world ($4.25–4.95). Everyone faces the screen, so chatting is hard. Not all seats are "parked cars"—request one if you want it. Kid's menu $4.99.

Table | American | Noisy | Priority seats strongly recommended | Call 90 days | Med. waits | 11 am–4 pm | 4 pm–closing

Eatery descriptions and ratings are explained on page 204.

Disney-MGM Studios Eateries

(continued)

Jennifer's Rating | Dave's Rating | Readers' Rating

Toluca Legs Turkey Co. [G-3]	L/D/S	$9	4	4	5

Part of the outdoor Sunset Ranch Market mini-food court on Sunset Blvd. As you may have guessed, you can get a turkey leg ($4.49) to munch on. You can also get foot-long hot dogs with chili and/or cheese ($3.69-4.89). Seating is outdoors at covered picnic benches. Other stands nearby offer burgers, chicken strips, soup, ice cream, McDonald's fries, and fresh fruit.

Counter · American · Noisy · Med. waits · 11 am–closing

Toy Story Pizza Planet [B-5]	L/D	$10	3	4	6

The name is familiar, but this pizzeria/arcade doesn't look all that much like the pizza palace in Toy Story. Choose from individual pizzas ($5.29–5.79) or "meal deals" that combine pizza, a side salad, and drink ($8.49–8.99). There's also a Greek Salad ($5.29) and cookies ($1.79) It's an OK place to eat and rest while your little "Andy" or "Jessie" hits the arcade. Seating upstairs and outside.

Counter · American · Very noisy · Long waits · 11 am–closing

Fantasmic! Dining Package

If you're thinking about a table service dinner at Disney-MGM Studios, consider the Fantasmic! Dinner Package. You get a meal at Hollywood Brown Derby, Mama Melrose, or Hollywood and Vine *plus* seats in the reserved section at the Fantasmic! nighttime show (no waiting in those long lines!), at the price of the meal alone. To qualify, everyone in your party must order the fixed-price meal—$19.99-36.99 for adults, depending on the restaurant, and kids are $9.99. Fantasmic! meal reservations require a credit card deposit. Call 407-WDW-DINE to make reservations and pre-pay up to 90 days in advance, or ask about it at Guest Services at your Disney resort hotel or at Guest Relations in the park. Availability is very limited. See map on page 153 for the location of Guest Relations. Note: Restaurants and details may change, lunch may be available in some seasons (ask) and Fantasmic! may be cancelled in bad weather.

Disney-MGM Studio's Snack Shops and Carts

Name	Location	Specialties
Dinosaur Gertie's Ice Cream	Echo Lake	Soft-serve ice cream
Min & Bill's Dockside Diner	Echo Lake	Shakes & malts, stuffed pretzels
Peevy's Polar Pipeline	Echo Lake	Frozen slushes, bottled drinks
Tune-In Lounge	Echo Lake	Alcoholic beverages, snacks
Anaheim Produce	Sunset Boulevard	Fresh fruit, drinks
Hollywood Scoops	Sunset Boulevard	Hand-dipped ice cream
Starring Rolls Bakery	Sunset Boulevard	Cookies, pies, pastries, coffee
Fairfax Fries	Sunset Boulevard	McDonald's fries, beverages
Studio Catering Co.	Mickey Avenue	Ice cream, popcorn (may be closed)

Note: Some shops and carts may be seasonal.

Disney's Animal Kingdom Eateries

(park map on page 163)

Jennifer's Rating / Dave's Rating / Readers' Rating

Eatery	Meals	Price	Jennifer's	Dave's	Readers'
Flame Tree Barbecue [E-4]	L/D/S	$13	6	6	6

Although we're not sure how barbecue fits in with the Animal Kingdom motif, at least one of us can't knock it, because it's good stuff. Pork, chicken, and beef is smoked right on premises and is available sliced on sandwiches ($6.79) and arrayed on platters ($7.99-8.49). The condiment stations offer traditional and mustard-based barbecue sauces. A green salad with BBQ chicken in a garlic bread shell ($6.99) and the fresh fruit salad ($7.29) are light alternatives. PB&J and "Beanie Weenies" for the kids ($3.49). Shaded outdoor seating in a lovely Asian garden or on decks overlooking the river. May be open seasonally.

Counter · American/Barbecue · Quiet · No priority seating · Med. waits · 10 am–5 pm

Eatery	Meals	Price	Jennifer's	Dave's	Readers'
Pizzafari [B-4]	L/D/S	$10	4	4	7

This popular pizzeria serves individual cheese and pepperoni pizzas ($5.49–5.79), chicken Caesar salad ($5.99), and a hot Italian sandwich ($6.19). You can also get a basket of breadsticks ($3.99). There's lots of indoor, air-conditioned seating in brightly decorated, uniquely-themed dining areas. Not surprisingly, the menu makes this a popular family dining spot. Some folks love Pizzafari, but we find the noise levels, crowds, and the scramble for tables to be a bit much. Look for quieter seating outside on the patio (seasonal).

Counter · Italian · Very noisy · No priority seating · Long waits · 10 am–5 pm

Eatery	Meals	Price	Jennifer's	Dave's	Readers'
Rainforest Cafe [B-7]	B/L/D	$47 ($32)	5	6	7

Environmentally conscious dining in an artificial rainforest hidden behind a two-story waterfall? It even rains indoors! The Rainforest Cafe puts on quite a show and piles your plate with tasty, inventive foods representing many different cuisines. Hearty breakfasts ($7.99-12.99), enormous sandwiches ($9.50-12.99), personal pizzas ($9.99-11.99), pastas ($12.99-21.95), steaks ($22.99-23.99), comfort foods ($13.99-19.99), and mountainous salads ($11.99) overflow the menu. Smoothies and specialty alcoholic drinks are very popular. Located just outside the gates (no park admission required). This is the only table-service restaurant at Disney's Animal Kingdom. There's a special entrance for folks exiting and re-entering the park. For discounts, see page 203.

Table · American · Very noisy · Priority seats strongly suggested · Call 90 days · Long waits · 8:00 am-6:30 pm

Eatery	Meals	Price	Jennifer's	Dave's	Readers'
Restaurantosaurus [E-6]	B/L/D/S	$11	5	5	8

Disney and McDonald's teamed up to bring you DinoLand's only sit-down meal. Choices include "Dino-Size" 1/2 lb. burgers with McDonald's fries ($6.59), hot dogs with fries ($5.49), grilled chicken salads ($5.99), veggie plates (on request), and Chicken McNuggets ($5.49). McNuggets Happy Meals are $3.79. Donald's "Breakfastosaurus" is a fun character buffet ($16.95/8.95 kids) serving traditional morning fare (vegetarians can make special requests) and featuring that lovable duck, Donald (see pages 232–233). Priority seating accepted and recommended at breakfast. The food is not thrilling, but the indoor, air-conditioned dining areas are fun—it's a weathered, dig site bunker with broken equipment, humorous signs, and educational displays.

Counter · American · Very noisy · Priority seating at breakfast · Call 90 days · Long waits · ~7:30-10:30 am 11am-3:30 pm

Eatery descriptions and ratings are explained on page 204.

Tip: Flame Tree Barbecue, when open, has quiet, relaxing dining areas that are rarely full. Even if you don't buy food from Flame Tree, you can get food from a nearby snack stand and enjoy it in the Flame Tree gardens.

Disney's Animal Kingdom Eateries

(continued)

Jennifer's Rating | Dave's Rating | Readers' Rating

Tusker House Restaurant [B-2] **B/L/D/S** **$14** 7 7 8

Savory, moist rotisserie chicken ($7.99) with garlic potatoes and veggies takes center stage at our favorite eatery at Disney's Animal Kingdom. A marinated vegetable sandwich ($7.29), a turkey wrap ($7.29), a huge grilled chicken salad in a bread bowl ($7.29), fried chicken sandwich ($6.99), and grilled salmon ($7.99) round-out the menu at this no-red-meat establishment. Try the carrot cake ($3.29) for dessert. Kids can order macaroni and cheese or a peanut butter & jelly sandwich ($3.49). Breakfast sandwiches are $4.99-5.29, cereal is $1.99, and the scrumptious cinnamon rolls are $2.79. There's lots of cool, indoor seating, but tables on the dining terrace or by the shaded Dawa Bar are a pleasant alternative, especially when there's a live African band playing.

Counter
American
Noisy inside
Quiet outside
No priority seating accepted
Med. waits
8:30-10:30 am
11am-3:30 pm

Where Are All the Restaurants?

You may have noticed that Disney's Animal Kingdom doesn't offer many eateries, and it has only one table-service restaurant. Why is this? We think it's because Disney's Animal Kingdom closes in the late afternoon, before most folks sit down for dinner. This makes for slim pickings during your day, but it provides an excellent opportunity to sample the eateries at your resort or Downtown Disney in the evening. You could even take a direct bus to Epcot for an excellent meal and IllumiNations. Another option is to arrive early and leave in mid-afternoon, stopping for lunch when you return to your resort or hop to a new park. If you do eat in the park, look for a special discount meal program (see page 203).

Disney Animal Kingdom's Snack Shops and Carts

Name	Land	Specialties
Chip 'n' Dale's Cookie Cabin	Camp Minnie-Mickey	Cookies, ice cream sandwiches
Dawa Bar	Africa	Beer, cocktails
Harambe Fruit Market	Africa	Fresh fruit, juices, beverages
Kusafiri Coffee Shop & Bakery	Africa	Pastries, cappuccino & espresso
Tamu Tamu Refreshments	Africa	Ice cream, sundaes, floats
Anandapur Ice Cream	Asia	Ice cream and floats
Chakranadi Chicken Shop	Asia	Chicken stir-fry, pot stickers
Dino Bite Snacks	DinoLand, U.S.A.	Ice cream, sundaes, nachos
Dino Diner	DinoLand, U.S.A.	Ice cream, drinks
Petrifries	DinoLand, U.S.A.	McDonald's French Fries

Note: Some shops and carts may be seasonal.

Tip: Want to enjoy the flavors of Walt Disney World at home? Pick up "Mickey's Gourmet Cookbook" (Hyperion Books) or download recipes at http://familyfun.go.com/recipes/disney/specialfeature/dm0303_sf_disney

Downtown Disney Marketplace Eateries

(map on page 183)

Jennifer's Rating | Dave's Rating | Readers' Rating

Cap'n Jack's Restaurant — L/D — $47 — 7 4 6

This casual, nautically-themed restaurant hovers over the Lake Buena Vista Lagoon. Tables and chairs line the outer rim of the six-sided main dining room, giving each table glittering views through floor-to-ceiling picture windows. The lights of Downtown perform an enchanting dance on the waters, providing a romantic setting that the lackluster kitchen can't quite match. The menu includes crab cake ($11.99) and shrimp cocktail ($9.99) appetizers, chowder ($4.49), sandwiches at lunch ($7.99–11.99), and entrees that include seafood pasta in a lobster sauce ($19.99), steak ($19.99), smoked pork ribs ($15.99 & $21.99), crab-stuffed filet of grouper ($22.99), and a pound of king crab legs ($29.99). Consider Ghirardelli for dessert and Fulton's for superior seafood.

Table | Seafood | Med. noise | Priority seating not accepted | Short waits | 11:30 am-10:30 pm

Ghirardelli Soda Fountain & Chocolate Shop — S — $8 — 6 6 8

Who can resist the pleasures of San Francisco's famed chocolatier? Sundaes, sundaes, and more sundaes ($4.75–6.50) tempt dessert fans, or share an eight-scoop Earthquake ($19.95). If that's too much, shakes, malts, and frozen mochas beckon ($3.75–3.95). Their whipped cream topped hot chocolate ($2.50) is perfect on cool winter evenings. Sugar-and-fat-free ice cream, too.

Counter | American | Med. waits | 10:30 am–12:00 am

Rainforest Cafe — L/D — $47 ($32) — 5 6 7

Another Rainforest Cafe? Yes, and it's very similar to the one at Disney's Animal Kingdom (see page 218 for menu items and descriptions). Differences include a smoking volcano atop the restaurant (rather than a waterfall) and lunch and dinner only (no breakfast). This is a very popular stop for families. Show up, sign up, and be prepared to wait. And wait. And wait. Occasional live animal demonstrations help pass the time. If the wait is too long, you can sit at the Juice Bar and order from the regular menu, or browse the Rainforest gift shop or the nearby Art of Disney shop. Near the Downtown Disney Marketplace bus stop. Open until midnight on Fridays and Saturdays. Priority seatings accepted at 407-827-8500. For discounts, see page 203.

Table | American | Very noisy | For priority seating, call 407-827-8500 | Very long waits | 10:30 am-11:00 pm

Ronald's Fun House (McDonald's) — B/L/D/S — $8 — 2 2 5

This is a classic "Mickey D's" with Big Macs ($2.59), McNuggets ($2.69–6.29), and fries ($2.09–2.79) at familiar prices. What sets it apart from the typical Golden Arches is the imaginative, Disneyfied architecture. The eatery is a huge McDonaldland-styled clockworks, filled with oversized gears and springs connected to a clock tower outside. It's next door to Lego and World of Disney, so it's a happy stop for young families. Open 'til 2 am on Fridays and Saturdays.

Counter | American | Very noisy | Med. waits | 8:00 am–1:00 am

Wolfgang Puck Express — L/D/S — $13 — 6 6 7

Fast food for the trendy, upscale set. Puck's famous wood-fired pizzas ($8.25), rotisseried rosemary garlic chicken ($10.95), and soups ($4.25) are served hot. A wide choice of salads ($3.95–7.95), sushi ($8.95), and appetizing sandwiches ($5.95–6.95) are available in the refrigerator cabinet. Desserts are $3.95–4.25, and childrens items are $2.95–7.95. Drink homemade lemonade, frozen cafe mocha, wines by the bottle and glass, and beer on tap. Dine outside, or take-out. See page 223 for Wolfgang Puck Grand Cafe over at the West Side.

Counter | American | Med. noise | Med. waits | 11 am–11 pm (or 11:30 pm on Fri & Sat)

Eatery descriptions and ratings are explained on page 204.

Downtown Disney Pleasure Island Eateries

(map on page 193)

Jennifer's Rating / Dave's Rating / Readers' Rating

D-Zertz — S — $6 — 6 5 7

End your evening on Pleasure Island with a sweet something from this little cafe. Baked goods, ice cream, and frozen yogurt ($1.95–4.95), plus cappuccino and espresso to wash it down. Or pick up pastries for your breakfast the next morning. As at other Pleasure Island snack shops, convenience trumps quality.

Counter | American | Med. waits | 7 pm–2 am

Fulton's Crab House — L/D — $65 — 6 7 8

A boatload of seafood, served in a replica of a riverboat (sans paddlewheel) outside the gates of Pleasure Island. The fish is flown in fresh every day, and the prices suggest it flew First Class. If you're looking for a fish feast, this is the right place. Preparations are straightforward–grilled, steamed, fried, or raw, with appropriate sauces. Crab lovers will be in seventh heaven, with nearly a dozen items featuring crab ($22.95–44.95). Lobster ($36.95), and the finest seasonal fish, shrimp, oysters and clams ($23.95–25.95) also appear in many forms. Steaks make a strong showing, too ($28.95–$39.95). Dave just might dive into the Seafood Boil (lobster, clams, mussels and snow crab–$32.95). Prices aren't too bad if you avoid crab and lobster. Kid's menu $4.95-12.95. Priority seating arrangements may be made at 407-WDW-DINE.

Table | Seafood | Very noisy | Priority seating accepted | Call 90 days | Med. waits | 11:30 am-4:00 pm, 4 pm-11 pm

Missing Link — S — $10 — 3 2 7

Quick, cheap eats at Pleasure Island, for those who can't stand to leave the party. Greasy cheeseburgers, uninspiring nachos, cheese steaks, hot dogs, grilled sausage, and chili cheese fries make for an artery-clogging dinner (we admit to having done this more than once). Patio tables outdoors. Go down the stairs next to the Adventurers Club for quieter outside dining.

Counter | American | Noisy | Med. waits | 7 pm–2 am

Portobello Yacht Club — D — $56 ($28) — 5 6 8

This is a nice way to start your night at Pleasure Island. Contemporary Italian specialties are served in a bustling setting. Meals are robust and flavorful, and sometimes memorable–we've been disappointed by mediocre meals and excess noise, but we enjoyed our most recent dinner and loved our first. Specialties focus on grilled meats and fish, including veal chops ($31.95), rack of lamb ($27.95), and prosciutto-wrapped yellow fin tuna ($25.95). Pastas from $17.95-24.95. There's a fine, if expensive, wine list. Desserts include sinful chocolates, fresh fruits, and sorbet ($4.95–6.95). Call 407-WDW-DINE for priority seating.

Table | Italian | Very noisy | Priority seats accepted | Call 90 days | Med. waits | 5–11 pm

Tip: The **Earl of Sandwich** has landed at Downtown Disney Marketplace, opening a new sandwich shop/cafe on the site of the former Gourmet Pantry. Yes, the real Earl (seven generations removed from the sandwich's inventor) is involved, although his second son, Orlando (appropriate, no?), is the real driving force behind this business (the company already runs a thriving delivery business in London). If one Earl isn't enough, Robert Earl of Planet Hollywood fame is an investor, and probably adds a bit of chain-restaurant savvy to the team. The shop opened too late to be included in this edition, so look for future updates.

Downtown Disney West Side Eateries

(map on page 183)

Jennifer's Rating | Dave's Rating | Readers' Rating

Bongos Cuban Cafe L/D $31	4 6 7
The lively Latin sounds and flavors of Miami's South Beach make Gloria Estefan's Bongos a popular choice for Downtown Disney dining. This is robust, savory fare, with not a chili pepper in sight. Black bean soup ($4.95), seafood stew ($27.95), garlic shrimp ($21.95), skirt steak ($18.95), ropa vieja ($12.95), fried plantains ($3.25), and flan ($5.25) are some of the authentic Cuban choices. The lunch menu offers mainly sandwiches ($6.95–8.50). Tastes may be too exotic for some diners, and our most recent meal was disappointing. The bar serves classic rum drinks, including the Mojito, a refreshing mix of white rum, mint, and sugar. Open to 12:30 am on Fri and Sat. An outdoor counter serves sandwiches and snacks (avg. meal cost=$16) from 9:30 am–midnight.	**Table** Cuban Noisy No priority seating Long waits (allow 20 to 60 min.) 11:00 am-11:30 pm

FoodQuest L/D/S $12	5 6 6
FoodQuest serves a wide, appealing variety of salads ($3.95–6.50), hot wraps ($6.95), sandwiches ($5.75–6.95), hot dogs ($3.95), and burgers ($4.95) to guests at DisneyQuest (you must have DisneyQuest admission to dine here). Kid's hot dog available for $2.75. FoodQuest is operated by the Cheesecake Factory, which means there's also a good selection of desserts and beverages.	**Counter** American Noisy 11:30 am-10:30 pm

Wetzel's Pretzels S $4	- - -
Former Disneyland Jungle Cruise cast member Rick Wetzel has become king of the gourmet soft pretzel. This new shop in the former Forty Thirst Street Cafe offers a variety of fresh, hand-rolled soft pretzels, "pretzel dogs" (pretzel dough-wrapped weiners), fresh-squeezed lemonade, fruit drinks, and Häagen-Dazs ice cream. A second kiosk can be found at Downtown Disney Marketplace.	**Counter** American Med. noise 10:30 am-11:00 pm

House of Blues L/D $44 ($30)	8 7 8
The funky House of Blues' menu is "Nawlins" Blues, with enough Cajun and Creole dishes to chase the blues away. The fried catfish starter ($8.95) gumbo ($3.95/5.25), jambalaya ($18.95), and étouffée ($13.95) are two beats ahead of any place similar in the "World," and you can get fine burgers ($9.45), steaks ($24.95–25.95), salads ($5.50–10.95), pizza ($9.95), and sandwiches ($9.95–10.95), too. Located near Cirque du Soleil and DisneyQuest, "HOB" looks like a weatherbeaten wharfside dive. Inside is an equally aged interior with comfy booths. Live blues bands keep the joint cookin' (and make conversation difficult). Headliners play at the concert hall next door. A Gospel Brunch is held every Sunday (see page 236 for details). Open to 1:30 am on Thurs–Sat.	**Table** American Very noisy Priority seats at 407-WDW-DINE Call 90 days Long waits 11:00 am-11:30 am

Eatery descriptions and ratings are explained on page 204.

Tip: We enjoy eating at Downtown Disney West Side before or after a night out, but we find the lack of priority seating and the long lines frustrating. To offset the waits, try visiting at times least likely to be crowded (late afternoon and late night). If you can't avoid the peak times but need a good meal, try the bar seating at Wolfgang Puck Grand Cafe—seats open up frequently and you usually don't need a host to be seated. You can order any item off the regular menu at the bar, too.

Downtown Disney West Side Eateries
(continued)

Jennifer's Rating | Dave's Rating | Readers' Rating

Planet Hollywood — L/D — $40/28 — 5 5 6

Everyone will be entertained and well-fed inside Planet Hollywood's big, blue globe full of movie and TV memorabilia. Every visitor gets the Hollywood treatment—you have to pass by the bouncers at the bottom of the stairs and walk under a long awning to reach the front door. There's seating on several levels, with views of projection video screens showing TV clips and movie trailers. You don't really come for the food, or do you? The menu can please almost anyone, with entree salads ($8.95-$12.45), sandwiches and burgers ($8.95-13.95), pastas ($10.95-15.95), fajitas ($13.95), and grilled and roasted meats ($13.95-19.95). Kid's meals run about $11.00. Portions are huge, quality is average, and service can be slow. You won't get bored, though.

Table | American | Very noisy | Priority Seating at 407-WDW-DINE | Call 90 days | Med. waits | 11 am–1 am

Wolfgang Puck Grand Cafe — L/D — $41 ($32) — 7 6 7

Puck is famous for nearly single-handedly popularizing California cuisine and for putting wood-fired, individual pizzas on the map. Menu favorites include Chinois Chicken Salad ($10.95), four cheese pizza ($11.95), stir-fried Pad Thai noodles ($12.95-16.95), ribeye steaks ($20.95), seafood ($19.95) and rotisserie chicken ($13.95). Ooops! Let's not forget his fabulous sushi and California Rolls ($4.95-$24.95)! The decor is trendy, the tables for two are too small, service is spotty, and dinnertime seating requires long waits. If you're in a rush, dine at the bar or outdoors. Conditions are much nicer at lunch. Note: "Grand Cafe" refers to the three restaurants under one roof. Priority seating can be made for dining times between 11:30 am–6:00 pm and 9:30 pm–closing.

Table | American | Very noisy | Priority seats at 407-938-9653 | Very long waits | 11:30 am-11:00 pm

Wolfgang Puck Dining Room — D — $56 — 8 8 8

Climb the broad staircase inside Wolfgang Puck Grand Cafe and you'll reach the upscale Dining Room. This is a popular site for private parties, but when it's open to the public it offers refined respite from the crowds below. Seafood items include tuna tartare, smoked salmon, pan-seared rare tuna "Nicoise," and sushi ($10–27)—notice a trend? Main courses include tandoori-spiced lamb chops ($28), pumpkin ravioli ($18), honey-lavender pork tenderloin ($26) and Wienerschnitzel ($25). Call 24 hours in advance for the five-course Chef's Table menu ($65). Call 407-938-9653 for reservations and parties.

Table | American | Noisy | Reservations recommended | Call 60 days | Long waits | 6-10:30 pm

Wolfgang Puck Express — L/D — $13 — 5 6 8

Fast food for the trendy, upscale set. Puck's famous wood-fired pizzas, rotisseried rosemary garlic chicken, real macaroni and cheese, soups, and pastas are served hot. Enjoy a wide choice of salads and appetizing sandwiches, soft drinks, and alcoholic beverages. Part of Wolfgang Puck Grand Cafe. Dine outside, or takeout. See page 220 for Wolfgang Puck Express at Marketplace.

Counter | American | Med. noise | Med. waits | 11 am–11 pm

Wonderland Cafe — S — $8 — 7 7 7

This is truly a coffee and dessert wonderland! This is the place to go for virtually every possible kind of hot and cold coffee drink plus to-die-for desserts, such as cheesecakes ($4.75-5.50), mud pie blackout cake ($4.95), and hot fudge brownie sundae ($4.95). Comfy seating. The Cheesecake Factory runs the joint. Located inside DisneyQuest—admission required.

Counter | American | Med. noise | 10:30 am-11:45 pm

Resort Restaurants

(Disney's Animal Kingdom Lodge and BoardWalk Resorts)

Jennifer's Rating | Dave's Rating | Readers' Rating

Disney's Animal Kingdom Lodge Resort Restaurants

Boma–Flavors of Africa — B/D — $30 — 7 | 8 | 9

Savor the many flavors of Africa at a fabulous buffet (breakfast is $14.99/adults and $7.99/kids; dinner is $23.99/adults and $9.99/kids). At dinner a dazzling array of unusual soups, stews, salads, veggies, and wood-grilled meats tempt both timid and adventuresome diners (including kids and vegetarians). The wood-burning grill and exhibit kitchen adds extra flavor to the marketplace décor. And the dessert station is fabulous–be sure to try the Zebra Domes. Breakfast is equally wonderful but more down-to earth. This has become one of Disney's most talked about restaurants. Diners are consistently amazed by the wide variety of pleasing new tastes, and even plain meat and potatoes lovers are delighted. Book ahead and arrive early. Even the line to check-in can be long. Enjoy the Animal Kingdom Lodge's lobby and animal overlooks while you wait to be seated.

Buffet | African | Very noisy | Priority seats strongly suggested | Call 90 days | Long waits | 7:30 am-11:00 am, 5:30-10 pm

Jiko–The Cooking Place — D — $51 — 9 | 9 | 9

African flavorings meet Californian and Asian influences with grace and style at Jiko. Savory appetizers like crispy cinnamon-spiced beef roll and duck firecracker come from wood-burning ovens ($7.25-12.00). Entrees include heavenly steamed Golden Bass "in a bag" ($24.00), buttermilk-curry shrimp ($24.50), pomegranate-glazed quail ($23.50), grains and veggies with tandoori tofu ($17.50), and wood-grilled pork tenderloin with mushroom ragout ($23.50). Star chef Anette Grecchi Gray can now boast of a AAA Four Diamond rating, among other honors. Under her direction fish and vegetarian items are now taking the limelight, and you'll also find a stronger Afro-Mediterranean influence. For dessert, try the Tanzanian chocolate candies ($7.00). Phenomenal South African wine cellar. The kids have their own menu with appetizers ($1.75) and entrees ($5.50-8.75).

Table | African | Noisy | Priority seats strongly suggested | Call 90 days | Short waits | 5:30 pm-10:00 pm

BoardWalk Resort Restaurants

See pages 230-231 for Beach Club eateries

Big River Grille & Brewing Works — L/D — $42 ($32) — 3 | 4 | 4

No, you won't see Brewmaster Mickey, but this brewpub chain is a popular family dining spot at the BoardWalk (ESPN Club seems to siphon-off the rowdier drinking crowd). Choices range from chicken quesadilla ($8.99) to a grilled chicken cashew salad ($10.99), barbecue sandwich ($7.99, lunch only), burgers ($8.99-10.99), or grilled porkchops ($19.99). Steaks and ribs are also plentiful ($13.99-24.99). The decor and seating is simple–we suggest you dine outdoors on the boardwalk in good weather. A recent visit was disappointing, with lackluster service, mediocre food, and a dirty floor. They do take reservations 24 hours in advance, and priority seatings on the same day at 407-560-0253.

Table | American | Noisy | Reservations 407-560-0253 | Med. waits | 11:30 am-midnight

ESPN Club — L/D — $34 — 4 | 4 | 7

100 TVs pipe the big games into every nook and cranny of this very popular (and loud) sports bar. You can even go on camera for a live sports trivia quiz. The lineup is familiar–hot wings ($8.99), chili ($5.99), burgers and sandwiches ($7.99-11.99), grilled meat or fish ($13.99-15.99), plus beer and mixed drinks. Sit at booths or on stools. Open until 2 am on weekends. No priority seating.

Table | American | Very noisy | Med. waits | 11:30 am-1 am

Eatery descriptions and ratings are explained on page 204.

Resort Restaurants

(BoardWalk, Caribbean Beach, and Contemporary Resorts)

Jennifer's Rating | Dave's Rating | Readers' Rating

BoardWalk Resort Restaurants *(continued)*

Flying Fish Cafe	D	$65	8 8 8
This is a Disney dining hot spot and one of our favorites, serving uniquely-prepared, fresh seafood in a trendy-but-fun atmosphere. The menu changes to suit the season and the catch. Appetizers are special. Dave was blown away by plump steamed mussels in a pastis-flavored cream. The "Chef's Thunder" portion of the menu offers daily specialties, such as coriander-crusted Yellowfin Tuna ($28), while the main menu may offer a remarkable red snapper in a crispy, sliced-potato wrapper with leek fondue ($29), or oven roasted grouper with clams and chorizo ($30). There's strip steak, chicken, and pasta for the fish-shy ($20-34), and not-to-be-missed desserts. The crowds here are loud—ask for a quieter table under the "canopy" in the back. Open to 10:30 on Fri. and Sat.			**Table** Seafood Very noisy Priority seats strongly recommended Call 90 days Med. waits 5:30 pm-10 pm

Spoodles	B/D	$42	6 7 6
Fresh seafood, grilled meats, oak-fired flatbreads, pastas, and other Italian, Greek, and Spanish specialties grace the menu. A satisfying breakfast offers popular items plus Italian frittata and breakfast pizzas ($5.99-12.99); try the all-you-can-eat breakfast platter ($10.99). At dinner start with flatbread or tapas, or make a meal of these Spanish-style appetizers ($4.99-7.99). A tapas platter is $19.99. Entrees include a Moroccan spiced tuna ($21.99); flavorful pasta with chicken and spinach ($15.29); and grilled pork porterhouse with polenta and figs ($19.50). Desserts ($1.99-6.99) include a chocolate velvet cake and a key lime ice cream. A take-out pizza window is open for lunch.			**Table** Mediterranean Noisy Priority seats recommended Call 90 days Short waits 7:30-11 am 5:00-9:50 pm

Caribbean Beach Resort Restaurant

Shutters	D	$40	6 6 6
Serving American cuisine inspired by the flavors of the Caribbean, this new, 120-seat, casual family restaurant has a breezy, island atmosphere. In all ways, a big improvement over the old Captain's Tavern. Menu items include a delicious black bean soup ($4.29), pan-seared shrimp skewers ($18.99), and marinated pork tenderloin ($16.99). Their signature smoked prime rib ($17.99/$19.99) is just average. For dessert, go with the French toast bread pudding ($7.99- serves two).			**Table** Caribbean/American Priority seats suggested ~5-10 pm

Contemporary Resort Restaurants

California Grill	D	$58	8 8 8
High atop the Contemporary Resort, overlooking the Magic Kingdom, the California Grill pours fine wines, serves excellent California cuisine, and keeps getting better! The noise can be deafening, but the fireworks bursting over Cinderella Castle are spectacular. The menu changes weekly, but count on inventive sushi ($9.50-$25.00), flatbreads ($9.00-9.75), grilled or roasted seafood and meats ($19.75-$33.50), and sinful desserts. Perennial picks include Yellowfin Tuna ($23.00) and grilled pork tenderloin ($21.95). Vegetarians are well-served, too. The trio of créme brulée ($7.25) is a sinful dessert. When available, the peaceful Wine Room has the same menu, and you may see Epcot's IllumiNations. Sushi bar seating, too. Kids menu $6.75-9.00. No tank tops.			**Table** American Very noisy Priority seats strongly recommended Call 90 days Long waits 5:30 pm-10:00 pm

Resort Restaurants

(Contemporary, Coronado Springs, and Fort Wilderness Resorts)

Jennifer's Rating | Dave's Rating | Readers' Rating

Contemporary Resort Restaurants *(continued)*

Chef Mickey's	B/D	$30	6	6	8
Chef Mickey's fills the Contemporary's cavernous lobby with all sorts of Goofy antics (not to mention Mickey, Minnie, and friends). Mickey's offers separate adult and kid's dinner buffets ($23.99/10.99 kids 3-11), and a sundae bar. Breakfast buffet ($16.99/8.99) includes omelettes and pancakes cooked to order. Dinner items change, but on our last visit we had flavorful roast beef, tasty pork loin, and cod with a curry crust, all of a quality and presentation befitting a deluxe resort. Note that your picture is taken before you're seated—you may purchase the photo during your meal. The place is huge, but it's broken up into smaller areas. See pages 232-233 for character meal details.			Buffet; American; Very noisy; Priority seats suggested; Call 90 days; Med. waits; 7-11:30 am, 5:00-9:30 pm		

Concourse Steakhouse	B/L/D	$42	6	7	8
Appealing touches on the appetizers and entrees lift the Concourse a cut above your typical steakhouse. Situated in the towering lobby of the Contemporary, you may see Goofy at neighboring Chef Mickey's, but it's a sane alternative when the California Grill upstairs is busy. Concourse's appetizing morning menu ($7.99-16.99) includes a breakfast quesadilla ($8.99). Lunch brings pizzas and sandwiches ($7.99-10.99), and grilled salmon salad ($13.99). The dinner menu includes shellfish bisque ($5.99), mushrooms and pasta ($13.99), steaks and prime rib ($16.99-23.99), and herb-crusted salmon ($18.99). If noise is a concern, ask to be seated at a table away from Chef Mickey's.			Table; Steakhouse; Noisy; Priority seats suggested; Call 90 days; 7:30-11 am, noon-2:30 pm, 5:30-10 pm		

Coronado Springs Resort Restaurant

Maya Grill	B/D	$45	5	6	5
Alas, this formerly inventive spot has become a plain steakhouse, with some Mexican/Southwestern items among the appetizers, catering to the resort's conventioneers. If you're hankering for Mexican food, try the resort's food court instead. The restaurant is almost too elegant for a moderate resort, with grand, soaring architecture evoking a Mayan temple in warm yellows and accents of deep blue, shimmering gold and rich woods. The breakfast buffet offers the standards, with a Southwestern flair ($11.95/6.95). The dinner menu includes pork chops ($14.99-17.99), BBQ ribs ($17.99), a bone-in strip loin steak ($22.99), and salmon filet ($19.99). Kid's menu available ($8.25-8.50).			Table; American; Med. noise; Priority seats suggested; Call 90 days; Short waits; 7-11 am, 5-10 pm		

Fort Wilderness Resort Restaurant

Trail's End Restaurant	B/L/D	$20	7	6	6
One of the best dining deals on Disney property. While the vittles at Trails End won't win awards for elegance, the food is plentiful, fresh, and tasty. Breakfasts ($9.99/5.99 kids 3-11) are hearty and heavy on home-style classics—eggs, french toast, Mickey waffles, hash, donuts, breakfast pizza, cereals, yogurt, and fruit. Lunch ($9.99/5.99) brings rib-stickin' fare like fried chicken, mac and cheese, BBQ, pizza, turkey wraps, and a passable salad bar. Dinner is a gentle $15.99/6.99 and you still get a tasty soup, salad bar, peel and eat shrimp, chicken, ribs, a carved meat, fish, good veggies, pizza, a daily regional specialty like venison stew, and fruit cobblers for dessert. Soup & Salad bar is $10.99			Buffet; American; Med. noise; No priority seating; Short waits; 7:30-11 am, noon-2:30 pm, 4:30-9:30 pm		

Eatery descriptions and ratings are explained on page 204.

Resort Restaurants

(Grand Floridian Resort)

Grand Floridian Resort Restaurants

Jennifer's Rating | Dave's Rating | Readers' Rating

Cítricos — D — $58 — 9 | 8 | 9

A grand restaurant at the Grand Floridian, Cítricos blends the fresh flavors of Florida and the Mediterranean with simplicity and elegance. Warm colors, tall windows, and well-spaced tables make this a very comfortable place. The menu changes frequently, but the sauteed shrimp ($12) and pan seared quail ($9) are appealing appetizers. A wonderful braised veal shank is available as an entree ($33), along with seasonal fish specialties ($25–$28), roasted duck breast ($25), and basil crusted rack of lamb ($29). The wine pairings—three wines selected to match your meal ($25)—are a fine idea, and the desserts ($8) are gorgeous! Closed Mondays and Tuesdays. Kid's menu ($6-12) available.

Table | Floridian | Med. noise | Priority seats suggested | Call 90 days | Short waits | 5:30-10:00 pm

Garden View Lounge — S — $25 — 8 | 7 | 5

If you've ever yearned for afternoon tea, this is the place for it. The quiet, genteel Victorian setting is perfect for tea sandwiches, scones, and pastries ($3.50-12.50), or do it right with an all-inclusive tea "offering" ($12.50-24.50). A good variety of teas is served. A kid's "Mrs. Pott's Tea" is available for $8.50.

Lounge | English | Priority seats | 2-6 pm

Grand Floridian Cafe — B/L — $33 — 5 | 6 | 6

This "informal" cafe features an American menu with all the extra flourishes found in finer restaurants. Hearty breakfasts include homemade corned beef hash ($9.99), eggs Benedict (9.99), and a traditional Japanese breakfast ($19.99). Lunch brings salads ($8.99-14.99), shrimp and pasta ($14.99), sandwiches including a Reuben, Catch of the Day, and the "Earl"—grilled ham and turkey ($9.99-13.99). At this writing the Cafe no longer serves dinner, but it may return.

Table | American | Very noisy | Call 90 days | 7-11 am, 11:45 am-3 pm

Narcoossee's — D — $66 — 8 | 8 | 8

Narcoossee's open kitchen serves an ever-changing menu of grilled seafoods with savory accompaniments. Perched on the edge of Seven Seas Lagoon, the restaurant has a sedate and casual dockside atmosphere, with lots of bare wood, and windows affording views of the Magic Kingdom fireworks and the Electrical Water Pageant. The huge appetizer of steamed mussels was heavenly ($11), as were the grilled salmon ($27) and pan-roasted red snapper ($29). Coriander Crusted Ahi Tuna ($28) and jumbo scallops ($30) are also tempting choices, and meat lovers can order filet mignon ($30) glazed free-range chicken breast ($26) or grilled pork tenderloin ($28). Desserts ($6-7) include assorted berry pyramid and Key Lime créme brulée. Kids menu ($6-12) available.

Table | Seafood | Noisy | Priority seats recommended | Call 90 days | Short waits | 5-10 pm (lounge open 5-10 pm)

1900 Park Fare — B/D — $30 — 7 | 7 | 7

Daily character meals in a jolly Victorian setting, complete with an orchestrion ("player" organ). The upscale buffet breakfast ($16.99/9.99 kids 3–11) features Mary Poppins, Alice in Wonderland, and their friends. Waits can be long, but Mad Hatter may be on hand to keep the little ones occupied. At dinner time ($23.99/10.99), Cinderella and friends take their turn hosting. You don't really come for the meal, but this is one of Disney's finest buffets (keep your eyes open for the strawberry soup—it's scrumptious). The Wonderland Tea Party is held here for kids on Mondays–Fridays. See pages 232-233 and 244 for details.

Buffet | American | Very noisy | Priority seats recommended | Call 90 days | 7:30-11:30 am | 5:15-9 pm

Resort Restaurants

(Grand Floridian, Old Key West, and Polynesian Resorts)

Jennifer's Rating | Dave's Rating | Readers' Rating

Grand Floridian Resort Restaurants *(continued)*

Victoria & Albert's	D	$115	10	10	9

You have to dress up for Walt Disney World's five-star dining experience—jackets are required and a tux or gown isn't entirely out of place. The Continental, five-course, prix fixe menu ($90) is redesigned daily, a harpist fills the air with music, and all the hosts and hostesses answer to "Victoria" or "Albert." For an extra-special evening, reserve the "Chef's Table," an alcove in the kitchen where you observe and interact with the chef and staff ($120, reserve six months in advance). Consider a wine flight ($45-50) to perfectly match your meal. Is it all worth it? Without a doubt! Your dinner is elegantly prepared, and each course brings new delights. It's just the place for that extra-special occasion. State special dietary needs in advance. Call to confirm 24 hours in advance.

Table | French | Blissfully quiet | Priority seating required | Call 90 days | Short waits | 6 pm & 9 pm

Old Key West Resort Restaurant

Olivia's Cafe	B/L/D	$40	6	6	5

Olivia's Cafe serves an enticing array of Southern- and Caribbean-tinged specialties in a homey, small-island atmosphere. Breakfast includes the classics and a lineup of healthy items ($7.29–10.79). Lunchtime brings conch chowder ($3.29–4.49), salads ($4.59–13.59), BBQ pork and Po' Boy sandwiches ($8.99–11.99). At dinner the shrimp fritters ($5.99), filet mignon with lobster-stuffed shrimp ($21.99), seafood ($16.99–19.99), and barbecued ribs ($18.99) will make you smile, and don't pass up the Key Lime Pie ($4.99). The character breakfast here was discontinued in 2001. Priority seats not always necessary.

Table | Floridian | Med. noise | Short waits | Call 90 days | 7:30-11 am, noon-5 pm, 5-10 pm

Polynesian Resort Restaurants

See page 235 for the Polynesian Luau

Kona Cafe	B/L/D	$42	8	7	8

A stylish spot for coffee and full meals. Its Asian/eclectic menu brings welcome sophistication to the Polynesian Resort. Breakfasts include banana-stuffed "Tonga Toast" ($7.99) and tropical fruit punch ($3.59). Lunch offers a huge teriyaki beef salad ($10.99), a satisfying Asian noodle bowl ($12.99), and a tasty blackened fish sandwich ($9.99). The appetizers are attractive, and dinners offer steaks, chicken, and seafood with an Asian flair ($13.99–24.99), including Macadamia-crusted Mahi Mahi ($19.99). Fabulous coffee bar and desserts, too (the specialty is "Ko Ko Puffs")! Sunday hours are 7-11:45 am, noon-2:45 pm, and 5-9:45 pm.

Table | International | Noisy | Priority seats recommended | Call 90 days | 7-11:20 am, noon-2:45 pm, 5-10 pm

'Ohana	B/D	$39	8	6	7

Aloha, cousins! The Polynesian Resort welcomes you warmly to 'Ohana, a great, fun spot for families and groups. This is an all-you-can-eat feast ($23.99/$9.99 kids 3–11). Appetizers (salad, wonton, and wings) and veggies are served family-style, then the enthusiastic cast members circulate with long skewers of grilled steak, turkey, shrimp, and pork. Kids can participate in coconut races and hula hoop contests, and live entertainers sing Hawaiian melodies. It's a fun place for the outgoing, or just to relax and enjoy. If you work things right you may even see the Magic Kingdom fireworks! Beverages and desserts ($4.99) cost extra, especially the rum drinks in unusual containers. 'Ohana also hosts a character breakfast (see pages 232–233) for $16.99/$8.99 kids.

Table | Polynesian | Very noisy | Priority seats strongly recommended | Call 90 days | Long waits | 7:30-11 am, 5-10 pm

Eatery descriptions and ratings are explained on page 204.

Resort Restaurants

(Port Orleans and Swan and Dolphin Resorts)

Jennifer's Rating | Dave's Rating | Readers' Rating

Port Orleans Riverside Resort Restaurant

Boatwright's Dining Hall — B/D — $38 — 7 | 5 | 7

Cajun cooking from down the bayou fits the bill perfectly. In keeping with the restaurant's theme a wooden boat hangs overhead and a fascinating collection of boat builders' tools hangs on the rustic walls. This is a place for hearty, Southern-style breakfasts such as the breakfast calabash ($8.99), big omelettes ($7.59), sweet potato hotcakes ($6.99), and stuffed french toast ($7.99). Dinner offers chicken gumbo ($4.99), cajun wings ($6.99), jambalaya ($16.99), pasta topped with blackened seafood ($17.59), bourbon-glazed chicken ($14.99), pot roast ($16.79), "butcher's tender" steak ($19.99), prime rib ($19.59), crab-stuffed salmon ($16.59), and pork chops ($16.99). Kid's menu ($5.29) available.

Table | American | Med. noise | Priority seats recommended | Call 90 days | Short waits | 7-11:30 am, 5-10 pm

Swan and Dolphin Resorts Restaurants

Gulliver's Grill at Garden Grove [Swan] — B/L/D — $52 ($39) — 5 | 6 | 8

By day this is the Garden Grove Cafe, offering breakfast and lunch. There's a satisfying breakfast buffet ($13.95/8.50 kids 3–11), a Japanese breakfast ($17.95), a la carte selections, and a character breakfast on Saturday from 8–10 am ($16.95/$8.50). Lunch offers salads, sandwiches, and light entrees ($8.50–14.95). Each night of the week, this eatery is transformed into Gulliver's, an a la carte character dining experience (see pages 232–233). Dinner offers hearty entrees ($17.95–29.95), pizzas, and sandwiches ($10.75–14.95). Reserve at 407-934-1609.

Table | American | Noisy | Call 90 days | 6:30-11:30 am, 11:30 am-2 pm, 5:30-10 pm

Kimonos [Swan] — D/S — $44 — 6 | 7 | 6

In search of excellent late night sushi, drinks, and karaoke? Try the Swan! Dinner is possible ($19.00–$22.50), or snack on sushi by the piece ($3.00–10.95), and hot appetizers ($3.25–9.95) while you get up the nerve to sing (if you want). Very noisy. No priority seating; reservations for 6+ (call 407-934-1609).

Table | Japanese | Noisy | 5:30 pm-12 am

Palio [Swan] — D — $54 ($40) — 7 | 8 | 9

The Swan resort is home to this refined Northern Italian restaurant. Service is gracious and attentive, and the decor honors Palio, the city of Siena's famed horse race. The menu features an enticing list of appetizers including carpaccio (thinly sliced raw beef) with parmesan ($10.50), risotto with mushrooms ($8.50), and stuffed eggplant ($8.25). There's also a selection of wood-fired pizzas ($13.95–14.75). Pastas and entrees include tortellini with lobster ($23.50), veal saltimbocca ($24.25), hearty seafood stew ($28.50), osso bucco ($24.95), and marinated swordfish ($23.50). Excellent choice of Italian wines and pastries ($7.50). Dine at linen draped tables in an elegant atmosphere.

Table | Italian | Quiet | Priority seats suggested–call Disney or 407-934-1609 | Call 90 days | 6-11 pm

bluezoo and Fresh come to the Dolphin Resort

Two new restaurants are expected to open in late 2003—bluezoo will open in the spot formerly occupied by Coral Cafe, and Fresh replaces Juan and Only's. bluezoo will feature coastal cuisine under the direction of Todd English, the chef/owner of 13 restaurants. Fresh will offer breakfast and lunch daily, and possibly a character breakfast. Watch for more details on our web site!

Resort Restaurants

(Swan and Dolphin Resorts, Wilderness Lodge, and Yacht and Beach Resorts)

Jennifer's Rating · Dave's Rating · Readers' Rating

Swan and Dolphin Resorts Restaurants *(continued)*

Shula's Steak House [Dolphin] — D — $73	8 · 8 · 9
This is the most upscale steakhouse on Disney property. Beautifully grilled, flavorful beef is the focus (if you finish the 48 oz. porterhouse they'll engrave your name on a plaque!) but perfectly succulent fish ($21.95-23.95) gets the utmost respect. Grilled meats cost from $20.95-$65.95. If you need to ask the "market price" of the 4 lb. lobster, you can't afford it! With dark wood paneling, Sinatra on the speakers, gilt-framed football photos, and formal, attentive service, you may prefer to wear a jacket or dress. Veggies are $5.95-7.95 (split an order, and get the potato pancake, too) but the "garnish" of peppers, watercress and mushrooms on every plate may be enough. The wine list is expansive and expensive. And order the chocolate soufflé for two ($13)!	**Table** Steakhouse Med. noise Priority seats suggested; call 407-WDW-DINE Call 90 days Short waits 5 pm-11 pm

Wilderness Lodge Resort Restaurants

Artist Point — D — $55	10 · 9 · 8
This visually stunning restaurant serves flavorful contemporary fare from the Pacific Northwest, and is among our favorites. The dining room is a soaring, log-beamed space graced by large murals of Western landscapes, and furnished with comfortable, Mission-style tables and chairs. The menu changes seasonally. For starters, try the grilled sausages ($7), braised mussels with lemon and fennel ($12), or smoky portobello soup ($6). The old-standby Cedar Plank Salmon ($28) is always rewarding, or try pan-seared pork chop ($24), grilled buffalo sirloin ($30), a mixed grill of lamb, venison, and rabbit sausage ($34), or seafood and vegetarian entrees ($19-25). For dessert, the hot berry cobbler is a must ($10). The wine list is excellent—try a wine pairing.	**Table** American Med. noise Priority seats suggested Call 90 days Short waits 5:30 pm-10:00 pm

Whispering Canyon Cafe — B/L/D — $39	8 · 6 · 8
If you hanker for really fine barbecue in a rustic Wild West setting, sashay over to the Wilderness Lodge. There are a la carte choices ($15.99-26.99 at dinner), but most get the family-style, all-you-can-eat "skillets," heaped with breakfast fare ($9.69/$5.89 kids 3-11). Lunch ($13.99/$7.39) and dinner ($21.99/$8.79) brings barbecued chicken, ribs, pork, sausage and all the fixin's. This is "dry" barbecue—marinated and smoked, with four sauces on the side. Just don't ask for ketchup. Trust us! There are activities for the kids, and the servers make sure all have fun. Hours: 7:30-11:00 am, noon-3:00 pm, and 5:00-10:00 pm.	**Table** Barbecue Very noisy Priority seats recommended Call 90 days Long waits 7:30 am-10 pm

Yacht and Beach Club Resorts Restaurants

Beaches and Cream — L/D/S — $20 ($9)	8 · 6 · 8
This small, seaside-style ice cream parlor is always jammed. Sure, you can get classic luncheonette items like burgers ($6.99-8.99), prime rib subs ($10.99), veggie burgers ($6.99), and hot dogs ($5.99), plus shakes and malts ($4.99), but you know everyone is here for the ice cream. Why not cut to the chase and go for an ice cream soda, float, ice cream, frozen yogurt, or sundae ($2.49-7.99). Or get the Kitchen Sink ($21.99), a huge sundae with every topping. Sit at tables, booths, or at the counter. The average meal costs above are for a "light" meal and a snack (dessert and soft drink). No priority seating. Take-out also available.	**Table** American Very noisy No priority seating Long waits 11:00 am-11:00 pm

Resort Restaurants

(Yacht and Beach Club Resorts and Miscellaneous)

Jennifer's Rating | Dave's Rating | Readers' Rating

Yacht and Beach Club Resorts Restaurants *(continued)*

Cape May Cafe [Beach Club] B/D $32 — 7 | 7 | 8

It may not be outdoors, but it's a real nice clam bake! Seafood lovers line up for this dinner buffet ($23.99/9.99 kids 3–11), which is within walking distance of Epcot and five resort hotels. An endless supply of chowder, steamed hard shell clams, mussels, baked fish, corn on the cob, and all the trimmings will make any seafood lover happy as a clam (although it's not quite genuine New England). They'll also steam-up crab legs for an extra $11.99. There's plenty for the fish-shy, a kid's buffet, a dessert bar, and they bring taffy with the check. A character buffet ($16.99/8.99) is held in the mornings that is prized for its relaxed atmosphere (see pages 232–233). Chairs and booths.

Buffet | Seafood | Noisy | Priority seating recommended | Call 90 days | 7:30-11 am, 5:30-9:30 pm

Yacht Club Galley [Yacht Club] B/L $34 — 4 | 5 | 8

This casual-yet-typical hotel café offers pleasant surroundings at breakfast and lunch. Traditional favorites and a healthy helping of meat and seafood dishes are the specialty here. Breakfast offers a buffet ($13.99/6.99 kids 3–11) and predictable a la carte selections ($4.99–12.99). Lunch brings salads ($6.99–11.99), half-pound cheeseburgers ($11.99), a crab and shrimp cake sandwich ($12.99), seared beef tips ($12.99), and a Yacht Club sandwich ($9.99). This is a fairly laidback restaurant without much theming.

Table | American | Med. noise | Short waits | Call 90 days | 7:30-11 am, 11:30 am–2 pm

Yachtsman Steakhouse [Yacht Club] D $65 — 7 | 7 | 9

Until Shula's opened, Yachtsman Steakhouse was considered to be the best steakhouse in the "World." Hardwood-grilled steaks are the main attraction at dinner, but vegetarians ($19.99 daily special) haven't been neglected. Appetizers include Oysters Rockefeller ($11.49), chipotle bbq shrimp ($6.99), and salads ($6.99–10.99). Plain and sauced steaks ($30.99–44.99) including a bourbon-glazed strip steak ($30.99), rack of lamb ($34.99), and prime rib ($26.99) fill the menu, plus scallops, sea bass, and a steak/lobster tail combo ($26.99–49.99). Excellent wine and beer list. It's been reported that this is chairman Michael Eisner's favorite restaurant on Disney property.

Table | Steakhouse | Med. noise | Priority seats strongly suggested | Call 90 days | 5:00 pm-10:00 pm

Miscellaneous Restaurant

(Wide World of Sports)

All-Star Cafe L/D $31 ($25) — - | 5 | 8

Super Star-powered decor fills this sports bar offering American cuisine, 55 televisions for watching the game, a video game arcade, and unique sports memorabilia. The predictable lineup of munchies ($4.99–8.99), salads ($4.49–$9.99), sandwiches ($7.99–9.99), rib-eye steak ($16.99), chicken tenders ($9.99), and smoked ribs ($10.99/18.99) is available, along with some pasta and seafood. Desserts ($3.99–4.99) include a warm apple crisp. Ask for one of the rooms off to the side to cut down on the noise levels. Expect long waits at game time. Open Thurs.–Sun.; closed when no events are held at Wide World of Sports.

Table | American | Very noisy | Priority seats not accepted | Short waits | 11:30 am-9:00 pm

[E]atery descriptions and ratings are explained on page 204.

Character Meals

Disney offers many opportunities to dine with characters, both those i full guise (like Mickey Mouse) and "face characters" in costume (lik Cinderella). While they don't actually sit with you throughout your mea they do roam around the restaurant and visit your table for interludes Character meals are generally more expensive than regular meals (usuall $17-35 for adults and $9-18 for kids), but the chance to meet the character in an unhurried atmosphere makes it worthwhile. Even if characters aren' at the top of your menu, character dinners are a good deal—the cost o these buffets and family-style meals is usually less than comparable full service meals when you factor all costs. Character meals are *extremel* popular—make priority seating arrangements as far in advance as possibl at 407-WDW-DINE. Bring your camera and an autograph book!

Be aware that there's a mad rush for priority seating at Cinderella's Roya Table in the Magic Kingdom. Folks start phoning at 7:00 am Eastern time exactly 90 days prior to their desired date, and tables are often gone in matter of minutes. If you get a table at Cinderella's, expect to pay a depos of $10/adult and $5/child by credit card—this deposit is refunded if yo cancel 24 hours in advance. If you miss out, don't despair. Try again onc you get to Walt Disney World. Cancellations are common, so it never hurt to ask for a table, even as you're walking through Cinderella Castle. If yo are set on dining with a princess, try the Princess Storybook Breakfast a Restaurant Akershus (see photo) or the character dinner at 1900 Park Fare

✔ Some character breakfasts start prior to park opening. All Disney resorts offer specia Disney bus transportation to the early character breakfasts.

✔ For the best character experience, dine off-hours. While Mickey may only give you quick hello during busy mealtimes, you might end up with a close, personal relationshi when tables are empty.

✔ Don't be shy, grown-ups! Even if you aren't dining with kids, the characters visit your table. If you'd rather sit things out, they will simply give you a nod or handshake.

✔ The "head" characters don't speak, but that doesn't mean you have to keep quiet. Talk to them and they'll pantomime and play along!

Cinderella and Snow White greet diners at Akershus

Character Dining Location Chart

To help you pick the meal that best suits you, we've created a chart of all the character meals known at the time of writing. The location of each meal is given in parentheses, along with the meal served (B=breakfast or brunch, L=lunch, D=dinner, All=all three meals), the type (buffet=buffet-style, family=family-style, plate=buffet items brought to you on a plate, menu=from the menu), and the prominent characters (note that a specific character's appearance is not guaranteed). Note: As of 2003, Hollywood & Vine no longer offers character meals.

Restaurant	Meal	Type	Characters
Cape May Cafe (Beach Club)	B	Buffet	Goofy, Chip, Dale, Minnie
Casual, beach party atmosphere and good, standard breakfast foods. (Page 231)			
Chef Mickey's (Contemporary)	B/D	Buffet	Mickey, Minnie, Goofy, Chip
Bustling, popular destination. Superior food. Try to dine at off-hours. (Page 225)			
Cinderella's Royal Table (MK)	B	Plate	Cinderella, Peter Pan, Belle
Gorgeous setting, hottest reservation at WDW. Original "princess" meal. (Page 205)			
Crystal Palace (MK)	All	Buffet	Pooh, Tigger, Eeyore
A favorite spot for satisfying meals in bright and airy surroundings. (Page 205)			
Donald's Breakfastosaurus (AK)	B	Buffet	Donald, Mickey, Goofy
Crowded and noisy, but lots of fun. Hearty, DinoLand-themed foods. (Page 218)			
Fresh (Dolphin)	B[1]	Buffet	Pluto, Goofy, Chip, Dale
Have a breakfast buffet, or order a la carte from a hearty menu. (Page 229)			
The Garden Grill (Epcot)	L/D	Family	Farmer Mickey, Chip, Pluto
Tasty dining in an unusual setting. Good spur-of-the-moment choice. (Page 210) Also: An ice cream social is offered with the same characters—see page 210.			
Gulliver's/Garden Grove (Swan)	B/D[2]	Menu	Timon or Goofy
A la carte menu makes this the most expensive character dinner. (Page 229)			
Liberty Tree Tavern (MK)	D	Family	Minnie, Pluto, Donald
Thanksgiving-style feast with Colonial-garbed characters. (Page 206)			
1900 Park Fare (Grand Floridian)	B/D	Buffet	Mary Poppins (B) Cinderella (D)
First-rate food, comfy Victorian surroundings, and lots of character. (Page 227)			
'Ohana (Polynesian)	B	Family	Mickey, Goofy, Chip, Dale
Aloha, Cousins! A relaxed atmosphere (no more Minnie, alas!). (Page 228)			
Restaurant Akershus	B	Family	Snow White, Belle, Jasmine
Dine in a castle with princesses (but don't expect Cinderella). (Page 208)			
Wonderland Tea Party (GF)	Tea[3]	Snack	Alice in Wonderland
"Tea," stories, and cupcakes with Alice at 1900 Park Fare. (Page 227)			

1 *Character breakfasts are on Sundays at 7:30–11:30 am only.*
2 *Character breakfasts are Saturdays at 8:00–10:00 am; dinners are held 6:00–10:00 pm every night (Timon and Rafiki on Mon. and Fri., and Goofy and Pluto on all other nights).*
3 *Wonderland Tea Parties are held Monday through Friday, 1:30–2:30 pm.*

Dinner Shows

Hoop-Dee-Doo Musical Revue

The Hoop-Dee-Doo Musical Revue is a **hilarious hoedown** in an Old West-style dance hall at the Fort Wilderness Resort. The song-and-dance vaudeville act relies heavily on slapstick humor, hokey gags, corny puns, and lots of audience participation. The Wild West performers interact with the audience, and guests celebrating birthdays and anniversaries may be singled-out for special attention. The all-you-care-to-eat meal includes salad, barbecue ribs, fried chicken, corn, baked beans, and bread, with strawberry shortcake for dessert (kids can request mac and cheese and hot dogs instead). Complimentary beverages include soda, beer, and wine—cocktails can be ordered but they are not included in the price. The dinner show costs $49.01/adults and $24.81/kids 3–11 (prices include taxes and gratuities). Shows are at 5:00, 7:15, and 9:30 pm nightly. Inquire about discounts for the last show. Note that a family photo is taken before the show, and you can purchase photo packages from a cast member who circulates during dinner. This show is very popular and reservations go early—reserve up to two years in advance at 407-WDW-DINE. Hoop-Dee-Doo Musical Revue is located in Pioneer Hall at the Fort Wilderness Resort. See travel directions below.

Mickey's Backyard Barbecue

This old-fashioned, open-air barbecue features good ol' Disney characters (Minnie, Mickey, Goofy, Chip, and Dale), live country music, carnival games, and line dancing. Vittles include chicken, hot dogs, burgers, ribs, salads, corn, cole slaw, beans, vegetables, rolls, and (of course!) watermelon—all served buffet-style at picnic tables under a huge pavilion. Typically held on Tuesday and Thursday at 6:30-9:00 pm. Cost: $39.01/adults and $25/kids 3-11 (prices include all taxes and gratuities). Note that the barbecue continues to be held at the pavilion near the River Country water park even though the water park is closed. Call 407-WDW-DINE to inquire about availability and reservations.

Getting to the Fort Wilderness Dinner Shows

To get to either Hoop-Dee-Doo or Backyard Barbecue, take the boat to Fort Wilderness from the Magic Kingdom, Contemporary, or Wilderness Lodge. Special buses run to and from some resorts, or take any Fort Wilderness-bound theme park bus. Driving (parking is free) is an option, too. The Hoop-Dee-Doo is in Pioneer Hall; Backyard Barbecue is next door at River Country. Allow 60 to 90 minutes for travel.

Spirit of Aloha Dinner (Polynesian Luau)

Aloha! The Spirit of Aloha Dinner is an exotic, South Pacific-style celebration of color, style, history, music, and dance. Everything you expect from a luau is here—women in "grass" skirts, men in face paint, fire dancers, plus traditional music and a little bit of Elvis—showcasing the cultures and traditions of Polynesia and connecting them all to the modern Hawaii seen in Lilo and Stitch. The show is held together by Auntie Wini, the heart of a group of young islanders who have learned to love traditional values including 'ohana (family). The show is held nightly in Luau Cove, an outdoor stage surrounded by a torch-lit garden. Upon arrival, guests are presented with a complimentary lei and entertained in the garden before dinner. While you wait for the show, you can buy drinks and souvenirs, and have a family photo taken. Guests are seated at long, wooden tables that fan out from the stage, all under shelter in the event of rain. The all-you-care-to-eat meal, served family-style for your party, includes salad, fresh pineapple, roasted chicken, bbq ribs, rice, and sautéed vegetables, with a special "volcano dessert" (the name is the most exciting part). Included with your meal is your choice of unlimited soda, coffee, iced tea, milk, beer, and wine. Specialty drinks are extra. The show begins after dinner with Hawaiian music and plenty of South Seas dancing by both men and women. Children are quite welcome at the Luau. Although it's not as kid-friendly as the long-departed Mickey's Tropical Luau, the Lilo and Stitch tie-in helps, and the young ones will be invited on stage for a special dance number. Photos can be picked up after the show. The Polynesian Luau costs $49.01 for adults and $24.81 for kids 3–11 (prices include taxes and gratuities). Shows are held at 5:15 and 8:00 pm, Tuesdays through Saturdays. We prefer the later seating as the darkness adds to the mystique and romance of the show. Annual passholders may get a discount on the late show (ask when you call). In the cooler months the late show may be cancelled. We highly recommend you make your reservations as early as possible—the best tables near the stage go to those who reserve first. Travel directions are detailed below.

Getting to the Polynesian Dinner Show

To get to the Polynesian Luau, you can drive directly to the Polynesian Resort. From the Magic Kingdom, take the resort monorail. From other parks, bus to the Polynesian. From other resorts, bus to the Magic Kingdom and take the monorail (daytime) or bus to Downtown Disney and transfer to a Polynesian bus. Once inside the resort, follow signs to Luau Cove. Allow plenty of time for travel, especially if coming from another resort.

Special Shows

Holidays

Holidays are always special at the Walt Disney World Resort. The parks and resorts overflow with special entertainment and decorations that vary from season-to-season and year-to-year (see pages 256–257 for details). The Christmas and New Year's season is especially magical, with all kinds of celebrations throughout the property. One big Christmas favorite is the Candlelight Processional at World Showcase in Epcot, which is available free to Epcot guests (show only) or as a dinner package offering special seating for the show (call 407-WDW-DINE).

House of Blues

House of Blues has a concert hall separate from its restaurant (page 222) which features performances by top musicians. On Sundays at 10:30 am and 1:00 pm, they serve an all-you-care-to-eat Gospel Brunch with soul food and glorious gospel music—price is $30/adults and $15/kids 3–9. Reservations can be made up to a month in advance at the House of Blues box office (or call 407-934-2583). Tickets for evening performances are available through the box office or Ticketmaster, and range from $15-30. The House of Blues is located at Downtown Disney West Side.

MurderWatch Mystery Dinner Show

The Grosvenor Resort, a Hotel Plaza Resort on Disney property (see page 104), stages a popular murder mystery dinner show at 6:00 and 9:00 pm on Saturday nights in Baskervilles restaurant. (Note: The Treasure Chest Quest game show is now held at the Westgate Lakes Resort.) The show includes an all-you-care-to-eat buffet and a healthy serving of (optional) audience participation. Tickets may be reserved in advance ($39.95/adult and $10.95/kids 9 & under) at 407-827-6534. Ask about discounts, too! Visit http://www.murderwatch.com for more information.

Restaurants With Entertainment

Several Disney restaurants offer performances or entertainment during meals. At the Magic Kingdom, a piano player may tickle the ivories at Casey's Corner. At Epcot, Biergarten has traditional German music and dancing, Restaurant Marrakesh features belly dancing and Moroccan musicians, and Rose & Crown plays host to pub performers. At Disney-MGM Studios, 50s Prime Time Cafe has TVs, the Hollywood Brown Derby may have cast members impersonating Hollywood personalities, and the Sci-Fi Dine-In Theater Restaurant shows old movie trailers. Both 'Ohana (Polynesian Resort) and Whispering Canyon Cafe (Wilderness Lodge Resort) offer fun activities for the kids (big and little).

Special Dining Opportunities

During Epcot's International Flower & Garden Festival (April 16–May 30, 2004) you can experience the **Food Among the Flowers Brunch**. This is an elaborate meal offering dozens of inventive and tantalizing choices—some may even include edible flower blossoms. Then, during the Epcot Food & Wine Festival (October 16 - November 14, 2004), there are special **wine tasting dinners** and other special meals (see page 214 for more about the Festival). Finally, during **Christmas season**, when all the familiar eateries are overflowing there is often a **holiday buffet** at a special location. For all these meals, call 407-WDW-DINE for information and reservations, but walk-up diners are often welcome at the holiday buffet.

Holiday dinners at the resorts and selected theme park restaurants usually go unheralded. Disney has no need to promote attendance during their busiest seasons, but you can be fairly certain that many resorts will have something happening on Easter Sunday, Mother's Day, Father's Day, Thanksgiving Day, Christmas Day, and New Year's Eve. Start by phoning your Disney resort to see whether the restaurants there are serving a special holiday dinner. If you strike out at your resort, call around to the various Deluxe resorts (holiday meals aren't always listed with 407-WDW-DINE). Magic Kingdom and Epcot full-service restaurants are also good candidates. Call 407-WDW-DINE to see if special meals are being offered at the theme parks during your visit.

The restaurants and cafes around Epcot's World Showcase are also likely to celebrate one or more of their **national holidays**. Check your park times guide and keep your eyes open as you travel about the World Showcase, you never know what you may find.

Lunch with an Artist and **Lunch/Dinner with a Disney Imagineer** are recent additions to the Disney-MGM Studios dining lineup. These special dining opportunities are typically available several days a week, and feature intimate conversations with a Disney artist or imagineer. Held in a private room at the Hollywood Brown Derby (see page 216), guests are served a special four-course meal while they learn about "their" artist's or imagineer's work. Each guest receives an autographed souvenir when the meal is over. Available for groups of 2-10 guests. Lunch is $60.99/adults ($34.99/kids 3-11) and dinner is $99.99/adult ($34.99/kids 3–11, although we do want to point out that it's not really a kid's event. Reserve up to 30 days in advance at 407-WDW-DINE.

Looking for the **Fantasmic! Dinner Package**? See page 217.

Meal Worksheet

The first step in planning your meals is determining your needs. Start by checkmarking the meals you'll need in the worksheet below. Next, write down where you would like to eat your meals—be specific ("cereal in room" or "Brown Derby at MGM"). Circle the meals that require priority seatings, then use the worksheet on the next page to make the arrangements.

Meal	Location	Meal	Location
Day One—Date:		**Day Six—Date:**	
❑ Breakfast		❑ Breakfast	
❑ Lunch		❑ Lunch	
❑ Dinner		❑ Dinner	
❑ Other		❑ Other	
Day Two—Date:		**Day Seven—Date:**	
❑ Breakfast		❑ Breakfast	
❑ Lunch		❑ Lunch	
❑ Dinner		❑ Dinner	
❑ Other		❑ Other	
Day Three—Date:		**Day Eight—Date:**	
❑ Breakfast		❑ Breakfast	
❑ Lunch		❑ Lunch	
❑ Dinner		❑ Dinner	
❑ Other		❑ Other	
Day Four—Date:		**Day Nine—Date:**	
❑ Breakfast		❑ Breakfast	
❑ Lunch		❑ Lunch	
❑ Dinner		❑ Dinner	
❑ Other		❑ Other	
Day Five—Date:		**Day Ten—Date:**	
❑ Breakfast		❑ Breakfast	
❑ Lunch		❑ Lunch	
❑ Dinner		❑ Dinner	
❑ Other		❑ Other	

Priority Seating Worksheet

Once you've determined what meals you plan to eat in table-service restaurants, note them in the chart below along with your preferred dining time. Next, call 407-939-3463 to make priority seating arrangements. Note the actual meal time and confirmation number below. When dining arrangements are finalized, transfer the information to your PassPockets.

Our Resort:
Our Arrival Date:

Before calling, fill in everything ← to the left of this line.

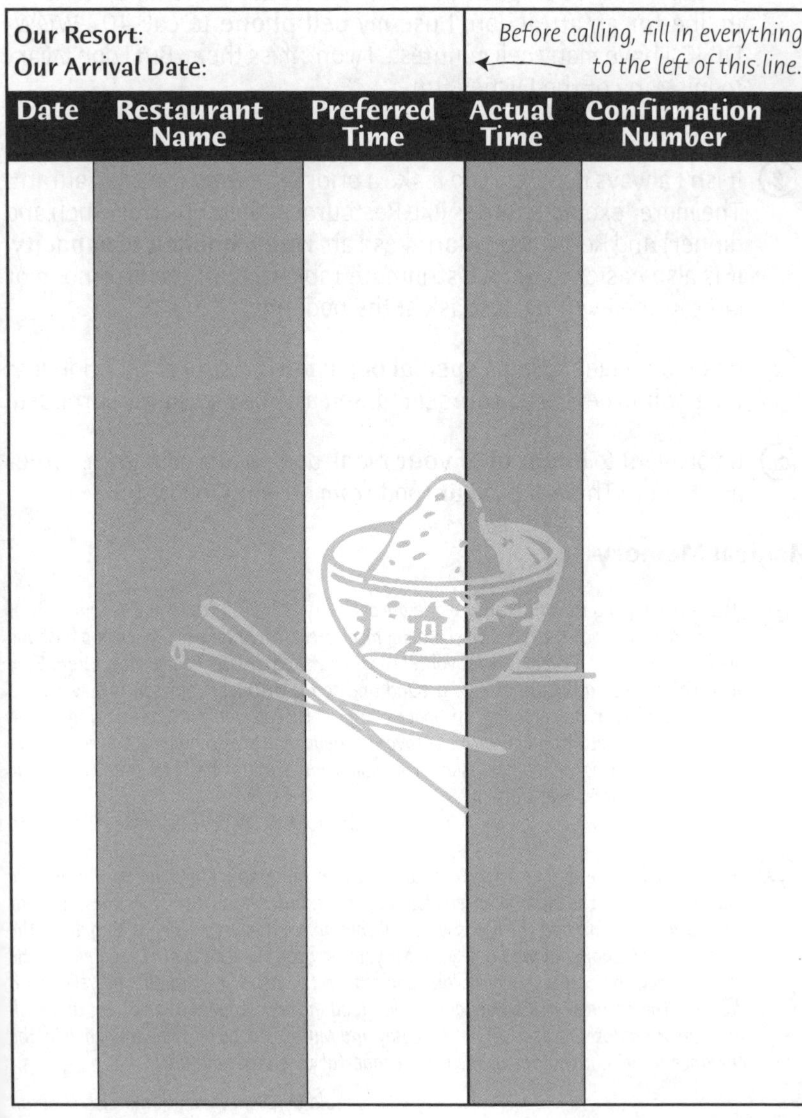

Date	Restaurant Name	Preferred Time	Actual Time	Confirmation Number

A Recipe For Fun

Make the most of your dining experience at Walt Disney World with these tips and tricks we've collected over the years:

- I get so excited about playing in the parks all day that I never know what I'll feel like having for lunch or dinner later in the day. Even though I may be steps away from where I decide to dine, while I'm in line for an attraction, I use my **cell phone** to call 407-WDW-DINE. I have many cell minutes... I won't miss them. But I don't want to miss any of the Disney fun.
  – Contributed by Cynthia Olsen, a winner in our 2003 Dining Tip Contest

- It isn't always necessary to make a priority seating for a restaurant. The more "exotic" eateries like Restaurant Akershus (for lunch and dinner) and Restaurant Marrakesh are **rarely booked to capacity**. It is also easier to get a last-minute table later in the afternoon or later in the evening. Just ask at the podium.

- If you are celebrating a **special occasion**, be sure to mention it at the podium before you are seated. You may be pleasantly surprised.

- If you want to **linger over your meal**, don't place your entire order all at once. This keeps your food from arriving too fast.

Magical Memory

"We've been going to Walt Disney World almost every year since our son was four. One of the things we do each trip is book a character meal, breakfast or dinner. My son and husband are big Tigger fans (Eeyore is my favorite) so we've visited Crystal Palace most often. Each year we've taken a picture of my husband and son with Tigger. Our son is now 15 and there's a gallery of him growing 'up Tigger's stripes.' He still thinks it's a fun thing to do—each of us get pictures taken with our favorite friends (all over the place). We're going to Disney in December and when asked if he still wanted to do this, I received the typical teenager response... 'well duh!'"

...as told by Disney vacationer Liz Myrato

"We enjoyed a late dinner at the Crystal Palace in the Magic Kingdom. By the time we finished our meal the park had been closed for 45 minutes. Main Street was deserted but the music played on and the lights were still shining. We took our time walking down the street, window shopping the whole way! My youngest son turned toward Cinderella Castle and watched the castle change colors, amazed by it. When it turned blue he yelled with delight, 'The castle is my favorite color!' We stood in the middle of Main Street and took some great photos. Our kids sat with the Roy and Minnie statue on the park bench by the entrance for a photo op! It was the most wonderful way to end our day!"

...as told by Disney vacationer Lisa Frieman

Making More Magic

FIND the hidden attractions at Disney

You're bold. You're daring. You're a Disney vacationer. Now, here's your passport to an even more magical Walt Disney World Resort vacation!

Once you've tasted the Walt Disney World Resort you'll hunger for more. Most visits can only *nibble* at the many wonders the "World" holds. There is much, much more that can be done to make your vacation magical. We've been to Disney more than most and yet there are *still* things we haven't done, and we add new discoveries to the wish list after every trip. It can all be a bit overwhelming, not to mention habit-forming. If you tried to keep up with each new activity on the Disney horizon, you'd have a full-time job on your hands.

To help you undertake your own magical explorations of the Walt Disney World Resort, we present a collection of useful information about some of its lesser-known aspects and attractions. This is our "everything else" chapter. To begin we give you a backstage pass to the guided tours, special classes, and educational programs Disney offers—from peeks behind-the-scenes to dives under-the-seas. From there we lead you on a treasure hunt for fun tucked away inside the parks—both real "treasure hunts" and hunts for items you'll treasure. We've even added a mini-worksheet for those of you who love to shop! Next we share our special tricks for feeling and looking like a VIP on your trip—a little extra-special attention can go a long way! Then we give you the lowdown on childcare programs. Your kids may find these more fun than the theme parks themselves—no kidding! Special occasions and events aren't forgotten either, with ideas, tips, and details on celebrating birthdays, engagements, honeymoons, anniversaries, holidays, and more. Before we say goodbye, we'll leave you with information for explorations beyond the Walt Disney World Resort at other Disney vacation spots—from exotic ports of call, to foreign lands, to home lands.

So get out that pixie dust and don your sorcerer's hat—we're making magic, Disney-style!

Tip: Sections highlighted in light blue (like the one below) indicate additions or significant changes at Disney since our previous edition! Rest assured that we updated all prices, too.

Backstage Passes

Disney does such a good job of hiding the figurative ropes and pulleys that you'll be disappointed if you hope to catch a glimpse of what makes Disney really work. To meet the growing demands of interminably curious guests, Disney offers tours and programs that satisfy the need to "peek."

Guided Tours

Unless otherwise noted, advance tour reservations may be (and should be) made at 407-939-8687, or through your resort's Guest Services desk. Some discounts are available to Annual Passholders, AAA Diamond, or Disney Vacation Club. Tours are only open to guests 16 and older unless otherwise noted. Many tours require substantial walking and most are wheelchair accessible. No photos of backstage areas are allowed on any of the tours. Cancel 48 hours in advance to avoid penalties. Tours which require regular park admission are noted with the ticket ( ) icon.

Backstage Safari Tour [Disney's Animal Kingdom] (ticket icon)

A three-hour, behind-the-scenes peek at the Disney's Animal Kingdom park to see how they care for our four-legged friends. No photography is allowed in backstage areas. Tours depart at 8:45 am on Mondays, Wednesdays, Thursdays, and Fridays. Park admission is required (not included in price).	**$65** Ages 16 & up Backstage peek

Backstage Magic [Magic Kingdom, Disney-MGM Studios, and Epcot]

This seven-hour tour of three major parks explores how Disney's magic is created and maintained. Go beneath the Magic Kingdom to explore the underground "utilidors," observe Disney animators at the Disney-MGM Studios, and see the computer systems at Epcot's Body Wars. Tours depart at 9:00 am. Price includes lunch. Park admission is not required. Reserve well in advance.	**$199** Ages 16 & up Backstage peek at three theme parks

Epcot Aqua Seas Tour [Epcot]

A 2 1/2-hour scuba-assisted snorkel dive that takes place in the largest indoor aquarium in the world at the Living Seas pavilion. You do not need to be SCUBA certified; equipment and instructions are provided. Actual snorkel time=30 min. Held daily at 12:30 pm. Guests ages 8-17 must be with a participating adult.	**$100** Ages 8 & up Backstage peek

Family Magic Tour [Magic Kingdom] (ticket icon)

This fun, two-hour tour offers guests an interactive adventure through the Magic Kingdom in the company of a Disney villain (such as Captain Hook or Maleficent) to solve a mystery. The tour is open to everyone and is offered daily at 10:00 am. Reservations are accepted, but those without reservations may still find room by asking at City Hall. Park admission required.	**$25** All ages On-stage only (no backstage)

Gardens of the World [Epcot] (ticket icon)

This three-hour walking tour explores the lush gardens of Epcot's World Showcase pavilions. A Disney horticulturist explains the basic concepts, theming, and practices used in creating the gardens, and offers ideas for home gardens. Tours leave at 10:00 am (same-day and advance reservations accepted) on Tuesdays and Thursdays. Park admission is required. A special version of this tour is offered during the Flower and Garden Festival (see page 256).	**$59** Ages 16 & up On-stage only (no backstage peek)

Looking for Epcot's Behind the Seeds tour, Dolphins in Depth, or Divequest? See page 245.

Hidden Treasures of World Showcase [Epcot]

This three-hour walking tour focuses on the unique design and construction of the World Showcase pavilions. Tours leave at 9:00 am on Tuesdays and Thursdays. Park admission is required. 20-person maximum tour size.	$59 Ages 16 & up On-stage only

Keys to the Kingdom [Magic Kingdom]

This 4 1/2-hour guided tour of Magic Kingdom gives an overview of the park's highlights, history, and backstage areas, plus lunch. The route varies, but usually visits five attractions and two backstage areas (the "utilidors"). Tours are offered daily at 8:30 am, 9:00 am, and 9:30 am (a 1:30 pm tour is available seasonally). Reservations can be made 45 days in advance. Guests without reservations can inquire at City Hall. Price includes lunch. Park admission is required.	$58 Ages 16 & up Backstage peek (including the utilidors)

The Magic Behind Our Steam Trains [Magic Kingdom]

Railroad fans get an inside look at the Walt Disney World Railroad in the Magic Kingdom. Join the opening crew, view the roundhouse, and explore Walt's passion for steam trains. The tour is held on Mondays, Tuesdays, Thursdays, and Saturdays at 7:30-9:45 am. Park admission is required.	$40 Ages 10 & up Backstage peek

Undiscovered Future World [Epcot]

This 4 1/2-hour walking tour of the pavilions in Future World goes backstage. Tour highlights include a visit to a VIP lounge, a walkthrough of the Cast Services building, an opportunity to meet an International Ambassador, and a peek at where the IllumiNations barges are stored. Guests may receive discounts off lunch and purchases in the China pavilion plus special seating for IllumiNations that evening. Tours are offered on Mondays, Tuesdays, Fridays, and Saturdays at 10:30 am. Park admission is required.	$49 Ages 16 & up Backstage peek (including Epcot marina)

VIP Tours

Custom-designed five- to eight-hour tours may be booked by individuals or groups of up to ten people. Tours must include a meal. Cost is about $75 per hour per tour guide and does not include park admission. VIP Tours may be booked from 24 hours to three months in advance. Blackout dates apply; call 407-560-4033 for availability and reservations.	$75/hour All ages On-stage only (no backstage)

Welcome to the Magic Kingdom [Magic Kingdom] (English & Japanese)

Get a great introduction in English or Japanese with this 90-minute walking tour. Japanese tours leave at 9:30 am on Sunday–Wednesday and Friday; English tour leaves at 8:30 am on Thursday. Kids under 10 are free.	$20 All ages On-stage only

Wild By Design [Disney's Animal Kingdom]

This three-hour walking tour takes you around Disney's Animal Kingdom to learn about the represented cultures, historic artifacts, and storytelling. Guests wear headphones to hear the tour guide better. Tours leave at 8:30 am on Tuesdays, Thursdays, and Fridays. Price includes a light continental breakfast.	$58 Ages 14 & up On-stage only

Yuletide Fantasy [Theme Parks and Resort Hotels]

Offered during the holiday season Monday–Saturday, this three-hour tour gives a behind-the-scenes peek at the magical holiday transformations. The tour visits theme parks and resorts to view and discuss the decorations. Guests under 16 must be with an adult. Price includes a snack. Park admission is not required.	$59 Ages 16 & up (Ages 12-15 with an adult)

Children's Tours, Parties, and Activities

Fun stuff for kids! You can reserve fee-based activities by calling 407-WDW-DINE up to 120 days in advance; free activities take no reservations.

Pirate Cruise [Grand Floridian Resort]

Ahoy, mateys! Cast off from the Grand Floridian marina on a cruise around the Seven Seas Lagoon in search of treasure. Little buccaneers get a bandanna to wrap around their heads, hear a reading of "The Legend of Gasparilla," learn pirate songs, and receive a bag of a "loot" (treats). Lunch is included.	**$28.17** Ages 3-10 10 am–12 pm Mon.-Thu.

Wonderland Tea Party [Grand Floridian Resort]

Take tea with Alice in Wonderland! Kids make and eat cupcakes, participate in projects, and meet Alice, the Mad Hatter, and friends. Held in the 1900 Park Fare restaurant in the Grand Floridian Resort on Monday–Friday.	**$28.17** Ages 3-10 1:30–2:30 pm

My Disney Girl Princess Grand Tea Party [Grand Floridian Resort]

Pure pampering for your little princess. This five-part party is held in the Grand Floridian's Garden View Tea Lounge, and includes a visit from Princess Aurora. Includes tea, brunch, dessert, a My Disney Girl doll, and other gifts. Additional children are $135 each, and adults are $65 each. Limited availability.	**$200.00** Ages 4-12 10:30–noon (Limited)

Grand Adventures in Cooking [Grand Floridian Resort]

Kids listen to a story, get aprons and chef's hats to decorate, then share their kitchen creations. Grand Adventures is held at 10:00–11:45 am on Tuesdays and Fridays in the Mouseketeer Club. A $5 fee is charged for no-shows.	**$23.47** Ages 3-10 10-11:45 am

Boma Kids' Activities [Disney's Animal Kingdom Lodge]

Daily activities for kids—such as cookie decorating—are available in the restaurant (Boma) and lobby of Disney's Animal Kingdom Lodge. Ask for the daily schedule of events at the hotel's front desk or at Boma.	**Free** Ages 3-12 Times vary

Junior Chef Program at The Land [Epcot]

Don your chef hats and help the grown-ups make a batch of yummy chocolate chip cookies! Just go to the bright yellow "bakery" downstairs in The Land (near Sunshine Season Food Fair) to participate. Typically held every half hour.	**Free** Ages 3-10 Times vary

Recreation and Water Sports

A wide variety of recreation options are available at many of the resort hotels, water parks, and the Downtown Disney marina. While not all activities are offered in all locations, you can expect to find biking (regular and surrey), fishing, canoeing, boating, sailing, parasailing, water skiing, wakeboarding, tubing, surfing, horseback riding, and carriage rides somewhere in the World. Call 407-WDW-PLAY or your resort to get details on recreation. Sammy Duvall's Watersports Centre at the Contemporary offers personal watercraft excursions, waterskiing, parasailing, and wakeboarding (included in some vacation packages)—call 407-939-0754. Tip: Look for money-saving programs at your resort that offer the use of boats and bikes for four hours (Family Plan—$115 for any group size) or for the length of your stay (Captain's Plan—$199 for up to four people).

Classes and Educational Programs

Behind the Seeds: A Special Guided Greenhouse Tour—This one-hour walking tour delves deeper into the innovative greenhouses seen in the Living with the Land exhibit at Epcot. Cost is $6/adult and $4/child 9 & under (no minimum age requirement), 13 people max. per tour. Park admission to Epcot is required. Sign up at The Land's Green Thumb Emporium or call 407-WDW-DINE. Tours leave throughout the day.

Disney Institute—A special educational and enrichment program for conventions and corporations. Groups of 10 or more are welcome, whether their focus is business or pleasure. For more information, visit http://www.disneyinstitute.com.

Dolphins in Depth—This unique 3½ hour program highlights the dolphin research at The Living Seas in Epcot. Guests play an active part in the research as they learn about dolphin behavior. Guests must be 16 or older, and 16-17 year olds need a signed waiver. Offered on Mondays–Fridays beginning at 9:45 am. Cost is about $140/person and includes a videotape, soda, and a souvenir T-shirt. Dolphin interaction is not guaranteed. Park admission to Epcot is required to participate in this program.

Epcot Divequest—Open Water SCUBA-Certified divers ages 16 and older can dive the 5.7-million gallon pool at The Living Seas. The 2½ hour program includes a presentation on marine research and conservation. Divers suit up and are guided in small groups for a 30- to 40-min. dive. The cost includes use of gear, refreshments, a certificate, a dive log stamp, and a shirt. Proof of certification must be shown and divers have to sign medical and legal waivers. Dives are daily at 4:30 and 5:30 pm. Cost is $140/person. Park admission to Epcot is not required to participate in this program. Advance reservations are required. Tip: There's also a snorkel-based version (Epcot Aqua Seas Tour)—see page 242.

Typhoon Lagoon Learn-to-Surf Program—Surf's up! This exciting class at Typhoon Lagoon water park teaches guests surfing basics. Learn on dry land for the first half-hour, then try your new skills on the big waves in the park's huge wave pool for the remaining two hours. The 2 ½ hour class is offered on Tuesdays and Fridays at 7:30 am, though starting time may vary with park operating hours (class is held before park opens). Class is open to resort guests ages 8 and older who are strong swimmers. Cost is $135/person. Call 407-WDW-PLAY for reservations. See pages 171–174 for more details on Typhoon Lagoon. (You can also book special surf events for groups at Typhoon Lagoon—call 407-WDW-SURF for details.)

Planning | Getting There | Staying in Style | Touring | Feasting | Making Magic | Index | Notes & More

Treasure Hunts

There is hidden treasure at the Walt Disney World Resort. While it may not consist of golden doubloons, it is every bit as priceless. There are countless sets of often-hidden and always-valuable Disneyesque items for you to find during your vacation. Sometimes these items are purposefully hidden, other times they are out in plain view for all to see but few to notice. Hunting for your favorite item can add a new dimension to your vacation! Here are our favorite things to collect:

Disney Characters and Autographs
Live Disney characters abound, and kids of all ages delight in spotting them. You can discover where some characters are "hiding" by checking with Guest Relations at each major park. If you want to "bag your catch," take photographs—and try to get yourself or your family in the picture! Keep in mind that characters are popular and crowds will form. If you know when your characters will appear, show up early to greet them. You can also collect autographs from characters who are able to sign their name. Special autograph books are available at most shops, or you can bring your own. Or use the PassPorter's autograph space on pages 274–277. Try to bring a wide-barreled pen or marker so the character can hold it easily—their costumes may cover their fingers. You can also have the characters sign hats or shirts (which must be Disney or non-commercial), but shirts cannot be worn while they are being signed and you need something to slip under the fabric to provide a writing surface.

Pressed Pennies and Quarters
One of the least expensive souvenirs at the Walt Disney World Resort is pressed coins. Souvenir Pressed Coin machines, found throughout the "World," press different Disney designs onto pennies or quarters. Cost is 51 cents for a pressed penny and $1.25 for a pressed quarter. Designs differ from machine to machine, making a complete collection a worthy achievement. Bring rolls of shiny pennies and quarters along with you—the hunt for a money-changing machine isn't as much fun. While there are comprehensive lists of pressed coin machine locations on the Internet (try http://www.liss.olm.net/ec), finding them is half the fun! **Tip**: Buy a keepsake book at Disney's gift shops to store your coins.

Free Stuff
Disney may seem to be a mecca to capitalism, but there are still free things for the taking and they make great souvenirs! Some may even become collector's items one day. You can collect guidemaps, brochures, napkins, cups, plates, containers, bags, menus, resort "newsletters," and more.

Hidden Mickeys

Believe it or not, Disney intentionally hides "Mickeys" all over the place! The internationally-recognized Mickey Mouse head (one big circle and two smaller circles for the ears) has been discovered hidden in murals, fences, shows—you name it, you can probably find a Mickey hidden somewhere in it! Disney fans maintain lists of these hidden Mickeys—try http://www.hiddenmickeys.org for one of the largest collections. You will also enjoy the "Hidden Mickeys" field guide by Steven M. Barrett, available in bookstores and at our web site (http://www.passporterstore.com/store). We made a list of our favorite Hidden Mickeys for a rainy day activity—how many hiding places can you find? Write your answers below.

# Location	Hint	Hiding Place
1. General	Isn't it good to know Disney cares for the environment?	
2. General	Ka-ching! Look at what you get when the cash register rings!	
3. General	Bubble, bubble, toil, and trouble, look to laundry for three bubbles.	
4. Magic Kingdom	Clippity clop, clippity clop! I pull a trolley past the Main St. shops.	
5. Magic Kingdom	Look to your feet for the holes in the street.	
6. Magic Kingdom	Grinning ghosts set the table, find the mouse if you're able!	
7. Epcot	Life's a Wonder, can't you see? The mural hides a green Mickey.	
8. Epcot	As you stand in Maelstrom's line, find him in the hands of time.	
9. Epcot	Now turn your glance to the gardens of France.	
10. Disney-MGM Studios	Look for a tower and we'll bet if you say "terror" you're all wet.	
11. Disney-MGM Studios	All around the park I run, my thin black bars protect the fun.	
12. Disney-MGM Studios	We won't leave you in the lurch. Look at New York Street's church!	
13. Disney's Animal Kingdom	Amid the trees near Simba's fest hangs a house that holds a nest.	
14. Disney's Animal Kingdom	Near Pangani you'll pass some fruit. Don't squish Mickey under your boot!	
15. Disney's Animal Kingdom	There is a froggie near Pizzafari. Now that's the end of this safari!	

Hidden Mickey hiding places are found on page 259.

Photographs and Memories

Many vacationers bring a camera or a camcorder to record their trip. Most seem content to simply take pictures as the mood strikes them, but you can also "collect" pictures as well! Here are some ideas for fun photograph collections: Disney puns and visual gags that often go unnoticed (try "holding up" Spaceship Earth or the monorail track in your photos); your favorite spot at different times of the day; all of the "Kodak Picture Spot" signs; and pictures through the eyes of your children (give them their own camera). How about a photo of each family member next to their favorite attraction? If you take these same photos on return trips, you can make a "growth chart" over time. Another idea is to hold a family photo scavenger hunt for fun things and places around the "World."

Souvenirs

If you enjoy taking home souvenirs but you're tired of the usual T-shirts or postcards, consider beginning a new collection. Chances are that if you can collect it, Disney has it somewhere on their property. Here are favorite collectibles: enamel pins (see page 251 for details), patches (you can sew them onto your packs), mugs (our favorite), figurines, hats, clothing, stuffed animals, mini bean bags, and the new Pal Mickey (see below). Love shopping? Here's a mini-worksheet to help you organize the items you want to purchase for yourself and others at Walt Disney World!

Who	What	Size/Color	$$	✓

Pal Mickey – "The Talk of the Parks"

Who's 10 inches tall and is destined to become the most popular tour guide at Walt Disney World? Pal Mickey! Pal Mickey is Disney Imagineering's latest, plush innovation, a soft, loveable toy that plays games wherever he goes, and becomes an instant tour guide whenever he enters a Walt Disney World theme park. While Pal Mickey is no substitute for a real tour guide (be that a person or a guidebook) and he mainly appeals to kids, he's still an amusing diversion. We recommend you rent one first ($8/day), and then apply the rental towards an outright purchase ($60) if you decide to keep it–this also means you turn in the rented one and get a new, boxed Mickey to take home. Be sure to keep his black nose pointed outward and uncovered, as he is literally guided by his nose.

In Search Of...

Quite often we're on the lookout for specific items, whether they be souvenirs or necessities. To help hunt down your treasures, here is a partial list of places to find some of the more sought-after items:

Alcohol—You can buy a mixed drink or beer at any of the resorts or parks with the notable exception of the Magic Kingdom. You can also purchase alcohol at most resort general stores and at Downtown Disney.

Baby Needs—The baby care centers in the four major parks sell common baby items, such as diapers, powder, and formula. Your resort's gift shop stocks these items as well.

Groceries—Snacks are available at most of the resort stores, and a small selection of groceries is available at resorts with in-room cooking facilities. For more serious marketing, visit Gooding's Supermarket at the Crossroads Shopping Center near Downtown Disney.

Gum—Gum is not sold on Disney property nor at the airport to avoid messes. If you need it, bring it with you or buy it off-property.

Lost Items—Lost and Found centers are located everywhere you go—generally near the front of the park or complex. Jennifer dropped a favorite scarf at Downtown Disney and within 15 minutes she had recovered it at Lost and Found (much to her relief). You can also call Lost and Found at 407-824-4245. Lost and found items are generally kept at each park only until closing. After that they are usually transferred to Central Lost and Found at the Transportation & Ticket Center (inside the Kennel).

Medicine—Order prescription and over-the-counter drugs through Turner Drugs at 407-828-8125 from 8:00 am to 8:00 pm. Deliveries are available between 9:00 am and 9:00 pm. Over-the-counter medicine and band-aids are kept under the counter at many Disney shops—ask a cast member. Aspirin and band-aids are also available at no charge at the first-aid stations located in each park, which are staffed by licensed medical personnel.

Missing or Lost Persons—Should the unthinkable happen, immediately alert a cast member or go to Guest Relations. Teach kids how to recognize cast members. A message system is available at Guest Relations and Guest Services to help coordinate things, even if you aren't lost (yet). It's a good idea to choose a meeting place each day in the event you are separated from your family or friends. You may also find it helpful to give each member of your party a two-way radio to stay in touch with one another.

Money—ATMs (cash machines) are located in all the parks and resorts. See our park maps or Disney's guidemaps for locations. The Walt Disney World Resort accepts American Express, MasterCard, Visa, Discover, The Disney Credit Card, JCB, Diner's Club, travelers checks, cash, Disney Dollars, and Disney Visa Reward Vouchers (see page 10 for details on the Disney Visa card). Personal checks are also accepted (with two forms of identification) in most spots.

Rain Gear—If you didn't bring an umbrella or poncho along, Disney will sell you one at virtually any shop. You may need to ask, but chances are they'll have something. Tip: If your poncho rips, bring it back to any shop and they'll replace it. Note: In late 2003 Disney began selling clear ponchos (instead of the traditional yellow) to make it easier to spot your companions in the rain. No more "sea of yellow!"

VIP Tips

Wake Up Call

If you're staying at a Disney resort, start your day with a call from Mickey. Just use the phone system to arrange a wake up call and when the phone rings, Mickey or one of his friends welcomes you to the new day! When the phone rings with your wake up call, press the speakerphone button so everyone in the room can hear it! Reader Jenn Reall suggests you make your wake up call for an off-time, such as 7:03, to ensure you get Mickey.

Box Seats

Monorail—If you're at one of the monorail resorts, ask the cast member on the platform about riding in the front cab. The view is fabulous! Keep in mind that you may need to wait for a specific monorail to arrive. Monorail cab rides are available on the Express and Epcot lines when traffic and crowds permit, too. Seating is limited to four guests. The front cab is not available when boarding a resort monorail from the Magic Kingdom or Transportation & Ticket Center (TTC). Note that wheelchairs cannot ride in the front cab; ask for a "license" in lieu of riding up front!

Contemporary Resort—Enjoy a drink in the California Grill lounge during the Magic Kingdom fireworks (the music that normally accompanies the fireworks is broadcast in the restaurant). On our last visit, the observation deck on the 15th floor was open to the general public. And there's another viewing area on the north end of the Grand Concourse (4th floor).

Fireworks Cruises—Do you have something to celebrate? Rent a pontoon boat, the Breathless speedboat, or the Grand 1 Yacht to view the fireworks at the Magic Kingdom or Epcot. Cruises are booked per boat rather than per passenger, and all include a pilot. Call 407-WDW-PLAY for rates and reservations. Note: These are sometimes called "specialty" cruises by Disney, as they can't promise that the fireworks won't be cancelled.

Leave a Legacy

Leave a Legacy is a huge, outdoor photo gallery at Epcot. Row after row of polished granite monuments line the entrance plaza. The monuments are decorated with shining metal plaques, each displaying dozens of one-inch square, laser-etched portraits. The photos have been reduced to stark black on silver, so they're not always the most flattering. We were among the first to leave our legacy—find our smiling faces at West 6-A-3-10-8 (west side, sixth monument, column A, 3rd plaque, 10 images up, and 8 images from the left). Leave your own legacy for $35 (one face) or $38 (two faces in one image). Annual Passholders get a 10% discount.

Trading Pins

Colorful, enameled commemorative pins are a favorite Disney collectible, available at nearly every shop. Disney designs hundreds of these colorful, cloissone pins, which commemorate the theme parks, resorts, attractions, characters, and events. Over the years, Disney stepped up pin trading activity by introducing Pin Trading Stations at the parks and the Disney's Pin Traders shop at Downtown Disney at which you can buy and swap pins. Bring (or buy) your own Disney pins, and trade pins with other guests and with cast members wearing special pin-trading lanyards. Note that cast members wearing green lanyards trade only with children. Pin trading is a fun way to meet fellow vacationers and learn more about the world of Disney. Buy a Disney pin lanyard, or display your pins in a scrapbook, or on a vest or hat (see photo to the right).

© MediaMarx, Inc.

Jennifer displays a few pins from her collection on her hat and lanyard.

Name Badges and Pins

Show everyone how special you are with an oval Disney name badge, personalized with your first name. The badges make great conversation starters—you may even get more personal attention from cast members while wearing one. You can purchase badges in the parks and at Downtown Disney for $6. Have an unusual name? Visit the engraving shop at Disney-MGM Studios or at Disney's Days of Christmas at Downtown Disney. Another option is our own PassPorter Badge, which our readers requested to help them spot fellow fans in the parks. (Jennifer is wearing her badge in the photo above.) PassPorter Badges are $4 and also come with free personalization. You can order PassPorter Badges at our Web site. We also issue our own collectible, cloissone PassPorter Pins for $6. And if you're looking for a way to recognize outstanding cast members, visit the folks at http://www.whatwouldwaltdo.com for special cast-only award pins!

Park Passports

Disney has passports, too! The Epcot Passport is a great way to tour the World Showcase. Once you have a passport, you can get it "stamped" at each pavilion or land by a cast member. The passports—which kids love—can be purchased at shops and carts for about $10, and include an "I'm a World Showcase Traveler" pin and a set of stickers. A similar passport is available at Disney's Animal Kingdom.

Childcare Programs

"We're going to Walt Disney World. Why in the 'World' would we need childcare?" The Walt Disney World Resort is an adult playground, too! The "World" offers an exciting nightlife and leaves lots of room for romance. All you need is a sitter. Not surprisingly, Disney delivers with a variety of childcare options and a few programs that may seem like childcare to you (but don't tell the kids). The two main options are childcare programs at the resorts and private, in-room baby-sitting.

Each of Disney's deluxe resorts offer childcare programs. These childcare programs are a good bit like daycare, but unlike daycare, their "day" usually starts at around 4:00 pm and runs until midnight. They offer a variety of structured activities and entertainment, and usually include a full meal. All programs accept children from 4–12 years of age and all children must be potty-trained. Rates are $8–10/hour, and some programs have minimum stays. Programs usually also have an overtime rate—the kids won't be evicted if your coach turns into a pumpkin on the way back from Cinderella Castle. Parents are given pagers, too. Some programs are available only to Disney resort guests, and some only for guests staying in that particular resort. Make your status clear when you phone so there are no disappointments. No matter which program you contact, we recommend you call well in advance and ask plenty of questions. Reservations can be made with the club itself, or at 407-WDW-DINE. Each resort offers different services and rules, and all are subject to change. Cancel at least 24 hours in advance to avoid a $15/kid fee. Allie's KidTip: "It's cool to stay at the kids clubs so you can do what you like to do and grown-ups can do what they want to do." Read on for more of Allie's KidTips on the clubs she's visited.

Childcare Near Epcot and Disney-MGM Studios

Sandcastle Club [Beach Club]	407-934-3750
Large club with plenty of Legos, games, computers, and video games (free) to play with. Meals are served at 6:00, 7:00, or 8:00 pm. Allie's KidTip: *"You might get to choose the movies to watch and there are fun games to play."*	**$10/hour** 4:30 pm-midnight
Harbor Club [Boardwalk Inn & Villas]	407-939-6301
Smaller club with kid-friendly activities. Price includes a meal and a snack—meals are served at 6:00, 7:00, or 8:00 pm. Closed Mondays and Tuesdays. This club closed for a while in 2003, but is expected to be open in 2004.	**$10/hour** 4:00 pm-midnight
Camp Dolphin [Swan and Dolphin]	407-934-4000 ext. 4241
Kids have fun with arts and crafts, video games, and movies. Price includes a meal at 7:00 pm—kids are taken to either Tubbi's or the Dolphin Fountain eateries in the resort. Note that participation is limited to Dolphin guests.	**$10/hour** 5:30 pm-midnight

Childcare Near Disney's Animal Kingdom

Simba's Cubhouse [Disney's Animal Kingdom Lodge]	407-938-4785
The club with a view of the savannah and animals. Plenty of movies and games. Price includes a meal (serving time varies). **Allie's KidTip:** *"This is my first choice! I liked the people and the decorations. And I loved watching the animals."*	**$10/hour** 4:30 pm-midnight

Childcare Near the Magic Kingdom

Mouseketeer Clubhouse [Contemporary]	407-824-1000 ext. 3038
This is a smaller club but it seems to be a big favorite with the kids. Price includes a meal served at your specified time. Two-hour minimum stay.	**$8/hour** 4:30 pm-mid.

Mouseketeer Clubhouse [Grand Floridian]	407-824-2985
A medium-sized club with movies, games, and crafts. Price includes a meal if child is checked-in by 6:30 pm (meal is at 7:30 pm). Two-hour minimum stay.	**$10/hour** 4:30 pm–mid.

Cub's Den [Wilderness Lodge]	407-824-1083
A smallish club with structured activities, movies, arts and crafts, and games. Price includes a meal (choice of hot dog, hamburger, cheeseburger, chicken strips, mac & cheese, or PB&J, plus ice cream) served between 6:30–8:00 pm.	**$10/hour** 4:30 pm-midnight

Never Land Club [Polynesian]	407-824-2000 ext. 2184
This is the largest, most creatively-themed club! Price includes a meal (buffet of kid-friendly items) served 6:00–8:00 pm. Open house daily from noon–4:00 pm for kids (and their parents). **Allie's KidTip:** *"I like the people here, and the toy stairs are fun to sit on and watch movies. The TV here is big!"*	**$10/hour** 4:00 pm-midnight

Other Childcare Options

Kids Nite Out offers Disney-sanctioned, private in-room baby-sitting, day and night (they replaced KinderCare in 2002). Two other independent agencies, **Fairy Godmothers** and **All About Kids**, offer similar services. The professional sitters will take kids to the theme parks if you make arrangements in advance, and watch infants and children with some special needs. The sitters show up equipped to keep the kids occupied with games and activities. They are well-trained, bonded, and insured. Rates vary, depending on the age and number of kids under care. For reservations, call Kids Nite Out at 407-828-0920, the Fairy Godmothers at 407-277-3724 or 407-275-7326, or All About Kids at 407-812-9300.

KinderCare provides structured daycare services to Disney guests on a limited, space-available basis. Hours are 6:00 am–9:00 pm Monday–Friday, and 6:00 am–6:00 pm on weekends for kids from 1-12 (must be able to walk and eat table food). Rates are $45/10-hour day or $10/hour. Weekend reservations may be made one month in advance. Weekday reservations must be made same-day (call in the morning). Call 407-827-5437.

Special Occasions

It seems natural to celebrate a special occasion at Disney. It's designed for fun and comes pre-decorated! So whether you plan a trip around a special day, or want to celebrate one that falls during your vacation, you can do it at Disney! Here are our tips and tricks for a magical celebration:

Birthdays–What better place to celebrate a birthday than at Disney? If you're at a Disney resort, press "0" and ask for the special "birthday message." Be sure to request a free "It's My Birthday!" pin at the Guest Relations desk at the theme parks. If you want to celebrate in style, all sorts of birthday parties and cruises can be arranged in advance–you can even "invite" Disney characters (though they're very expensive). For kids ages 4-12, you can arrange a birthday party at the BoardWalk or the Yacht & Beach Club–call the resorts directly for more information (phone numbers are found in the Staying in Style chapter). For parties in other restaurants, call 407-WDW-DINE. Birthday cruises (407-WDW-PLAY) are also available–we surprised Dave's father with one and he loved it! And in March 2003, Jennifer surprised her mom Carolyn with a special birthday event, planned in part by Gifts of a Lifetime (see sidebar below).

Jennifer's mom Carolyn celebrates her birthday at Restaurant Akershus

Engagements–Disney is a magical place to propose to a loved one. Devise your own scheme, or get ideas from Disney by calling 407-824-5130.

Weddings–Of course you can get married at Disney, too! From intimate to traditional to themed, Disney's Fairy Tale Weddings have something for virtually every budget. Visit http://disneyweddings.com or call 407-828-3400. Visit http://www.yourfairytale.com, where you can get unofficial Disney wedding and honeymoon details, and order the "Disney Weddings" e-book by Andrea Rotondo Hospidor ($20).

Special Services for Special Occasions

It's a challenge to organize a special occasion long distance. An innovative company, **Presentations: Gifts of a Lifetime**, helps you shop for that perfect gift, arrange a magical event, and even put on the whole show! To learn more, visit their Web site at http://www.giftsofalifetime.com or call 407-909-0593.

You can also have the **Walt Disney World Florist** (407-827-3505) prepare a fruit or snack basket and deliver it to a guest room.

Need a little help remembering that special occasion? Another unique service, **MouseMemories**, can create custom memory albums from your own photos. If you prefer to create your own memory albums, they offer scrapbooking supplies. To learn more, visit http://www.mousememories.com.

Honeymoons—Walt Disney World is the #1 honeymoon destination in the world, believe it or not. Not only are romantic spots found around virtually every corner, but Disney goes out of its way to make newlyweds welcome. Special honeymoon packages, romantic rooms, candlelit dinners, and adult-oriented entertainment abound. Even if you do nothing more than mention that it is your honeymoon to cast members, you're in for a special treat. For details, call Disney at 407-934-7639. We recommend the book "Walt Disney World for Couples" by Rick and Gayle Perlmutter for an excellent guide to romance at Disney.

Anniversaries—Like birthdays, anniversaries are always in style at the Walt Disney World Resort. You can plan a special night out at a romantic restaurant, or shape an entire vacation around your special day. The Garden Grill at Epcot offers an anniversary "re-hitching" celebration—call 407-WDW-DINE. Be sure to mention your anniversary when making priority seatings (especially at Cinderella's Royal Table)—you may be pleasantly surprised. If you're staying at a resort, mention your anniversary at check-in, too.

Group Events—With all the conventions they host each year, Disney is a pro at group parties and functions. We've planned several ourselves and found plenty of options and many helpful cast members. And with the introduction of "Magical Gatherings" (see sidebar below), group events are even easier to plan! You can have a private party virtually anywhere in the "World," for small or large groups. For parties in any of the resorts, call 407-828-3074. If you're interested in having a private party at one of the parks, including Pleasure Island (can we come?), call Group Sales at 407-828-3200. We can't say it'll be cheap, but you can plan one within a reasonable budget if you're careful. Of course, you can go all-out, too—companies rent entire theme parks. Planet Hollywood at Downtown Disney hosts private functions, too. In fact, your authors host special gatherings for PassPorter readers who want to meet us and other like-minded folks who just can't get enough of Disney. If you'd like to learn about our next PassPorter Gathering, please visit us at http://www.passporter.com/gathering.htm.

A jolly PassPorter Gathering with friends Russ, Cindy, Don, Ashley, Jason, Nancy, and Dave at Biergarten in Epcot

Magical Gatherings

Disney kicked off a new program in October 2003 designed to help bring friends and family together at Walt Disney World. If you've got eight or more people staying at a Walt Disney World resort, you can book special experiences only available to groups. These events include the International Storybook Dinner (with storytelling and a VIP viewing of IllumiNations at Epcot), Good Morning Gathering (a Magic Kingdom character breakfast with Mickey Mouse), Safari Celebration Dinner (an end-of-day safari followed by a dinner reception at Tusker House with characters, live entertainment, and animal experiences), and the Magical Fireworks Voyage (an evening cruise to view the new Wishes fireworks show over Magic Kingdom). Disney also provides helpful services to plan your gathering, such as web-based tools to help your group stay in touch and build consensus. And Disney has increased the number of restaurants that accommodate larger parties. To plan a Magical Gathering, call 407-WDISNEY or visit http://www.disneyworld.com/magicalgatherings.

Planning | Getting There | Staying in Style | Touring | Feasting | Making Magic | Index | Notes & More

Special Events and Holidays

Disney really knows how to celebrate. Nearly every holiday seems to have at least one event, and Easter, Halloween, Christmas, and New Year's Eve spark extended festivities. Disney also is a master at battling periods of slow attendance with specially-themed events throughout the year. Call Disney's main information line at 407-824-4321 or visit their Web site at http://www.disneyworld.com for more information.

Sports

January brings the sell-out **Walt Disney World Marathon**—it's Jan. 9–11 in 2004 (call 407-939-7810). The **Atlanta Braves** baseball spring training begins in February, and the **Tampa Bay Buccaneers** football team may have their training camp again in July and August. The PGA's top golfers gather for the **FUNAI Golf Classic** in October. For more details, visit http://www.disneyworldsports.com.

Celebrations at Pleasure Island

Pleasure Island throws special parties throughout the year. **Mardi Gras** is February 24, 2004, and the island throws a party to celebrate for several days. Celebrate **Black Music Month** in June. Get a jump on Independence Day with **July 3 fireworks**. September sees salsa during **Latin Rhythm Nights**. And November has the **Pleasure Island Jazz Fest**.

Festivals and Fun

Magic Kingdom, Epcot, and Disney-MGM Studios host special events. The **Epcot International Flower & Garden Festival** (April 16–May 30, 2004) fills the park with exhibits, seminars, tours, demonstrations, the Food Among the Flowers Brunch (page 237), and special entertainment at the America Gardens Theatre. **Grad Nights** party down at the Magic Kingdom (April 23, 24, and 30 and May 1, 2004) from 11:00 pm to 5:00 am—for details visit http://www.disneyyouthgroups.com. The Friday and Saturday after Labor Day brings the popular **Nights of Joy** to Magic Kingdom to celebrate contemporary Christian music ($35; see http://www.nightofjoy.com). The **Epcot International Food & Wine Festival**, held October 16–November 14, 2004, turns the World Showcase into an even greater gourmet delight (see page 214). November is also heaven for soap opera fans—**ABC Super Soap Weekend** brings many favorite soap stars to Disney-MGM Studios.

Easter *(April 11, 2004)*

Spring crowds reach a peak during Easter week. The BoardWalk has fun stuff to do. Some restaurants offer Easter dinners, such as Chef Mickey's (see page 225). Note that Magic Kingdom no longer has an Easter parade.

Halloween *(October 31, 2004)*
Mickey's Not So Scary Halloween Party brings kid-friendly spookiness to Magic Kingdom for 10 nights (7:00 pm–midnight) in late October (usually the Friday and Sunday before Halloween, plus Halloween night). Enjoy a costume parade, trick-or-treating, fireworks, and access to most rides. Advance tickets are $31.90/adult, $26.58/child. Call 407-934-7639.

Thanksgiving *(November 25, 2004)*
Crowds take a bump-up for this All-American holiday. Disney's holiday decorations are on their way up, and a number of the full-service restaurants at the parks and almost all of the Disney resorts host special holiday dinners, with and without Disney characters.

Christmas *(December 25, 2004)*
Christmas is a very special time, with delightful decorations, holiday entertainment, and countless ways to enjoy the season. Decorations go up around Thanksgiving, so there's over a month of merriment. Try to come during the first two weeks of December when the crowds are thinner, the party is in full swing, and the "World" is decked with holiday cheer. **Mickey's Very Merry Christmas Party** is a big favorite. Packed full of special shows and special fun, the Magic Kingdom is open for five extra hours for 12 nights in early December. Snow falls on Main Street, fireworks and music fill the air, and the big rides are open. Advance tickets are $38.29/adults, $27.64/kids (add $5 if you buy at the gate). At Epcot, the **Candlelight Processional** runs 2-3 times nightly. A celebrity narrator, chorus, and orchestra present the Christmas tale. No extra admission required, but a special dinner package offers reserved seating (call 407-WDW-DINE). Be sure to **view the resort decorations** (try the Yuletide Tour—page 243) and enjoy merriment at **Downtown Disney**. For the status of the **Osborne Family Spectacle of Lights**, see page 158.

New Year's Eve *(December 31, 2004)*
Magic Kingdom, Epcot, Disney-MGM Studios, Pleasure Island, and Atlantic Dance at the BoardWalk all host big New Year celebrations. The theme parks overflow during the Christmas-New Year's week, and reservations at resorts are extremely hard to get. Disney charges regular admission to the parks on New Year's Eve, but Pleasure Island hosts a $129/person event featuring headline entertainment, food, and a holiday toast. Recent celebrations have been extra busy, with Disney promising park admission only to resort guests. When we visited in 1999/2000, the roads and parking lots closed early and only Disney's transportation got through.

Other Holidays and Observances
All parks participate in February's **Black Heritage Celebration**. The first long weekend in June (June 2–7, 2004) is **Gay Weekend** (for information visit http://www.gayday.com). Special fireworks displays mark **July 4**.

Planning | Getting There | Staying in Style | Touring | Feasting | Making Magic | Index | Notes & More

Beyond Walt Disney World

We're pretty infatuated with Disney, but there is life beyond Walt Disney World. At least that's what we hear. We don't venture far beyond the gates, preferring to spend more time immersed in Disney's magic rather than battle traffic to get to another park. We do know that families hope to visit other theme parks during their visit to central Florida, so here is a list of Florida parks and attractions, along with their numbers and Web sites. You may also be interested in "The Other Orlando" guidebook by Kelly Monaghan, available at our web site and at your local bookstore.

Name	Number	Web Site
Busch Gardens	813-987-5082	http://www.buschgardens.com
Gatorland	800-393-JAWS	http://www.gatorland.com
Green Meadows Farm	407-846-0770	http://greenmeadowsfarm.com
Kennedy Space Center	321-452-2121	http://kennedyspacecenter.com
Medieval Times	407-396-1518	http://medievaltimes.com
Sea World	407-363-2613	http://seaworld.com
Splendid China	407-396-7111	http://www.floridasplendidchina.com
Universal Studios/Islands of Adv.	407-363-8000	http://www.usf.com
Wet 'n' Wild	407-351-1800	http://www.wetnwild.com

(Note: Cypress Gardens closed in April 2003, but was purchased in September 2003 by a conservation group who plans to sell it to someone who will re-open it. Watch for news!)

Beyond Orlando

Like any other forward-thinking organization, The Walt Disney Company has expanded into other locales. Here are a few of them:

Disney Cruise Line—"Take the magic of Disney and just add water!" The Disney Cruise Line set sail in 1998 with the same enthusiasm and energy you find at the Walt Disney World Resort. See pages 100–101, and pick up a copy of our popular guidebook, "PassPorter's Field Guide to the Disney Cruise Line and its Caribbean Ports of Call" (available in bookstores or order at http://www.passporter.com/dcl—more details on page 284).

Disneyland Resort (California)—The original "Magic Kingdom," near Los Angeles. Disneyland was the model for the Magic Kingdom in Florida and still keeps a step or two ahead of its offspring, since Disney's Imagineers live close by. The official Disneyland hotels are right next door if you want to make a week out of it. A whole new park, Disney's California Adventure, opened in 2001. We plan to cover the entire Disneyland Resort and other area attractions such as Universal Studios, in a brand new book "PassPorter® Disneyland® Resort." For details on the book's release and to pre-order a copy, visit http://www.passporter.com/dl (see page 284).

isneyland Paris Resort (France)—The first (and only) Disney resort ı Europe, this park was originally known as Euro Disneyland. The park as a similar layout to Disneyland, with the major change being a ıbstitution of Discoveryland for Tomorrowland. It is said by many to be ıe most beautiful of all the Disney parks, and it certainly has the latest ɛchnology in planning, architecture, and attractions. In April 2002, the ew Walt Disney Studios theme park opened, featuring a number of the ıost popular attractions from the Disney-MGM Studios in Orlando. For ıore information, visit http://www.disneylandparis.com.

okyo Disney Resort (Japan)—Disney, Japan-style! Tokyo Disney Resort located in Urayasu, just outside Tokyo. It is similar to Disneyland in alifornia, incorporating the quintessential "American" things. When nnifer visited in 1992, she found it squeaky clean and definitely Disney, ith just a touch of Japanese peeking through. In 2001, the new Tokyo isneySea theme park opened immediately adjacent to Tokyo Disneyland. he new aquatically-themed park has seven lands and a new resort, Hotel liraCosta. Visit http://www.tokyodisneyresort.co.jp and click English.

isney's Vero Beach Resort—Vero Beach, Florida, is Disney's first ceanside resort, a two-hour drive from Orlando. Relaxing and definitely id-back compared to the parks, Vero Beach Resort offers the chance to et some real rest. But there's also plenty to do—nightclubs, theatre, ovies, restaurants, cultural events, recreation, and, of course, walking ı the beach (very important). Call 561-234-2000 for more information, visit http://www.disneyvacationclub.com, and click Resorts.

isney's Hilton Head Island Resort—For southern grace and charm, xperience the Carolina Low Country lifestyle at Disney's Hilton Head land Resort. Hilton Head is a golfer's nirvana, boasting twelve nearby olf courses. The tennis and beaches are also big draws. It's an ideal spot r small group retreats. For more information, call 843-341-4100.

isneyQuest—Though we've already described this indoor amusement ark on pages 186–189, it deserves another mention here. Plans originally alled for DisneyQuests around the country, but only one outside of rlando was built—in Chicago. Alas, Chicago's closed in September 2001. on't expect new locations to open. Visit http://www.disneyquest.com.

dden Mickey Hiding Places (from list on page 247)

1) In the Disney Recycles logo on bags, napkins, etc.; 2) On cash register receipts; 3) The "Soap Stop" vend machines in the resort laundry rooms; 4) Main Street Vehicle horse harnesses; 5) In the center of manhole covers Plates in The Haunted Mansion's dining room; 7) In "broccoli" in the mural over entrance to Body Wars; 8) Drill platform worker's watch; 9) Hedges trimmed into circles; 10) Earffel water tower; 11) The ironwork fence arou Disney-MGM Studios; 12) Stained-glass windows in church; 13) Birdhouse near Festival of the Lion King; 14) On sidewalk near the Harambe Fruit Market; and 15) On the frog statue outside of the women's restroom near Pizzaf

Your Own Walt Disney World

Make Walt Disney World your personal playground with these tips:

Create your **own shirts**! I used Avery Dark T-shirt Transfers to mak personalized shirts for all five members of our family. I four inexpensive Hanes shirts in a different color for each day and use Disney's Magic Artist software and clip art from Disney web sites create a different design for each set of shirts. I also added som personalization to the designs, like 'Powell Family Vacation.' Th shirts helped me keep track of my husband and three boys. We als got extra attention from cast members who would say things lik 'Have a great day, Mr. Powell!' etc. At least 10 people chased us dow to ask where we got our shirts. The shirts only cost around $6 eac

— Contributed by Kris Powell, a winner in our 2003 Magic Tip Conte

Write to us and **share your experiences, memories, and tips**. we use them, we'll credit you in the PassPorter and send you a autographed copy! Drop us a note at P.O. Box 3880, Ann Arbo Michigan 48106 or e-mail us at memories@passporter.com.

Magical Memories

"We made plans for a family trip to Walt Disney World—there were 10 of us going (11 you count my being 3 months pregnant!), grandparents included. From the time bought our airline tickets until the time we left for the airport, I gave everyone da updates and trip ideas. Most of them I got from the PassPorter web site! I made folde up and printed up restaurant menus from all over the 'world' and out-of-the-way f stuff (like the butterfly gardens in Epcot and the Mickey head in the Haunted Mansi on the banquet table). I printed out all our reservation info for each family, and ma coloring pages for the little ones to color while the months passed slowly by! And I se the group daily e-mails and Disney facts each day! Time still passed too slowly for taste, but it gave us that light at the end of a long dreary winter tunnel! I even we online and ordered Disney name tags for the kids through Gifts of a Lifetime, a these were a hit! The kids wore them everyday and cast members called them by nam In short, the anticipation of the trip became as much fun as the trip itself!"

...as told by Disney vacationer Tami Roma

"When my mother Evelyn passed away, my daughter Jennifer promised me that we'd ta a special trip to Walt Disney World together. It so happened that the trip coincided w my birthday, and Jennifer pulled out all the stops. She made up inspirational cards a birthday goodie bags themed to our next visit to place on my pillow each night and morni she brought me 'It's My Birthday!' pins at all the parks, and she decorated our ho rooms in honor of the event. As a finale, she arranged a special event through Gifts o Lifetime, during which I had to follow a series of hidden clues to find the birthday ca that 'Tinker Bell' had hidden in Fantasyland. Jennifer said that my reaction whe discovered the surprises in the end was just priceless... as I actually shrieked in deligh

...as told by Disney vacationer Carolyn Tody (Jennifer's Mo

Index

We feel that a comprehensive index is very important to a successful travel guide. Too many times we've tried to look something up in other books only to find there was no entry at all, forcing us to flip through pages and waste valuable time. When you're on the phone with a reservation agent and looking for that little detail, time is of the essence.

You'll find the PassPorter index is complete and detailed. Whenever we reference more than one page for a given topic, the major topic is in **bold** and map references are in *italics* to help you home in on exactly what you need. For those times you want to find everything there is to be had, we include all the minor references. We have plenty of cross-references, too, just in case you don't look it up under the name we use.

P.S. This isn't the end of the book. More nifty features begin on page 274!

Symbols

A

D

Web Site Index

Site Name	Page	Address (URL)
Adults at Walt Disney World	vii	http://www.adultsatwdw.com
All Ears Newsletter	6	http://www.allearsnet.com
Along Interstate 75	15	http://www.i75online.com
American Express	11	http://www.americanexpress.com
Amtrak	18	http://www.amtrak.com
AutoPilot	15	http://www.freetrip.com
Badger's Disney Countdown	vii	http://nhed.com/countdown
Best Western Resort	107	http://www.orlandoresorthotel.com
Busch Gardens	258	http://www.buschgardens.com
Care Medical Equipment	35	http://www.caremedicalequipment.com
Comfort Inn Lake Buena Vista	108	http://www.comfortinnorlando.com
Courtyard Inn	104	http://www.courtyardorlando.com
Disney's Magical Gatherings	255	http://www.disneyworld.com/magicalgatherings
Disney Cruise Line	100-101	http://www.disneycruise.com
Disney Desktop	vii	http://www.disneydesktop.com
DisneyDollarless	7, 11	http://www.disneydollarless.com
DisneyEcho	7	http://www.disney
DisneyQuest	188	http://www.disneyquest.com
Disney Vacation Club	102-103	http://www.disneyvacationclub.com
DisneyZone	vii	http://www.disneyzone.actusa.net
DoomBuggies.com (Haunted Mansion)	130	http://www.doombuggies.com
DoubleTree Guest Suites	107	http://www.doubletreeguestsuites.com
Drive I-95	15	http://www.drivei95.com
DVC By Resale	103, 283	http://www.dvcbyresale.com
EarPlanes	23	http://www.earplanes.com
eGuides To Go	vii	http://www.eguidestogo.com
Expedia	16	http://www.expedia.com
Florida Department of Transportation	15	http://www.dot.state.fl.us
Florida Orlando Tickets	117	http://www.floridaorlandotickets.net
Friends of Bill W. in Orlando	112	http://aaorlandointergroup.org
Gatorland	258	http://gatorland.com
Gay Days	257	http://www.gayday.com
Gifts of a Lifetime	255	http://www.giftsofalifetime.com
The Globe Pequot Press	202	http://www.globepequot.com
Green Meadows Farm	258	http://greenmeadowsfarm.com
Greyhound	18	http://www.greyhound.com
Grosvenor Resort	104	http://www.grosvenorresort.com
Hard Rock Hotel	107	http://www.hardrockhotelorlando.com
Hidden Mickeys of Disney	vii, 247	http://www.hiddenmickeys.org
The Hilton	105	http://www.hotel-inside-the-park.com
Holiday Inn Family Suites	108	http://hifamilysuites.com
Holiday Inn SunSpree	109	http://www.kidsuites.com
Hotel Royal Plaza	105	http://www.royalplaza.com
Howard Johnson Maingate	109	http://www.orlandohojomaingate.com
Iago & Zazu's Attraction of the Week	vi	http://aotw.figzu.com
Intercot	vii, 7	http://www.intercot.com
Interstate 95 Exit Information Guide	15	http://www.usastar.com/i95/homepage.htm
Kennedy Space Center	258	http://kennedyspacecenter.com
LaughingPlace.com	vi	http://www.laughingplace.com
Lynx (local buses)	19	http://www.golynx.com

Site Name	Page	Address (URL)
Magical Disney Cruise Guide	103	http://wdwig.com/cruise/cruise.shtml
Magictrips.com	vii	http://www.magictrips.com
Marc Schwartz's Unofficial Disney Golf	194	http://www.wdwgolf.com
Medieval Times	258	http://medievaltimes.com
MouseEarVacations.com	6, 282	http://www.mouseearvacations.com
MouseMemories	255	http://www.mousememories.com
MousePlanet Trip Reports	12	http://www.mouseplanet.com/dtp/trip.rpt
MousePlanet Disney Vacation Club	103	http://www.mouseplanet.com/dtp/dvc
MousePlanet Trip Planner	vii	http://www.mouseplanet.com/dtp/wdwguide
MouseSavers.com	vii, 11	http://www.mousesavers.com
MurderWatch Mystery Dinner Show	236	http://www.murderwatch.com
Orbitz	16	http://www.orbitz.com
Orlando Houses of Worship	112	http://www.orlandowelcome.com/pray/pray.htm
Orlando International Airport	17	http://www.orlandoairports.net
Orlando Magicard	11	http://www.orlandoinfo.com/magicard
Our Laughing Place	vi	http://www.ourlaughingplace.com
PassPorter Online	281	http://www.passporter .com *(see more on page 281)*
PassPorter Book Updates	4, 281	http://www.passporter .com/customs/bookupdates.htm
Perri House	109	http://www.perrihouse.com
Portofino Bay Hotel	107	http://www.portofinobay.com
Premier Vacation Homes	109	http://www.premier-vacation-homes.com
Pressed Coin Collector Page	246	http://www.liss.olm.net/ec
Priceline	16	http://www.priceline.com
Priority Seating Calculator	201	http://pscalculator.net
Quality Inn Plaza	109	http://www.qualityinn-orlando.com
Radisson Resort Parkway	106	http://www.radissonparkway.com
Rainforest Cafe	203	http://www.rainforestcafe.com
Rodeway Inn International	109	http://www.rodewayinnorlando.com
Royal Pacific Resort	107	http://www.loewshotels.com/hotels/orlando_royal_pacific
Sea World	258	http://seaworld.com
Selective Limo	19	http://www.selectivelimo.com
Shades of Green	96	http://www.shadesofgreen.org
Sheraton Safari	106	http://www.sheratonsafari.com
Sheraton's Vistana Resort	109	http://www.sheraton.com
Sierra Suites	109	http://www.sierra-orlando.com
Spencer Family's Disney Page	vi, 62	http://home.hiwaay.net/~jlspence
Splendid China	258	http://floridasplendidchina.com
Steve Soares' Disney Entertainment	122	http://pages.prodigy.net/stevesoares
Swan and Dolphin Resorts	99	http://www.swandolphin.com
TicketMania	117	http://www.ticketmania.com
Tiffany Towncar	19, 282	http://www.tiffanytowncar.com
Travelocity	16, 29	http://www.travelocity.com
Travelodge Maingate East	109	http://www.orlandotravelodgehotel.com
Universal Studios Florida	258	http://www.usf.com
Unofficial Disney Information Station	vii, 7	http://www.wdwinfo.com
Unofficial Disney Weddings Guide	254	http://www.yourfairytale.com
Unofficial Walt Disney World Info Guide	vii, 7, 203	http://www.wdwig.com
Vegetarian World Guides	202, 204	http://www.vegetarianworldguides.com
Walt Disney Travel Co.	8	http://www.disneytravel.com
Walt Disney World Resort	7, 120	http://www.disneyworld.com
Walt Disney World Sports & Rec.	194	http://www.disneyworldsports.com
Wet 'n' Wild	258	http://www.wetnwild.com
What Would Walt Do	251	http://www.whatwouldwaltdo.com
Wyndham Palace Resort & Spa	107	http://www.wyndham.com/hotels/MCOPV/main.wnt
YourRide	19	http://www.yourride.net

Notes & Autographs

Whether you run out of space somewhere else or want to get your favorite character's autograph, these pages stand ready!

Scribbles & Doodles

Whether you scribble and doodle or just scoodle and dribble, this page is specially treated to accept ink and resist moisture!

(Ok, so all paper does this... but hey, we just can't resist mentioning hidden features!)

Autographs

Kids and kids-at-heart love to get autographs from Disney characters! These two pages beg to be filled with signatures, paw prints, and doodles from your favorite characters. We've even provided places to write the actual name of the character (they can be hard to read—they are autographs, after all), plus the location you discovered the character, and the date of your find. Even if you bring or purchase an autograph book, use these pages when you fill it up or just plain forget it. (Been there, done that!) Be sure to see page 246 for tips and tricks on how to get character autographs, too!

Character: *Location:* *Date:*

Character: *Location:* *Date:*

Character: *Location:* *Date:*

Autographs Anonymous

We know. We understand. Bouncing tigers and giant mice can be intimidating. After several months of research and development, we came up with the following system that can help both the interminably-shy and the over-stimulated. Just write your name in the blank below, take a deep breath, and hold out your book. Now, wasn't that easy?

Hi, my name is ____________. May I have your autograph?

(write your name here)

Character:
Location: *Date:*

Character:
Location: *Date:*

Character: *Location:* *Date:*

Character: *Location:* *Date:*

Register Your PassPorter

We are **very** interested to learn how your vacation went and what you think of the PassPorter, how it worked (or didn't work) for you, and your opinion on how we could improve it! We encourage you to register your copy of PassPorter with us–in return for your feedback, we'll send you coupons good for discounts on PassPorters and gear when purchased directly from us. You can register your copy of PassPorter on the Internet at http://www.passporter.com/register.htm, or you can fill-in-the-blanks below (it's fun and painless!) and mail it to P.O. Box 3880, Ann Arbor, Michigan 48106. Or just send us a postcard or letter. Thanks!

Dear Jennifer and Dave,

We vacationed from ____________ to ____________, which was our ❑ first ❑ second ❑ third ❑ _____ trip to the Walt Disney World Resort! There were _____ of us along for the trip, ❑ with ❑ without kids. We got your book ❑ long before ❑ _________ before ❑ right before our vacation ❑ as a gift ❑ from a bookstore ❑ from the Internet!

We planned our trip ❑ carefully ❑ some ❑ by the seat of our pants, and the book helped ❑ tremendously ❑ a lot ❑ a little ❑ very little. Specifically, we liked the chapters on ❑ planning ❑ traveling ❑ lodging ❑ touring ❑ eating ❑ making more magic. In addition to the PassPorter, we relied upon ❑ the Internet ❑ another book ❑ ______________.
The best thing about the PassPorter was ______________.
The worst thing about the PassPorter was ______________.
Overall, we think the PassPorter is ❑ the best thing since sliced bread ❑ helpful ❑ not bad ❑ in need of improvement ❑ ______________

Comments/suggestions/questions/contributions: ______________

____

____

Please ❑ do ❑ don't send us updates via e-mail periodically. Our e-mail address is: ____________@__________.____ (i.e., someone@somewhere.com)

Sincerely, ______________________________

Address ______________________________

Phone ______________________________

PassPorter Walt Disney World 2004: First Printing

PassPorter PassAlongs

Have you noticed curious glances when you crack open your PassPorter? Do you know someone going to Walt Disney World who always seems to have "just one more question?" Envious people and Disney novices may ask you about your PassPorter and wonder how to get one. Wonder no more! These little "PassAlongs," requested by our readers, are yours to pass along to friends, family members... even complete strangers. The front side, which you may enjoy reading yourself, bears fun quotes from readers. The back lists the "PassPorter Pledge" and ordering details.

The Dancing PassPorter

"I brought my PassPorter to my daughter's dance class for a whole 45 minutes of uninterrupted reading while she was in class! Some of the moms sitting near me noticed I had a 'Disney Guide.' That started a wonderful conversation about trips to Disney. And after my positives raves of the PassPorter, a couple of the moms actually bought their own copies of PassPorter!"

– Lori Enders

I Caught You!

"I brought along my PassPorter on a recent trip. My husband gave me one of those looks that says 'you're nuts for taking this with you everywhere.' One day at lunch I pulled out my trusty PassPorter to work on plans. While we ate, I noticed my husband moving closer and closer to me. I glanced at him. To my surprise, he was heavy into reading my PassPorter and our plans!"

– Cindy Seaburn

Thanks to the Tribune!

"About the same time I was considering a family trip to Disney, the Chicago Tribune did story on the PassPorter. They gave the PassPorter such high praise, I immediately ran out to get a copy. The PassPorter guide and the Web site were instrumental in helping us plan the most wonderful family vacation we have ever had!"

– Kathleen Dahm

'It's Disney!'

"As a mother of a toddler I've seen books destroyed, so I try to keep PassPorter safe. One day my little guy kept poking the cover and saying 'It's Disney!' I then realized the PassPorter really is Disney! It's all the details, excitement, and magical memories packed into one place! Then he grabbed a pen and drew on the cover... Oh well!"

– Jessica Sims

Mom's Disney Tradition

"In 1999 I got my first PassPorter and carried it everywhere. My family laughed at me and called it 'Mom's Disney Bible.' Before too long, my daughters were so taken with it that I had to buy each a copy. I got myself a deluxe edition. Now the PassPorter is a tradition, and I get a new one each year!"

– Patricia Chandler

PassPorter, Take Me Away!

"I work hard year-round so I can be a relaxed and lazy tourist. The PassPorter is a handy reference, and its little golden pockets make planning so easy. Everything is tucked safely and easily within reach. I can use the time it saves to caress a cool Dole Whip instead of reams of papers. PassPorter, take me away!"

– Melinda "Moley" Brickhouse

Using PassPorter PassAlongs

If you enjoy the PassAlong stories on the reverse side too much to "pass along," feel free to make a photocopy of these two pages. You may even want to pre-cut the PassAlongs and place them in a PassPocket! If you need more PassAlongs, you can get new pages (with new stories) at http://www.passporter.com/wdw/passalongs.htm. Oh, and before you hand out a PassAlong, we recommend you write your personal information under the front cover flap—just in case someone can't wait to get their own copy of PassPorter!

*PassPorter readers, including the person who gave you this PassAlong, are special people who appreciate the magic of Disney! In accepting this you agree to the PassPorter Pledge. Raise your right hand and say, "I thank you for this PassAlong, and now I pledge to find a safe place to put it." It's traditional to offer the giver a **big hug** or send **a postcard from Disney**.*

***To order a PassPorter** (and get a place to put this PassAlong), call 1-877-WAYFARER or visit us at http://www.passporter.com/store. PassPorter is also available in fine bookstores.*

*PassPorter readers, including the person who gave you this PassAlong, are special people who appreciate the magic of Disney! In accepting this you agree to the PassPorter Pledge. Raise your right hand and say, "I thank you for this PassAlong, and now I pledge to find a safe place to put it." It's traditional to offer the giver a **big hug** or send **a postcard from Disney**.*

***To order a PassPorter** (and get a place to put this PassAlong), call 1-877-WAYFARER or visit us at http://www.passporter.com/store. PassPorter is also available in fine bookstores.*

*PassPorter readers, including the person who gave you this PassAlong, are special people who appreciate the magic of Disney! In accepting this you agree to the PassPorter Pledge. Raise your right hand and say, "I thank you for this PassAlong, and now I pledge to find a safe place to put it." It's traditional to offer the giver a **big hug** or send **a postcard from Disney**.*

***To order a PassPorter** (and get a place to put this PassAlong), call 1-877-WAYFARER or visit us at http://www.passporter.com/store. PassPorter is also available in fine bookstores.*

*PassPorter readers, including the person who gave you this PassAlong, are special people who appreciate the magic of Disney! In accepting this you agree to the PassPorter Pledge. Raise your right hand and say, "I thank you for this PassAlong, and now I pledge to find a safe place to put it." It's traditional to offer the giver a **big hug** or send **a postcard from Disney**.*

***To order a PassPorter** (and get a place to put this PassAlong), call 1-877-WAYFARER or visit us at http://www.passporter.com/store. PassPorter is also available in fine bookstores.*

*PassPorter readers, including the person who gave you this PassAlong, are special people who appreciate the magic of Disney! In accepting this you agree to the PassPorter Pledge. Raise your right hand and say, "I thank you for this PassAlong, and now I pledge to find a safe place to put it." It's traditional to offer the giver a **big hug** or send **a postcard from Disney**.*

***To order a PassPorter** (and get a place to put this PassAlong), call 1-877-WAYFARER or visit us at http://www.passporter.com/store. PassPorter is also available in fine bookstores.*

*PassPorter readers, including the person who gave you this PassAlong, are special people who appreciate the magic of Disney! In accepting this you agree to the PassPorter Pledge. Raise your right hand and say, "I thank you for this PassAlong, and now I pledge to find a safe place to put it." It's traditional to offer the giver a **big hug** or send **a postcard from Disney**.*

***To order a PassPorter** (and get a place to put this PassAlong), call 1-877-WAYFARER or visit us at http://www.passporter.com/store. PassPorter is also available in fine bookstores.*

PassPorter Online

A wonderful way to get the most from your PassPorter is to visit our active Web site at http://www.passporter.com/wdw. We serve-up valuable PassPorter updates, plus useful Walt Disney World information and advice we couldn't jam into our book. You can swap tales (that's t-a-l-e-s, Mickey!) with fellow Disney fans, play contests and games, find links to other sites, get plenty of details, and ask us questions. You can also order PassPorters and shop for PassPorter accessories and travel gear! The latest information on new PassPorters to other destinations is available on our Web site as well. To go directly to our latest list of page-by-page of PassPorter updates, visit http://www.passporter.com/customs/bookupdates.htm.

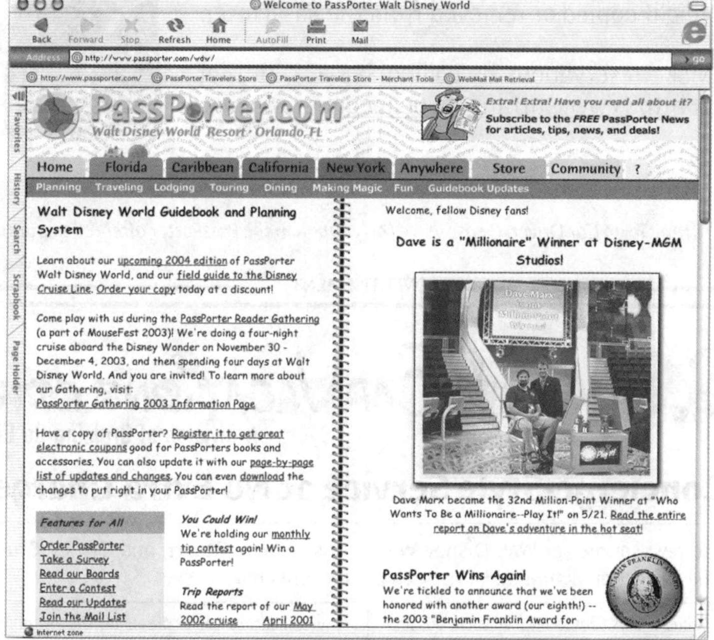

PassPorter Web Sites	Address (URL)
Main Page: PassPorter Online	http://www.passporter.com
Walt Disney World Forum	http://www.passporter.com/wdw
PassPorter Posts Message Boards	http://www.passporter.oards.com
PassPorter: Best of Times Links Page	http://www.passporter.com/wdw/bestoftimes.htm
Luggage Log and Tag Maker	http://www.passporter.com/wdw/luggagelog.htm
Rate the Rides, Resorts, Restaurants	http://www.passporter.com/wdw/rate.htm
Register Your PassPorter	http://www.passporter.com/register.htm
Resort Room Request Form	http://www.passporter.com/wdw/resortrequest.htm
PassPorter Deluxe Edition Information	http://www.passporter.com/wdw/deluxe.htm

Money-Saving Coupons & Offers

Money-Saving Coupons & Offers

Free PassPorter Pin with Online Purchase

Receive a free 2004 cloissone PassPorter Pin ($6 value) when you place an order of $17 or more in merchandise from our Online Store.

shown actual size

Add to your pin collection with our new cloissone pin! This is the second in a series of limited edition pins.

To redeem, visit our special pin offer page (before you place your order) located at http://www.passporter.com/store/freepin.htm and have this PassPorter handy.

Valid for online purchases only. Limit one coupon per order, and one free pin per order. This limited edition pin may sell out—if it does, another PassPorter Pin will be offered with this coupon.

More PassPorters

You've asked for more PassPorters—we've listened! At our readers' request, we developed the Deluxe Edition of same book you hold in your hands—it's proven phenomenally popular! In 2003 we introduced "PassPorter's Field Guide to the Disney Cruise Line and its Caribbean Ports of Call," and our new "PassPorter Disneyland Resort and Southern California" book (ISBN: 1587710048-spiral and 1587710056-deluxe) debuts in 2004. To learn more about new PassPorters, visit http://www.passporter.com.

PassPorter Deluxe Edition

Design first-class vacations with this loose-leaf ring binder. The Deluxe Edition features the same great content as the PassPorter Walt Disney World spiral guide. Special features of the Deluxe Edition include ten interior storage slots in the binder to hold guidemaps, I.D. cards, and a pen (we even include a pen). The Deluxe binder makes it really easy to add, remove, and rearrange pages... you can even download, print, and add-in updates and supplemental pages from our Web site, and refills are available for purchase. You can learn more and order a copy at http://www.passporter.com/wdw/deluxe.htm. The Deluxe Edition is also available through bookstores by special order—just give your favorite bookstore the ISBN Code for the 2004 Deluxe Edition (1587710137).

PassPorter's Field Guide to the Disney Cruise Line and its Caribbean Ports of Call—Second Edition

Get your cruise plans in shipshape with our updated field guide! This take-along travel guide and planner covers the Disney Cruise Line in incredible detail, and includes deck plans, stateroom floor plans, original photos, menus, entertainment guides, port/shore excursion details, and plenty of worksheets to help you budget, plan, and record your cruise information. This is the only guidebook devoted to the Disney Cruise Line! Learn more and order at http://www.passporter.com/dcl or get a copy at your favorite bookstore (ISBN: 1587710161). Our cruise guide is also available in a Deluxe Edition with PassPockets—you can order this on our Web site or through a bookstore (ISBN: 158771017X).

(march 2004)

To order any of our guidebooks, visit http://www.passporterstore.com or call toll-free 877-929-3273. PassPorter guidebooks are also available in your local bookstore. If you don't see it on the shelf, just ask!

Note: The ISBN codes noted above apply to our 2004 editions. For later editions, just ask your bookstore to search their database for "PassPorter."

PassPorter Goodies

PassPorter was born out of the necessity for more planning, organization, and a way to preserve the memories of a great vacation! Along the way we've found other things that either help us use the PassPorter better, appreciate our vacation more, or just make our journey a little more comfortable. Others have asked us about them, so we thought we'd share them with you. Order online at http://www.passporterstore.com, call us toll-free 877-929-3273, or use the order form below.

PassPorter® PassHolder is a small, lightweight nylon pouch that holds passes, I.D. cards, passports, money, and pens. Wear it around your neck for hands-free touring, and for easy access at the airport. The front features a clear compartment, a zippered pocket, and a velcro pocket; the back has a small pocket (perfect size for FASTPASS) and two pen slots. Adjustable cord. Royal blue. 4 7/8" x 6 1/2"	**Quantity**: ____ x $7.95 
PassPorter® Badge personalized with your name! Go around the "World" in style with our oval pin (see page 251). Price includes personalization with your name, shipping, and handling. Please indicate pin color(s) and name(s) with your order.	**Quantity**: ____ x $4.00 lemon yellow or lime green Name(s): ________
PassPorter® Pin is our collectible, cloissone pin. Our 2004 version depicts our colorful PassPorter logo and reads "1999 ★ 2004 ★ Five Years of Magic." More details and a coupon for a free pin is on page 283. Watch for new pins to be introduced each year!	**Quantity**: ____ x $6.00 

Please ship my PassPorter Goodies to:

Name ....

Address ....

City, State, Zip ....

Daytime Phone ....

Payment: ❑ check (to "MediaMarx") ❑ charge card

❑ MasterCard ❑ Visa ❑ American Express ❑ Discover

Card number .... Exp. Date. ....

Signature ....

Sub-Total:

Tax*:

Shipping**:

Total:

* Please include sales tax if you live in MI or NJ.

**Shipping costs are:
$5 for totals up to $9
$6 for totals up to $19
$7 for totals up to $29
$8 for totals up to $39
Delivery takes 1-2 weeks.

Send your order form to P.O. Box 3880, Ann Arbor, MI 48106, call us toll-free at 877-WAYFARER (877-929-3273), or order online http://www.passporterstore.com.

Planning
Getting There
Staying in Style
Touring
Feasting
Making Magic
Index
Notes & More

Vacation At-A-Glance

Create an overview of your itinerary in the chart below for easy reference. You can then make copies of it and give one to everyone in your traveling party, as well as to friends and family members who stay behind.

Name(s):	
Departing on: Time: #:	
Arriving at:	
Staying at:	Phone:
Date:	Date:
Park/Activity:	Park/Activity:
Breakfast:	Breakfast:
Lunch:	Lunch:
Dinner:	Dinner:
Other:	Other:
Date:	Date:
Park/Activity:	Park/Activity:
Breakfast:	Breakfast:
Lunch:	Lunch:
Dinner:	Dinner:
Other:	Other:
Date:	Date:
Park/Activity:	Park/Activity:
Breakfast:	Breakfast:
Lunch:	Lunch:
Dinner:	Dinner:
Other:	Other:
Date:	Date:
Park/Activity:	Park/Activity:
Breakfast:	Breakfast:
Lunch:	Lunch:
Dinner:	Dinner:
Other:	Other:
Date:	Date:
Park/Activity:	Park/Activity:
Breakfast:	Breakfast:
Lunch:	Lunch:
Dinner:	Dinner:
Other:	Other:
Departing on: Time: #:	
Returning at:	